From Crisis to Crisis
PAKISTAN 1962–1969

From Crisis to Crisis

PAKISTAN 1962–1969

HERBERT FELDMAN

London
OXFORD UNIVERSITY PRESS
LAHORE   KARACHI   DACCA
1972

Oxford University Press, Ely House, London W.1

GLASGOW NEW YORK TORONTO MELBOURNE WELLINGTON
CAPE TOWN IBADAN NAIROBI DAR ES SAALAM LUSAKA ADDIS ABABA
DELHI BOMBAY CALCUTTA MADRAS KARACHI LAHORE DACCA
KUALA LUMPUR SINGAPORE HONG KONG TOKYO

ISBN 0 19 215192 4

© Oxford University Press 1972

PRINTED IN GREAT BRITAIN
BY EBENEZER BAYLIS AND SON LIMITED
THE TRINITY PRESS, WORCESTER, AND LONDON

FOREWORD

This book is the sequel to my *Revolution in Pakistan*[1] which surveyed the Martial Law administration initiated on 7 October 1958, by the then President of Pakistan, the late Major-General Iskander Mirza and General (as he then was) Ayub Khan. The present work examines the administration of the country by Field-Marshal (as he became) Ayub Khan through the instrumentality of the Constitution promulgated by him and brought into effect on the abrogation of Martial Law on 8 June 1962. Thus the two books cover two distinct but consecutive periods in the history of Pakistan during both of which Field-Marshal Ayub Khan was President of the country excluding a brief period of three weeks from 7 to 27 October 1958, when Major-General Iskander Mirza occupied that office. Taken together, these two periods amount to rather more than ten years and these ten years can very properly be treated as an organic whole. For one thing, Field-Marshal Ayub Khan was continuously in office during that time, except for the three weeks already noted. For another thing—and this is much more significant—the period began with the institution of Martial Law and the sweeping away of the parliamentary system of government and of direct elections through universal adult suffrage. It ended with the offer, by Ayub Khan, acting under irresistible public pressure, to reinstate these institutions; an offer followed by the resumption of Martial Law and his departure from the office of President.

It was thus Ayub Khan's disagreeable lot to propose the dismantling of the constitutional structure which he had devised, and in which he had expressed so much faith, in order to give effect to institutions in which, according to himself, he had no confidence and which he considered unsuitable for Pakistan. These latter proposals were not immediately implemented because, almost at once, the entire Constitution was abrogated. In due course, we shall consider the reasons for the failure of his constitutional theories. Meanwhile, there are some other things to be said.

[1] London, 1967.

It may appear that many of the opinions expressed or conclusions stated in the present work are decidedly *ex post facto*—wisdom after the event. Concerning this, I had noted in *Revolution in Pakistan*[2] that it was doubtful whether Ayub Khan ever succeeded in convincing all his countrymen of the validity of his opinions relating to Pakistan's constitutional needs. I drew attention to the unsatisfactory circumstances which attended the introduction of the Constitution he had framed, or which had been drafted for him on the basis of his thinking, and I suggested that sooner or later his system would give way to, or would mature into, something similar to its predecessor.

I do not claim credit for having foreseen so swift, so decisive and so dramatically emphatic a rejection of his Constitution, nor was I pessimistic enough to feel that the intervention of military authority would again be necessary, but I had little doubt that the Constitution Ayub Khan had given his countrymen enjoyed but small chance of survival. As time passed, these opinions were fortified by various happenings, a record of which will find its place in later pages. Here it may be said that the Constitution itself was the object of so much change and amendment by Ayub Khan and his Government that, at times, it appeared as if they were floundering in a quagmire of irresolute views, conflicting opinion, and apprehensions for the future. In his broadcast to the nation on 1 March 1962, Ayub Khan, when announcing the new Constitution, said: 'I believe in every word . . . and have complete faith in it.' Notwithstanding his profession of total confidence, this Constitution, during the five and a half years that immediately followed, was amended by Ayub Khan in no less than eight separate enactments. These included the Preamble and also Part II, Chapter 1, which was totally recast. In addition, thirty-nine Articles were changed, some very drastically and some of them two or three times. The Third Schedule was likewise altered, two additional Articles and two more Schedules added. It is true that not all these changes were initiated by Ayub Khan, nor were they all congenial to him. Further, it is doubtless the case that some of the changes were the simple result of the mechanics of necessary consequential

[2] ibid., pp. 113–16, 197–8, 210.

alteration, but even so it became increasingly difficult to believe in the initial soundness of the conception and in the worth of its intellectual foundations.

As far as concerns the weight of the observation and opinion contained in this book and in *Revolution in Pakistan*, the documentary sources are clear enough from the notes. Their adequacy may be called into question, but a work of contemporary history is, by its nature, debarred from access to state papers and other authoritative material which law, or convention, or both, may require to be withheld until after the lapse of a period deemed necessary or appropriate. It is at least arguable that this limitation is mitigated by the contemporary record that this book presents. What is narrated here is the observation of a person resident in the country where the events described took place, at the time they occurred, and having the opportunity to witness them sometimes more, sometimes less, closely. Since September 1965 I have maintained a diary of facts, documents, and opinions expressed at the time and these have often enabled me to perceive patterns in the sequences of events described which might not be so evident to someone writing without the advantage of such a day-to-day record.

Earlier in this Foreword I remarked that the two periods of Ayub Khan's administration—under Martial Law and under his presidential system—can be treated as an organic whole. Events during the period from 1962 to 1969 would, if plotted in terms of Ayub Khan's power and personal prestige, form a rising graph whose peak was reached when he achieved a decisive victory in the presidential election of January 1965. Thereafter, a series of successful tours abroad (which *The Times*, London, of 12 April 1965 referred to as his 'diplomatic quadrille') and a sense of national satisfaction at home with the course of economic development sustained him at that level until he blundered into Kashmir in August and September in that year.

However much the morale of Pakistan may have been fortified by its performance against India in September 1965, there can be no doubt of the disastrous consequences to Ayub Khan. He was wise in cutting his losses and in agreeing to a ceasefire, but he could not escape those further inroads upon his stature which began with the Tashkent Declaration. From this time onward, his image began to shrink and although there remained to him three more years of power and although, with the celebration of the Great Decade, in 1968, it seemed as if he were as firmly entrenched as at any time since 1958, it was evident to a discerning eye that, more and more, he was depending upon publicity rather than upon performance to sustain his name before the people.

To some extent, therefore, the period from 1962 to 1969 can be divided between the events that culminated in the year of optimum power—1965—and those which culminated in the collapse of Ayub Khan's presidential system and his own demission. On the other hand, the dichotomy was not so marked as to make it possible to treat the period as two fully integrated halves of one whole and these circumstances create problems of construction in any attempt to write the history of Pakistan during that time. The best that can be done, so far as I am able to find a solution, is to indicate the rising trend from 1962 to 1965 and, thereafter, deal with each category of events as it leads towards the final act of abdication. Unfortunately, some going back and forth in time can scarcely be avoided. These are blemishes of structure to which the only alternative would be to write the history in two or more periods, covering all aspects of each. But that way, it seems to me, lies hopeless confusion since there are so many important matters which, in their own way, overleap 1965, developing as they do from events and circumstances prior to that year.

Inevitably, some assessment of Ayub Khan, the man, must be included. He has been identified with this period in the country's history so closely and with such deliberation that the relationship between himself and the period of his administration has been forged into a complete unity. The cult of his personality has lodged in the public mind a deeply rooted sense of his total association with everything that occurred, for better or worse, during the period in which he held office. This creation of a powerful image was energetically pursued with the consequence that his character, personality and talent were automatically put in issue.

The manner in which this was done has since been very heavily criticized and indeed, if Ayub Khan's ultimate fate is any test, the effort must be deemed to have been ill-judged, ill-advised and to have failed.³ His total identification with the administration of the country inevitably placed upon him a personal liability for everything that happened, and especially for everything bad. It is not, therefore, surprising that a political opponent, who happened also to have been a former Commander-in-Chief of the Pakistan Air Force, Air-Marshal Asghar Khan, was moved to say: 'The rejection of President Ayub Khan is utter and complete. In his person, President Ayub Khan, rightly or wrongly, symbolises in the eyes of the people all that is evil in our society.'⁴ There can be no doubt that these harsh words objectified much that, at the time of their utterance, was agitating the public mind. Ayub Khan was deemed responsible for the rapidly deteriorating state of public order, for a mounting political crisis, and even for the loss of life and for injury to persons and to property during periods of riot and tumult. Air-Marshal Asghar Khan's words were spoken when feeling was running high and when the political temperature was feverish and a good deal might be read into them. Here, I will be content with two points. The first is that publicity and the creation of a public image form a delicate and subtle art. The second is that determined publicity, unsupported by achievement, must end finally in hollow collapse. This second statement brings into question just what the achievement amounted to in the case of Ayub Khan. I do not intend to suggest that there was none and I defer the point to its due place in the story to be narrated.

³ In a despatch to the *New York Times*, 9 March 1969, Mr. C. L. Sulzberger referred to a '... slavish propaganda ministry studded with incompetents'. If this refers to the Ministry of Information and Broadcasting the use of the word 'incompetents' conveys a false impression. The trouble was not a want of ability in the abstract but of professional skill and a totally misconceived approach. The *Observer*, London, 30 March 1969, also heavily criticized the public relations work undertaken on behalf of Ayub Khan. In a diary entry dated 26 September 1967, I noted: 'Ayub's personality cult ... will end in disaster....' This opinion had as much to do with the manner in which his personality was being projected as with the fact of projection itself. Curiously, however, *The Times*, London, 17 November 1966, said that President Ayub Khan was little given to flamboyance and personal publicity. It is difficult to understand how this conclusion was reached. In fact, during 1964, or soon thereafter, an official direction was issued to the effect that all national activity relating to development, improvement, progress etc. was to be so reported and expounded as to reflect well on Ayub Khan's sagacity, leadership, wisdom, etc.

⁴ *D*, 27 January 1969.

No doubt it was with knowledge of where events had led him that, addressing the nation in his famous broadcast of 21 February 1969, Ayub Khan appealed to his countrymen to *forgive and forget*. Yet a man should know that ten years of history, in which he himself has played so uniquely prominent a part, cannot be erased from the recollection of his countrymen nor, indeed, from that of the world at large. Field-Marshal Ayub Khan must, willy-nilly, occupy whatever place just and mature judgement may assign to him and even if the verdict prove painful to himself, his family, and his friends, there is no alternative to acceptance.

The intimacy of association between Ayub Khan and the administration during the period with which this book deals, provides an inescapable pattern. Both are so inextricably interwoven that it is impossible to write of the one without constantly impinging on the other, and if this work sometimes takes on the aspect of a critique of Ayub Khan's career as a political leader and as an administrator, that simply cannot be avoided.

This being so, we should remind ourselves what is, and ought to be, the prior purpose of such studies as this. Field-Marshal Ayub Khan, like the rest of us, is mortal. So, too, has proved the kind of Pakistan with which this book deals. The history of the sub-continent is littered with the debris of lost empires, shattered thrones, abandoned republics and broken dictatorships. And even today, when one surveys the course of events in Pakistan and India, it is difficult to accept without considerable misgiving the suggestion that the present political structures will endure. Indeed the history of the entire world is no less strewn with the wreckage of kingdoms, republics and other causes that could not, or did not know how to, survive. But life goes on, as the saying is, and it is with people rather than with political artifacts that our concern is greatest.

To some extent, therefore, I have moved, in my own thinking, from the assertion with which the previous volume, *Revolution in Pakistan* ended. There it was claimed that what was needed was understanding of the emergent nations. By the time that book was published, this sentiment had become a cliché and my own ideas had undergone modification. Today,

I am convinced that the problems of the group of countries of which Pakistan is naturally one, are hindered in their solution, not by a lack of sympathy and understanding on the part of other nations (although this may well exist) but by a lack of understanding of themselves. Their particular misfortune is well stated by Dr. Henry A. Kissinger. 'History . . . is made by men who cannot always distinguish their emotions from their analysis.'[5] In my view, this precise definition of an ever-present dilemma applies with special force to the poorer countries and more especially to those which have a long background of colonial rule.

It is true that other factors contribute to their difficulties. We are accustomed to hearing much about corruption, nepotism, and dishonesty and these, as elsewhere, play their deleterious part, along with indolence, which I hold to be more pernicious than the first three put together. Still, none of them can or will account for the quixotic miscalculation, the fierce, unguarded reaction, an extraordinary capacity for rationalizing situations and a well-exercised ability in the deadly and destructive art of self-persuasion. These are, indeed, the products of a confusion between emotion and analysis and out of them have been generated many unwise decisions and crippling errors of judgement.

Since this book was completed, a great deal has happened, particularly in East Bengal, which is of the gravest import. It is therefore necessary to emphasize that the present work is intended to be a study of the period from June 1962 to March 1969 and if I have sometimes strayed outside these limits in time, it has only been to underline something which falls within them. To the events which followed General Yahya Khan's declaration of Martial Law on 25 March 1969, I hope to return in a later volume.

As to the rest, the story must be allowed to tell itself. It remains only to acknowledge certain debts of gratitude which cannot easily be repaid. I owe much to the unfailing kindness of the librarians the Directorate of Archaeology of the Government of Pakistan, the National Bank of Pakistan, the Pakistan Institute of International Affairs and the State Bank

[5] Henry A. Kissinger, *The Troubled Partnership*, New York, Anchor Books, 1966, p. 63.

of Pakistan. Major Ibnul Hasan, Mr. Ronald Harrison, Mr. M. F. H. Beg and Mr. Guy Feldman were kind enough to read chapters and to give me the benefit of their knowledge and judgement. To them also, as to Squadron Leader M. Afzal (retd.), Mr. Jamiluddin Aali, and (though in a very different context) Sheikh Abbas, I am indebted for a great deal of valuable and light-shedding discourse. All this kindness contributed much to the writing of this book, but for those errors and omissions such as may be found, I alone am responsible.

H.F.
Karachi, 1970–1

CONTENTS

		Page
	Foreword	v
	Abbreviations	xv
I	From Martial Law to the Presidential System	1
II	The Political Structure, June 1962	12
III	Constitutional Change, 1962–5	24
IV	Economic Growth under the Presidential System	34
V	Political Events prior to the Elections, 1964–5	53
VI	The Presidential Election, 1965	68
VII	Foreign Relations, 1962–9	85
VIII	Indo-Pakistan Relations I	125
IX	Indo-Pakistan Relations II	138
X	East Pakistan	167
XI	West Pakistan	190
XII	Constitutional Change after September 1965	213
XIII	The Great Decade	226
XIV	The Last Phase	237
XV	Field-Marshal Mohammad Ayub Khan—An Assessment	272
	Epilogue	298

APPENDICES

A	Altaf Gauhar—A Profile	301
B	Wealth acquired by Captain Gohar Ayub Khan	305
C	Pakistan and Indian Armed Forces prior to September 1965	307

		Page
D	Karachi, September 1965—An Eye-witness Account	310
E	Zulfikar Ali Bhutto	313
F	Section 144 of the Criminal Procedure Code	319
G	The Pakistan Democratic Movement	321
H	Coup or Conspiracy?	323
I	The Fate of the '303'	328
J	The Tashkent Declaration	330
	Index	333

ABBREVIATIONS

D — *Dawn*, a daily newspaper published in English in Karachi. Although not a National Press Trust newspaper it was, particularly after the presidential election of 1965, *plus royaliste que le roi*. It is very useful for verbatim reproductions of official papers and documents.

FNM — *Friends not Masters* by Field-Marshal Mohammad Ayub Khan, O.U.P., London, 1967.

NAD — National Assembly Debates.

PO — *The Pakistan Observer*, a daily newspaper published in English in Dacca. Founded in 1949, it played an important part in the language movement in East Pakistan which led to the acceptance of Bengali as a national language. During the entire government of Ayub Khan, it was in opposition and has published some illuminating material.

TRANSLITERATION

The problem of transliteration is an abiding one and, unfortunately, Pakistan has not adhered to the excellent system of Roman-Urdu which was devised for the old British-Indian Army. This partly accounts for the inconsistencies and variations in the spelling of names of which *Mohamed* is the most conspicuous example. Certainly it accounts for many inconsistencies which may be noticed in this book. Of course, a man may spell his name as he likes—Smith, Smithe, Smyth, Smythe. In Pakistan, a man whose name is spelled *dal*(D), *yih*(EE), *noon*(N) can transliterate it to read *Deen, Dean, Deane* or whatever so long as it gives that result when uttered.

The want of system in Pakistan has led to such spellings as *Quaid* which looks as if it ought to be pronounced 'kwade' or 'kwide' and *Eid* which looks as if it ought to be pronounced 'ide'. All are wrong. The worst cases are provided by the film industry which in the sub-continent pursues an esoteric method of its own. We find such instances as *Bees Din* which does not mean the noise created by swarming honey-gatherers but signifies, in fact, 'Twenty Days'.

Our present destiny is to move from crisis to crisis. For us, there can be no rest or relaxation.

Field-Marshal Mohammad Ayub Khan

I

From Martial Law to the Presidential System

WHEN, at 8.30 a.m. on 8 June 1962, Pakistan's form of government changed and Martial Law gave place to the Constitution drafted in accordance with Field-Marshal Ayub Khan's ideas of a structure which, to use his own words, his countrymen 'could understand and work',[1] certain things had already become apparent.

It was certain that his countrymen were far from unanimous in their approval of his constitutional theories and of the form of the constitution he had promulgated. Moreover, those of dissentient views were not unanimous among themselves, including some holding what we may call progressive opinions and others guided by an intense Islamic orthodoxy. In particular, the system of Basic Democracy which, according to Ayub Khan was 'probably unique',[2] continued to be suspect and none of the arguments which he had employed to rebut the criticism made of it had succeeded in convincing everyone. It is true that the sycophantic chorus in Pakistan, and elsewhere, hailed the new Constitution as the work of political genius and, on this point, it suffices to glance at the Pakistani newspapers of that time. But there were others a great deal more reserved in their opinions.

Public misgiving could not be dispelled by the apologetics which the Government had earlier published on the provisions of the new Constitution, especially those relating to the electoral machinery.[3] It was, moreover, widely felt that the views of some, if not of everyone, concerned with the preparation of the new Constitution, had been shouldered very brusquely aside, and although Ayub Khan had expressed his special thanks to the Chairman of the Constitution Commission, a former Chief Justice of Pakistan, the late Mr. M.

---

[1] Broadcast, 8 October 1958. [2] Broadcast, 1 March 1962.
[3] On this, see Feldman, *Revolution in Pakistan*, pp. 114 et seq.

Shahabuddin,[4] it was widely rumoured that Mr. Shahabuddin disapproved of the new Constitution and had sent a statement to the press to the effect that it was not in accordance with the recommendations of his Commission. Publication of this statement, so people said, was not permitted and, years later, Mr. Shahabuddin affirmed the truth of all this.[5]

A great deal has been written about the Constitution which Ayub Khan promulgated on 1 March 1962 and it is not intended to give any elaborate description of it here. Generally, it has been spoken of as based on the presidential system although one learned commentator remarked: 'Our present Constitution conforms neither to the Parliamentary nor to the Presidential pattern.'[6] This author advanced several reasons to support his assertion and their substance was that under the Constitution which Ayub Khan instituted, the measure of his responsibility to the Legislature and to the electors was minimal and his executive power almost unlimited. Whether these reasons suffice to establish the author's point is, it seems to me, doubtful and, in any case, it seems clear that there are as many presidential systems as there are constitutions with presidents. Much more significant is the fact that the reasons adduced by Mr. Munir do indicate, very clearly and very accurately, the true nature of the Constitution by which Pakistan was governed from 8 June 1962 to 25 March 1969. It was authoritarian and, in the hands of its sometimes adroit and sometimes clumsy manipulator, proved to be democratic in name rather than in fact. With the Head of the State there reposed a wide range of executive powers on the exercise of which there was no restraint whatsoever and, as we shall see later on, it was this great quantum of authority, on the retention of which Ayub Khan was so eagerly bent, that contributed much to his ultimate undoing.

[4] Broadcast, 1 March 1962.
[5] *PO*, Dacca, 10 December 1968. Views supporting Mr. Shahabuddin's statement were also published by a former High Court Judge and one-time Secretary to the Government of Pakistan in the Law Ministry, Mr. Hamid Ali. *D*, 15 December 1968.
[6] M. Munir, *Constitution of the Islamic Republic of Pakistan*, Lahore, 1967, p. 254. Mr. Munir is a former Chief Justice of Pakistan and was the first Minister of Law and Parliamentary Affairs to be appointed by President Ayub Khan when the new Constitution came into effect in June 1962.

In bare fact, the nation had been asked to accept a Constitution in which neither the President nor the Ministers chosen by him were responsible to the National Assembly, itself a diminutive body, bearing in mind that it represented a nation of about one hundred million persons. It comprised only 156 members of whom six were women elected to seats reserved for them.[7] This tiny chamber was elected, not by direct voting on the basis of universal adult suffrage, but by an Electoral College consisting of eighty thousand persons, themselves elected on the basis of universal adult suffrage, and divided equally between the two Provinces. These eighty thousand persons[8] were otherwise known as Basic Democrats and it was in this capacity that they provided the elected membership of those bodies which carried on, at various levels, the local government of the country. Basic Democrats also had other responsibilities. They provided the members of the Conciliation Courts for settling minor disputes between individuals and for dealing with disputes relating to matters of marriage and divorce among Muslims in accordance with the Family Laws Ordinance. They were directly concerned with the operation of the Rural Works Programme and sometimes with the local distribution of foodgrains and other necessities when there was shortage or disaster. It was their dual character, by which membership of the Electoral College and that of local government bodies were combined, which made possible the purchase and retention of their allegiance. Thus, as time passed, it was generally believed in Pakistan that the Basic Democrats had, for the most part, been thoroughly corrupted by Ayub Khan and his political henchmen. This had more than a formal relevance, for the institution of the Basic Democracy system and the creation of Basic Democrats were intimately associated with the name of Ayub Khan. They comprised one of the first great changes made during his Martial Law administration,

[7] Women could also be elected to unreserved seats. In 1967, the National Assembly's membership was increased to 218 members, divided equally between the two Provinces. The number of seats reserved for women was increased to eight, and ten seats were reserved for persons who had held high office, or had distinguished themselves by way of professional or academic eminence, or who had not less than ten years' practical experience in law, medicine, engineering, or journalism.

[8] In 1967 the number was increased to 120,000, also divided equally between the two Provinces.

and the Basic Democracies Ordinance was promulgated on 27 October 1959, on the first anniversary of what was held to be the day when his 'revolution' began. The Basic Democracies system was one in which Ayub Khan took special pride and for which he claimed special credit.

The truth of the assertion that the Basic Democrats had been suborned from their duties cannot be totally denied, although it is just as evident that by no means every one of them had been so corrupted. Certainly, in the presidential election of 1965, no less than 28,000 out of 80,000 Basic Democrats voted against Ayub Khan and in favour of Miss Fatima Jinnah, sister of Quaid-i-Azam Mohamed Ali Jinnah, who was the Combined Opposition Parties' candidate. It is also said that but for electoral gerrymandering on that occasion the number who voted for Miss Jinnah would have been higher. To this point I shall return in a later chapter.

Not only was the National Assembly small in itself; its powers were considerably limited, especially in relation to financial matters. Over national expenditure it had no control whatever, except with respect to what was called 'new expenditure', and this represented by far the minor aspect of the subject. In respect of voting money supplies, although a Budget was presented to the Assembly and members could criticize it as they might wish, there was no power to refuse.

Such, in very brief outline, was the form of government which Ayub Khan had, doubtless with the help of others, devised. The allotment of responsibility for many of its provisions has remained substantially obscure, although I have already remarked on the disclaimer of the Chairman of the Commission on the Constitution. Ayub Khan himself took credit for having contributed the salient points[9] and, in later years, he said that over this constitutional system he had 'sweated blood' and would not see it trifled with, although he conceded that it could be amended or changed in the light of experience.[10] In fact, as will appear in the next chapter, the first person to trifle with it was Ayub Khan himself, exactly four days after the Constitution came into effect.

Secondly, both public and literary images revealed that his

---

[9] Broadcast, 1 March 1962.   [10] *FNM*, p. 221.

thinking was neither penetrating nor profound and that the development of his political thought in particular had no extensive, well meditated background.[11] His attitude to the solution of his country's problems was based on a combination of solid common sense allied to a set of notions conspicuous for their simplistic naïveté. He could be wise enough on clear-cut issues and could see his way towards necessary and practical ends as these revealed themselves, but as soon as he strayed into the less substantial realms of theory and projection, his grip faltered and he was liable to make himself look foolish.

Thirdly, there was the question of his personality. Notwithstanding the impressive exterior and the choice of blunt soldierly language, it had already been demonstrated that his was no stern and unrelenting character, firm in its decisions and in the determination to pursue to the end clearly defined objectives. On the contrary, he had shown himself to be, in essence, a conciliator, a man ready to compromise and come to terms with any movement, organization or individual, even within the country itself, wherever there was a genuine point of view and the courage to pursue it. This is not to say that anyone visited with his displeasure might not be made to feel its sting, but that had more to do with a sensitive vanity and an easily provoked feeling of injured pride. In some material respects it had long been evident that he was not a man to press convictions *à outrance* and part of his ability to remain in office for more than ten consecutive years consisted in a talent for flexible and timely manœuvre.

This explains why some of the reforms initiated by him during the Martial Law administration were not implemented. Open defiance on the part of the students led to a suspension of many of the proposed reforms in education. At the instance of more occult influences, the recommendations of the Commission on Company Law remained a dead letter. His Land Reforms, which applied only to West Pakistan, were far less effective in their scope than insistent publicity had claimed and, in the

---

[11] He claimed, in the broadcast quoted above, to have given wide study as well as deep and prolonged thought to the constitutional problem. In *Revolution in Pakistan*, however, I drew attention to the simplistic nature of Ayub Khan's political ideas and his later abandonment of some of them. Op. cit., pp. 110, 112, and 118.

case of certain influential landlords, their effect had been greatly mitigated.[12]

On the other hand—and it is fair that this should be clearly pointed out—there were important social measures, instituted by Ayub Khan, and opposed in many orthodox quarters, with which he had persevered. Conspicuous among them was the Ordinance on Muslim Family Laws which had liberated many Pakistani women from the unfair exercise of certain Islamic institutions, notably plural marriage and divorce by *talaq*.[13] Not only did certain groups dislike these changes, but they maintained a steadfast opposition to them which, to this day, has not been entirely silenced, although it seems unlikely that the law either will, or could be, changed back. In any case, the number of legal notices appearing in the newspapers by wives obviously aggrieved and probably deserted, is testimony enough to the utility of the changes which Ayub Khan brought about.

Similar things can be said about his proposals for a country-wide movement to encourage family planning and the wise limitation of families. He clearly saw, and had more than once remarked to the effect, that without some limitation on population growth, all economic progress would be nullified simply by reason of the proliferation of hungry mouths. But these opinions did not fall on unanimously willing ears, and the orthodox saw in family planning yet another impious subversion of the Divine Scheme.

But whatever might be said about the want of firmness in Ayub Khan's character, about the scope of his reformist endeavours and the measure of their success, the paramount fact was that the impact of his personality was sufficiently strong,

---

[12] Report on the Land Reforms in West Pakistan, Vol. 3, 1967, Appendix IV, p. 188, gives the names of nine persons allowed to retain on lease additional areas out of proprietary lands under para. 9(d) of the Land Reform Regulations. The areas ranged from 74 acres in the case of Mian Mohd. Hyat Nangiana of Sargodha District, to 18,619 acres in the case of the late Nawab Malik Amir Mohd. Khan and his sons, of Kalabagh, Mianwali District. All these nine persons came from the class of great landed proprietors and these retentions on lease appear to have been allowed as a solace to injured feelings.

[13] Divorce by *talaq* simply means that with a mere verbal pronouncement the husband can break the marriage tie. It is the method which Islam most clearly condemns and the method which Muslims most commonly use except in those countries where its use has been restricted or abolished.

and his position still sufficiently well entrenched, to enable him to resist any encroachment on his authority. Indeed, at that time, he could well afford to disregard the possibility of any such attempt for although there were groups who remained in opposition, none of them deployed the kind of power which could make any inroad on his well-fortified position and it is probable that his ascendancy in the public mind was still such as to rob those opposition groups of confidence in themselves.

At that time, it was indisputable that he enjoyed the support of the generality of the people. They still felt that here was a man who could maintain a stable order and thereby make it possible for the nation to progress along the path of economic and social progress. If the voice of criticism was not entirely still, at any rate it mostly went unheeded. Even abroad, where there were people who looked askance at the kind of authoritarian government Ayub Khan had established, it was frequently conceded that the advantages conferred by political stability must mean more to a country where poverty and illiteracy abounded than freedom for politicians to wrangle noisily in the market-place.[14]

Although Article 226 of the new Constitution somewhat cavalierly nominated Field-Marshal Ayub Khan as the first President, for a term of approximately three years expiring in March 1965,[15] there was some feeling that he should continue the work he had successfully begun. In particular, it was considered desirable that the impact of his personality and drive, in relation to planning for economic growth, should continue to be felt.

In this last respect, evidence was not wanting to support such ideas. Based on constant factor cost for the year 1959–60, the national income *per capita* had risen from Rs.315 in 1957–8 to Rs.337 in 1961–2. Unfortunately, the family planning movement had not yet had time to achieve any substantial results

[14] India was no exception, where General K. M. Cariappa was the frequent and injudicious mouthpiece for attacks on politicians. Perhaps the best-known instance was his reference to 'dog eating dog' reported in the *Indian Express*, 19 July 1965. This remark became the subject of a privilege motion in the Hyderabad State Assembly, but General Cariappa was not discouraged and his advice to his countrymen continued for years afterwards.

[15] The authority for this was stated, in the same Article, to be the referendum conducted in February 1960 when Ayub Khan was the only candidate, no others being permitted.

so that the rate of population growth remained at the disastrous figure of more than 2 per cent. But for this, the income *per capita* would have shown a greater improvement.

Taken in greater detail, some departments of national economic activity appeared to be doing rather well. Large-scale manufacturing had risen from Rs.138·7 crores in 1957–8 to Rs.219·1 crores in 1961–2. Electricity, gas, water and sanitary services had risen from Rs.6·9 crores to Rs.12·5 crores for the corresponding years. The index of agricultural production had risen from 108 to 119 after a drop to 91 in the year 1960–1.[16] Further, reserves in gold, dollars and sterling, which stood at Rs.76·58 crores in September 1958 had risen to Rs.112·83 by June 1962.

Satisfactory though this might be, there were also disquieting signs. The cost of living had undoubtedly gone up. If the 1961 figure is taken as 100, the cost of food, in Karachi, had risen from 96·38 in 1957–8 to 101·78 in 1961–2. Housing and household expenses showed very small increases for those years, but clothing had risen by 15 per cent and general living costs by 8 per cent.[17] Much more sinister, perhaps, was the fact that East Pakistan continued to lag behind.

In that Province, 81·3 per cent of all households had monthly incomes of Rs.200 ($42·50) or less. In West Pakistan, the corresponding percentage was 68·5, and of a total personal income for the entire country of Rs.3,912 crores, 51·7 per cent accrued to West Pakistan and 48·3 per cent to East Pakistan although, according to the 1961 Census, East Pakistan had a population of 50·8 million as against 42·8 million in West Pakistan. The disparity in income was particularly marked in the rural areas where, for East Pakistan, the *per capita* figure was Rs.305 whereas in West Pakistan it was Rs.373. Of East Pakistan's share in the total national personal income, 44·3 per cent came from rural areas and only 4 per cent from urban areas. In West Pakistan, 37·2 per cent came from rural areas

[16] 1959 equals 100. The availability of food-grains *per capita* continued to hover around 14 oz. a day, although population increase had much to do with this. Wheat production, however, was still inadequate. The practice, in Pakistan, of lumping all food-grains together for statistical purposes is highly misleading.

[17] This information is based on consumer price indices prepared in respect of clerical personnel employed by the Government and commercial firms. It is taken from the Economic Surveys prepared annually by the Government of Pakistan.

and 14·5 per cent from urban areas. Thus, not only was West Pakistan in all respects better off, its urban development far exceeded that of East Pakistan.[18]

Another menacing factor, although not then explicitly regarded as such at that time, was the extent to which the Export Bonus Voucher System had become integrated into the economy, making it doubtful whether the economy could ever be wrested free of it. It was unduly optimistic to assert as it then was, that a day would come when the stimulus provided by the Bonus Voucher System would no longer be required for the export trade and, in particular, for the export of manufactured goods. In a sense, this was only stating the obvious since it is a condition precedent to the adoption of any such system that its success will ensure its superfluity and if the system is not progressively self-eliminating, the conclusion must be either that it has failed or, at best, that it has not been suitably operated.

It was easy enough to describe the system as an export incentive but no such euphemism could conceal the fact, which the passing years underlined more and more clearly, that the Export Bonus Voucher System was nothing other than a form of devaluation expressed through a series of multiple exchange rates and that the prospects of doing away with the system, short of an explicit devaluation, were as remote as ever. It was also becoming increasingly evident that the longer the system was retained, the more difficult it would become to have recourse to that explicit devaluation which, in the end, would not only be more expedient but a great deal more just to all sections of the community. By permitting the use of Bonus Vouchers to be extended to a lengthening list of non-essential goods, including some which could only be described as luxuries, the market rate at which Bonus Vouchers could be purchased was kept high. This had the effect of soaking up inflationary funds in circulation, but at the same time raising the landed cost of necessary goods brought in by this means.[19]

---

[18] These figures are based on a sample survey undertaken in 1963–4, by the Central Statistical Office, Government of Pakistan.

[19] The price of an Export Bonus Voucher, i.e. the percentage premium over its face value in rupees, at which it could be purchased in order to import goods, fluctuates considerably. Fluctuation depends on (a) the categories of goods permitted to be imported; (b) the availability of ordinary import licences and (c) the

In short, the consumer was paying and the price, like the gentle rain from Heaven, fell on rich and poor alike. The introduction of extortionate rates of customs duty on certain luxury items such as motor cars whose c.i.f. value exceeded Rs.11,000, on air conditioners, and on refrigerators above a certain cubic capacity, had very little impact on the wealthy few and had no relevance at all to the weight with which rising prices for essentials fell on the impoverished many.

It was somewhat in this context that people remembered those unfulfilled assurances—many of them no doubt reckless and others unconvincing from the start—which, at various times, Ayub Khan, or members of his Martial Law administration, had bestowed upon the people. There was the little matter of a country-wide food-drive that was to bring self-sufficiency in food-grains within two years.[20] Early in the following year a pilot project was launched to abolish beggary.[21] Not long after this, Mr. Mohd. Shoaib, the Finance Minister, was bold—or imprudent—enough to express the view that, within two years, Pakistan would become self-sufficient in the manufacture of sugar.[22] Notwithstanding the economic advance said to have been made during Ayub Khan's administration, sugar was still being imported when he gave up the office of President in March 1969, and by that time it was on ration. Lieut.-General Burki, who tended to be more venturesome in his pronouncements than other members of the Martial Law administration, had promised social legislation by the end of 1961,[23] and about the same time as he gave this promise, he expressed the view that by the end of the Second Five Year Plan, i.e. by June 1965, there would be medical aid for all in Pakistan and that no tuberculosis or malaria would exist.[24]

Politicians' promises are notoriously fragile. We need not attach too much weight to the comforting, though evanescent

general state of trade and the availability of goods within the country. In the course of a year, fluctuation might lie within a range of 40 per cent. However, the tendency has been for Bonus Vouchers to rise as the finances of the country have weakened. This, too, has been reflected in the free market rate for the Pakistani rupee which has fallen steadily since June 1962.

[20] *D*, 5 April 1960.
[21] *D*, 5 February 1961.
[22] *D*, 4 April 1961.
[23] *D*, 12 November 1961.
[24] *D*, 24 November 1961.

FROM MARTIAL LAW TO THE PRESIDENTIAL SYSTEM

visions that Ayub Khan and his colleagues held out, but a time was to come when people would recall them. When in later years that day came, Ayub Khan was operating on a basis of publicity rather than on achievement, and many compared the substance of what they actually had with the shadow of what they had been persuaded to believe in. These were discoveries that many, still finding Ayub Khan credible in June 1962, were to make years afterwards when his credibility had taken wings for ever. Still the fact is that when, in June 1962, Martial Law gave place to the presidential system of Ayub Khan's devising, he was still regarded as credible and he still enjoyed the confidence of the majority.

II

The Political Structure, June 1962

To understand the constitutional and political structure that sprang into being when the new Constitution became effective in June 1962, it is necessary to retrace steps a little.

In his broadcast to the nation on 1 March 1962, when President Ayub Khan announced the new Constitution, he indicated that elections would be held for the purpose of selecting, in advance, members of the National and Provincial Assemblies for which the new Constitution made provision. He also made it clear that for the purpose of these elections no formation of political parties, which had been abolished in 1958, would be permitted. For this he adduced two reasons. The first was that, until the Constitution came into effect, Martial Law remained. The second lay in his hope, shortly to be abandoned, that it would be possible to organize the nation's political life without the party system in which case 'we shall have cause to bless ourselves'.[1] With no possibility of appeal to party considerations, therefore, candidates would be chosen on the basis of personal merit, and in these circumstances it would be left to each individual seeking election to make felt the substance of his talent and personality when electioneering began. For this purpose the State would provide means by which candidates could present themselves to members of the Electoral College and impress them with the extent of their abilities and qualifications.

Three weeks later, in another broadcast, Ayub Khan announced his Manifesto, a long document containing a series of claims, declarations, and exhortations. Its purpose seems to have been that of guiding electors in favour of candidates who declared themselves supporters of the President and his policies, and although, in the same broadcast, he was careful

[1] Broadcast, 1 March 1962.

enough to explain that he had no political party of his own, the Manifesto provided something round which support for him might coalesce. He also claimed to have no interest in any individual candidates and he made it clear that the election would be a matter of free and unfettered choice by the electorate, which comprised 80,000 Basic Democrats. To these he addressed a special word of guidance emphasizing the gravity of their responsibilities.

On 25 March it was announced that elections to the National Assembly would be held on 28 April 1962 and to the Provincial Assemblies on 6 May. Shortly afterwards there appeared the National and Provincial Assemblies (First Elections) Order which made provision for the conduct of these elections. This legislation was necessary since the Constitution was still not in force. Pursuant to this Order, nomination papers for candidates for the three Assemblies were required to be filed before 5 April and on that day it was stated that some 600 persons had offered themselves as candidates for the 112 National Assembly constituencies and more than 1,800 persons had offered themselves for the 224 Provincial constituencies.

On 6 April, the day following that on which nomination papers were filed, it was announced, to no one's great surprise, that Prince Aurangzeb, heir to the Wali of Swat, had been declared returned unopposed to the National Assembly for Constituency No. NW-18 (Swat-Peshawar Agencies III). Two days later, on 8 April, the Nawab of Dir, the neighbouring state, was likewise declared elected unopposed for Constituency No. NW-17 (Peshawar Agency III).

However, there were still three weeks to polling-day. Arrangements were made at public expense for candidates in each constituency to appear at what were called meetings 'to face the electorate'. Candidates were permitted to issue their own manifestoes, but anything in the nature of party activity was prohibited, and to enforce this prohibition, a further National and Provincial Assemblies (First Election) Order was published which forbade any candidate to claim membership of a political party or the support of any such party.

The public meetings held to face the electorate were joint affairs, held under the chairmanship of the District Magistrate or some other civil service functionary. All candidates sat on the platform and each was allowed the same number of minutes in which to address the audience. The audience was not restricted to members of the Electoral College, but members of the general public were admitted and could ask questions along with the others.

In these circumstances, it is not surprising that the elections passed off in a largely tranquil atmosphere. Moreover, the proceedings were simplified as time went on because there were many withdrawals from the poll and the patience of the electors was not unduly taxed. When polling-day arrived, the average number of candidates for each of the 112 National Assembly constituencies could not have exceeded three or four. The results, when declared, were peculiar and unfamiliar. Instead of the more customary figures that ran into thousands, candidates with one or two hundred votes were successful while the unsuccessful might have none, or a mere handful. The reason was that the Electoral College was divided by constituency and, in all, about 80 per cent of them voted. It was all very simple and there was not the least difficulty in counting 65,000 votes divided among 112 constituencies. None of this, however, deterred many unsuccessful candidates from disputing the elections for one reason or another and for the adjudication of such objections the Settlement of Disputes (First Election) Order was promulgated.[2] Not long afterwards, in somewhat similar circumstances, elections for the two Provincial Assemblies were held.

Thus it was that when the new Constitution came into force, a National and two Provincial Assemblies were ready to be summoned. In fact, the National Assembly was summoned on 8 June 1962, to hear an address by President Ayub Khan commending the new Constitution to them and reminding them of their duties to it and to the nation. Four days later a curious thing happened. Reference has been made to it in the previous chapter and it concerns Ayub Khan's attempt to change an important provision of the Constitution which had been the object of so much study by so many learned men and in whose every word Ayub Khan had expressed complete faith.

It was soon to become characteristic of a great deal that Ayub Khan did and said, usually with much show of fore-

[2] Two years were to elapse before all these disputes were finally decided.

thought and decision, that having done or said it, he thereupon proceeded to alter it. Just as characteristic is the fact that, as in the instance about to be described, he ran into legal difficulties, sometimes at once.

By virtue of Article 103 of the Constitution, a person appointed to be a member of the President's Council of Ministers would, if he happened at the time of appointment to be a member of the National Assembly, be obliged to relinquish that membership. This was clearly a material feature and its point needs no emphasis. Nevertheless, ninety-six hours after the Constitution had come into effect, it was announced that an Ordinance would shortly be made, under Article 224, so that members of the National and Provincial Assemblies could be appointed to the President's and the Governors' Councils of Ministers, without losing their Assembly seats.[3] However, Article 224 happened to be one of the transitory provisions of the Constitution, to remain in force only for three months after the Constitution came into effect, and its purpose was to enable the President to make such Orders as might be necessary to remove any difficulties arising in the course of bringing the new Constitution into operation. For that matter, a number of Orders were so made and it is clear that temporary authority to make possible the solution of unforeseen difficulties was a reasonable safeguard. It is, however, just as clear that the question whether or not Ministers could retain their Assembly seats had no bearing whatsoever on the problem of giving the Constitution practical effect. The application of Article 224 to make what was, in reality, a change in the constitutional structure, was not a legitimate use of this temporary power but an abuse of it. The Order, Removal of Difficulties (Appointment of Ministers) Order, No. 34, was nevertheless made, though its validity was challenged in the High Court in East Pakistan, in the case of Mohd. Abdul Haque *vs.* Fazlul Qader Choudhury, where it was held that the Order was *ultra vires* the terms of the Constitution. On appeal, this decision was upheld in the Supreme Court.

This decision, announced in May 1963, had important repercussions which are worth noting. As a result of it, all Ayub Khan's Ministers holding seats in the National Assembly,

[3] *D*, 12 June 1962.

i.e. six out of eight, lost them and so the slender majority in the House on which the Government could rely was reduced until by-elections could be held. Ayub Khan thereupon took the opportunity of making ministerial changes. Mr. A. T. M. Mustafa was brought in as Education and Information Minister and Mr. Mahmud became Minister of Industries and Natural Resources in place of Mr Z. A. Bhutto who had become Foreign Minister in place of Mr. Mohamed Ali Bogra who died on 23 January 1963.[4]

However, we must not go too far ahead and should return to the events of June 1962. Lieut.-General Burki, one of Field-Marshal Ayub Khan's colleagues in the first Martial Law administration, was appointed Special Assistant to the President with the privileges of a minister but without Cabinet rank. On the same day the late Maulvi Tamizuddin Khan was elected unopposed as the first Speaker of the new National Assembly. Tamizuddin Khan was a highly respected figure with several claims to fame. He was Speaker of the Constituent Assembly which the then Governor-General, Ghulam Mohamed, had dismissed in 1954, and he had sought, through the medium of the Courts, to resist Ghulam Mohamed. More conspicuous, perhaps, is the fact that he is about the only person among Ayub Khan's political contemporaries for whom Ayub had a good word to say in his book.[5] As First Deputy Speaker, Abul Qasem of Rangpur, in East Pakistan, another greatly respected member of the old Muslim League, was elected, also without opposition. The Second Deputy Speaker, Choudhury Afzal Cheema, was elected after a close contest with Raja Hasan Akhtar. Both of these men were from West Pakistan.

[4] There were other interesting repercussions. In June 1966, Mr. Mahmood Haroon and Mir Ghulam Qadir of Lasbela resigned as Ministers of the West Pakistan Government. Their resignations appear to have been forced on them in consequence of their support, in a by-election for the National Assembly, for Mir Ghaus Baksh Bizenjo who was contesting the seat (in Karachi) against Khan Bahadur H. M. Habibullah, the Government-sponsored candidate. In the West Pakistan Assembly it was proposed to discuss the circumstances in which the two Ministers resigned, but the Speaker disallowed the debate on the ground that the Ministers were not members of the House. 'This,' he explained, 'is the difference between the presidential and the parliamentary system.' (West Pakistan Assembly Debates, June 1966. See also *Daily News, Evening Star* and *Leader*, Karachi, 7 June 1966.)

[5] 'I always admired his courage.' *FNM*, p. 206.

Important political events occurred quickly. On 12 June, the late Mohamed Ali (Bogra), a former Prime Minister, launched in East Pakistan a heavy attack in the National Assembly on Mr. Manzur Qadir, at that time Foreign Minister and closely associated with President Ayub Khan in the drafting of the new Constitution. Mr. Mohamed Ali described Manzur Qadir as 'a political upstart' and proceeded to attack the new Constitution, saying it was by no means perfect. As we shall see, boldness paid on this occasion.

Next day seven members of the President's Council of Ministers were sworn in. They comprised:

Mr. M. Munir—Law and Parliamentary Affairs
Mr. Mohamed Ali (Bogra)—External Affairs and Leader of the House
Mr. Abdul Qadir—Finance
Mr. Abdul Monem Khan—Health, Labour and Social Welfare
Mr. Habibullah Khan—Home and Kashmir Affairs
Mr. Wahiduzzaman—Commerce
Mr. Zulfikar Ali Bhutto—Industries and National Resources
Mr. Abdus Sabur Khan—Communications
Mr. A. K. M. Fazlul Qader Choudhury—Agriculture and Works

Of these, Mr. Munir, Mr. Abdul Qadir, Mr. Habibullah Khan, and Mr. Z. A. Bhutto were from West Pakistan and the rest from the Eastern Province. Mr. Abdul Qadir was a former civil servant and Mr. Munir a former Chief Justice of Pakistan. Of this first Council of Ministers, Mr. Sabur Khan survived until the very end in March 1969. Mr. Monem Khan likewise survived but as Governor of East Pakistan. All the others went their several ways and may well have congratulated themselves since that they departed when they did.

Politics were now very much in the air. Shortly after these appointments were announced, Mr. Mohamed Ali (Bogra) made public the formation of a 'democratic group' from among National Assembly members comprising forty-six like-minded persons who, as it happened, all came from his own Province of East Pakistan and they prepared a seventeen-point programme.[6]

[6] *D*, 17 June 1962.

Soon afterwards, Sardar Bahadur Khan, a brother of the President, announced a group of some forty like-minded members of the Assembly whose distinguishing characteristics were that they all came from West Pakistan and had a seven-point programme which included elections based on direct, universal adult suffrage.[7] On the following day an independent group of thirty, consisting mostly of members of the old Muslim League, announced a twelve-point programme which included a proposal for direct elections based on universal adult suffrage and another proposal by which the Budget was to be made fully subject to the vote of the National Assembly.

Thus it was that although the Constitution was ratified by a vote of the National Assembly[8] and although President Ayub Khan had expressed the hope that Pakistan would manage its affairs without the intervention of party considerations, party groupings emerged within a fortnight of the Constitution taking effect and these party groupings bore an aspect of provincial division. Moreover, on 15 July the President assented to a Bill permitting the formation of political parties, which had been explained in a somewhat lame statement by the President issued on 21 June 1962 and again, on 17 July 1962, when he said that he considered the formation of such parties to be necessary.

Known as the Political Parties Act, 1962, this brief measure permitted the formation of political parties which were not 'foreign aided' and whose objects did not conflict with Islamic ideology or with the integrity or security of Pakistan. The most interesting provision was in Section 8(2) which said that if a person, elected to the National or a Provincial Assembly, as a candidate or nominee of a political party, withdrew from that party, he would, from the date of withdrawal, be disqualified from being a member of that Assembly for the unexpired period of his term as a member, unless he were re-elected at a by-election caused by this disqualification. The idea was to put an end to the frequently witnessed farce of members of the national and provincial legislatures crossing and re-crossing the floor, with no reference to the electorate which put them there or to the political programmes they had professed to support when canvassing. In this respect the Act was neither unreasonable nor unsound but even this provision was, in due

[7] *D*, 22 June 1962.   [8] *D*, 18 June 1962.

time, to lose its weight because of Ayub Khan's own manipulations.

Party politics were now fully resumed, beginning with an announcement concerning the reactivation of the Muslim League which, along with all other parties, had been abolished in October 1958. Early in August, former Muslim League leaders met in Dacca at the house of the much respected Muslim League veteran, Maulana Akram Khan.[9] A few days later, it was stated that the Council of the Muslim League would meet on 29 September 1962[10] and the revival of the League was specifically reported two days afterwards. However, six days after this,[11] Maulana Akram Khan cancelled the arrangement by which the Council was to meet on 29 September. He gave no reason for this announcement, and he refused to state a reason when asked.[12] On the same day, 19 August, it was reported that arrangements were being made for a 'broadbased Muslim League Convention' to be held in Rawalpindi, but this was later modified and a convention was arranged for Karachi on 4 September to which one thousand delegates would be invited. At first, it was not known whether Maulana Akram Khan would be invited, but a few days before the convention was held it became known that he would not be present.[13] In an atmosphere of mystification and mounting excitement, President Ayub Khan announced that he had no desire to lead any political party.[14]

An invitation to preside over the convention was declined by the Raja of Mahmudabad, yet another greatly respected veteran of the All-India Muslim League.[15] In his place, Choudhury Khaliquzzaman was then appointed Chairman and Chief Organizer, but although he had long been associated with the Muslim League, his political credentials by no means matched those of the Raja of Mahmudabad and it was widely felt that the choice was unfortunate.[16] The convention itself

[9] He belonged to East Pakistan and died in Dacca on 18 August 1968.
[10] *D*, 12 August 1962.
[11] *D*, 18 August 1962.
[12] *D*, 19 August 1962.
[13] *D*, 29 August 1962.
[14] *D*, 27 August 1962.
[15] *D*, 3 September 1962.
[16] *D*, 10 September 1962.

was anything but a harmonious affair. There were noisy scenes, vociferous protests, and walk-outs. At one stage of the proceedings students were invited to the platform in the hope that their youthful appeals for order might quell the angry rivalries among the audience. There was indeed a time when it seemed that the whole business might end in a 'fiasco of fisticuffs'.[17]

Later that month, seventy-two members of the old Muslim League gave notice to Mr. Abul Qasem, Senior Joint Secretary (and First Deputy Speaker of the National Assembly) requisitioning a meeting of the Muslim League Council, in terms of the old League Constitution. This notice was given on 21 September and a decision was taken that the requisitioned meeting would be held not later than 27 October 1962.

In this fashion was created the dichotomy which led to the existence of two Muslim Leagues—one known as the 'Convention' League and the other as the 'Council' League. The background to these events may never be clearly known, but certain facts are established. It is clear from Ayub Khan's statement, issued at Rawalpindi on 21 June 1962, that the need or desirability of his joining or leading a political party had been suggested by his friends and the question acquired fresh urgency upon the passing of the Political Parties Bill.[18] It is probable that if Ayub Khan could have been certain of joining Maulana Akram Khan and other members of the old Muslim League Council and of assuming leadership when he did so, or soon afterwards, the question of a convention would never have arisen, but it is precisely here that the doubt and the difficulty lay.

It is possible that in the self-appointed role of saviour of Pakistan, Ayub Khan saw himself as the heir of Jinnah and Liaquat Ali Khan and that, for this reason, he considered that the mantle of legitimacy should properly fall on him, but of this eventuality he could not be sure. He was aware, even then,

---

[17] ibid.
[18] 'The result of this law, i.e. the Political Parties Act, was that the President had to create a party of his own or join one of the old parties.' Munir, op. cit., p. 63. On 22 May 1963, Ayub Khan announced that he had been invited to join the Muslim League Party which had 'supported my programme within and without the legislature'. (This, of course, was the Convention League.) He stated that he accepted the offer gratefully 'with the prayer that this action . . . will be of some assistance to the cause of the country'.

of Miss Jinnah's hostility and opposition, of which there was ample evidence. There was, too, the patent risk of unacceptability since it was he, along with Iskander Mirza, who had abrogated the Constitution of 1956 and had abolished all political parties. It was Ayub Khan, in particular, who had expressed his dislike for politicians with so much emphasis and even venom. And, in other respects, his claims were small. His connexion and identification with the old Muslim League—either before or after independence—was negligible, as befitted a professional soldier who has no place in a political organization. There were also his associations with the former Governor-General, Ghulam Mohamed, whose Defence Minister Ayub Khan became after Ghulum Mohamed's *coup* of 1954, and, of course, with the former President, Iskander Mirza.

It became apparent, as soon as Maulana Akram Khan summoned the Council meeting, that for political parvenus like Ayub Khan there was no place. The intention was clearly to entrust the revival of the League to the hands of those men who had never deserted the Muslim League at any time since, and even before, Partition, the men who, in their hearts, had never changed their allegiance. They themselves pointed, not without some show of scorn, at those who had not been so steadfast, the opportunists, the men who had wavered in their loyalty, and had joined other parties even before Martial Law was declared in 1958. There were also those who had hastened to accept Ayub Khan and his Martial Law administration and had approved his animadversions against party politicians and party politics. Yet again there were those who had curried favour with the Martial Law administrators and had turned their backs on old political associates, especially those in trouble. It was these men, the defectors, splinter-group makers and those who had behaved traitorously to their fellow-politicians who, it now seemed, were seeking to find their way back to the party they had deserted and to do so in a manner that might well drive the old and faithful stalwarts out of party office. It was all very well to criticize the notion of 'first-class citizens' (those who never wavered) and 'second-class citizens' (the pliant persons who did)[19] but loyalty has its worth and people who knew how to turn their coats once, could be relied

[19] *D*, 19 August 1962.

upon to do it again should occasion arise. Thus the dichotomy went as deep as it could do, with the Convention League sympathetic to the existing régime and the Council League firmly in opposition.

At the same time, other parties were either reviving themselves or coming into existence. Mr. H. S. Suhrawardy who, on 3 January 1962, had been released from detention under the Security of Pakistan Act, was now travelling the country seeking support for the National Front which he hoped to forge from opposition parties in both Provinces. In October 1962, he announced the formation of a National Democratic Front and claimed that he had the support and collaboration of no fewer than fifty-four leading men from both Provinces. He published a list of these names as well as a statement defining the terms of his new organization and started a campaign to mobilize public opinion in its favour.[20] Although Suhrawardy retained the confidence of most, if not all, of his old Awami League colleagues, his National Democratic Front was not a success and he died of heart failure in Beirut some months later.

In the same month, October 1962, Abdul Qayum Khan, a former Chief Minister of the old Frontier Province, was released from detention following an order by the Review Board. However, the West Pakistan Government placed a ban on his political activities for a period of six months under Section 5 of the West Pakistan Public Order Ordinance.

By this time, in the National Assembly itself, political grouping was taking a much clearer shape. Late in November seventy-eight members of the Assembly formed what they called the Democratic Group, led by Mohamed Ali (Bogra) at that time Foreign Minister and Leader of the House. Under the leadership of Sardar Bahadur Khan, a loose coalition of opposition groups was forming. It included members of the old Council Muslim League, old Muslim League men who did not accept the revival of the pre-Martial Law organization, members of the Nizam-i-Islam Party, of the National Awami Party and the Awami League. It was calculated that the maximum number of members which the Opposition could muster in the House would be sixty-five so that it could be assumed that some ninety-one members would support the

[20] *D*, 5, 6, and 7 October 1962.

Government. On 27 November, Sardar Bahadur Khan was elected Leader of the Opposition, his deputies being Masihur Rahman (from East Pakistan) and Khair Baksh Marri (from West Pakistan). This opposition comprised thirty-nine members from East Pakistan who formed the Peoples' Party Group and twenty-one members belonging to the Council Muslim League of whom sixteen were from West Pakistan and five from East Pakistan.

Thus, the membership supporting Ayub Khan's Government had a clear majority over the opposition although, in terms of the Constitution, it would not have mattered had the reverse been the case. The Government might be defeated on every conceivable issue but that would not, as the Constitution then stood, have brought it down. The really important point was that, as the grouping emerged, it was clear that the Government could not be sure of commanding the 105 votes necessary, under the terms of the Constitution, to secure such amendments as it might desire. This would not have mattered greatly had Ayub Khan not found it necessary to change the Constitution so soon and so frequently, but as he did insist on making whatever amendments he desired, the longer-term effect of all this upon his political position was a decisive factor in his ultimate fall.

In this way, then, within six months of the change from Martial Law to the Presidential system, party politics reappeared in Pakistan. The practice now grew up of naming the member's party affiliation when reporting the debates in the House and so, in all respects, it could be said that parties and party politics had been firmly re-established. It remains only to add that before the end of 1962 Mr. M. Munir and Mr. Abdul Qadir gave up their portfolios. In their places, Sheikh Khursheed Ahmed became Law Minister and Mr. M. Shoaib took over the Finance Ministry. Rana Abdul Hamid also joined the Government as Minister for Health, Labour, and Social Welfare in place of Mr. Monem Khan who had been appointed Governor of East Pakistan in place of Mr. Ghulam Faruque. The circumstances in which Mr. Faruque relinquished this appointment will be discussed in the chapter on East Pakistan.

III

Constitutional Change, 1962–5

THE protean nature of the Constitution devised and promulgated by Ayub Khan has already been sufficiently indicated. He did not at any time claim finality for its terms and on more than one occasion had said that the Constitution could be changed in the light of experience and to meet those necessities to which time might give birth. However, the distinction to be made is obvious enough. Constitutional evolution is one thing. Manipulation of constitutional provisions is another.

Many of the changes which were made in the period with which this chapter is concerned involved little that could not have been thought of when the Constitution was first in draft. The necessary conclusion is either that they were not thought of, which would belie the claim that the Constitution of 1962 was the object of much profound cogitation by many able minds, or that they were thought of and rejected. But if rejected then what made these matters desirable so soon thereafter? In some respects, as we shall see, Ayub Khan's hand was forced, or he felt it to be forced by the trend of the times. A man engaged in politics is entitled to study his own survival and it may well be that in his conclusion Ayub Khan was right, but it necessitated a recantation of much that he had preached. There is the further point that in assessing the terms of the original Constitution, and the changes that he later made, Ayub Khan was doubtless much dependent on the advice of others. He was not, after all, a constitutional lawyer and he could reasonably expect to be properly guided in those matters where legal expertise was necessary. It is fair to him to say that in this, as in many other respects, Ayub Khan was sometimes given advice of very doubtful worth.

But it is also evident that, as time went on, he became more reckless in his attitude towards his Constitution. He did not seem to understand that a cavalier disregard for its solemn and abiding worth in the very person claiming to be its author told not only of irresponsibility in him, but of his inability to grasp the essential point that such careless indifference would, sooner or later, be shared by everyone. Why should the nation respect what he obviously did not? Now that the Constitution of 1962 has been cast aside and, in some important respects, utterly rejected in the public mind, it is scarcely a productive exercise to examine all the verbal minutiae of many of the changes made, but the fact that they were made, and the form and manner in which they were made, throws light on the course of events in Pakistan's troubled constitutional history. These matters also tell something of the pressures exerted on Ayub Khan and of his own efforts to endure.

In this chapter, we shall confine ourselves to the first four of the eight Acts amending the Constitution. There are three reasons for this. The first is that it will be inconvenient if we travel too far ahead in time; the second that these four include the second amending Act which had so vital a bearing on the presidential election of 1965 and on the interpretation of which amendments so many people drew adverse conclusions with respect to Ayub Khan's intentions. The third reason is that in September 1965 there occurred the hostilities with India which form so prominent a benchmark in the history of Pakistan and of the sub-continent as a whole.

Of these first four amending statutes, the first—Constitution (First Amendment) Act, 1963—was placed before the National Assembly in the form of a Bill in November 1962, that is eight months after the Constitution was first promulgated and five months after it became effective. This Bill proposed a number of drastic changes by no means conformable to Ayub Khan's thinking. They had to do with fundamental rights and the Islamic emphasis, subjective issues with a troublesome potential, but not matters over which he was going to create further opposition to himself. Although the Bill did not receive his assent until 10 January 1964, there is no indication that he was prepared to resist these changes to the point of crisis.

The main burden of this amending Act was to re-write the First Chapter of the Constitution and to give to this chapter a new and highly significant title—*Principles of Law-Making*

2*

became *Fundamental Rights*. The effect was to endow these guiding principles of legislation with an inherent character and, by an amendment to Article 98, they were made justiciable and, therefore, enforceable at law provided, of course, the Courts could determine their correct interpretation and application. Next, the Islamic features of the previous Constitution of 1956 were restored and thereby, in the new Constitution, a much heavier emphasis was laid on the Islamic aspect which, too, became armed with a measure of legal enforcement. Here, then, we have yet other issues on which Ayub Khan had evidently failed to convince his countrymen. It was his belief, a by no means frivolous one, that by giving a fundamental and justiciable character to the rights set out in chapter one of the Constitution, the door would be opened to endless litigation. With somewhat similar considerations in mind, it had also been his intention to import into the Constitution the spirit of Islam without necessarily burdening it with the letter. It is, however, clear, that he had not succeeded in persuading the entire nation of the wisdom of these views.

He gave way, realizing that he would not be able to withstand the pressures that must inevitably follow. The earlier appearance of a private Bill seeking to make these changes left no alternative but to accept and, doubtless, he judged it worthwhile to take the credit for having done so. As matters then stood, his term was due to expire three years and sixty days after 8 June 1962, that is on 7 August 1965, and prior to the presidential election there would be elections to the National and Provincial Assemblies.[1] And, even before any of these things were possible, the electoral law, not as yet enacted but required by Article 158, had to be framed and passed. Thus a great deal was still to be done before the elections could be held and all of it politically very sensitive and controversial. As we have seen in the previous chapter, by November 1962 political grouping had taken a very definite shape in the National Assembly and the Opposition was by no means negligible either in numbers or in its capacity to make its voice heard. So far as concerned this first amendment, therefore, with its religious and moral import, Ayub Khan doubtless

---

[1] This arrangement was changed in the second amending Act.

felt that there was no sense in alienating further the orthodox section of public opinion which had already discovered plenty to criticize in his efforts at social reform. Paris, in short, was worth a Mass.

The first amending Act, then, represents changes which Ayub Khan would have avoided if he could, but since they were so congenial to popular sentiment he had no intention of trying. This was entirely consistent with the development in his political awareness which grew in sensitivity and penetration since the day he entrusted part of his political future to the people he felt he could control—the Basic Democrats. But he could not control them merely by the exercise of authority, only by sharing with them the sweets of office, and he had no intention of arousing their antagonism with reference to something as harmless to himself as the terms of the first amending Act.

The second amending Act—a matter of his own devising assisted by his political friends—was a much more contentious business which represented Ayub Khan's first successful attempt at manipulating the Constitution. In substance, it changed the order in which elections would be held in Pakistan as between the President, the National Assembly and the Provincial Assemblies. The details of these changes will be stated shortly. Meanwhile, it is necessary to know that Article 164 of the Constitution provided that elections and referendums, required to be held by the Constitution, would be conducted and decided in the manner provided by law. The law had yet to be provided and during the course of 1964 legislation for this purpose was enacted.[2]

The second amending Act received assent on 23 June 1964, after a great deal of bitterly expressed dissent in the National Assembly. Its passage into law, after a number of amendments to the Bill were accepted by the Government, resulted in alteration to ten Articles of the Constitution and the addition of Article 173A. This additional Article was itself an interesting exercise in the retention of authority in the hands of the President. It had to do with representation of the Tribal Areas, as defined, in the Electoral College, the National

[2] The Electoral College Act, 1964, the Presidential Election Act, 1964, and the National and Provincial Assemblies (Election) Act, 1964.

Assembly and the West Pakistan Provincial Assembly for which purposes the President could make such provision as *he*[3] deemed fit. This apart, the result of the changes led to a new constitutional situation in which:

(a) The sitting president would remain in office until his successor was *elected*;
(b) The election of a new president would precede the election of a new National Assembly;
(c) The selection of presidential candidates under Article 167 (which provided that if the number of candidates exceeded three a joint sitting of the National and Provincial Assemblies would select three as candidates for election, though for this purpose, a candidate then holding office as president would not be included)[4] would be carried out by the existing Assemblies and not by newly elected Assemblies;
(d) The date of elections would be advanced by limiting the sitting President's term of office so that it would expire on 22 March 1965.

The gravamen of the case against these proposals lay first of all in their non-necessity. The electoral provisions contained in the Constitution devised by Ayub Khan and his advisers had not yet been tested and even those who were reserved in their opinion of the Constitution as a whole had never suggested that these provisions would operate inequitably or inefficiently. Why were these changes proposed before these constitutional arrangements had ever undergone a test? The next objection to the proposals lay in the suggestion that Ayub Khan's re-election would be facilitated since the sitting Assembly would be influenced in his favour and through it the Electoral College also. This second objection, it was naturally argued by the Government and its supporters, was entirely hypothetical and it was urged that the new arrangements would remove administrative and other difficulties that would ensue if the existing arrangements were retained.

It was doubtless true that the argument raging about these proposals was founded upon speculative and hypothetical

---

[3] My italics.
[4] Ayub Khan had no intention of running any risks!

considerations. The point was that the Opposition did not trust the President and they trusted the new proposals still less. Ayub Khan's own attitude to them, when commending the second amending Bill to the nation in his broadcast on 1 May 1964 was expressed as follows: 'If this amendment does not go through, heavens are not going to fall. But if it does go through, as I hope it will, the Constitution will become tidier—which is the only object of putting it forward.' In other words, if the amendments are passed, it is well, but if not, they still had all they started with. The question why this well-meditated Constitution was not sufficiently tidy at the start need no longer be asked.

The fact is that the merit, or lack of it, in this contention no longer justifies examination and the most important thing about the episode is the bitterness with which the proposals were resisted in the Assembly. During many hours of debate, some thirty-five in all, feeling rose high and language grew acrimonious. Accusation and counter-accusation were flung across the floor of the House and right up to the last minute it seemed doubtful whether the Government would succeed in securing the 105 votes necessary to carry the proposals. In fact, the votes were secured, but only just, and only after eight persons defected from the Opposition benches of whom two at least displayed the grossest want of good faith. One of these, resigning from his party, was afterwards appointed a Judge of the West Pakistan High Court.[5] At the same time, there is no doubt that those who changed their allegiance in order to vote for the Government did so under the heaviest kind of pressure including, in some cases, threat of personal ruin. It does not seem that those who quitted the Opposition in order to vote with the Government suffered the penalties laid down in the Political Parties Act, but this exoneration may be attributable to the fact that when they were elected such parties did not formally exist.

To what extent the second amending Act contributed to Ayub Khan's successful election in 1965 must always remain a matter of conjecture. What can now be said with certainty is that the unflinching resolve with which these amendments were forced through the House, convinced many people that

[5] Mr. Justice Afzal Cheema.

Ayub Khan had made up his mind, election or no election, to remain in office for at least one more term.

The third amending Act was likewise, although in a different way, disquieting. It received assent on 15 June 1965, and it dealt with the question of persons disqualified from being elected to membership of the Assemblies. Article 103(2) stated that a person was so disqualified if he held an office of profit in the service of Pakistan. There were of course other forms of disqualification, but we are now concerned with this particular one. The third amending Act changed the provisions of Article 103(2) by making an exception in the case of persons occupying offices specified in a new and Fifth Schedule to the Constitution. This new Schedule listed seven different categories of persons exempted from this particular form of disqualification. The last of these groups provided that a person could be elected a member of any Assembly even if he held *any*[6] office so long as it was declared by an Act of the Central Legislature not to disqualify him from doing so.

A broader exemption than this it is impossible to imagine. In theory, it would have been possible to man all three Assemblies with permanent civil servants although this would have involved an act of political suicide on the part of the sitting members. But even political suicide was not unknown among them as will later be seen. Some of the other exempted groups were reasonable enough. They included Army, Navy and Air Force reservists and holders of part-time jobs. So, too, the holders of certain elective offices in the hierarchy of local government which enjoyed small stipends. More doubtful, however, were the cases of persons holding the office of *lambardar* (a minor, sometimes part-time official assisting in the collection of land revenue);[7] of *inamdar* (a person enjoying a reward from Government, usually in the form of a piece of agricultural land); of *safedposh* (literally a person who always wears clean, white clothes and, by inference, a man respected in the community who enjoys some official benevolence); of *zaildar* (a minor revenue functionary); others too there might

---

[6] My italics.
[7] It has been held in the High Court of West Pakistan that a *lambardar* does not hold any office of profit in the service of Pakistan. Sajjad Ali Khan *vs.* Fazal Illahi. P.L.D. 1957, Lah. 940.

be 'whether called by this or any other name'. Without reading too much that is sinister into everything Ayub Khan did, the intention was not simply to make it possible for men of these categories to secure election to an Assembly but, to encourage them to do so because although they were persons of minor degree, their influence in their own localities could be substantial. This interpretation is supported by the general tenor of the amendment whose evident purpose was to place minimal restrictions on the selection of candidates by Ayub Khan's party from among those whom it deemed suitable.

The fourth amending Act, which received assent on 11 August 1965, is a more complicated and significant affair. It is somewhat densely worded and in order to construe its provisions and consequential provisions with detailed accuracy it would be necessary to possess a knowledge of the rules governing the employment of persons in the public service. These, in turn, are governed with reference to what are known as the Fundamental and the Supplemental Rules and the subject is by no means simple. It is well known that the terms and conditions of public employment everywhere tend to be complicated and nowhere more so than in Pakistan where the rules of service are encrusted and overlaid with an immensity of interpretations and departmental decisions.

This said, the background to the Fourth Amendment must now be sketched in. Prior to independence, the age of retirement from public service was fifty-five years. On rare occasions, an official due to retire was given an extension of service, usually for six to twelve months and usually for some special reason such as there not being a suitable replacement immediately available. The reasons for this somewhat early age of retirement had to do with the fact that so many Englishmen were employed in Government service in the sub-continent in those days. Retirement at the age of fifty-five offered them some assurance of a few years of leisure in their own country. It was thought that the wearing nature of the climate of the sub-continent justified an earlier retirement age than was customary in Europe. Lastly, it was recognized that life-expectation among people born in the sub-continent was less than in western countries. Although this retirement age was continued after independence and the creation of Pakistan, opinion began to strengthen that the reasons which had given rise to retirement at fifty-five were no longer fully valid. Englishmen were no longer in the service and the average life-expectation in the sub-continent had increased. Moreover, conditions of life and work in the service were no longer so harsh. Finally, in view of the shortage of trained and experienced senior civil servants, the country could not so easily afford to dispense with the services of such men of this category as it had. Ayub Khan gave effect to these views in December 1962 when retirement age was raised to sixty.[8]

About two and a half years later, Ayub Khan appeared to reject all this. The Fourth Amendment provided that in the case of any person in the service of the Central Government the President could at any time direct that person's retirement after completion of twenty-five years of pension-qualifying service or after completing fifty-five years of age. Similar provisions were enacted with respect to persons in the service of each provincial Government except that in this case the directing authority was the Governor.

The fourth amending Act provoked much dispute. It seemed to place in the hands of the President the prospects of every civil servant who had completed twenty-five years of pension-qualifying service. Fine distinctions were purportedly drawn between *pension, superannuation* and *retirement,* but the substance of the amendment lay in the fact that this sudden lowering of the retirement age, after its advance by Ayub Khan to sixty, not only led to the retirement of men who had reason to hope for longer time in service, but enabled Ayub Khan to relieve of their duties those men who were not congenial to him and who, as it happened, fell within the mischief of the clauses of the Fourth Amendment.

Thus, in a period of two years and five months from the date of first promulgation, Ayub Khan amended his Constitution in four distinct statutes, quite apart from those other attempts which proved nugatory when challenged in Court. These four amending Acts imported very drastic alterations and they led to the popular belief in Pakistan that the Constitution over which Ayub Khan had meditated for so

[8] Ministry of Finance Notification No. F5(8)RI(RWP)/62 dated 1 December 1962. This notification was the basis of a new Fundamental Rule 56-A.

long was simply a plastic instrument in his hands, to be shaped and moulded by him as circumstances and convenience might dictate.[9]

[9] This frequent fiddling with the Constitution was a fruitful cause of the administrative 'laxity and chaos' to which General Yahya Khan referred in his address to the nation on 26 March 1969 (see Epilogue). It is wrong to suppose that Ayub Khan's firm hand restored some kind of administrative discipline which had gone to pieces before October 1958. It may have gone to pieces as he suggested, and for a time he may have restored some system and order, but after his Constitution was promulgated the old evils soon crept back. To take but one example, during his administration the reports of the Auditor-General on the yearly accounts of the Central and the provincial Governments fell more and more heavily into arrears and action upon them even more so. This circumstance made possible much defalcation and misuse of public money. So far as concerns the Fourth Amendment, we shall see that seven months afterwards Ayub Khan again amended these provisions, retaining the age limit of fifty-five but making possible extensions of service or re-employment after the due date of retirement on such terms as the 'competent authority' might deem fit.

IV

Economic Growth under the Presidential System

PROMINENT in the list of achievements with which Ayub Khan is generally credited is that of actively encouraging economic growth. It has often been said that it was during his administration that the country was made planning conscious and that the spirit of enterprise in the private sector was most powerfully stimulated. Pakistan, it was asserted, was a richer country in March 1969 than it was in October 1958 and this accretion of wealth was mainly the result of Ayub Khan's own belief in and enthusiasm for economic development.

In this chapter I shall examine these claims, but with less regard to the achievement or otherwise of the years 1962 to 1969 and of Ayub Khan's administration, than to some other matters which, it seems to me, now press very urgently upon us. In this, I do not mean to rob Ayub Khan of any praise to which he may be entitled and it is important, also, to measure the quantum of growth and the extent to which its measure is truly meaningful. It is, furthermore, necessary to consider the extent to which everyone in Pakistan has participated beneficially and to enquire also whether it is true that Pakistan is within measurable distance of the day when the economy will be self-generating. Is there any real breakthrough from the state of grinding poverty which has oppressed the major part of the population and are people, in general, in any respect better off? Such questions as these are surely important, but I think they have, after the lapse of a generation since independence, to be considered in a matrix of ideas different from those which have served till now.

The time has passed when the bare statistics of overall increases in growth rates, usually expressed as percentages, in power generation, in acreages sown, in spindles installed and in the range of articles manufactured, can be considered

ECONOMIC GROWTH

sufficient evidence of real progress. There was a time when such things could satisfy because such figures showed that, in countries newly released from foreign rule, something was being done and that people were on the move. Today, none of this will answer because what is happening is simply not enough. It may well be that with, without, or in spite of Ayub Khan, Pakistan has in twenty-three years of independence witnessed a substantial measure of industrial, commercial and agricultural advance. It may well be there are good grounds for saying that Pakistan has done a lot better than many, if not most, countries that have emerged since World War II, yet the fact remains that Pakistan still shares with all those countries a condition of poverty, illiteracy and backwardness that is as distressing as it is alarming. The truth of the matter is that Pakistan, a poor country in 1958, was not a great deal richer in March 1969. During this period the income *per capita* taken at constant prices, grew by Rs.82, or Rs.8·2 per annum, which equals U.S. $1·72 at the official rate of exchange. In these circumstances what really matters is not what Ayub Khan deserves credit for, but rather the question why more was not achieved, whether more could have been achieved and, indeed, what prospects there are for a speedier advance to the stage when most, if not all of the population, can enjoy an adequate diet, decent housing, enough to wear, and educational and medical facilities.

What poverty means in Pakistan is vividly disclosed by the National Sample Surveys, undertaken by the Central Statistical Office of the Government of Pakistan in 1963-4 and again in 1966-7. The analysis shown on page 36 is a summary of the figures obtained by a survey of some 13,000 families, distributed between the two Provinces, in rural and urban areas, and covering all ranks of society.

On the basis of these figures, it is evident that during Ayub Khan's administration there has been a slightly favourable shift away from a condition of the most abject poverty. If, in 1963-4, 5·2 per cent of all families lived on an income of less than fifty rupees a month, that number had fallen to 1·9 per cent by 1966-7. The same kind of shift is reflected until we get to the highest income group, but here a true comparison is not possible as the surveys were not carried out in identical terms.

		1963-4						
Monthly Household Income Group (Rs.)	All Pak.	Rural Pak.	Urban Pak.	East Pak.	Rural	Urban	West Pak.	Rural	Urban
				(all in percentages)					
Less than Rs.50	5·2	5·6	2·0	7·2	7·3	4·5	2·8	3·2	1·2
Rs.50–199	67·9	69·5	57·6	72·8	73·5	54·5	61·9	63·5	56·2
Rs.200–899	21·2	24·5	37·4	19·6	18·9	39·1	34·4	32·7	40·6
Rs.900 and over	0·7	0·4	2·0	0·4	0·3	1·9	0·9	0·6	2·0
		1966-7							
Less than Rs.50	1·9	2·1	0·3	2·7	2·8	0·9	0·7	0·8	0·2
Rs.50–199	69·3	72·0	50·7	76·0	76·5	52·0	60·0	62·0	58·1
Rs.200–999	28·3	25·7	46·7	21·1	20·5	45·3	38·5	37·0	39·4
Rs.1,000 and over	0·5	0·2	2·3	0·2	0·2	1·8	0·8	0·2	2·3

It must be remembered, however, that the incomes are taken at the levels prevailing at the time of survey in each instance and there is no doubt that salaries and wages did increase. So, likewise, did prices as we shall have occasion to see.

The major points that stand out so very clearly are, first, the dominating position of the rural groups and, second, the concentration of incomes, comprising 70 per cent of all families, in the group whose monthly earnings range from Rs.50 ($10·50) to Rs.199 ($42). In the year 1966–7, the *per capita* income at current prices was Rs.491 and the average number of persons in each family lying in this income group was 4·7 so that the share in the Gross National Product for each such family was Rs.2,308. In fact, the average annual income for such families was Rs.1,440 so that, on this basis, 70 per cent of all families in Pakistan received about two-thirds of their share in the Gross National Product.

It will be understood that the preceding analysis is a gross over-simplification. It is very difficult to determine whether and to what extent *everyone* shares in the country's economic growth. The social structure of Pakistan does not comprise a series of income groups, divided between town and country, each of them homogeneous. Indeed, in countries like Pakistan, the complexities of the social fabric have little parallel in the more prosperous countries. This may make the poorer countries more interesting and, as they say, more colourful but it is less satisfactory in other respects. The application of averages and plausible generalizations have very restricted meaning in countries such as Pakistan. We are here dealing with nations within which there are substantial communities, part of the nation in a legal sense and yet, for one reason or another, living more or less outside the economy and even outside the general social pattern. Such people may receive money wages which it may be possible to assess accurately and they may use money to procure food and other necessities, but it remains doubtful where and how they fit into the general social and economic pattern, and to what extent their ideas and attitudes can be identified with the generally accepted understanding of what, for example, the Pakistani nation is.

In West Pakistan, for instance, there are nomadic or migratory groups, with their own tribal affinities and rendering obedience to their *sardars* (chiefs) rather than to the state, which provide a labour force for such occupations as the construction industry and for other unskilled or semi-skilled work. They form self-contained societies, living on daily wages and the livestock that they own, travelling by foot from one job to another, taking their modest belongings on ox-carts and constructing temporary camps whenever they halt for the purposes of work. Apart from the contribution they make through their labour, it is difficult to know how else they signify in the national life.[1] Similar remarks might be made of other groups such as the fishermen of the Manchhar Lake in Sind, who form a community of their own and whose dependence on, or integration into, the national economic system is minimal. There is, too, the practice of *begar* (a word which, strictly speaking, has much the same meaning as *corvée*) which is still extensive although efforts have been made to suppress it and to liberate the unfortunate people, mostly young men, who find themselves bound to oppressive masters. However, owing to the poverty of the countryside, many of them drift back to their exploiters with whom there is, at any rate, a chance to work and eat.

The truth of the matter is that, with countries like Pakistan,

[1] An interesting instance will be found in Pehrson and Barth, *The Social Organisation of the Marri Baluch*, Aldine, Chicago, 1966.

to think of them as undeveloped in the sense that one day they may become developed as this word is understood in the industrialized countries of Europe, North America and the Far East, is to start with a premise as false as can be. Before such a transition is possible, there must be a change in attitudes, in values, in social institutions and in political ideologies as well as what has been called the intelligent and responsible manipulation of our own global ecosystem.[2] I do not mean to imply that such a metamorphosis is not possible, but I do assert that judgements made today, with respect to Pakistan as it now is, must not be founded upon such false premises as those of which I have given one example. It may be that this shows unfair prejudice and pessimism, but I do not see how this conclusion can be avoided and there can be no true assessment of what has been done, is being done, or ought to be done in and for countries such as Pakistan except in the light of this understanding.

In most of the discussion relating to the development and growth of that group of less prosperous countries to which Pakistan belongs, there has been a general failure to realize, not that we are talking about a different kind of society, founded upon a set of different circumstances, but to realize how and in what significant ways it is different. The result has been one false conclusion coupled with disappointment followed by another.

Pakistan is an example of that form of social and economic organization which has been exhaustively analysed by Professor Karl A. Wittvogel in his great work *Oriental Despotism*.[3] It is a consequence of our failure to understand clearly what this particular kind of organization means and imports, that we pursue the erroneous and misleading practice of speaking of countries such as Pakistan in a terminology that may be

[2] See address by Professor Thayer Scudder on *Some Problems of the Emerging Nations*, Report on Conference on *The Next Ninety Years*, California Institute of Technology, March 1967, p. 123. I have slightly paraphrased what Professor Scudder said.

[3] New Haven, Yale University Press, 1957. The title is, I think, unfortunate in that it tends to create a vision of eastern satraps brandishing scimitars and surrounded by bevies of beautiful but submissive slaves. The book is far from that. I suspect the title to have been taken from a despatch sent by Karl Marx to the *New York Daily Tribune* which appeared in that newspaper on 25 June 1853 and was entitled 'The British Rule in India'.

specifically and definably meaningful only in countries where the European tradition prevails.

Thus, by way of example, we may, if we wish, refer to feudalism in Pakistan or to the existence of a class of feudal landlords but, if we do, we must bear in mind that the use of the word *feudal* in such a context is metaphorical and imprecise. The institution of feudalism, as it is known and understood in Europe, is not and has never been known in the Indo-Pakistan sub-continent or in other Asian countries.[4] Strenuous efforts were made to establish the existence of feudalism in the sub-continent by men like James Tod in the *Annals and Antiquities of Rajasthan,* but it is clear that Tod was moved by a romantic attachment to the Rajputs rather than by scholarly endeavour, and James Mill, who was a senior official of the East India Company in London, objected in rather acid terms to strained analogies between forms of land tenure in the sub-continent and the feudalism of Europe. Wittvogel refers to the interpretations of the Asian social and economic structure which appear in the works of Marx and Lenin and he mentions Lenin's use of the word *pharisaic* when describing attempts to equate European and Asian institutions,[5] but there is no doubt that on this subject both Marx and Lenin retreated from their earlier position in the better interests, one must presume, of scientific socialism.

So, too, with the word 'democracy' which seldom means the same thing in countries where the European tradition does not prevail. This is so even where there are parliamentary institutions with direct elections based on universal adult suffrage and all the other apparatus devised to give expression to the popular will. The reason lies in economic and cultural considerations and it is a meaningful, even if cruel, coincidence that whereas, for Ayub Khan, the letters B.D. stood for Basic Democracy, for Wittvogel they signify Beggars' Democracy.[6]

The position of the bureaucratic hierarchy in such countries as Pakistan has been a constant source of complaint invariably giving rise to exhortations and threats to institute reform.

---

[4] Wittvogel, op. cit., p. 270.
[5] ibid., p. 378. In the English translation of Lenin's *Works*, published in 1964, I cannot find this reference. It appears that Wittvogel used the edition in Russian.
[6] ibid., p. 126.

It has been constantly alleged that the bureaucracy has wielded too much power, is selfish, dictatorial and unmindful of its public duty. In India, Pakistan and other countries which have emerged from British rule, the former rulers have been blamed for this on the ground that they instituted a civil service which was distant, superior and overbearing. However true this may be, it is perfectly clear that the administrations which preceded the advent of the British were just as distant, superior and overbearing and to suppose that the present attitude of the civil services in Pakistan is solely attributable to British rule in the sub-continent is quite unhistorical and a false interpretation.

The Civil Service of Pakistan, lineal heir in its own country to the former Indian Civil Service, has been heavily and in some respects justly criticized although the extent to which the grounds of criticism stem from the past is debatable. Proposals have been made for the evolution of a more homogeneous civil service and one more attuned to the necessities of the times,[7] but to what extent this will provide a cure is also questionable. As has been said, 'the men of the apparatus easily control the secular and religious variants of the Beggars' Democracy'.[8]

To these ideas there will be occasion to return, but now it will be useful to consider some figures which illustrate what was done to develop the economy during Ayub Khan's administration.

In the year 1949–50, the G.N.P. was Rs.2,446·6 crores based on Constant Factor Cost in the year 1959–60. On the same basis, the G.N.P. for 1958–9 was Rs.3,014·4 crores, an advance of Rs.567·6 crores; for the year 1967–8, the G.N.P. was Rs.4,828·0 crores, an advance of Rs.1,813·6 crores. On this basis, therefore, the rate of economic growth was higher during Ayub Khan's administration than before and we shall in due course see in what forms this growth manifested itself. However, between the years 1949–50 and 1967–8, the population increased by forty-three million so that the *per capita*

---

[7] See the Report of the Pay and Services Commission better known as 'The Cornelius Report'. This Report, completed in 1960, was withheld from the public until September 1969.

[8] Wittvogel, op. cit., p. 328.

income, based on the same constant factors, only grew from Rs.311 (U.S.$65·5) to Rs.397 (U.S.$83·00). It is, therefore to Ayub Khan's credit that compared with the trifling and sometimes negative growth rates experienced during the years that preceded his administration, the years that followed witnessed a steady expansion in the economy with a growth rate that averaged 4·97 per cent for the decade that ended in 1967–8.[9]

Some figures tabulated below help to illustrate the rise in industrial production. The periods have been selected to show what was done during the years that preceded Ayub Khan's administration and the years that followed the declaration of Martial Law in 1958.

Product	1947–8	1957–8	1966–7
Mill-made cotton cloth (millions of yards)	85·8	555·8	738·6
Jute goods ('000 tons)	nil	154·1	403·7
Paper and paper board (tons)	nil	9,644·0	26,142·0
Art silk and rayon ('000 sq. yards)	nil	12,383·0	45,538·0
Sugar (tons)	35,000	133,730·0	416,499·0
Vegetable cooking oil (tons)	2,000	19,204·0	87,851·0
Cement ('000 tons)	351	1,057·0	2,009·0
Chemical fertilizers (tons)	nil	1,337·0	186,241·0

The preceding brief list of manufactures has been selected for its importance as well as for the picture it provides of growth since 1947 and again, since 1958. The list is not fully representative since it omits such manufactures as woollen textiles, leather manufactures, matches, cigarettes, sulphuric acid, soda ash, soaps and paints and other articles of consumption. There was also, at the same time, a corresponding advance in electrical power production, in mining, in the development of transport, docks and harbours including the important inland waterways of East Pakistan.

In 1949, the total money supply was less than Rs.300 crores

[9] The statistical information used in this chapter, unless otherwise indicated, is taken from the Economic Surveys published annually by the Government of Pakistan.

and, in 1958, it was rather more than Rs.500 crores. In 1967, it had grown to more than Rs.1,000 crores. The total number of bank offices—both Pakistani and foreign—was slightly more than 200 in 1950. In 1958, there were about 380 and in 1967 there were more than 2,300 of which about 2,200 were Pakistani bank establishments. So, too, with insurance. Total life business in force in 1948 was about Rs.26 crores. In 1958, the total was in the order of Rs.850 crores and in 1965 this had grown to about Rs.2,900 crores. Of this total, Rs.1,891·5 crores was written by Pakistani companies and the rest by foreign companies operating in Pakistan.

From this brief statement, it will be obvious that industry started long before Ayub Khan, and in some instances the rate of growth was greater prior to his administration than during it. Nevertheless, it became the fashion to speak of the economic miracle of Pakistan which became the object of much praise uttered by economists and others from many countries. To what extent this miracle has real meaning, particularly for the masses, it is difficult to understand and the misfortune is that, for reasons which can only be surmised, there is a common and widespread practice among such visiting economists and others, belonging to richer countries and visiting their poor relations as it were, to indulge in much fulsome flattery which may be intended to prop up morale, but is usually as meaningless as it is insincere. To quote one such instance, the *New York Times*, in its issue of 18 January 1965, said: 'Pakistan may be on its way to an economic milestone that so far has been reached by only one other populous country, the United States of America.'[10]

What is to be made of a statement such as this? In 1968 the United States had a G.N.P. of about $4,000 *per capita*, as against $80 in Pakistan—a ratio of fifty to one. In 1995 it is expected that the United States will have a G.N.P. of about $15,500 *per capita* and, in Pakistan, if the targets of the present Twenty Year Perspective Plan are realized, the G.N.P. in 1995 should be around $300, which is roughly the same ratio. On this basis perhaps the *New York Times* was right in the sense

---

[10] Quoted by Dr. Gustav Papanek, *Pakistan's Development*, Harvard, 1967, p. 1. Dr. Papanek's close association with and intimate knowledge of economic planning in Pakistan confer a special value on his work.

that the two countries are keeping pace, but other than this it is impossible to discern any economic relationship between them except the contrast in riches and poverty. One is pursuing the culture of affluence and the other is pursuing the culture of poverty and the fact that they are doing these things at the same rate of increase does not seem important. The idea, moreover, of a linear progression to a state of affluence by the simple process of annual increases in production and in the areas of economic activity, measured as increments on the starting base, is a grossly oversimplified notion.

A word should now be added about agriculture which, as is so well known, forms the basis of Pakistan's entire economy and livelihood. Here too there is a similar picture of rising production and development and in the period 1962-9 the promotion of agriculture took two forms. The first was the extension of the infrastructure on which agriculture directly depends and the second was the provision of more equipment and more inputs for better crops and higher yields.

The extension of the agricultural infrastructure was most marked during this period, due mostly to the signing of the Indus Waters Treaty with India in 1960, one of the most significant events in Ayub Khan's administration and one of his major contributions to progress in his country and in the entire sub-continent. This led to a vast programme of dam, barrage and canal construction, the completion of the great Mangla Dam, and the initiation of the even greater Tarbela Dam. In addition, a vast increase in the availability of electrical power carried by new transmission systems to thousands of villages, made possible the beginning of the tubewell schemes known as SCARP (Salinity Control and Reclamation Project).

West Pakistan had long been suffering from the destructive consequences of water-logging and salination of agricultural land and these schemes involved the drilling of thousands of tubewells and the installation of electrically-operated pumps. The pumping reduced the water-table and the water so raised was used to flush out injurious salts which had accumulated in the soil, rendering it unfertile. By the time Ayub Khan left office, at least four SCARP projects were in progress in West Pakistan and a fair acreage of land had been reclaimed.

It is no doubt true that for the major part of Ayub Khan's administration agriculture had been left largely to itself until it was realized, during the course of the third Five Year Plan, that the stagnant condition of agriculture was hampering the growth of the economy as a whole. The necessity to correct this state of affairs led to a change of policy and a concentration on the development of high-yield varieties of wheat (Mexi-Pak) and rice (IRRI) and to the rapid establishment of more factories, using Pakistan's extensive resources in natural gas for the production of nitrogenous fertilizers. For this purpose the private sector, which had hitherto been excluded from the industry, was invited to enter, and it was hoped that by 1970 fertilizer production would reach about three million tons in terms of ammonium sulphate and triple super-phosphate. Although these targets were not achieved, progress in fertilizer manufacture did make considerable strides as is evident from the statistical detail set out earlier.

The policy of encouragement to agriculture was given much publicity during the later years of Ayub Khan's administration and there is no doubt that he was relying on bumper crops to justify the many claims he had made for the success of his policies. In fact, when he left office, the benefit of his efforts remained to be seen. High-yield varieties of wheat depend heavily on water, which is not cheap when it requires an artificial system of irrigation, and ample supplies of fertilizer which must be balanced as between nitrogen and phosphorus. Pakistan does not appear to have natural resources in rock phosphate so that phosphatic fertilizer must either be imported or manufactured in Pakistan from imported rock. There was also a failure to realize that, to maintain the quality and yield of hybrids, it is necessary to seed from fresh crossings and not to rely on seed harvested, year after year, from the hybrids themselves. At the close of Ayub Khan's administration agriculture had not really emerged from the doldrums, as the following figures, based on yields per acre, will show.

For the year 1968–9, it was estimated that the total availability of food grains, *per capita* (comprising rice, wheat, barley, maize and millet) was 16·5 oz., the highest figure since 1947–8, but this estimate depended in turn on an estimated wheat crop of 6·985 million tons, an estimate which

Crop	Approximate average yield per acre prior to 1968–9	Approximate average yield per acre 1968–9
Rice	900 lb.	1,066 lb.
Wheat	830 lb.	1,041 lb.
Sugar-cane	15 tons	15 tons
Jute	1,300 lb.	1,066 lb.
Maize	900 lb.	900 lb.
Barley	560 lb.	508 lb.
Cotton	270 lb.	270 lb.
Tea	650 lb.	600 lb.

was not, in fact, realized. In September 1969, Pakistan was still seeking to purchase wheat from the United States on P.L.480 terms.

While it is true that progress has been made in agriculture, particularly with the all-important food grains, this has been achieved through increased acreage sown, including marginal lands with their obvious difficulties and economic limitations, rather than through improved yields or better methods of cultivation. The benefit of effort made in that direction has yet to be experienced. Moreover, it is simply not enough to measure progress in agriculture by sole reference to rice and wheat, vital as they may be. Man does not live by bread alone, and agriculture in Pakistan is far from providing the nation with an adequate and balanced diet. The fact that the *per capita* availability of food grains may be better than it was (although this is by no means certain) offers no assurance that people are getting enough to eat. Protein deficiency is a grave nutritional problem and the production of milk, edible fats, poultry, eggs, fish, meat and vegetables simply does not suffice to meet the national requirements. Today, as for many years past, people go hungry or partly hungry, and what they get to eat provides inadequate nourishment. The general shortage of food is clearly indicated by a constant progression of rising prices in which the price of food has risen most.

If one takes 1959–60 as 100, the index for the wholesale price of food in 1956–7 was 93·7. Ten years later, in 1966–7, it was 139·6. It is true that all other groups of consumer articles showed increased prices for this period, but none of them has advanced to a comparable degree and in East Pakistan food prices showed an acute increase. In that Province, the index for 1966–7 was 148·5, an increase of nearly 50 per cent over 1959–60.[11]

One of the principal sources of public discontent, leading ultimately to Ayub Khan's political defeat, lay in the uncontrolled and apparently uncontrollable burden of rising prices. Corruption, nepotism, bureaucratic tyranny and the absence of direct, political representation certainly had their influence on the public mind, but the effect of rising prices hurt most. Mr. Zulfikar Ali Bhutto might proclaim, as he did when he was Ayub Khan's Foreign Minister, that the people of Pakistan would eat grass rather than submit to pressures designed to thwart their pursuit of just claims and inalienable rights, but however noble these motives, grass is a poor diet, and there was no reason to suppose that the people of Pakistan would accept it in order to keep Ayub Khan in office.

In a later chapter on the Great Decade, we shall have occasion to notice how, with Ayub Khan's multiplying claims for great economic progress and, in particular, for an important break-through in agricultural production, not only did the prices of food continue to rise, but there were even times when common articles of diet grown in Pakistan were not available. Never in the days of the corrupt politicians whom Ayub Khan had censured so often and so vigorously had such high prices been known, and never had the extraction of white flour been prohibited as happened towards the end of Ayub Khan's administration. Thus it was all very well to talk about the economic miracle and the achievements of the Great Decade, but the fact was that for the most part people were hungry, ill-nourished, ill-clad and ill-housed.

Ayub Khan has frequently been attacked for allowing, and even encouraging, the concentration of the nation's wealth in the hands of a few, to the detriment of the many. No doubt, this process of concentration was plainly visible during his administration and it had much to do with his policy of

[11] *20 Years of Pakistan in Statistics*, Central Statistical Office, Government of Pakistan, 1968, p. 198.

granting to supporters, and others whose influence he needed, permits to set up industries. In many cases these permits were farmed and so found their way into the hands of the country's great capitalists. The effect of this was to foster the process by which industry, banking, insurance and commerce were concentrated within a comparatively small group. Still, it is true to say that these methods and their consequences did not start with him. From the very beginning, in 1947, there had been no effort to prevent the rich from growing richer and the granting of import licences and industrial permits for political purposes was current practice long before Ayub Khan came into power. One of the distinctive and perhaps inevitable features of Pakistan's economic growth since 1947 has been the rise of what have been described as the 'robber barons'[12] and no matter how much they prospered in the days of Ayub Khan, they certainly had their origins before 1958.

This subject received a great deal of publicity after Dr. Mahbubul Huq, Chief Economist in the Planning Division of the Government of Pakistan, stated, in April 1968, that 66 per cent of all industrial projects, 97 per cent of all insurance funds and 80 per cent of all bank deposits were in the control of some twenty families.[13] Although earlier comment had not been quite so forthright or specific, Dr. Huq was not the first or only person in Pakistan to remark on the concentration of economic power in a few hands and, during Ayub Khan's administration, in response to this kind of criticism there were lukewarm references to reform. They came mostly from his Finance Minister, Mohamed Shoaib, who in 1963 announced that cartels would be broken up,[14] but as time passed his pronouncements on this subject became feebler. Later, in the same year, he said that steps would be taken against cartels,[15] but he moderated this assurance with the remark that the subject should be tackled judiciously.[16] In his Budget speech, he made reference to anti-cartel measures,[17] but followed this up with the innocuous suggestion that the liquidation of cartels

[12] Papanek, op. cit., chapter entitled 'The Robber Barons' Progress'.
[13] *PO*, 2 May 1968.
[14] *D*, 9 January 1963.
[15] *D*, 8 August 1963.
[16] *D*, 26 May 1965.
[17] *D*, 15 June 1965.

should be undertaken voluntarily.[18] Eventually the subject was dropped. Ayub Khan himself had little or nothing to say on the matter, although he was fond of referring to socio-economic objectives for the benefit of the common man and for the attainment of the welfare state.

It should be explained that although the word *cartel* is commonly used in Pakistan to refer to family groups of financiers and industrialists, the more appropriate term would be *conglomerates*. These concentrations of economic power are not so much in the form of associations to control production and prices in a particular industry, but rather each is a motley group which could include a bank, an insurance company, a textile, jute, or paper mill as well as a cement or chemical plant, or indeed anything else which is profitable. But these enterprises are not uniformly successful and some have been distinct failures, ill-judged and ill-advised from the start. It is fair to suggest that a broader and wiser selection of entrepreneurs than those to whom these various enterprises were entrusted might have secured better as well as more equitable results.

Yet it is clear that on the national issue of a fairer distribution of wealth it is difficult to know what Ayub Khan or any other person at the helm could or can do about it. In poor countries, where illiteracy and superstition prevail, there is no possibility of distributing wealth but only poverty, and the control of such wealth as there is must find its way into the hands of a few, whether in the public or private sectors or both. According to the National Sample Survey, to which reference has already been made, the number of families in Pakistan which possess an income exceeding Rs.2,000 a month (U.S.$421) is 0·1 per cent. The average number of persons in such families is about ten and the number of earners is not less than two. Out of this trifling percentage, a very small fraction enjoys very much larger wealth, but it is clear that an income exceeding Rs.2,000 a month is by no means princely, especially when ten people have to live out of it. Further, it is evident that the total income represented by this group is but a small part of the total Gross National Product which, at current

---

[18] *D*, 24 June 1965. Interesting details concerning these groups will be found in the *Pakistan Times*, Lahore, 6, 7 and 8 October 1969.

prices, is the equivalent, at official rates of exchange, of about U.S. $13 billion for a nation of 120 million people. The primary problem is that of creating real wealth. Thereafter, the question of distribution is likely to find a solution.

It is possible that Pakistan may decide to seek a new approach through a centrally controlled system on communist lines or through the nationalization of banks, insurance companies, and major industry. Whether the incentives provided by the sense of national ownership would make a decisive contribution to economic growth it is hard to say. In Pakistan opinion ranges between those who see no need for change to those who believe that a solution lies in the strict application of Islamic teaching, or to those who believe in what is called Islamic socialism, or, again, to those who believe in socialism, pure and simple, with special reference to the Peking canon.

During Ayub Khan's administration, the pace of economic growth picked up a little and under the impulse of his encouragement, many in Pakistan became more conscious of the need for, as well as the opportunities of, economic growth. But this advance was really quite trifling and the spectre of poverty is as haunting and as ominous as ever.

In any case, the programmes of development for industry, banking, shipping and agriculture did not represent planning in its most constructive sense. It was, and still is, *étatism* in the worst sense. The situation prevailing, for example, in Pakistan is correctly stated in an economic appraisal of Turkey published in 1949. 'What we see in Turkey looks, not like a planned economy, but a poorly managed capitalist economy in which most of the capital happens to be supplied by the Government.'[19] Whether the money comes from the Government's own resources or from aid and lines of credit which the Government obtains from foreign sources and then makes available to the public and private sectors, does not make any difference. Clearly, the operative word in the sentence quoted is 'managed'.

It is possible that the situation is inescapable, in view of the nature of the social and economic framework in countries such

[19] M. W. Thornburg and Others, *Turkey—An Economic Appraisal*, New York, 1949, p. 19.

as Pakistan. 'Recognition of the peculiarity of hydraulic society is the decisive stumbling-block for any unilinear scheme of development. It is crucial in the formation of a multilinear pattern of societal evolution. And it is the starting point for any institutional analysis of the recent changes in the East.'[20]

It should be emphasized that in Pakistan plans are of course made, schedules of acceptable industries are prepared, and targets fixed. These things are not done haphazardly or at random but only after investigation of potentialities, of requirements, and of priorities. Moreover, these studies are often carried out with the help of foreign experts and specialists most of whom are genuinely sympathetic in their approach to the task. But if we leave aside the question whether politics take precedence over planning or *vice versa*, it is evident that the planning we have seen is not always relevant to the people's needs. After fifteen years of planning, it is possible, in Pakistan, to enjoy a dozen or more varieties of internationally known popular, sweet, fizzy drinks, but processed cheese remains an expensive luxury which only a few people in the top income group can afford. It is also generally true that as manufactured articles tend to be made or assembled in Pakistan, instead of being imported from other countries, their prices often rise.[21]

We know and hear a great deal about planning, the application of economic doctrine, the models and the targets, but we hear much less about the cost of financing individual projects, whether the most suitable equipment is obtained, and whether the most suitable people are entrusted with these projects. Little indeed is said about operating costs with respect to results obtained, and whether productivity bears a satisfactory relation to the capital invested and the labour employed. These questions are not often asked and less frequently answered. This is not to suggest that all industry in Pakistan and similar countries is inefficient and costly, but

---

[20] Wittvogel, op. cit., p. 413. By 'hydraulic society' the author means one whose distinguishing characteristic is its agricultural base depending upon the state control of water, i.e. irrigation, flood control, and protective measures. Marx, at any rate for most of his life, upheld the view that the form of development of the oriental state rose from 'government directed waterworks'. ibid., p. 374.

[21] See Nurul Islam, 'Pakistan's Efficient Industrialists', in *Forum*, Dacca, Vol. 1, No. 6, 27 December 1969.

mostly it will be found that the prosperous cases belong to those industries which may be termed indigenous to the land. The cotton textile industry is the classic instance in the Indo-Pakistan sub-continent. One lesson which still needs to be learned is that industries, like nature's vegetation, flourish better in some soils than others and, in still others, may not flourish at all.

It is quite possible that Pakistan has simply shared in a general misconception about the need for longer views than have hitherto prevailed. To quote an American observer: 'There are so many pressures in the direction of making a showing within a short time ... I often feel that if we had taken a twenty-year view of the problem when we had first started our assistance efforts abroad, they [i.e. the countries to whom assistance was given] would be much further ahead than they actually are.'[22] Pakistan can be credited with having prepared a Twenty Year Perspective Plan in 1965 based on an annual rate of growth of 7·2 per cent compound during the entire period and for the whole country. This was certainly forward thinking, but there remains the question of execution.

During Ayub Khan's administration, the need and the desire to impress were paramount considerations. Let more acres be sown, more equipment purchased, more factories set up and statistics swell so long as the country seemed to burgeon with a hitherto unheard of prosperity. Whether the acres were fertile in an economic sense, i.e. yielding a crop that paid for the labour and other inputs, whether the factory buildings were put to early and full use, the equipment productive and the statistics meaningful, were questions seldom answered because they were uncomfortable. No one cared to think, at least in public, about how much equipment there was in Pakistan entirely unused, partly used or misused. This, perhaps, is the real measure of criticism of Ayub Khan's economic administration.

Nevertheless, if Ayub Khan did not do more than he did during his years as President, it must be allowed that in matters of economic planning and industrial efficiency he had to depend on others. His own mistakes have been mentioned and

[22] Harrison Brown in *The Next Ninety Years*, op. cit., p. 16.

many of these can be attributed to his personal ambition.[23] Whether others, in his place, would have done better than he, or would have done differently, is doubtful. Pakistan's experience demonstrates that although a new generation has grown up since World War II, both rich and poor countries are far from knowing how to solve the problems of poverty and limping progress. Or perhaps they do know, but cannot face the implications.

[23] For example, Ayub Khan's resolute refusal to allow a devaluation of the Pakistan rupee, which involved the retention of the Export Bonus Voucher System, was one source of grave economic injury to the country and, in particular, to the poor. No doubt the actual mode of operation of the System, leading to multiple exchange rates, contributed to its adverse effects.

V

Political Events prior to the Elections, 1964–5

THE election—he might claim re-election—of Ayub Khan as President of Pakistan in 1965, and its circumstances, form so central an event in the history of those years that some knowledge of it, and of the political developments and influences that preceded it, are indispensable. Ayub Khan's election in January 1965, not only armed him with the mandate he required from the nation, but was thought by the world at large to confer upon him exceptional authority with respect to Pakistan's affairs. For these reasons we should consider domestic political events during 1963, 1964, and the election at the beginning of January 1965.

Something has already been said about the political background that developed when Martial Law gave place to Ayub Khan's presidential system, and also about constitutional developments after the new Constitution was promulgated. In this chapter, something will be said about the influences and events which appeared during the two years that preceded the presidential election in 1965.

The burgeoning of political activity was marked by a proposal to amend the Elective Bodies Disqualification Order, one of the earliest measures instituted by Ayub Khan's Martial Law administration. Its effect was to disqualify certain persons from election to representative bodies, a disqualification that was to last until 31 December 1966. Better known as EBDO, this was one of the measures designed to purify public life and purge it of those undesirable elements which, according to Ayub Khan, had done so much injury to Pakistan. The amendments proposed now appeared to have for their object some form of exemption for certain people living under the restraints imposed by EBDO. The history of this proposal is obscure but evidently it was not actively disapproved of, or opposed, by Ayub Khan. Had the proposed change been accepted by the National Assembly, it could have been used by him to attract a number of experienced people ready to come to terms with him in the political struggle that lay ahead. If this was the purpose the proposal did not receive the sanction of the National Assembly whose members saw no reason to provide themselves with competitors experienced in political life and, in some cases, with territorial influence or substantial wealth. Since the elections were due, as matters then stood, in 1965, there would have been little sense in liberating anyone from his EBDO disqualification, and so they remained until the appointed day, 31 December 1966.

There were signs, too, that the political temperature was rising and early in 1963 Ayub Khan made a fighting speech at a meeting at Campbellpur, headquarters town of Campbellpur District, adjacent to his own District, Hazara. Speaking to his audience in Urdu, he was for the most part occupied in replying to various charges laid against him by Choudhury Mohamed Ali who had been carrying on a campaign of severe criticism of Ayub Khan's administration and policies. He had accused Ayub Khan of ruling the country with the rod and with permitting corruption to grow. He had also challenged the manner in which the economic affairs of the country were being conducted and he charged Ayub Khan with hanging round the country's neck a millstone of unproductive, or inadequately productive, foreign debt. Considering the broad measure of praise that had been bestowed on Ayub Khan's development and economic programmes, both abroad and at home, this was a very sensitive area of criticism indeed and in his Campbellpur speech, Ayub Khan pulled no punches.

The vigorous nature of his reply can be judged by this quotation, intended to be descriptive of Choudhury Mohamed Ali. 'He is a gentleman, but I have yet to meet a person who would trust him.' There was one other observation which rings strangely since the publication of *Friends not Masters*. '. . . he [Choudhury Mohamed Ali] referred to our ex-President Iskander Mirza and praised him. . . . Perhaps this was the only occasion when Choudhury Sahib persuaded himself to praise someone.'[1]

[1] Several reviewers of *FNM* took note of the fact that throughout the entire book, Ayub Khan had scarcely a good word for anyone but himself.

In making specific reference to this speech, it is not intended to imply that Ayub Khan had hitherto played the role of the reticent or silent dictator who preferred to remain closeted and out of sight. On the contrary, he always had plenty to say and much advice to give and one of his favourite occupations was that of providing his countrymen with what were referred to as *guidelines*. The Government of Pakistan published eight volumes of his speeches and statements.

There are three reasons for mentioning the Campbellpur address. First, although it contained much that was mere party contention, it was a good deal livelier than the sustained flattery heard from others and the dreary self-praise that so often fell from the lips of Ayub Khan himself. Second, it provided evidence of the fact that the voice of opposition was not totally silenced, that people could and did criticize, and that Ayub Khan was sensitive to such criticism and did not hesitate to give a Roland for an Oliver. Those who took interest in Pakistan's political future found some comfort in this otherwise unprofitable cut and thrust. Third, it pointed to the fact that Ayub Khan was being drawn more and more into the political arena and that, therefore, he would be privately measuring the influences that were likely to weigh in the shaping of his political life.

A more tangible premonition of Ayub Khan's political intentions appeared in May 1963, when he joined the (Convention) Muslim League. This he did apparently at the invitation of that party whose members, as he said,[2] had consistently supported his programme in the legislature and outside it, and had consequently expected that he would eventually join them. Whether, as has often been suggested, this was all a clever affair devised since proposals to revive the Muslim League had first been heard, it would, I think, be difficult to prove, but as soon as political parties re-entered Pakistan's political life, the formation of his own party, or the adherence to one already existing, became inevitable for Ayub Khan. He enlisted under the banner of the (Convention) Muslim League, becoming a member twice over—once from East Pakistan and once from West Pakistan. In this way he buried finally his dream of non-party politics, though at the same time

[2] In a statement dated 22 May 1963.

as he announced his party membership he sought also to maintain the image of a just father-figure, emphasizing that, as President, he would act impartially in all things.

Among the influences that came to occupy men's minds in those days, one can be succinctly stated by mention of Choudhury Mohamed Ali's reference to *the rod* which implied, of course, the nature of Ayub Khan's authoritarian system in practice. So far as this relates to East Pakistan, we shall deal with the subject in a later chapter on the problems of that Province. Here we shall be concerned rather with the weight of this authority as it appeared in West Pakistan and as it found expression through the personality of its Governor, the late Malik Mohamed Amir Khan, Nawab of Kalabagh in Mianwali District.

Mohamed Amir Khan of Kalabagh belonged to what is known as Pakistan's class of feudal[3] landlords and he was by nature and upbringing an overbearing man, highly conscious of his ascriptive privileges, and although by no means uneducated or ignorant, he was conservative, obscurantist and unprogressive. The relationship between Ayub Khan and himself was very close and dated back to a friendship between their respective fathers.[4]

Kalabagh was appointed Governor of West Pakistan in June 1960, having previously occupied the position of Chairman of the Board of Directors of the West Pakistan Industrial Development Corporation in which job he acquired the reputation of a man of quick and firm decision. He also enjoyed the reputation—which never left him—of being personally incorrupt and of insisting that members of his family remained the same if they desired to remain on good terms with him. He remained Governor of West Pakistan until September 1966, when he retired 'for private reasons'. Ayub Khan accepted this 'very reluctantly' and 'his personal regard was in no way diminished'.[5]

[3] See p. 39.
[4] It is said that Kalabagh's father paid for Ayub Khan's education at Aligarh, having been impressed with the youthful Ayub's ability and personality. Since Ayub Khan's father was certainly not rich, it is possible that Kalabagh's father, out of friendship, provided some financial help.
[5] *D*, 18 September 1966. In place of Kalabagh, General M. Musa, former Commander-in-Chief of the Pakistan Army was appointed.

In spite of this, the two men did not part on good terms and after his resignation Kalabagh was greatly troubled by police and other enquiries.[6] When Kalabagh visited Karachi in August 1966 the security arrangements were quite extraordinary and attracted much public attention especially as rumours of his impending retirement were already abroad. The nature of the harassment after his resignation can be gauged by the fact that in December 1966, his maternal uncle, Haji Nawab Khan, applied to the Court for bail before arrest, alleging that many false charges were being brought against him including charges of murder, theft and the possession of unlicensed arms.[7]

The actual cause of the rift, about which there were stories as early as June 1966 is not fully clear, but it seems to have had much to do with the defeat of Khan Bahadur H. M. Habibullah by Ghaus Baksh Bizenjo in a National Assembly by-election at Karachi. It seems that between Kalabagh and Habibullah, who was the official (Convention) Muslim League candidate and therefore approved by Ayub Khan, there was long-standing enmity and Kalabagh appears to have used his influence, as Governor, to ensure Habibullah's defeat. At any rate, Habibullah failed to secure election and not long thereafter stories of sharp differences between Ayub Khan and Kalabagh became common.[8]

In the course of his governorship, Kalabagh acquired the reputation of being a dictatorial person who disliked opposition and had no hesitation in crushing those who attempted to oppose him or who had offended him. His character was said to possess a strong element of vindictiveness and he allowed no one who had done him any injury to escape his vengeance.[9] While this may well be correct, an over-emphasis upon it has obscured the marked strain of spitefulness in Ayub Khan's character. What was done in West Pakistan, apparently at the

[6] Some of this came out at the trial of Malik Asadullah Khan in 1969. See below.
[7] *Daily News*, 15 December 1966 and *D*, 16 December 1966.
[8] This by-election was productive of many consequences. See Ch. II, note 4.
[9] Without wishing to press this unfairly or too far, it is worth noting that the Awan tribe of Punjabi Mussulmans to which the Kalabagh family belongs and of which it is the traditional head, has been described as: '... sensitive to opposition and offence ... pursues its enmities to the bitter end'. *Government of India Handbook for the Indian Army—Punjabi Mussulmans*, 2nd Edition, 1935.

instance of and with the authority of Kalabagh, was often at the wish of Ayub Khan himself. In the application of oppressive methods in West Pakistan, the two men worked closely together until they parted, but that was not before much injury was wrought, mainly by their reliance upon the police as one of the principal instruments by which Ayub Khan's authoritarian system was administered. It was for this reason that the public image of the police deteriorated to the point at which it came to be regarded as a conspiracy against the public welfare.[10] So unpopular did the police become that in May 1966 Kalabagh promised an impartial enquiry into alleged police excesses.[11] There is no evidence that such an enquiry was ever held and, as we shall see, the attitude of the public continued in hostility, reaching its lowest ebb in January 1969 when the outrage at Kharian Police Post occurred in West Pakistan. For much of the prejudice against the police, Kalabagh was to blame and although he served Ayub Khan as Ayub Khan desired to be served, he thereby made his own contribution to Ayub's ultimate fall.[12]

In all these circumstances, it cannot be said that Choudhury Mohamed Ali was entirely wrong when he spoke of rule by the rod, although this was figurative language and Ayub Khan would certainly have applied a different description to his

[10] Between police and students, for example, there had grown up a regular feud but this, it must be added, goes back to events long preceding Ayub Khan's administration. The part played by the police in Pakistan's affairs is a subject that deserves special study. Far too many police officers have occupied high places in Pakistan including governorships and the equivalent; ministerships both at the Centre and in the Provinces; top diplomatic posts; senior posts in the Secretariat as well as other important jobs in the civil service which have no relation to the normal duties and training of a police officer. The explanation was that Pakistan suffered from a want of trained, gazetted personnel and therefore recourse to police officers was necessary. It is not totally convincing.

[11] *D*, 1 May 1966. This promise arose out of the conduct of a junior police officer named Sipra who took objection to the presence of a newspaper photographer on an occasion in Karachi when civil commotion was expected. Sipra seized the photographer's camera, placed it on the road and ordered a truck driver to run over the camera until it was smashed. See editorial in *D*, 23 April 1966. The police were not always in the wrong, but the conduct of men like Sipra did much to make them appear so.

[12] In November 1967, Kalabagh was shot to death by his youngest son, Malik Asadullah Khan, in the course of a quarrel. Tried for his father's murder, Asadullah pleaded self-defence and was acquitted, in December 1969, on the ground that the prosecution had not established its case beyond reasonable doubt. The State appealed and at the time of this writing the outcome of the appeal was not known.

methods. What for one man is the enforcement of law and order, may well be, for another, unabashed tyranny. Much depends, as Clemenceau once said, on which side of the barricade one stands. However, it is a fair conclusion that the use of the police as part of Ayub Khan's administrative apparatus contributed substantially to the events that led to his departure from public life.

In this, as in other respects, the course of events after the withdrawal of Martial Law, had provided Ayub Khan with much to think about, particularly concerning the prospect that his policies would be approved by the National Assembly and implemented without obstructive opposition. The attitude of the Press, whose reception of his Constitution had been lukewarm, indicated clearly that he could not rely upon its loyal support and approval. This applied in equal measure in both Provinces, although in East Pakistan the Press, as well as other politically sensitive institutions, had been treated with more restraint. This explains why some newspapers in East Pakistan showed a capacity for speaking out, a capacity that has not in general been shared in West Pakistan.[13]

The attitude of the press could be gauged not merely from the criticism that appeared but from the less desirable practices of publishing unfair headlines and carefully sifted reports of speeches made in the National and Provincial Assemblies. Often what was said in the House originated in a form suitable for ostentatious display in the Press and was so intended. This must be tolerated in a society where freedom

[13] This does not mean that in East Pakistan the Press enjoyed complete liberty. In 1963, no fewer than eight periodicals, published in West Pakistan, were subject to pre-censorship before they could be distributed in East Pakistan (*NAD*, March 1963). In East Pakistan, some editors and journals suffered severely. Notable among these was *Ittefaq* (meaning 'unity') whose editor, Tofazzal Hossain, was frequently in trouble. On 30 September 1959, he was detained under Martial Law Regulation No. 24. In June 1966 he was again detained under the Defence of Pakistan Rules, apparently for the part that he and *Ittefaq* were playing in the Six-Point Movement. At the same time, the New Nation Printing Press, where *Ittefaq* was produced, was declared forfeit to the Government under Defence of Pakistan Rule No. 52(2). The effect was that *Ittefaq*, the weekly *Dacca Mail*, and the Bengali weekly *Purbani* all went out of circulation. Tofazzal Hossain was released in March 1967. On 9 February 1969, when Ayub Khan was visibly retreating on all sectors, the forfeiture order, relating to the Press, was rescinded. Toffazal Hossain did not live long to enjoy his triumph. A few weeks later he died suddenly of heart failure.

of speech prevails and the intention of all parliamentary debate is that the speaker's voice shall be heard outside the walls of the chamber. The unfortunate truth in Pakistan, however, was that soon after these Assemblies first met, the level of discussion deteriorated, reviving memories of the pre-Martial Law legislatures and the 'sustained nonsense'[14] that disfigured so many of their sessions.

Ayub Khan never underestimated his opponents in the same way as he did the nation. He neglected nothing that might contribute to the retention of power and he would not permit his opponents to exercise any advantage against him if he could prevent it. Thus, as much as two years before the 1965 election, he concluded that he could not necessarily rely on favourable Press reporting and a decision was taken to establish closer control of the fourth estate. Much rumour circulated about the future of the Press and about the possibility that working journalists might be required to take out licences to be followed by the first intimation of curbs on Press activity. In August 1963, a West Pakistan Press and Publications Ordinance, No. XXX of 1963, was issued.

The reaction was sharp and vigorous. On 6 September 1963, journalists held a countryside strike when black arm-bands were worn and some very hostile speeches made. Following a joint meeting of newspaper proprietors, editors and journalists, the Ordinance was declared unacceptable. Ayub Khan, with his capacity for compromise when faced with a determined and important opponent, agreed to a change. In October amendments were issued accordingly.

Like all men who are pliant as well as successful, Ayub Khan, and perhaps his advisers, displayed ingenuity. As a result, in addition to a truncated Press Ordinance, a National Press Trust was formed in 1964 with the energetic Mr. Ghulam Faruque as its first Chairman. The terms of the trust deed have never been made public, but this appears to be a private trust on which a number of businessmen settled money, some willingly and others less so. With these funds, the National Press Trust was able to acquire existing newspapers and periodicals and to establish others. The Board of Trustees comprised officially appointed nominees with a full time

[14] Feldman, op. cit., p. 24.

Chairman whose business it was to administer all the newspapers and periodicals of the Trust as a means of projecting Ayub Khan and his policies. It is not surprising that the expression 'Press Trust paper' acquired certain pejorative undertones.

Financial or administrative control of newspapers favouring the government of the day carries with it no assurance that those newspapers will be purchased or read. Nor does such control preclude other newspapers from winning readers, and it was therefore necessary to ensure that newspapers and journals not owned by the National Press Trust were encouraged to report favourably on the work of Ayub Khan's Government and to be restrained in their criticism. For this purpose, all official advertising was centralized either through the Central Government or through the provincial Governments thus placing an important form of patronage in the hands of the executive. Those newspapers and journals which incurred official displeasure could even be removed altogether from the list of officially approved media. This centralization affected such semi-autonomous organizations as the Industrial Development Corporations, the Water and Power Development Authorities, the State Bank of Pakistan and even the National Bank of Pakistan. The serious financial implications of this are obvious and, in the result, most newspapers and periodicals not owned by the National Press Trust found it wiser to conform as far as possible. Some, however, did not. The *Nawa-i-Waqt*, a newspaper published in Lahore in Urdu, carried on throughout Ayub Khan's régime without official patronage in the form of advertising and managed to do so in spite of the fact that even its sales were limited by official restriction on the quantity of newsprint available to it. Since the editor was shrewd enough not to give actual offence, *Nawa-i-Waqt* survived and copies used to pass from hand to hand, sometimes fetching a premium in the bazaar.

The Press Ordinance carried on the old practice of demanding, when necessary, cash security for good behaviour and it was possible for the Government to confiscate a printing press where an offending journal was produced. Editors, printers and writers could also be detained under security laws or prosecuted for defamation or sedition.¹⁵ A curious result of all these measures proved to be that very often National Press Trust newspapers tended to be more liberal and bolder, both in reporting and comment, than many that were not so controlled. This does not mean that the National Press Trust newspapers did not give fullest coverage to Ayub Khan, his activities, speeches and homilies, but they certainly published criticism tilting at the crimes and the follies of the day.¹⁶ Often they gave more space to critics and opponents of Ayub Khan than did independently owned newspapers. After the decision in 1968 to liberalize the attitude towards press reporting about the position, National Press Trust papers were among the first and the most prominent to take advantage of it. No doubt the editorial staff of those journals found the pure air oɩ freedom as invigorating as did others.

To what extent the Press was harnessed and muzzled during the period of Ayub Khan's administration, as compared with other countries, where general restraints are imposed on printed work, it is difficult to say. What is anathema in one country, is innocuous in another. Much depends upon the inherited tradition and the national outlook. In Pakistan, there was, during Ayub Khan's era, a good deal more freedom to publish than might be found in contemporary China. Much of the restraint in Pakistan was self-imposed and, as we have remarked elsewhere, a good deal of it derived from a dislike of printing unpleasant truths.

The injury done by Press restraints proved in the end to be less to the nation than to Ayub Khan. The damage to his image and that of his Government on account of the sycophancy of the Press was permanent, and much the same can be said oɩ efforts, during 1963 and 1964, to restrain individuals, political parties and other quasi-political organizations from actively engaging in opposition or criticism. Some of these individuals—

¹⁵ Ayub Khan did not invent or start all these things. Some of them stemmed from pre-independence days and had been carried on in India and Pakistan. A notable instance, in Pakistan, of the misuse of such legislation occurred during the prime ministership of the late Khwaja Nazimuddin when the *Times of Karachi* (no longer being published) commented sarcastically on some pronouncement made by Nazimuddin by printing a cartoon which showed East Pakistan in flames. The editor was prosecuted for sedition.

¹⁶ Notably the *Pakistan Times*, which published the refreshing satire of a clever young writer, Khalid Hasan.

Miss Jinnah for example—were beyond his reach. Although she seized every suitable occasion to publish a pungent, sometimes really blistering, statement in the Press, there was little that Ayub Khan could do.[17] Others, however, could be dealt with more or less efficiently and according to their potential for mischief. The late Mr. M. H. Gazdar managed to get himself arrested in April 1963 on the charge of having made a seditious speech in Karachi. Unlike other and less fortunate victims, he was acquitted by the Court only eight months later. The case of Sardar Ataullah Khan Mengal was a more serious affair and dragged on until 1968 when the departure of Ayub Khan soon afterwards led to its abandonment. The case was noteworthy for an illuminating statement by a defence witness who said that the camp for political *détenus* at Quetta was no better than a *qattalgarh* (slaughterhouse). Whether he spoke from experience or merely from prejudice against the Government is not clear, but it lent credence to the growing belief that physical maltreatment was becoming more and more common as a means of extracting evidence and confessions, or of forcing people to become state witnesses. It was this belief that caused people to accept as true statements made in the Agartala Case, five years later, by the accused who gave details of the forms of physical ill-treatment to which they had been subjected.

In some respects the most significant among the attempts made to stifle opposition was the arrest of eight persons, in May 1963, on charges of sedition.[18] They were all leading figures in the parties opposed to Ayub Khan and were prominently associated with a proposal to form a National Democratic Front for which purpose a meeting was held in Karachi, at Lakhem House, the residence of H. S. Suhrawardy. At the closure of this two-day conference, on 28 January 1963, a resolution was passed and, in consequence, the eight men named were arrested. Unfortunately, the terms of this resolution were not published,[19] so the public had no means of

[17] His revenge took the form of a coarse reference to Miss Jinnah, popularly regarded as *Madar-i-Millat* (Mother of the nation), calling her 'an old woman of 76'. *D*, 23 October 1964.
[18] Their names were: Z. H. Lari, Mahmoodul Haq Usmani, Sh. Abdul Majeed, Mian Mohd. Ali Qasuri, Tufail Mohamed, Maulana Abdus Sattar Niazi, Khwaja Mohd. Rafiq and Nasrullah Khan.
[19] Nor have I been able to obtain a copy despite much effort.

forming any opinion as to the gravity of the offence. Bail was granted subject to the condition that the accused would not make seditious speeches while at liberty and five of the accused declined bail on these terms since they denied any seditious activity or intent.

From such evidence as was reproduced in the newspapers, the resolution contained a long preamble critical of the prevailing situation and of Ayub Khan's methods of administering the country, and called for a united opposition against him. This resolution was officially interpreted as an attempt to provoke hatred and contempt for the Government and was, therefore, seditious. Nothing remains to be said about this except that, in April 1968, the Court accepted a bathetic petition by the Government requesting permission to withdraw the case and, in consequence, all the accused were discharged.

In the same month that these men were arrested, the West Pakistan Government was obliged to give way to a forceful public outcry in Karachi relating to an arbitrary assessment of higher taxes on property. The truth of this extraordinary matter is quite obscure and may never be known. The most that the citizens of Karachi knew about it was that without warning, property owners were confronted with enormously increased demands in respect of taxes on their buildings. The imposts were quite impossible and how submission to them could ever have been considered is beyond imagination. The manner of serving notice of these demands was aggressive and threatening and when the public had recovered from its initial surprise, it made known its defiance. This was an interesting instance of the arbitrary, dictatorial and even irrational methods of those times which ultimately became habitual. As often happened, the administration was obliged to retreat, leaving behind no sense of gratitude but only anger and suspicion. It was not surprising that in the elections of 1964–5, Karachi voted strongly against Ayub Khan.

The second prong of his attack on the opposition was directed against the Jama'at-i-Islami, an organization of strictly orthodox outlook. It was a formidable opponent for two reasons. First, its religious orthodoxy had a wide appeal especially in view of Ayub Khan's attempts at social reform with special reference to the Muslim Family Laws Ordinance and to the Family Planning Campaign. These measures were heartily disliked by many and the Jama'at-i-Islami exploited this feeling as actively as it could. It was not the only political organization which depended upon the orthodox Islamic appeal, but it was certainly the most effective. Led by Maulana Maudoodi, a clever, learned and strong-minded man, the Jama'at-i-Islami was a well-organized and disciplined party. It had, moreover, wide contact with the masses through its vigorous social work.

The Jama'at ran mobile dispensaries and maintained libraries. There was a strong bias towards education as understood by the orthodox Muslim of the Sunni school and on social welfare including help for the poor. The Jama'at-i-Islami was the only political party in Pakistan which attributed so much importance to this side of its work and, as a result, it acquired a substantial following. This has remained loyal in spite of not wholly fictitious charges against Maudoodi that his attitude to the Pakistan proposal, before Partition and Independence, was ambiguous. These charges were often repeated and formed the basis of the attack which Ayub Khan initiated in October 1963.

This began with a speech by Khan Habibullah Khan, then Ayub Khan's Minister for Home and Kashmir Affairs. He accused the Jama'at of creating a sense of frustration and despondency by its unwarranted criticism of Government policy and he said that Maudoodi was inspired by foreign sources. A few days later, it happened that the Jama'at held a three-day conference at Lahore and, on the first day, a man was killed by a pistol bullet fired by someone who appeared to have gone to the meeting in order to make trouble. The immediate upshot was an outburst of student unrest in Lahore, Rawalpindi and Lyallpur. Although a few days earlier Ayub Khan had claimed: 'My people believe in me,'[20] this unrest was directed against him, and soon afterwards, on 8 November, Ayub Khan made this clear when he blamed the Jama'at for fomenting student trouble. There could be no doubt that the Jama'at was pursuing a very active campaign of criticism because although none of its meetings was reported in the

[20] *D*, 2 November 1963.

newspapers, the regular, almost daily, attacks on the Jama'at, principally in speeches by Habibullah Khan, provided the mirror by which the situation could be judged.

On or about 17 December, three leading members of the Jama'at (including a Government official) were arrested in Karachi. They were granted bail of Rs.100,000 each although the prosecution opposed it. Here was another of those extraordinary contradictions in behaviour that so often made Ayub Khan's administration appear irresponsible. In opposing bail in this case, the prosecution informed the Court that the nature of the offences *could not be disclosed at that stage* in which circumstance all reasonable men were left wondering how the Court could decide whether bail should be granted or withheld.

Three weeks later, the Jama'at-i-Islami was banned throughout Pakistan and declared an unlawful association under the Criminal Law Amendment Act of 1908. Maudoodi and eighteen others were arrested under Section 3 of the West Pakistan Maintenance of Public Order Ordinance 1960. Some members of the opposition sought to raise the matter in the West Pakistan Assembly but the Speaker disallowed the motion on the strange ground that the subject concerned the ordinary administration of the law in the Province. Yet, having tried to silence the Jama'at in this way, Ayub Khan was once again thwarted. In July 1964 the High Court in Dacca held that the ban on the Jama'at was void, at any rate so far as that Court interpreted the law in East Pakistan. Two months afterwards, the Supreme Court held that the ban could not be upheld anywhere in Pakistan.

However, Ayub Khan's activities at that time were not all negative. In April 1964, increases of pay for civil and military officers were announced with retrospective effect from 1962 so far as they related to their application to service rules, but arrears were to be paid from 1 July 1963. It was a pleasant little gift of nine months' increase to be collected by each officer. The total cost of the sanctioned increases was estimated about Rs.150 million a year. Two months later, the West Pakistan Government followed suit with an announcement of increased pay for its own officials. In July, Ayub Khan attended the Commonwealth Conference in London and took this opportunity to visit four other countries. Accompanied by Zulfikar Ali Bhutto, he was considered to have achieved a notable success at the Conference and to have added much to Pakistan's international stature. He returned to his own country in an aura of glory and, so surrounded, was adopted, a month or two later, by the (Convention) Muslim League as its presidential candidate.

VI

The Presidential Election, 1965

THOSE who served with or under Ayub Khan, whether in the Army or during his period of office as President were all agreed on one point. He was a hard worker, attending diligently to files and writing his notes indefatigably. He also retained the thorough, industrious approach that he had displayed when Commander-in-Chief. This made itself apparent in his preparations for the presidential election, not only in the constitutional manipulations already described, but in a careful study of the tactics to be pursued during the campaign itself. He was doubtless aware that many of his countrymen regarded his success as certain, but this in no way deterred him from a single-minded application to the task of achieving it.

Since there was virtually no question about his own candidature, the initial problem for him was not that of his own nomination but to know what effective personality might come forward to oppose him. There was no doubt that determined opposition could be expected. The principal opposition parties in the National Assembly had already joined forces to bring about his undoing. Known as the Combined Opposition Parties, this group included the Council Muslim League, led by Khwaja Nazimuddin and Mian Mumtaz Khan Daultana; the Awami League, led by Sheikh Mujibur Rahman; the National Awami Party, led by Maulana Bhashani; the North-West Frontier group of the National Awami Party, led by Wali Khan, son of the famous Abdul Ghaffar Khan; the Nizam-i-Islam Party, led by Choudhury Mohamed Ali and Farid Ahmed; the Jama'at-i-Islami Party, led by Maulana Maudoodi, and to these were added other prominent political personalities determined to remove Ayub Khan.

It is easy to see the essential weakness of such opposition.¹ A common desire to defeat Ayub Khan in the presidential election was scarcely an adequate programme for a political coalition, whether in or out of office. Leaving aside those who genuinely believed in his leadership and in what he claimed to have done for Pakistan, there were others who felt that, whatever his shortcomings, the alternative offered by the Combined Opposition Parties was chaos. What guarantee, it was asked, could there be that, having defeated Ayub Khan, this combination of parties would not at once fall to quarrelling and then split up, leading to the very consequences that had brought about the Martial Law of 1958? Clearly there was none, and the known attitudes of this oddly assorted coalition offered every prospect of disagreement. This particular argument weighed heavily in the minds of many who were otherwise doubtful about Ayub Khan's personal integrity and motives.²

It should be remembered that before there could be an election of a new President, the Constitution required the election of members for a new Electoral College, comprising 80,000 Basic Democrats to be chosen, in equal numbers, by each of the two Provinces. Thus, the initial battle would be fought at this level and Ayub Khan hoped to ensure that as many persons as possible favourable to himself would be so elected. He might well expect to be successful in this since the election of the Basic Democrats would take place while he was still President and while his party had clear majorities in the National and Provincial Assemblies. His party members would use their influence in the constituencies they represented and would extract promises of support from the candidates they helped. This, as has previously been explained, was the purpose of the controversial Second Amendment to the Constitution, enacted in June 1964. Although it was *prima facie* desirable that as many members of the Electoral College as possible should be known to be favourable to Ayub Khan in order to simplify, if not to ensure, his re-election, it has also been said that it did not really matter who was sent to the

¹ Ayub Khan and his supporters referred to this association as the *Jugto Front*. *Jugto* is derived from the Bengali word *jug* meaning *world*. The implication is sarcastic, meaning *all and sundry*.
² The pros and cons are well examined in editorials which appear in *D*, 21 and 22 November 1964.

Electoral College since it would be easy to corrupt these people afterwards, with the help of Assembly members. This may appear too cynical a view but such fears—prompted by a general awareness of existing political corruption—caused the country to reject this particular part of Ayub Khan's constitutional structure.

Thus the programme was that elections to the Electoral College would take place in November 1964. The presidential election would follow and after that elections for new Assemblies—National and Provincial. In all this, the key election was for the office of President.

On 16 September 1964 it was announced, after much confabulation, that the Combined Opposition Parties had invited Miss Fatima Jinnah, sister of the Quaid-i-Azam, to be their candidate, an invitation she accepted although she had been virtually inactive in politics since her brother's death. It was, nevertheless, well known that Miss Jinnah was decidedly opposed to Ayub Khan and, in regular public pronouncements published on such occasions as 'Id-ul-Fitr', the anniversary of her distinguished brother's birthday, the undertone of criticism was notably waspish even in the days when Ayub Khan was treated, or treated himself, as being above any such *lèse-majesté*. Of course, as sister of the Quaid-i-Azam and one who had stood firmly by his side during all the years of endeavour to win Pakistan, Miss Jinnah was in a special position. There was not a great deal that Ayub Khan could do to *her*.[3]

At that time, the selection of Miss Jinnah was generally interpreted as having been more or less forced upon the Combined Opposition Parties among whom diversity of feeling and purpose prevented agreement on a mutually acceptable candidate. The selection was also interpreted as an attempt to influence the electorate simply by evoking the magic of Pakistan's most famous name and there were many who considered that Miss Jinnah should not have allowed

---

[3] Miss Jinnah died on 11 July 1967. She was buried at Karachi and the crowd that followed her bier was estimated at about half a million. The opportunity was taken to raise slogans against Ayub Khan and there was some rioting in which members of the Jama'at-i-Islami and left-wing groups were involved. The police had recourse to tear-gas and rifle fire. The dead were variously estimated between two and twelve.

herself to be made a party to such exploitation. In fact, as was subsequently revealed the Combined Opposition Parties were moved, in part if not in whole, by circumstances that were somewhat different.

About fifteen months after the elections were held, the vernacular Press published an interesting story about the manner of Miss Jinnah's selection. It stated that when the Combined Opposition Parties decided to unite for the purpose of selecting a candidate whom they would all support, it was agreed that such a candidate must be the object of unanimous agreement among all the constituent parties. To this, Maulana Bhashani is said to have added a further condition, that no one who had been associated with the Martial Law administration, which had assumed power in 1958 could possibly be acceptable. The reasonableness of this suggestion was difficult to refute among political parties so firmly opposed to Ayub Khan's methods of government and so firmly wedded to the democratic ideal. The effect, however, was to eliminate the possibility of Lieutenant-General Azam Khan's candidature. General Azam Khan was one of Ayub Khan's military colleagues associated with the declaration of Martial Law in 1958. Later, however, they quarrelled and General Azam came out in political opposition. As an election rival, he might well have proved formidable. Previously, he had been Governor of East Pakistan until his differences with Ayub Khan, and there he had been extremely popular, so popular that he might well have reckoned on carrying that Province in an election. In West Pakistan, those opposed to Ayub Khan might also have voted for him, in which case he might have gained an overall majority. However, his chances were nullified by Maulana Bhashani's stratagem, engineered by Ayub Khan's Foreign Minister, Zulfikar Ali Bhutto, working through his friend, Masihur Rahman, who happened to be one of Maulana Bhashani's countrymen.

By the time the story became known, the elections were many months old and Ayub Khan had been elected. The information did not create any great stir and, of course, its publication in the Press was unthinkable. Consequently, the matter disappeared from public notice until in 1969 new information was volunteered which, to some extent, lent credence to the story which had elicited so little interest in 1966. The *Daily News* of 27 November 1969 carried a fresh tale that before the election a deal had been negotiated by Bhutto with Masihur Rahman by which a sum of Rs.5 lakhs was paid and, in return, Maulana Bhashani's party was to ensure Miss Jinnah's defeat. The author of this story was Sheikh Karamatullah, General Secretary of the Tasnim-i-Islam, Karachi, who said that the information had been given to him by Mahmoodul Haq Usmani, General Secretary of the National Awami Party. Karamatullah challenged Ayub Khan and Bhutto to deny this on oath, an invitation they either declined or ignored. At any rate, neither of them ventured any public comment.

This was followed a few days later by a statement in the same newspaper by Mr. M. H. Saiyid, a former secretary to Mohamed Ali Jinnah and closely associated with Miss Jinnah during the election of 1965.[4] He confirmed what Karamatullah had said and added much more detail. Thereafter, the subject was allowed to drop although some political leaders in East Pakistan, not necessarily members of Maulana Bhashani's party, declared, apparently with reference to these disclosures, that the Maulana was incorruptible. Whether or not this is true, Ayub Khan certainly penetrated the Combined Opposition Parties' organization and was fully informed during the election campaign about his opponents' thinking and intentions.[5]

Lieutenant-General Azam Khan would have been a popular choice whatever opinions people might have held about his capacity for the job and the fact that his chances were cleverly frustrated created problems for the Combined Opposition. Even the proposal to invite Miss Jinnah, with its obvious advantages, had equally obvious dangers of which the first, perhaps, was the problem of her own personality. She was by no means young, and although her character was firm and

[4] *Daily News*, 4 December 1969.
[5] There is no doubt whatsoever that there was at least one treacherous person in the higher command of the Combined Opposition. It was intended to challenge Ayub Khan's candidature in the Supreme Court by reason of the fact that he was holding the rank of Field-Marshal, a challenge it might have been difficult to meet. This plan was betrayed and Ayub Khan took the necessary steps to have Army Orders issued, with retrospective effect, to regularize his position.

indomitable, the flesh might prove weaker than the spirit. She was, moreover, a difficult person to deal with, having a powerful will and a sharp, imperious temper. After her brother's death, her own political hopes were disappointed and she had pursued a life of retirement, a blighting experience after the activity and prominence she had known for many years. None of this had done anything to sweeten or appease her nature and were she to have been elected President, those who served under her as Ministers might well have found life difficult.

She was not equally acceptable to all the parties and groups which formed the Combined Opposition. There were some, particularly from East Pakistan, who had resented Miss Jinnah's attitude to Suhrawardy, particularly at the time of his death. On a rather different plane, there was the difficulty that others felt about a woman candidate and a woman President, were she to have been elected. For those who belonged to parties wedded to religious orthodoxy, for instance the Jama'at-i-Islami, this prospect raised grave questions of law and conscience. In fact, this point became an issue. A gathering of *'ulema* produced a *fatwa*[6] declaring that in Islam a woman could not be a head of state. In reply to this, Maulana Maudoodi, the head of the Jama'at-i-Islami announced that according to Islam a woman could be a head of state but it was not desirable. The Pir of Dewal Sharif went considerably further. He claimed that in the course of meditation, the Almighty had favoured him with a communication which indicated divine displeasure with the Combined Opposition Parties. An indignant public, which had shown no great concern with the question of the legality, in Islam, of Miss Jinnah's candidature, claimed that the Pir was criticizing Miss Jinnah, the sister of the Quaid-i-Azam and this the Pir promptly denied.[7] It does not seem that his

[6] A *fatwa* is an opinion with reference to Islamic law given with respect to a case stated. A juris-consult. *'Ulema* signifies persons learned in Islam. The singular is *Allama*.

[7] For this unsavoury exploitation of religion see *D*, 18, 23, and 24 December 1964. The Pir of Dewal Sharif, at that time, was a comparatively youthful man. He was well-educated and made a great impression on many people in West Pakistan. At one time it was widely said that Ayub Khan was one of his devotees but this seems very uncertain. In the photograph facing p. 165 of *Friends not Masters*, the figure in white robes is the Pir of Dewal Sharif.

revelations exercised any great influence on the course of the campaign.

In addition to the two prominent figures—Ayub Khan and Fatima Jinnah—there were two freak candidates of whom it may now be said that one, K. M. Kamal, secured thirteen votes and the other, M. Bashir Ahmed, did not get any. The purpose of these two unknowns in seeking nomination is obscure and many stories were current at the time. It seems that there was no real purpose except, perhaps, to gain a little notoriety. There may also have been interest in the lakh of rupees which, under the Constitution, each candidate could obtain from the Government to cover election expenses, but even this was done away with in November 1964. Still, the appearance of these two candidates, whose nomination papers were in order and which had been accepted, drew attention to a serious constitutional problem. Had both Ayub Khan and Miss Jinnah died on election day, would it have followed automatically that one of the other two would be deemed to have been elected?

From 1964 onwards, electioneering was in full swing and tempers began to rise. There were appeals for tolerance, for law and order and an abstention from mud-slinging, but none of these appeals had much effect. Trouble occurred at projection meetings and in the environs of Karachi there were brawls. Section 144 was imposed in the city to prevent gatherings of people bent on mischief. Quite apart from the sense of antagonism between parties which led, when encouraged and fostered, to violence, the state of public order in Karachi was further endangered by the systematic import of men from Ayub Khan's own District of Hazara. Each train, coming from the north, brought with it a fresh contingent of these easily identifiable men in grey *mazri* shirt and pyjama with a jacket for warmth. In the buttonhole, each wore a plastic rose, Ayub Khan's election symbol and the people of Karachi gazed askance at these surprisingly numerous visitors. Karachi did not then know that these were the storm-troopers with a part yet to be played.

Of course, all this cost money, but there was no doubt that Ayub Khan's party coffers were full. It soon became known that at least two of his Ministers, those whose portfolios brought greater contact with the business community, had been charged with the collection of funds. It appears that a regular tariff was fixed, based on the nature of the business. Trades who held import licence quotas contributed proportionately to the nominal value of the quota. In the case of jute, cotton and wool textile mills, the levy was based on the number of looms and spindles installed. Years afterwards, in 1969, the *Weekly Mail* of Karachi,[8] published facsimiles of the two secret letters dated 6 and 12 November 1964 circulated by the All-Pakistan Textile Mills Association to its members, asking them to pay their contributions to the funds of the Pakistan (Convention) Muslim League on the basis of Rs.2 per installed spindle and Rs.25 per installed loom. On the basis that 37,340 cotton looms and 2,952,580 spindles were in use at the time, the contribution to Ayub Khan's party chest from this source alone would have been in the order of Rs.15 million.[9]

Foreign businesses established in Pakistan were asked to contribute but these organizations submitted that they should not be expected to involve themselves in Pakistan's internal affairs, this being as undesirable from the point of view of Pakistan as it was of foreign business. This reasonable argument, with its implied references to the colonial past was accepted but not without murmured warning that the foreign business community would find itself called upon to contribute to some other national undertaking.

There was, however, other and better evidence of the funds available to Ayub Khan than the mere arrival in Karachi of a few thousand Hazarawals. Day after day, in leading newspapers—English and Pakistani languages—there appeared full-page advertisements extolling the virtues of Ayub Khan's administration and emphasizing the theme that only Ayub Khan could be relied upon to defend Pakistan against the Indian threat. What, it was inferred, could a mere woman do about this? In his election campaign Ayub Khan relied much upon India. On top of one of Karachi's prominent buildings there appeared an enormous neon sign, measuring forty feet

[8] 5 December 1969.
[9] At the time of Ayub Khan's fall from power, it was estimated that the funds of his party amounted to about Rs.40 million, or more than U.S. $8 million calculated at the official rate of exchange.

by thirty-six feet, and said to be the biggest in Pakistan. It displayed Ayub Khan's name, along with his rose symbol, all in vivid colours. Miss Jinnah had no neon signs and no full-page advertisements. Her campaign was fought through her own tours, by her supporters at the hustings, and through canvassing.

Clear-cut issues were presented to the electorate although, as the campaigning went on, it became more and more evident that the dominating issue was Ayub Khan's own personality and conduct. The general attack on his record was focused on the form of the constitution he had created. It was considered dictatorial, placed too much uncontrolled power in his hands, and the method of indirect election continued to be disliked. The Basic Democracies system was described as corrupt. His economic policy was criticized and he was accused of having loaded Pakistan with a foreign debt that would burden the country for years to come. The Indus Waters Treaty, signed with India, was the subject of a heavy onslaught and the exchange of polemics on this became acrimonious.

Ayub Khan's reply was that he had given the country some seven years of stable and orderly government. Pakistan's economic progress had been the object of much praise in many parts of the world and, for the first time in the country's history, planning had not only been explicit, but had been implemented. The social and economic benefits of the land reforms were emphasized and also the social reforms brought by his Family Laws legislation. Since he had first come to office, Pakistan's stature had been raised in the eyes of the world and in international councils Pakistan again spoke with a firmer voice to which attention was paid. Those who criticized him and desired his fall were enemies of Pakistan who, for their own interests, sought a return to the bad old days. Above all, with the threat from India hanging over them, an India armed to the teeth by the Soviet Union, the United Kingdom and the United States, the country required a firm hand at the helm and a person capable of understanding what was involved in the problems of defence. This was one reason why his constitution provided that the Minister of Defence must be a person holding, or who at least had held, the rank of Lieutenant-General (or the equivalent in the Navy or Air Force).

But, as has so often and so unfortunately been the case in Pakistan, the election was fought less with reference to the political and economic programmes offered by the contending parties, than with personalities, and in particular that of Ayub Khan. Was he corrupt? Was he a dictator? Was he guilty of nepotism and favouritism? Had he teamed up with the nation's great capitalists? These were the questions that almost exclusively preoccupied most electors' minds. In saying this, we must remember that the electors comprised 80,000 Basic Democrats, not the mass of the people, but the interest of the masses was reflected in the part they could play in influencing the men *they* had voted for, the Basic Democrats themselves.

In relation to Ayub Khan's personality and conduct, one of the most publicized questions was that of the considerable fortune said to have been accumulated by his son, Captain Gohar Ayub, who had retired from the Army after a few years' service and had entered the world of business in a very substantial way,[10] in association with his father-in-law, Lieutenant-General Habibullah Khan Khattak. Taxed with this, Ayub Khan made a long and prevaricating statement in which he avoided the real issue. The issue was not that Gohar Ayub had gone into business and had made money, but that he had used his father's position and influence to do so. He had obtained access to financial resources which no young man, Army officer or other, without substantial property or business experience, could ever hope to secure. The question was not whether the business had been acquired (substantially it consisted of the General Motors Corporation assembly plant located at Karachi) through wealth corruptly gained or whether the business itself was being badly or dishonestly conducted. The question was that of improper use of influence to which Ayub Khan had lent himself or, at any rate, had done nothing to prevent. His reply was not satisfactory and the case of Captain Gohar Ayub continued to be pressed against him.

On 3 January 1965, the result of the election was announced: Field-Marshal Ayub Khan 49,647 votes; Miss Fatima Jinnah 28,345 votes. The votes for the two freak candidates have

---

[10] See Appendix B. In the last chapter of this book, there is a different and probably more accurate estimation of Ayub Khan's attitude to his son's business ventures.

already been mentioned. Miss Jinnah had been soundly defeated, but by no means disgraced, despite alleged attempts on the part of Ayub Khan's supporters to corrupt members of the Electoral College[11] and alleged efforts by district officials and police officers to influence voters in Ayub Khan's favour. Moreover, in spite of all the difficulties and disadvantages that confronted Miss Jinnah, nearly 30,000 members of the Electoral College, representing a substantial body of public opinion, were prepared to vote against Ayub Khan, a point which Ayub Khan might claim as speaking well for his arrangements by which the voice of the people could be heard.

While it is improbable that Miss Jinnah could have won this election, she might have given Ayub Khan a closer run but for four circumstances. In the first place, many people did not like the political kaleidoscope which called itself the Combined Opposition Parties. It was considered to be a ramshackle agglomeration with no better purpose than to unseat Ayub Khan. Secondly, in East Pakistan, Maulana Bhashani remained inactive and if he did not actually do anything to thwart Miss Jinnah, there is not much to show that he did anything to advance her prospects of success. Thirdly, Miss Jinnah lost votes, particularly in the North-West Frontier, through the unwise action of Abdul Ghaffar Khan whose son Wali Khan was leader of a section of the National Awami Party and a prominent member of the Combined Opposition Parties' higher command. Abdul Ghaffar Khan, whose attitude to Pakistan and the question of a separate Pakhtunistan was only too well known, was in London at the end of December 1964, having sought a visa to enter the United States unsuccessfully. There were difficulties too about a proposed visit to Cairo and he therefore decided to return to Kabul where he was certainly *persona grata*. He was asked by his political friends to defer his return to Kabul until after the election, but he did not agree to this. Instead, he went back to Kabul just before the election. Ayub Khan's election managers did not overlook the potentialities of this and the newspapers raised the propaganda question: What is Abdul Ghaffar Khan doing in Kabul?

[11] The smallness of the Electoral College facilitated the buying of votes and such trafficking as went on during the election was one of the most important criticisms of the Basic Democracies system.

Opinion against Miss Jinnah was undoubtedly influenced by this.

The fourth consideration affecting the election result relates to whether, and to what extent, the election was rigged in Ayub Khan's favour. In its issue dated 7 December 1968, the *Economist* raised this point but without coming to any definite conclusion.[12] By this time, opposition to Ayub Khan had become vigorous and outspoken. During the heyday of his administration, public or printed discussion about whether the election was fair was not permitted, but when the public turned finally against him, after November 1968, the question was often voiced. Several people, notably Air-Marshal Asghar Khan, claimed that the presidential election had not been as clean as many people assumed. Mr. J. A. Rahim, the Acting Chairman of Bhutto's Pakistan Peoples' Party bluntly said the election had been corruptly managed. Some people, notably among Bhutto's opponents, thought that J. A. Rahim ought to know!

All of this had occurred five years earlier and unless anyone was prepared to come forward with a confession, it seemed unlikely that any new evidence would ever be disclosed. Still, it is also the case that soon after the 1965 elections there had been talk of irregularities and pamphlets were printed giving the details. This is not proof of such irregularities, but the Government was sufficiently apprehensive of their contents to issue prohibitions on publishing or bringing into the Provinces any document which contained allegations against the Election Commission regarding the election of the members of the Electoral College, of the President or of members of the National and Provincial Assemblies.[13]

The majority of the people seemed at the time to feel that the election had been reasonably well and fairly managed. In the towns and cities, chances of irregularity were less among politically sophisticated people, who would notice any election tricks. But in the rural areas the same vigilance was not possible and it may well be that some members of the public

---

[12] In 1968, the Pakistan correspondent of the *Economist* was a senior Pakistani journalist who was extremely well informed about the election of 1964–5 and had played a considerable part in it, although not on the platform.

[13] *D*, 14 February 1965 and 26 August 1965.

service who were over-enthusiastic in their regard for Ayub Khan lent themselves to his purpose.

On the evening of 2 January 1965, Ayub Khan broadcast his thanks to the nation. There were the customary assurances of fresh dedication to the service of Pakistan and he did not fail to observe that the nation had given him a clear mandate to pursue 'my internal and external policies'. He made a call for national unity and expressed goodwill to all, including Miss Jinnah, and he urged that 'no trace of malice, nor of revenge should inhibit us from rejoicing in the glory of the people'. He added: 'Together let us build, together let us accomplish; so that Pakistan may endure and prosper.' Unfortunately, things did not work out that way.

The morning of the 4 January revealed Captain Gohar Ayub, standing in a jeep, apparently firing pistols into the air in unrestrained paroxysms of delight,[14] and leading a procession of trucks through the streets of Karachi. These were all driven by Pathans since most of Karachi's trucking business was in their hands. It seemed as if every three-tonner in the city had been mobilized for what appeared to be a show of force and a reminder to Karachi that although it had voted for Miss Jinnah and not for Ayub Khan, there need be no doubt as to the outcome of the election. The procession not only caused a great deal of inconvenience but also raised the question of whether this was a breach of Section 144 which was in force in Karachi at that time, and if so, whether an exemption from the effect of the order had been granted by the Commissioner, Roedad Khan, who happened to be a Peshawar man. Further, people were asking themselves whether the exemption, if any, had been granted before or after the procession. It appeared improbable that Gohar Ayub would be troubled by such niceties and it did not seem that the Commissioner was the kind of man to insist on their observance.

In the circumstances, it may not appear that any of this was of much importance, and certainly nothing more would have

[14] Although I witnessed the processions described in these paragraphs, I did not myself see the *feu de joie*. Others claimed to have done so. It was also said that in the suburb of Liaquatabad, through which the procession passed, wanton discharge of firearms by the processionists killed several people. They are known as the Liaquatabad Martyrs and are mourned each year on 5 January. Liaquatabad will be further mentioned in this record of tragic madness.

been heard of it had not worse soon followed. That night, the Pathan henchmen went down into those areas, including Liaquatabad, known to have been solidly opposed to Ayub Khan and there wrought vengeance. Huts and dwelling-places were burnt down and people were fired upon. Those attacked promptly defended themselves and a night-long battle ensued. The injured were taken to hospitals with bullet-wounds and when order was restored the visible damage indicated the anger and determination with which the contending factions had fought and defended themselves.[15] The Army was called out and on 5 January was patrolling the streets in the areas which had been witness to these grim scenes. In such circumstances, there was little prospect of renewed fighting but there was danger that the attacked might sally out during the night looking for revenge.

According to the newspapers that appeared the day following, six people died in this affair. Later a figure of twenty was mentioned, but it was generally believed that the number of lives lost was very much greater than the official admission. Loss of lives and property were not the only consequences; Karachi became irrevocably opposed to Ayub Khan and the ground was laid for a feud between Pathans and the refugee communities from India which endured for a very long time and in the months that followed January 1965 sporadic acts of vengeance occurred.

The explanation was afterwards advanced that when Gohar Ayub took his procession through Liaquatabad later that day, stones were thrown at him, and his outraged followers, unable to contain their anger, went down that night to avenge the insult.[16] The causes of the attack were never published, but had there been no importation of supporters from Hazara, there might well have been no rioting in Karachi and no loss of life.

In consequence of this disturbance, the Government of West Pakistan, on 7 January, appointed a Committee of Inquiry comprising three officials. Seen in retrospect, the appointment of this Committee, its form, and its manner of proceeding, had

---

[15] I visited the area shortly afterwards. I have seen much rioting in the subcontinent but no devastation to exceed this.

[16] In August 1964, Ayub Khan was installed as chief of the Tareen tribe of Pathans. The chiefship was said to have passed from his ancestors when, 200 years before, they left Pishin for Hazara.

no other purpose than to ensure that no enquiry was ever made. To the frustration of this enquiry, some contribution was made by the Combined Opposition Parties, whose attitude was ambiguous and difficult to understand. The situation was further complicated by the registration of no fewer than twelve criminal cases by the police involving some seventy-five persons.[17] Not only this. While the Committee lawyers and others were debating the procedure to be adopted for the enquiry, events took a different turn which, as it happened, fitted very conveniently into the pattern.

On or about 18 January, a number of serious charges were made by one Shamsuddin against Gohar Ayub. This raised the question of whether the whole matter should be treated as being *sub judice*, since the persons central to the enquiry were now in court. The general public, detecting trickery, raised an outcry and the Governor of West Pakistan gave an assurance that the guilty would be punished.[18] However, it *was* finally decided that the case *must* be treated as being *sub judice* and, in those circumstances, there was nothing more the Committee of Inquiry could do, at any rate not until the Court had disposed of the cases before it. The Committee therefore adjourned *sine die* and the three officials returned to their respective duties. Thereafter, nothing more was heard of it.[19]

Concerning Captain Gohar Ayub, little remains to be said except for one curious consequence of this affair which will shortly be spoken of. The charges preferred against him at the instance of Shamsuddin soon found their way into the Supreme Court to which an appeal had been made for transfer of the cases from Karachi to Lahore. Out of this legal pettifogging nothing tangible emerged and to all intents and purposes the matter was forgotten or appeared so. But the day was to come when Karachi provided evidence of the fact that although people were silent about the events of January 1965, the memory remained.

---

[17] Nothing ever came of these. In November 1966, the Government of West Pakistan decided to drop all of them.

[18] All the daily newspapers of that time contain full accounts of these highly suspect proceedings.

[19] This was probably the only instance in the history of the sub-continent since around the middle of the nineteenth century, in which a riot leading to loss of life was not the subject of official, public enquiry.

The other principal victim of the Liaquatabad riot was Mr. Jacques Nevard, the correspondent of the *New York Times*. On the strength of his despatches, the *New York Times* of 19 January 1965 published news of the charges against Gohar Ayub with details of the alleged crimes. A few days afterwards, proceedings for contempt of court were instituted against Nevard who had done no more than communicate details, without comment, of the charges. This outcome was doubtless uncomfortable for Nevard who had acted quite innocently, but he was not committed further and it was probably not the Government's intention that he should be. In its judgement, the High Court said that the contempt had been purged by Nevard's expressions of regret and there the matter ended, but its principal purpose had been served. Thereafter, no newspaper in Pakistan and no foreign newspaper with a correspondent in Pakistan was likely to publish anything about Gohar Ayub and the crimes alleged against him in January 1965.[20]

Such were the closing scenes of the presidential election of 1965. Ayub Khan realized that these incidents cast a serious and lingering blemish on his success,[21] and had, moreover, belied his words to the nation on 2 January. But however much

[20] This was an interesting use of contempt proceedings to muzzle the Press. Four consequences flowed from it. The first was that any newspaper mention of *any* criminal complaint in Pakistan might become the object of such proceedings. The second was that any newspaper, published anywhere in the world, could become the object of contempt proceedings in Pakistan, it being sufficient to show, by affidavit, that some copies of the newspaper were received in Pakistan. The third was that foreign correspondents became wary in their reporting of matters relating to Pakistan, especially if they were posted in that country, and this was not necessarily to Pakistan's advantage. The fourth was that some resentment was felt in the profession over the treatment meted out to Mr. Nevard, and Pakistan's image abroad suffered as a result. The judgment in the *New York Times*'s case was published verbatim in *D*, 1 May 1965.

[21] In 1967, Gohar Ayub was appointed Chairman of the Karachi Provincial Muslim League Co-ordinating Committee whose principal task was to make preparations in Karachi for the presidential election which was to have taken place in 1970. In this capacity, he was given a good deal of front-page treatment in Karachi newspapers. When, in November 1968, on the occasion of the first Friday of Ramzan, he attempted to address the congregation at the Memon Mosque—a new and very large mosque erected in the heart of Karachi's commercial quarter—the congregation refused to hear him. He was roughed up and had to be rescued by the police. Thereafter, he was replaced by Begam Zahida Khaliquzzaman as Chairman of this Committee. It is difficult to understand why Gohar Ayub was given this particular job, after the events of January 1965. Was it supposed that Karachi had forgotten these, or was this an act of over-confident bravado? Altogether a very curious decision.

he may have regretted this unhappy stain, as well as his association with it in the person of his son, the violence which occurred presaged the tenor of his subsequent administration.

The presidential election did not, of course, end the business of voting. Thereafter, elections took place for the National and Provincial Assemblies, but these were tame affairs. With Ayub Khan firmly back in the saddle, the result was guaranteed. The only question that remained was the size of the majority which Ayub Khan's party would secure.

The importance of the election of 1965 had been made clear by Ayub Khan's speech of 2 January. His reference to the mandate he had received and to the approval by the people of his internal and external policies showed that he considered himself to have a free hand in the pursuit of his policies as he conceived them. His reputation abroad was that he enjoyed the full confidence of his compatriots and that there could be little effective opposition to the execution of his policies. Knowing this, it is not surprising that Ayub Khan proceeded as boldly as he did.

VII

Foreign Relations, 1962–9

On the subject of Pakistan's relations with the world, a Pakistani scholar and journalist developed the thesis that Pakistan's external behaviour had to be considered in the light of several factors, internal as well as external. He referred to the images of various nations created by the propaganda of their opponents. Thus, U.S.A.: wealthy, powerful, interventionist; U.S.S.R.: strong, idealist, revolutionary, powerful; U.K.: imperialist, cunning, would sell a refrigerator to an Eskimo,[1] etc. Utilizing a similar technique, although not as an opponent, I think it could be said of Pakistan: impulsive, generous, irrational.

The force of this is likely to become plainer as we proceed. Meanwhile, of more specific relevance is the fact that when Ayub Khan's presidential system began in June 1962, two very important movements in Pakistan's international relations were in train. The first lay in the changing attitude, in Pakistan to the United States and, to a lesser degree perhaps, to the United Kingdom. The second was the exercise, for the hundredth time, on 23 June 1962, by the Soviet Union, of the power of veto in the Security Council. The effect was to nullify a proposal calling upon Pakistan and India to enter into direct discussions with a view to settlement of the Kashmir question, in accordance with Article 33 of the United Nations Charter. This affair will be discussed more fully in a later chapter on Indo-Pakistan relations, but it can be added here that disappointment in Pakistan was considerable and a leading newspaper well represented that sense of disappointment when it stated, in an

[1] Kalim Siddiqui, 'Pakistan's External Development', *Asian Review*, January 1969. If any reader should think that the assessment given here of the Pakistani temperament is tinctured by prejudice, he should study an editorial entitled 'Nation Can't Be Hijacked' which appeared in *Pakistan Economist*, 24 April 1971. This deals, briefly but scathingly, with the emotionalism and hysteria which have played so prominent a part in the national character.

editorial, that in this way were 'probably sealed for ever hopes of a peaceful solution of the Kashmir dispute under United Nations auspices.'[2]

The deteriorating change of attitude in relation to the United States and the United Kingdom was the consequence of their supply of arms to India in large quantities, for the Sino-Indian border conflict had demonstrated considerable deficiencies in the Indian armed forces. Protesting strongly, Pakistan repeatedly urged the dangers of this policy to the tranquillity of the sub-continent, claiming that India's need for such supplies had been grossly exaggerated and that there could be no guarantee that India might not use these arms against Pakistan, despite assurances given by the two supplying Powers.

On the question of India's indifferent performance against the Chinese and its relation to inadequate supplies of suitable weapons, it seems probable that Mr. Krishna Menon's own deleterious contribution, as India's Defence Minister, to the efficiency of the country's armed forces, and the appointment of a Supply and Transport officer to command the troops engaged against the Chinese, had at least as much to do with China's striking success as did a shortage of weaponry. And clearly, there could be no effective guarantee on the question of safeguards against India's using the arms supplied by the Americans and the British against any nation other than China, although pressures might be exerted. For that matter, Ayub Khan had declared that, if necessary, all arms at the disposal of his country's armed forces would be used for purposes of defence.[3]

However, no argument and no appeal from Pakistan sufficed to persuade the two suppliers to abstain from their course of action, and in November 1962 there was a full-dress emergency debate in Pakistan's National Assembly to discuss the supply of arms to India. Several days were devoted to this debate and it was opened by the Foreign Minister, the late Mr. Mohamed Ali (Bogra). In the course of his speech, he mentioned that since 16 March 1951 India and the United States had been parties

---

[2] *D*, 24 June 1962. In fact, the two countries did agree, in November 1962, to meet and discuss the question. This will be referred to again.

[3] *D*, 21 January 1962. By implication this included arms received from the United States.

to a secret arms treaty. Describing this as a 'glaring example of hypocrisy and fraud', Mohamed Ali said that these matters had only just come to the notice of the Government and that the documents would be placed before the House.[4]

It does not appear that these papers were ever made public, but the debate afforded an opportunity for criticism of the SEATO and CENTO Pacts and for critics of these Pacts to call upon the Government to withdraw from them. It also provided an opportunity for Opposition members to invite attention to what they considered failures in the Government's foreign policy and they claimed that Pakistan had become abandoned and friendless. It was also an opportunity for Mr. Zulfikar Ali Bhutto to make a long speech in which he demonstrated his faith in China's friendship for Pakistan and laid the foundation for his personal commitment to a foreign policy based upon this premise.

In this, there is a matter of some significance. During the debate, Bhutto intervened frequently, drawing upon himself Opposition comment to the effect that the Foreign Minister ought to be present in the House to answer questions raised in the course of argument and counter-argument. As it happened, Mohamed Ali (Bogra) died suddenly on 23 January 1963 and Zulfikar Ali Bhutto was entrusted with the portfolio he so much desired and for which he considered himself so well qualified.[5]

Mr. Bhutto has since made it clear[6] that not only has he a penchant for international affairs, but that he had long been meditating the kind of policy that Pakistan should follow in order to secure its best interests. Among the conclusions he had formed was the necessity for developing a close attachment to China and there is no doubt that during his period of office in the Foreign Ministry, from January 1963 to June 1966, when he took 'long leave for reasons of health', this policy was sedulously pursued. Indeed, even before he was appointed Foreign Minister, he missed no opportunity to advance the merits of this policy and, as the records of the National Assembly will show, he intervened on a number of occasions to emphasize

[4] *NAD*, 22 November 1962.
[5] See the Preface to his book, *The Myth of Independence*, London, Oxford University Press, 1969.
[6] op. cit.

its importance. When he was appointed Foreign Minister he did not fail to utilize this opportunity, either in the promotion of his China policy or in the advancement of his ambition to figure prominently in international affairs. This he did with so much success in his own country that he eventually brought himself into rivalry with the man he was then serving—President Ayub Khan.

Whether this was done deliberately is doubtful, but when Bhutto proceeded on 'long leave', never to return to his post as Ayub Khan's Foreign Minister, a delicate situation had already grown up. This sprang from the widely held belief that it was Bhutto who, during the month of September 1965 and thereafter, had displayed the greater resolution. His image, as the young and forceful Foreign Minister who, at the Security Council, had defied India, and had more than compensated for S. M. Zafar's poor display,[7] occupied a large place in the public mind. By contrast, Ayub Khan was felt to have given away too much at Tashkent and although these matters will be considered in greater detail later on, it is relevant to consider the respective places occupied by Ayub Khan and Zulfikar Ali Bhutto in relation to foreign affairs.

Proceeding by train from Rawalpindi to Karachi in June 1966, Bhutto received tremendous ovations at intermediate stopping-places and anti-Ayub slogans were raised. The sympathy expressed for him, mostly by students and young people, was intense. In the bazaar, the rumour flew from lip to lip that 'Bhutto Sahib had been sacked because he was a friend to China which the Americans did not like'. Of all this, Ayub was highly conscious and his sense of Bhutto's impact was revealed the day after Bhutto's departure from Rawalpindi, when it was announced that there would be no change in the country's foreign policy of which President Ayub Khan was the architect and which had been initiated before Bhutto was entrusted with the Foreign Minister's portfolio.

Although this announcement was made to thwart Bhutto, it is also probable that Ayub Khan genuinely regarded himself as the author of this policy. Two chapters, comprising 41 out of the 227 pages of text in his book *Friends not Masters* are devoted to foreign policy.[8] Nor is it remarkable that in these

[7] See below, pp. 153-4.   [8] pp. 114-54.

two chapters, as in the book as a whole, the name of the man who served him as Foreign Minister during the most crucial period of his administration—Zulfikar Ali Bhutto—finds no place.

To be sure, *Friends not Masters* was published in 1967, long after all this, but there is no doubt that Ayub Khan considered himself rather good at foreign affairs and in his personal relationships with foreign dignitaries he got on well. One of the creditable achievements ascribed to his Martial Law administration was the raising of Pakistan's stature in the international community and for this Ayub Khan was considered responsible. But it is one thing to make a good impression by reason of a congenial personality and an engaging manner, and it is quite another to devise and pursue a skilful foreign policy which yields advantage and security to the State. Ayub Khan has given his own *ex post facto* account of the reasoning which led to a policy of bilateralism with special reference to the Great Powers, but whatever may have been his own contribution to its evolution, Bhutto also played a substantial part in it.

The situation speaks very plainly for itself. Ayub was firmly seated in office, wielding power with great political skill and ambitious to make his mark in Asia. Equally ambitious, Bhutto, having time on his side, might well regard himself as the legitimate successor, without succumbing to the temptation of rivalry. Moreover, he possessed those very qualities which were not only desirable, but which Ayub Khan conspicuously lacked. Ayub Khan was not deeply read and he certainly did not possess Bhutto's knowledge of history nor his legal training, particularly in international law, a subject on which Bhutto had once been a lecturer at the University of Southampton. On the face of it, the two men possessed a combination of abilities whose respective characteristics seemed complementary rather than incompatible—a combination of power, of knowledge and of a joint readiness to act upon decisions. If—although it was not so evident at the time—there were any seeds of disagreement, it could only have lain in Bhutto's desire to force the pace and it is clear enough that, after he became Foreign Minister, he did just this.

Such then, briefly stated, were the various factors which gave shape to the development of Pakistan's foreign relations during the period from 1962 to 1969. Undoubtedly, the very essentials were there—the men, the times, and the course of events—and it is impossible not to be impressed with a sense of dramatic inevitability. There were disappointments over the Soviet veto and over the return of the Kashmir question to cold storage; a weakening of ties with the western Powers, and distinct hostility towards them expressed by the public and particularly the students. Then, too, the sudden death of Mohamed Ali (Bogra) opened the way for Zulfikar Ali Bhutto and his partnership with Ayub; their shared purposes and complementary abilities, all of which boded so well and ended so ill. But that came later. At the beginning of 1963, the stage was set.

Armed with the courage that springs from a promising situation, Bhutto lost no time. He went to Peking and, on 2 March 1963, Marshal Chen-yi and he signed a Boundary Agreement which created much disturbance in India and evoked a lot of ill-informed comment. Acknowledging a telegram of congratulation from China's then President, Liu Shao-chi, Ayub Khan said that the Agreement was a significant landmark in the history of the two countries, but in those days Ayub Khan's communications with China were still guardedly balanced and he continued to demonstrate a characteristic caution, however much others might protest violently about American aid to India and other injustices to Pakistan.

The ambiguity of his frame of mind was demonstrated the very next month, as also was Bhutto's determination to sharpen the rate of development in Pakistan's foreign policy, when the Eleventh Session of the Council of Ministers of the Central Treaty Organization was held in Karachi. Ayub Khan sent a message of welcome in which he said, 'Pakistan believes that alliances such as CENTO have become necessary in the present-day world.' Two or three days later, this belief was modified as will shortly be seen.

The occasion appears to have been a rather heated one. Mr. Dean Rusk represented the United States and, from the United Kingdom came Mr. Duncan Sandys and the Earl (as he then was) of Home. It was popularly believed in Pakistan that these influential men had come not so much in the interests of CENTO as to persuade Pakistan to come to some settlement with India based on a partition of Kashmir. This will be discussed in more detail later.[9] Here, it may be said that whatever the purposes of these high-level representatives from the two western Powers, those of Mr. Zulfikar Ali Bhutto were different. As Chairman of the Session, he took it upon himself to *slate* (as the Pakistani newspapers had it) the western members of CENTO for their reprehensible attitude to their ally Pakistan, and to warn them of the possible consequences of this unfair approach. A day or two later, Ayub Khan followed this up with the further warning that if the United Kingdom and the United States continued to pour arms into India, Pakistan might have to consider seriously the need to leave the Commonwealth, CENTO, and SEATO.

CENTO and SEATO have since fallen into desuetude (some might say the Commonwealth, too), and the central fact in the development of Pakistan's foreign relations during the period 1962–9 is the ripening of the Sino-Pakistan attachment. In the last two years of Ayub Khan's administration, he, if no one else, began to experience a sense of disenchantment with China but in 1963 matters stood differently and the popular regard for China, as well as the importance ascribed to this association, was felt by everyone.

In Pakistan, China was—and still is—seen as a great Asian power, occupying an enormous, and therefore unconquerable, land-mass. Led by Mao Tse-tung and, as it then appeared, by a united Communist Party, this nation of industrious and intelligent people was evidently bent on making itself strong and secure without the least dependence on outside help. China manufactured arms of all sorts, including nuclear weapons and if it depended for its daily bread on Canadian wheat, at least China paid for it at world prices and in American dollars. For them, there was no soliciting, cap in hand, of free food or food paid for in local currency, but a policy of rigorous and manly independence. When the Soviet Union withdrew its technical support and its technicians the Chinese found other resources and other means. So far as India was concerned, had not the Chinese administered a brief but telling military reverse which had exposed the hollowness of Pandit Nehru's pretensions in several respects?

[9] See below, p. 113.

What, in Bhutto's view, China meant and means to Pakistan, he has succinctly stated. 'China's dominant place in Asia is assured. Pakistan is an Asian state whose destinies are forever linked with those of Asia and it is vital for Pakistan to maintain friendly relations with China for strengthening Asian unity.'[10] More explicitly what China means for Pakistan has been set out in a chapter entitled 'China's Impact' in a book by a well-known Pakistani writer on political affairs, Mr. Mushtaq Ahmed.[11] He says: 'The Revolution in China has opened a new chapter in Asian history. Its profound significance for the rest of Asia arises from the fact that it is an indigenous revolution, bred essentially in an Asian environment. The sources of its ideological inspiration apart, it does not owe its birth and fruition to foreign influence.... In the whole of Asia, including China, economic conditions were more or less similar.' The writer then goes on to speak of the agrarian problem, powerful landlords, the miserable, landless poor, the spectacle of the affluent few and the impoverished many but... 'In China alone, for the first time in history, the dormant energies of its overflowing population were released on a continental scale for the reconstruction of a new order based on opportunities for all and privileges for none.'

Mushtaq Ahmed's statement represents precisely what China has meant, and still means, for many people in Pakistan. It is not just a crude question of teaming up with the biggest power in Asia which is also on bad terms with India and in concert with which it might be possible to give India a first-class whipping. Satisfying as it might be to have so powerful a friend who came down fairly and squarely on Pakistan's side over the Kashmir question,[12] there were many in Pakistan who saw China in a much broader context. Here, to begin with, was an example that Pakistan would do well to emulate—the example of a poor nation, courageously working out its own salvation without help from others and systematically putting its own house in order by discipline, unity and hard work. There were many, especially among Pakistan's official classes, who, on

[10] Bhutto, op. cit., p. 131.
[11] Mushtaq Ahmed, *Pakistan's Foreign Policy*, Karachi, Space Publishers, 1969, p. 55.
[12] Or so it seemed. On this subject, China's pronouncements have not always been free from apparent ambiguity.

visiting China, came back deeply impressed by this striving Asian people whose sights were set high and whose aims seemed well within their grasp.[13] But it was not only officials who returned enthusiastic. Businessmen, intellectuals, Muslim divines, and officers of the armed forces returned to Pakistan full of praise for the single-minded determination of the Chinese people led by Chairman Mao. Nor could it be said that this admiration had been purchased for at that time China had made no contribution to Pakistan's development.

In 1964, Mr. Chou En-lai paid a visit to Pakistan which was returned in March 1965, when Ayub Khan paid a state visit, an event which marked the high point in Sino-Pakistan relations in those years. In the light of subsequent events, this visit must be regarded as most important. Its real meaning can be measured by the tremendous reception given to Ayub Khan, who was accompanied by a considerable entourage, including the indefatigable advocate of Chinese friendship—Zulfikar Ali Bhutto. A sixty-minute coloured film, very well produced by the Chinese, and showing the visit in elaborate detail, was exhibited throughout Pakistan. It conveyed the clearest possible idea of the enthusiastic welcome given to the President of Pakistan and of the fact that the Chinese Government had gone to considerable lengths to convince him of the importance they attached to his visit and to China's connexions with his country.

As I have said, the association of Pakistan and China is, for Pakistan, certainly one of the most important developments in its foreign relations and is particularly attributable to Ayub Khan's administration between 1962 and 1969. Unfortunately, the subject has not yet received the kind of full-length detailed study that it deserves, particularly relating to Ayub Khan's own declining enthusiasm for this association. The reasons for this are difficult to trace, but there is certainly the suspicion that, in its dealings with the Central Government of Pakistan and

[13] Notably, Mr. Qudratullah Shahab, at one time Private Secretary to Ayub Khan and afterwards Secretary to Government in the Ministry of Information and Broadcasting. In 1963, Mr. Shahab was posted as Ambassador at The Hague and it was popularly believed that this was done on American insistence because Mr. Shahab was so openly an admirer of the Chinese. This appointment was meaningful for other reasons. In his place, Mr. Altaf Gauhar became head of the Information Ministry. It was this gentleman who became so powerful an influence in Ayub Khan's administration. A brief profile of him will be found in Appendix A. See also p. 113, fn. 48.

in its activities in East Pakistan, China had been guilty of duplicity. There was, too, the feeling that out of the association, China was getting the major advantage.[14]

For most people in Pakistan, friendship with China is not only logical as Bhutto argues, and inspiring in the way described by Mushtaq Ahmed, it is also a policy of insurance against attack by India. China is a source of arms as well as of consumer goods which can be paid for by the exchange of goods produced in Pakistan. These arrangements have not always worked out well and the prosperity of some of Pakistan's nascent industries has been undermined by the supply, from China, of highly competitive products, such as light metal manufactures which, it seems, Pakistan has not desired, or has not been able, to refuse. On the other hand, the provision of important items such as coal and cement has been significant. China has also provided loans on easy terms for the purpose of industrial development and, at the end of 1968, the total amount so provided was U.S. $107·555 million. To this extent, therefore, Pakistan achieved a measure of independence from the rather demanding super-powers though this is mitigated by Pakistan's heavy dependence upon the United States for various forms of financial assistance and for large quantities of essential foodstuffs. Some of the advantages which Pakistan sees in its association with China are more hypothetical than real in that they can mature only if certain eventualities arise as happened, for example, in September 1965 when China presented India with an ultimatum. To that extent, it could be said that those eventualities did occur and that China responded to its obligations.[15]

For China, on the other hand, the advantages are solid and enduring. The association with Pakistan has opened fresh and important windows on the world[16] and has provided China with fresh bases from which to conduct intelligence operations

---

[14] The only well documented, analytical study available at the end of 1969 seemed to be that of B. L. Sharma, *The Pakistan-China Axis*, New Delhi, Asia Publishing House, 1968. Regrettably, the book is, to quote a review in *The Statesman*, Calcutta, 9 December 1968, 'polemical, propagandist and petulant'. Since the present book was completed, China has pledged much larger sums for the assistance of Pakistan's development.

[15] Written at the end of 1969.

[16] Quoting Feldman, op. cit., p. 177.

with respect to the U.S.S.R., India and Burma. The construction of roads linking Pakistan and China may well turn out to be significant factors in Asian affairs. In September 1966 it was recorded that roads built or being built would connect West Pakistan with Sinkiang through Gilgit. The Aksai-Chin road, passing through territory which India claims, would connect West Tibet with Sinkiang and if Pakistan should gain control in Kashmir, the road could then pass through the Kashmir valley and so down to Karachi as well as in a westerly direction. In September 1969 the old Silk Road, along which Marco Polo travelled, was reopened when a small caravan arrived from China. It reached Gilgit and goods were exchanged with local traders.

What appeared the most logical and promising development of the China policy, was the affiliation with Indonesia to form what, for a brief period, could be termed the China-Indonesia-Pakistan Axis. Bhutto energetically applied himself to this project, visiting Indonesia and apparently soon winning the confidence of the then Indonesian President, Sokarno and his close collaborator, Subandrio. When Sokarno visited Pakistan in 1963, he addressed a formal session of the National Assembly[17] and spoke with great enthusiasm about the new forces of democracy in Asia which the three countries were to create and lead. Two years elapsed, however, before relations between Indonesia and Pakistan were cemented by a Treaty of Collaboration, signed in March 1965,[18] and it could then be said, with some truth, that the triangular containment of India had been achieved.

Pursuing its policy of warm co-operation with Indonesia at the Commonwealth Relations Conference in London, in June 1965, Pakistan was able to secure the omission from the final communiqué of any reference to Indonesia as the aggressor in its dispute with Malaysia. This was treated in Pakistan as a considerable triumph and as evidence of Pakistan's influence in Commonwealth affairs.[19] As we shall in due course see, this incident earned its own requital three months afterwards, when the Indo-Pakistan hostilities were referred to the Security Council. In any case, the tripartite Axis, a shaky structure at best, did not last long. In October of the year of its formation,

[17] *NAD*, 26 March 1963.   [18] *D*, 4 March 1965.   [19] *D*, 30 June 1965.

a mob in Jakarta burned down the Chinese Embassy and in due course Sokarno was deposed from the office of life President.[20] Thus the triangular containment came to an end, but as we shall see some benefit did accrue to Pakistan, in September 1965, when Sokarno sent the Indonesian Navy into the Bay of Bengal and some ships, including at least one submarine, came to Karachi. To this must be added China's powerfully worded, but cautiously operated, *ultimata*, addressed to India.

Next in importance is the sedulous wooing of the Arab countries. This policy has immense popular appeal, especially in West Pakistan, with its sense of Middle East propinquity, where the theme of Muslim brotherhood is ecstatically, and sometimes hysterically, played upon. The difficulties of this policy are scarcely ever mentioned and any discussion of attitudes among the Arab states, not only towards Pakistan, but among themselves, is rarely seen or heard. There is a total unwillingness to grasp the fact that it is simply not possible to be on the side of all Arab states at once, but such subjects rarely come up for debate. The fact that the strengthening of ties with the United Arab Republic is likely to weaken ties with, let us say, Saudi Arabia, is ignored in public discussion about Pakistan's foreign policy. Such difficulties as these tend to be obscured or treated as mischievous suggestions. Indeed, as these matters are reported in the Press, it could be concluded that between all Arab states, as between all Arab countries, there prevails total unanimity and identity of view. The rivalries, and even embittered relations, that subsist among some of them are never spoken of. The result is a prevailing atmosphere of illusion in Pakistan.

It need scarcely be remarked that, during the brief war between Israel and some of its neighbours, in June 1967, Pakistan was passionately on the side of the neighbours. Ayub Khan's initial announcement, made when the lightning campaign opened, was distinctly reserved. It appeared verbatim in most Pakistan newspapers on 13 June and comprised about 150 words of encouragement, moderate in tone and with no marked enthusiasm for the Arab cause. This was not altogether surprising. The closing of the Suez Canal could only add to the

[20] *D*, 16 October 1965.

economic problems of Pakistan though this was less true for the eastern Province than for the western.

The tone changed as public sentiment in Pakistan rose quickly to feverish excitement founded upon the hope that the Egyptians, led by Nasser and armed by the Soviet Union, would deal out to Israel what one Pakistani journalist described as a 'tight-fisted punch'. When these anticipations were dashed, Nasser's crushing defeat was explained by reiterated references to American and British participation, to Israel's unwarranted aggression and to any and every excuse that came most conveniently to the purpose. But, one by one, all were exposed, shattered by the facts and even by Nasser's own admissions. Eventually people in Pakistan brought themselves face to face with the truth. Beneath their zeal for the Arab cause lay the realization that the Israelis had gained a brilliant victory founded upon skill, a high level of training, a sound plan and undeviating determination in its execution.

Nor could the Pakistanis help thinking of the Muslim martial tradition and of their own performance against India two years before. They have remained loyal to their pro-Arab sentiments, but there are many who cherish no illusions.[21] The very widely read newspaper *Jung*,[22] in its issue dated 21 September 1969, published this verse by Rais Amrohavi:

> *Jo sahibae nakhwat se sarshar hain*
> *Jo mahrum akhlaq-o-kardar hain*
> *Jo apas men sargram pekar hain*
> *Arab das arab hon to bekar rahen*

Crudely and briefly translated it means that useless people, even when they come in tens of millions, are still useless, and the point of the verse is a play upon the word Arab, signifying the people of that name, and *arab*, a word of Sanskrit origin, meaning one hundred crores or 1,000 million.

However, such reservations have not prevented a noticeable increase in anti-semitic sentiment in Pakistan. Apart from the familiar ranting about Jews and freemasons, there have been

[21] For a caustic article on the Arab summit conference at Rabat in December 1969, see *Holiday*, Dacca, 28 December 1969.
[22] It has the biggest circulation of any daily in Pakistan and is also published in the United Kingdom.

specific criticisms of commercial institutions and persons. Thus in June 1967 the shoe-making firm of Bata found it necessary to publish a newspaper announcement to the effect that it was not a Jewish organization, that the managing director in Pakistan, Mr. V. A. Samek, was a Christian and that no Jews were employed in the Company's establishments in Pakistan.[23] In the same month, the appointment of Mr. B. H. Oehlert Jr. as United States Ambassador to Pakistan was objected to, in some circles, on the ground that he was a Jew.[24] Shortly afterwards, at a Press conference in Karachi, the head of the Brooke Bond tea organization in Pakistan was obliged to deny that the group was Jewish and to deny that the Chairman of the group in the United Kingdom was a Jew. Even before the Arab-Israeli war of June 1967, traces of anti-semitism became visible from time to time. In June 1966, at a session of the National Assembly, one member desired to know why the Capital Development Authority had engaged the services of the American architect, Professor Louis Kahn, the reason for this enquiry, as stated in the question, being that Professor Kahn was Jewish. There have also been other more generalized incidents such as the publication of *The Protocols of Zion*, in a book which was later condemned by the Government of West Pakistan, not because it included this long-exposed forgery, but because it contained remarks disparaging of President Nasser.[25]

However, it is fair to say that although anti-Jewish sentiments in Pakistan have increased in volume and often in vulgarity, perhaps they are no worse than could be experienced or observed in many other countries not necessarily hostile to Israel. There are Pakistanis who have, on various occasions, publicly stated their admiration for the Jewish people and for the Israeli achievement, particularly in the development of Israel and in the high standard of living that the Israelis have created for themselves.[26]

On the whole, anti-semitism is not a very important issue in Pakistan. Many of the long-established, local Jewish community

[23] *Pakistan Times*, 26 June 1967.
[24] *Daily News*, 20 June 1967.
[25] *D*, 13 June 1967.
[26] A notable instance is that of Dr. I. H. Usmani, C.S.P., Chairman of Pakistan's Atomic Energy Commission who, in August 1969, made a most forthright statement on this subject and incurred the wrath of many smaller men.

have left the country and those who remain do not seem to be interfered with. This apart, the pro-Arab policy has its obvious logic for Pakistan. There is no reason why Pakistan, an avowedly Muslim country, should not look for friends among other Muslim countries. On the face of it, Pakistan is more likely to find them there than in, say, Israel. At the United Nations, Israel has only one vote, the Muslim countries between them have several and this fact is of particular importance in relation to Pakistan's disputes with India. There is also the question of finding markets, especially in the conveniently located Middle East, for Pakistan's manufactured goods, on the successful export of which Pakistan's programme of industrialization substantially depends. These are reasons enough for pursuing a strong pro-Arab policy. The difficulty does not lie in the reasons, but in the execution, which is marked by an over-emphasis on Islam that has proved injurious to Pakistan and irritating to others.

This was well illustrated when the Al-Aqsa mosque in Jerusalem was set on fire. Quite apart from the vehement language condemning Israeli 'vandalism', some newspapers ran banner headlines for several consecutive days and in a form which exceeded even those appearing at the time of hostilities with India.[27] More specifically, this over-emphasis has led to contradictions which have done Pakistan no good in the United Arab Republic, a country with which Pakistan's relations have ebbed and flowed despite Ayub Khan's visible efforts to improve them on a more permanent basis. Although a Muslim country, Egypt actually voted against Pakistan at the United Nations over the Kashmir dispute. Subsequently, Pakistan permitted itself to embark upon a campaign which appeared, in Cairo, to be an interference in the United Arab Republic's internal affairs. This occurred in August and September 1966, when three leaders of the Muslim Brotherhood, Sayyed Kotb, Youssef Hawas and Abdel Fattaz Ismail, were sentenced to death in Cairo. A campaign of protest began in Pakistan and, in particular, the Islami Jama'at-i-Talaba protested vigorously

[27] It has been said, however, that the great play made over the Al-Aqsa affair was to divert attention from the murder, in Dacca, of a student named Abdul Malek, springing from the rivalry between the Jama'at-i-Islami and left-wing groups. The issue seemed to offer a serious threat to law and order if allowed to be publicized.

against the death sentence passed on Sayyed Kotb, the head of the Muslim Brotherhood. All-India Radio was reported in Karachi's *Daily News* of 27 August 1966 as having said that, in Cairo, a Pakistani youth was arrested with Muslim Brotherhood literature in his possession. When the three men were executed on 29 August, this was reported in the same newspaper in a banner headline within a black border. All this can be read in conjunction with another movement which sprang up in Pakistan, three years later, when protests became current against the treatment of Muslim divines by the Baathist Government of Iraq.

Among those who appear to have been troubled by Pakistan's unrestrained religious enthusiasm is the present Shah of Iran,[28] with whose country Pakistan claims very strong ties through the association, which includes Turkey, known as the Regional Co-operation for Development. The zeal for this organization is not uniform among its three members and it seems that, of them, Iran exhibits the least interest while Turkey's ambitions to enter the European Common Market do not conduce to stronger economic ties with Pakistan. It is interesting that in a forty-three-page supplement on Iran, which appeared in *The Economist* dated 31 October 1970, this organization is not mentioned and in a volume entitled *Investors' Guide to Iran*, dated 1969 and published by the Bank Markazi Iran for the benefit of intending foreign private investors, it is stated that of Iran's total exports, 0·6 per cent went to Pakistan and Turkey while of Iran's total imports, 0·3 per cent came from the same two countries. The position is made more explicit, as regards Pakistan, from the following figures for which I am indebted to the Federation of Pakistan Chambers of Commerce and Industry. They are expressed in millions of Pakistan rupees, all conversions being at the official rates of exchange current in 1970. They are, of course, approximations relative to the period 1969–70, but they present a fair and valid picture.

Pakistan's total exports	Rs.3,271 million	
Pakistan's total imports	5,098 million	
Pakistan's exports to Iran	25 million	0·78%

[28] Not to mention the late, former King Farouk of Egypt, who is supposed to have said that Islam was not born until 14 August 1947.

Pakistan's exports to Turkey	Rs. 19 million	0·60%
Pakistan's imports from Iran	120 million	2·03%
Pakistan's imports from Turkey	1·3 million	0·02%
Iran's total exports	7,384 million	
Iran's total imports	8,923 million	
Iran's total exports to Pakistan	120 million	1·63%
Iran's total imports from Pakistan	25 million	0·30%
Turkey's total exports	2,422 million	
Turkey's total imports	3,467 million	
Turkey's total exports to Pakistan	1·3 million	0·50%
Turkey's total imports from Pakistan	19 million	0·57%

Pakistan's relations with Iran have, in the past, been injured by what was evidently a clash of personalities between Ayub Khan and Reza Shah Pahlavi in each of whom was only too visible the desire to figure prominently in eastern affairs.[29]

In view of the respective ambitions of Iran, Iraq, of Saudi Arabia and the United Arab Republic in the Middle East, and also the various claims that exist among them with respect to the Persian Gulf, the Trucial Coast, Bahrain, the Shatt-al-Arab and so on, the pursuit of a simple, all-embracing, pro-Muslim, pro-Regional Co-operation for Development, pro-Arab policy, cannot possibly yield any satisfactory answers to many complex questions, as Pakistan has discovered on several occasions.[30] Yet every Government of Pakistan has either ignored or has professed to explain adequately these same complexities. Often enough, however, these questions are not asked in Pakistan and people do not care to be reminded of conundrums which so palpably exist. For example, there are few in Pakistan who are aware of the several occasions between 1962 and 1969 when relations between Pakistan and Iran were really

---

[29] They were, also, literary rivals for each of them, while Head of State, had published a book, though it is possible they were less sensitive to each other's literary ambitions. It is said that the Shah was irritated by Ayub Khan's praise of Nasser in *Friends not Masters* and its serialization in a Teheran newspaper came to an abrupt end.

[30] A notable instance occurred at the conference of Muslims at Rabat, in September 1969, when President Yahya Khan threatened to *walk out* if India were admitted to the conference. India was not admitted, but the invitation given to it was not withdrawn either.

quite testy nor do many know why it was necessary for Ayub Khan to fly to Teheran in October 1966, on what was described as 'a private visit'.[31] Pakistan has also had cause for annoyance, particularly when Iran's Shahinshah offered in January 1969 to mediate between Pakistan and India, to which latter country he was then paying a state visit.[32] The fact is, of course, that the simple, all-embracing, pro-Muslim policy, signifying friendship, support and commitment for and to all Muslims everywhere, has no more political sense in it than if, in other circumstances, there somewhere existed a policy of Christians supporting all Christians everywhere or Communists supporting all Communists everywhere. As Europe's internecine wars have shown, and as contemporary history is showing, neither is possible. Indeed, Pakistan's pro-Muslim policy is not a policy at all but a sentiment, imposed by and willingly accepted by doctrinal attachment. This may have its weight and its place, but when confronted by other and more compelling issues, the weight is likely to prove minimal and the place illusory.

Thus with the Muslim country of Afghanistan Ayub Khan could make virtually no headway, although in May 1963 there was a resumption of diplomatic relations with an agreement

[31] The reason was that Pakistan had voted in favour of Bahrain being elected to a UNESCO body, implying that Bahrain was a sovereign state which Iran emphatically disputed. Much indignation was expressed in Iran, where newspapers came out with protesting headlines and articles were written enquiring why, in these circumstances, Iran should support Pakistan on the Kashmir issue?

[32] After General Yahya Khan became President of Pakistan, as from 25 March 1969, much was immediately set afoot to improve relations between the two countries through an exchange of visits at high level. It is possible that President Yahya and the Shah got along better because both are Shi'as and President Yahya's ancestors came from Iran. It does not, of course, follow that men who are both Shi'as and have a common ancestral background will automatically be fast friends, but the part occupied and played by the Shi'a community in West Pakistan is well deserving of special study. The Shi'as are in a heavy minority vis-à-vis the Sunni community and this may have something to do with the formation, in October 1969, of a Shi'a Political Party, an interesting instance of religious sectarianism invading the field of politics. There is no doubt that in the past the Shi'a community has felt difficulty with respect to its own religious traditions and particularly to the religious instruction given in Pakistan's schools to Shi'a children. The community also apprehends difficulty if political parties such as Maulana Maudoodi's Jama'at-i-Islami were to become a real influence in Pakistan's internal politics. It is a fact that, at various times in the history of Pakistan, Shi'as have been the object of organized attack by Sunnis, resulting in substantial loss of life.

signed at Teheran through the mediation of the Shah. In July 1964 Ayub Khan visited Kabul in an attempt to improve relations between the two countries, but in spite of this Afghanistan persisted obdurately in encouraging the Pakhtunistan movement. At a *Loe Jirga* (Grand Assembly) held in Kabul in September 1964, only two months after Ayub Khan's visit, approval was given to a Government-sponsored resolution which referred to the 'religious, national and historical' duty of the Afghans to 'support the rights of the Pathan people of Pakistan to self-determination' and the resolution added that Afghanistan was 'waiting for the day when the issue of Pakhtunistan will be settled on the basis of the true aspirations of the people and leaders of Pakhtunistan'.

Afghanistan has never failed to give hospitality and a refuge to Khan Abdul Ghaffar Khan, the older Frontier leader, as well as to others who have opposed the creation of Pakistan without ensuring autonomy for the Pathans. There is not much to be written about the subject of Pakistan-Afghan relations since the situation has scarcely changed since 1947—sometimes a little more cordial, sometimes a little less. It is noteworthy that in September 1965 the Afghans had nothing to say in support of Pakistan, but when Peshawar was bombed by Indian aircraft, the Afghan press and radio took the opportunity to express sympathy for the people of that city. Afghanistan has never omitted to publish maps showing Pakhtunistan immediately south-east of its own border, with Pakistan marked further south-east. One such map was prominently displayed in Karachi in the window of the sales office of Ariana Afghan Airlines, as late as 1969. The policy towards Afghanistan illustrates the hollowness of adopting Islam as its sole determining principle.

But the sentiments which have played an influential role in the determination of Pakistan's foreign policy and international attitudes are not confined to those Islamic in nature. If Islam is the worthiest among such influences, it does not, unfortunately, stand alone.

It is not necessary to be religious, or to possess a religious turn of mind, to understand that people who hold firmly to their faith, and in whose lives religion plays so prominent a part, may feel imposed upon them duties of the highest and most sacred character with respect to all who share that faith. For this reason, it is understandable that Pakistan may at all times be guided by a strong sense of obligation to all Muslims everywhere, but it is understandable only with the reservation that such a policy would not necessarily advance the cause of Islam, much less promote the international interests of Pakistan. No doubt, this is an issue for Pakistan to decide. The real difficulty lies in this, that it is clearly not Islam which solely provides the code of moral responsibility and the emotional impulses that have given shape to Pakistan's conduct in international affairs.

Indeed, any minute examination of that conduct makes it difficult to decide just what is that code and what are those impulses. Certainly, they do not spring solely from religion for whereas the United States, whose government is substantially in the hands of men who could be described as *Ahl-i-Kitab*,[33] is often castigated, the Soviet Union, whose government is in the hands of men of whom every one is a self-declared atheist, is never the object of criticism or reproach, and even when Czechoslovakia was invaded in 1968, Pakistan remained silent. Nor can it have a great deal to do with imperialism and neo-colonialism, for whereas the United Kingdom is often rebuked for its attitude to Rhodesia, France, second only to Portugal in its tenacious clinging to a colonial empire, is said to have 'left a salutary impression on the nations of the Third World'.[34] And even the principle of self-determination, to which Pakistan has so often declared its undeviating adherence, has acquired strange interpretations at times, for when the population of Gibraltar voted, almost to a man, in favour of the British connexion, Pakistan voted against the continuance of that connexion.[35]

Perhaps this should not be unduly laboured. The inconsistencies and irrationalities of government are only too familiar to us and have been the object of much satire, pleasant and unpleasant, ever since men learned to write. In the case of

[33] Those who believe in a revealed book of religion. It means, in general, Muslims, Christians and Jews.
[34] Bhutto, op. cit., p. 23. The 'Third World' refers to those smaller nations most of whom have emerged from colonial rule or colonial influences and are mainly members of the Afro-Asian group.
[35] At the United Nations in January 1969.

Pakistan, one suspects that a good deal of this inexplicable behaviour springs largely from a desire to cock snooks in the direction of the United States and, in some degree, the United Kingdom, and less from any integrated policy. Doubtless it all stems from the past. The United Kingdom has not yet really been forgiven for having conquered the sub-continent and for having deposed Bahadur Shah Zafar. As for the United States, the dismal truth is that most men and most nations resent a benefactor.

France, whose 'salutary impression on the nations of the Third World' has already been mentioned, provides a curious instance of this irrationality that has appeared in the conduct of Pakistan's foreign relations. During the years between 1962 and 1969, great play was made of the growing sympathies between Pakistan and France although why these sympathies should have thus grown is not particularly clear. It is true that the French attitude towards Israel and the Arab states in June 1967 was extremely gratifying to Pakistan, although it is just as true that that attitude was not adopted to gratify anyone, but simply to protect and, if possible, to extend French oil interests in the Middle East. It seems that General de Gaulle and Field-Marshal Ayub Khan got along well, sharing, perhaps, a similarity of authoritarian outlook and a sense of infallibility in the execution of their respective divine missions. On the whole, sentiment seems to be at the bottom of it, in which Ayub Khan and his advisers were much impressed by de Gaulle's independence of attitude towards the United States and by France's possession of an independent nuclear deterrent,[36] the *force de frapper*, which, unfortunately, has cost France so dear.

More tangible reasons are hard to find. As one of Pakistan's trading partners, France stands about seventh or eighth and its share in Pakistan's total foreign trade comes to about 3 per cent although it seems that, over the years, Pakistan has enjoyed a favourable balance. As a source of aid in development, France's contribution, until the end of 1968, was not conspicuous. A total amount of $106·061 million by way of export credits had been made available but by no means entirely disbursed. On capital account no loans or grants

[36] Bhutto, op. cit., p. 23.

whatsoever had been made. Lumping everything together, France stood behind Germany, Japan and the United Kingdom and, of course, far behind the United States. The comparable contributor is China which had made available a sum of $105·555 million by way of assistance on capital account.

But what really concerns Pakistan in its relations with Europe is the Soviet Union. In earlier years, the two countries were not particularly close, especially in the heyday of Pakistan's friendship with the United States, but in 1961 there was a change when Zulfikar Ali Bhutto went to Moscow to negotiate an agreement which led to a substantial programme of oil and gas exploration financed and operated by the Soviet Government in collaboration with Pakistan's state-managed Oil and Gas Commission. It was stated, at the time, by Pakistan's then Foreign Minister, Mr. Manzur Qadir, that the agreement was a purely commercial affair without any political implications.[37] Whatever may have been the weight of this assurance, the fact remains that from this moment on, relations between the two countries became warmer, with Pakistan the more insistent and with the Soviet Union plainly hesitating to endanger its long-standing relations with India.

Early in 1963,[38] the Soviet Government offered to provide economic aid to Pakistan 'without strings', as the cant phrase goes, and in this way the oil agreement of 1961 proved to have been the first in a series of understandings and arrangements between the two countries relating to air services, cultural exchange, assistance in agriculture and particularly in supplying farm equipment, power projects and the promotion of technology. But this changing attitude did not preclude the Soviet Union from giving arms to India fearing, perhaps, that assistance in this respect from the United Kingdom and the United States might loosen the ties between India and the Soviet Union unless such help were matched. News of this decision was received in Pakistan with expressions of dismay even if, on the whole, well moderated. In his broadcast on 1 October 1964, Ayub Khan said: 'In September, the event of gravest import to us was the announcement of large scale arms

[37] Conceivably this was said to reassure the United States, but it may have served also to restrain Bhutto's evident Foreign Office ambitions.
[38] *D*, 12 January 1963.

aid by Soviet Russia to India.' When taxed with the same subject, Zulfikar Ali Bhutto contented himself by saying that he regretted the help that the Soviet Union was giving to India in respect of armaments.[39]

However, relations between Pakistan and the Soviet Union were steadily pursued in spite of this disappointment. In April 1965 Ayub Khan paid a seven-day state visit, accompanied by Bhutto, and he was given a considerable welcome. On the part of the Russians, the signs of caution continued, but the joint communiqué, customary on the termination of such visits, contained a paragraph which Pakistan found exceptionally satisfying. It stated that the two Governments 'declare resolute support for the peoples who are waging a struggle for their national liberation and independence and for people who are fighting for the right to determine their future in accordance with their own will'. In Pakistan, this was received with much acclaim since it appeared to confirm, in decisive manner, a changing Soviet attitude to the Kashmir question. But, equally, it could not be denied that this paragraph could be taken to mean a good deal more than just the Kashmir question and the aspirations of the Kashmiri people. Paragraphs of this sort found their way into other communiqués issued from Moscow as, for example, after visits by the King of Afghanistan, in which case the meaning might be taken to be something very different indeed.

However all this might be, and however hesitant the Soviet Union might be to do anything that would disrupt or threaten its relations with India, it could not be doubted that the Soviet attitude to Pakistan was changing and, from Pakistan's point of view, for the better. Three months after Ayub Khan's visit, it was announced that in view of the modified approach in the United States, and other countries, on the question of economic assistance, the Soviet Union might step in with financial help for Pakistan's Third Five Year Plan. However, as it has since proved, the Soviet performance with respect to the provision of capital and export credits for Pakistan has been a lot less satisfactory than its promise and, indeed, the assistance given is notably less than that of several other countries, quite apart from the outstanding case of the United States. In fact, as at

[39] *D*, 6 October 1964.

31 December 1968, the Soviet Union stood tenth in the list, coming immediately behind China.

However, in more recent years, help given by the Soviet Union has been supplemented by trade arrangements and by the supply of some military stores the detail of which is not precisely known but which includes one squadron of Ilyushin light bombers. This matter will be referred to again.

The real and decisive change in Pakistan-Soviet relations came in January 1966, when Pakistan agreed to accept the Soviet Prime Minister, Mr. A. Kosygin, as sole mediator between India and Pakistan, at Tashkent. This was a very important development and although I do not think it was quite the diplomatic triumph for the Soviet Union as was stated at the time, it did bring about a new situation between the Soviet Union and the sub-continent. The effect was to place upon the Soviet Union new responsibilities and the necessity of adopting a more impartial attitude towards India and Pakistan. It has led also to a more pervasive Soviet presence in the sub-continent and has laid upon the Soviet Government complications of policy which, hitherto, it had avoided by the simple expedient of siding with India in everything.

The seal on this changed state of affairs was affixed when Kosygin and Mrs. Indira Gandhi met in July 1966. The meeting concluded with the publication of a long communiqué which indicated acceptance of Indian views on a number of important issues, but in terms which were not quite so satisfactory to the Indian Government.[40] The overall effect was that the Soviet Government was equating Pakistan with India and was relying more and more on an approach based on the necessity of mutual negotiation 'in the spirit of the Tashkent Declaration'.

The interesting consequence of this meeting was that in September 1966 the Soviet Deputy Foreign Minister, Mr. N. P. Firyubin, paid a three-day visit to Delhi and on 25 September flew to Rawalpindi and proceeded to Swat in order

---

[40] This new Soviet attitude was discussed at great length in India. A fair indication of the spirit of this discussion will be found in *The Statesman*, Calcutta, 16, 17 and 18 July 1966.

to meet President Ayub Khan. The visit was surrounded by close secrecy, but it was understood that its purpose was to pave the way for further efforts by Kosygin to bring the two countries together. In fact, these efforts, comparable with those of Dean Rusk and Duncan Sandys a few years earlier, failed. Thus, in a message to the Soviet Prime Minister on the anniversary of the Tashkent Declaration in January 1967, Ayub Khan said: 'I must confess we have not been able to convince India. . . .'

In January 1968 Kosygin again visited India and once more his attitude appeared to the Indians disappointingly ambiguous. On the subject of India's disputes with Pakistan he was evasive and he advised continued negotiation within the spirit of Tashkent. The real blow to India came when the Soviet Union expressed readiness to give assistance in the matter of arms and military stores. This, while not quite the clear-cut declaration that many people thought, was undeniably in the air, and Kosygin carried on with his attempts to bring the two countries together.

In April 1968 he visited Pakistan, the date having been proposed by himself. He was met at the airport by Ayub Khan and given a considerable welcome. In Pakistan, much importance was attached to this visit and a good deal of speculation went on as to its outcome. High hopes were expressed since prospects appeared to be much advanced by the news that Pakistan would not renew the lease, granted to the United States, of the communications installation at Peshawar.[41] As it happened, however, the visit did not prove to be as satisfactory as was hoped. It could easily be inferred from the communiqué that there were wide areas of difference and although the Soviet Union promised to help with a proposal for a steel mill at Kalabagh (subject to a feasability report) and perhaps also with the nuclear project at Rooppur in East Pakistan, there was no mention of Kashmir and no mention of arms. Still,

[41] Reported in *The Times*, London, 11 April 1968. The official announcement was made on 20 May 1968 and the lease duly expired. The installation was dismantled in 1969. Built in 1958, it used scatter radar and other methods to maintain watch on Turya Tam in the U.S.S.R., 647 miles distant, on Russian military installations beyond the Hindu Kush and the Karakoram and also on Chinese nuclear and rocket experiments. For technical reasons, the installation had lost much of its importance by the time it was dismantled.

indications were not wanting that, in private, Kosygin had expressed some sympathy for Pakistan's point of view concerning the Soviet supply of arms to India and had not closed the door to the idea that Pakistan might get some help also. This seemed to be confirmed when, two months later, the then Commander-in-Chief of the Pakistan Army, General Yahya Khan, went to Moscow to discuss, so it was understood, this very subject.

The idea that Pakistan might obtain arms from the Soviet Union was not new and the duty of impartiality, imposed by the Tashkent Declaration, had stimulated it. In May 1966, when Mr. Mazurov, First Deputy Prime Minister, visited Pakistan, he was questioned about a shipment of arms to India and he parried with the reply that Pakistan could have them on the same terms as those on which they were being supplied to India. Two months later, in July, Air-Marshal Nur Khan paid a visit to Moscow. However, the position remained somewhat vague until Kosygin's visit in 1968 and then the outcry in India was immediate.

Vociferously led by Mrs. Gandhi, who was determined to use this excellent material to steal Opposition thunder, an agitation swept the country, but it then transpired that Kosygin had promised to compensate India with more arms, equivalent to whatever aid might be given to Pakistan. Thus the Soviet Prime Minister had apparently led his country into a private arms race with itself. In spite of this, Indian feeling on the subject continued to be very strong and the Soviet Union tried hard to remove the evident bitterness. When President Zakir Hussain of India died, Kosygin attended the funeral and again, in May 1969, he visited Delhi for the express purpose of discussing Indo-Pakistan relations. The background to these talks involved a wider concept, incorporating an alliance to which Afghanistan, India, Iran, Pakistan and the Soviet Union would be parties. In India the subject was much canvassed in the newspapers and it was there alleged that Pakistan was committed to the proposal. However, in July 1969 Air-Marshal Nur Khan paid a visit to China and this seemed to give the lie to all such speculation.

Thus it was that during Ayub Khan's administration between 1962 and 1969, relations between Pakistan and the Soviet

Union underwent considerable change. The two countries drew closer together than ever before and the Soviet Union showed itself to be more sympathetic to the Pakistani point of view. Anxious always not to alienate Indian sentiment nor to do anything that might weaken ties built up since 1947 with India, the Soviet Union nevertheless veered towards a policy based not on a total commitment to India but rather—as with the United States—on the idea of promoting stability and tranquillity in the sub-continent. Not surprisingly, this shift of policy has not been entirely congenial to India which, at one time, assumed a special relationship with the U.S.S.R. exclusive to itself in much the same way as Pakistan had once assumed a similar relationship with the U.S.A. The new involvement of the Soviet Union in the sub-continent is a fact of considerable importance to Pakistan, but its first premise relates to Sino-Soviet relations. The threads which bind Pakistan and the Soviet Union are still tenuous and Pakistan is careful not to strain them.[42]

The improvement in relations with the Soviet Union contrasted with the deterioration in the American relationship. Signs of this began in 1961, after Pakistan signed its oil agreement with the Soviet Government, an event followed by heavy disappointment in the matter of Consortium Aid for the Second Five Year Plan. For this the United States Government was blamed, and it was suggested that Pakistan was being penalized or blackmailed because it had made an agreement with the Soviet Government. The process of decline was further accentuated when President Kennedy decided that India must be given maximum assistance in the provision of military equipment. In May 1962 Ayub Khan had remarked that American policy in this regard might cause Pakistan to look elsewhere which evoked a rejoinder from the American political writer, James Reston, to the effect that this prospect did not worry the United States. Pakistan came back with the retort that 'the United States' approach was childish and puerile'.[43] From this time onward, comment in Pakistan on the United States and

---

[42] This fear of offending Soviet susceptibilities is carried very far. Thus, in Pakistan, the film *Dr Zhivago* was banned, apparently for this reason, since any other reason is difficult to think of. It is an irony that the Soviet Embassy in Pakistan denied influencing this decision.

[43] *D*, 21 November 1962.

its affairs, has usually been waspish in a way which, so far, has never appeared in reporting or comment relative to the Soviet Union.[44]

At the beginning of 1963, therefore, sentiment in Pakistan had already become distinctly adverse to the United States and Ayub Khan was already referring to arms aid to India as a circumstance that might compel Pakistan to withdraw from SEATO and CENTO.[45] From then on, little opportunity was lost by Pakistan's publicists to poison the official relationship between the two countries which in fact was the outward expression of feelings and convictions which the United States did not, and could not, grasp.

In February 1963, the then American Ambassador, when in East Pakistan, made reference to heavier applications of aid for that Province in order to provide more effective impetus for development. This was promptly interpreted in Pakistan as 'interference' and was linked to a statement made by Mr. Robert S. Mcnamara to the effect that, 'India and Pakistan must now recognize that they face a common enemy to the north in communist China . . .'.[46] The idea of American interference in Pakistan's domestic affairs was further underlined by reference to a proposal whereby the emoluments of schoolteachers in Pakistan, and the cost of textbooks, should be subsidized out of the Counterpart Fund.[47]

Such was the atmosphere in which matters proceeded. In the very next month, reports appeared in the Pakistan press that an American employed in the Embassy had been heard to

---

[44] I have already referred to Ayub Khan's brief remarks about Soviet arms aid to India in his broadcast on 1 October 1964 and to Bhutto's expression of 'regret'. This bears interesting comparison with what Ayub Khan had to say in his broadcast on 1 July 1964 on the subject of American arms aid to India. 'The National Assembly and other leaders of the nation, in both wings of the country, have expressed themselves strongly against U.S. arms aid to India. There *was* [my italics] nothing but friendliness and goodwill for the United States in this country until she embarked on its [*sic*] present ill-advised policy of disregarding Pakistan's interests and jeopardizing her security for the sake of what is called U.S. global strategy.'

[45] Television interview, January 1963.

[46] Editorial, *D* 19 February 1963.

[47] There were other such incidents as, for example, an opinion poll organized by the American Embassy enquiring into the views held by Pakistanis on certain aspects of American policy. This provoked a newspaper outcry and the poll was dropped.

say in public that S. K. Dehlavi and Q. U. Shahab[48] were communists[49] and this report evoked further comment about the rising tide of feeling against the United States.[50] Relations had already been injured by an article in the American magazine *Newsweek*, on the subject of *Fasting and Feasting during Ramzan*.[51]

This campaign of unpleasantness continued at about the time that a series of meetings took place between Pakistan and India whose ostensible purpose was to find a solution to the Kashmir problem. This matter will be considered in more detail in a later chapter, but while these meetings were taking place, news appeared in Pakistan of a plan sponsored by the United Kingdom and the United States for a settlement of the problem based on a partition. The first intimation of this in the Pakistan press[52] was the quotation of a report and map which had appeared in the *Daily Telegraph* of London.[53] The partition plan received fresh mention in the following April in the *New York Times* and a report of this, along with the *New York Times* map, appeared in Pakistan's newspapers.[54] It is important to note, here, that the idea of a partition seemed, just then, to be falling on receptive ears. The Karachi newspaper *Dawn*, as always chauvinist, remarked that 'if there was to be a partition, then it would have to be on the same basis as that which gave birth to Pakistan that is, on the principle of contiguous Muslim majority areas based on districts or tehsils'. Meanwhile, American and British statesmen were very active and, in May, it was reported that Phillips Talbot and Duncan Sandys met Zulfikar Ali Bhutto in Karachi and then flew to Rawalpindi to meet President Ayub Khan. A proposal had been made in Delhi for assistance through foreign mediation in order to find a solution to the Kashmir dispute and India, it seemed, had

---

[48] At that time, Mr. Dehlavi was Secretary, Foreign Affairs and Mr. Shahab was Secretary, Information and Broadcasting.

[49] *D*, 11 March 1963. It should be mentioned that when, eventually, Mr. Shahab was appointed Ambassador at The Hague, an official statement appeared that this was at his personal request and had nothing to do with foreign influence. The official communiqué is in *D*, 31 August 1963.

[50] *D*, 12 March 1963.

[51] 25 February 1963.

[52] *D*, 21 February 1963.

[53] 16 February 1963.

[54] *D*, 17 April 1963, quoting the *New York Times*, 8 April 1963.

indicated acceptance of this idea,[55] though Ayub Khan took the view that foreign mediation would be premature.[56] In the result there was no mediation, no partition, no settlement and no solution.

Reference has been made to the belief that economic aid was used, particularly by the United States, as an instrument of political pressure and the year 1963 witnessed further developments in this respect also. Following the completion of an air agreement between China and Pakistan, it was announced that the United States had suspended a loan intended for the purpose of modernizing and improving Dacca Airport. This was interpreted as a clear case of aid-with-strings and even the Americanophile Finance Minister, Mr. M. Shoaib, said that Pakistan might be compelled to revise its foreign policy. Indeed, by this time, there is little doubt that relations between Pakistan and the United States were distinctly disturbed and on 3 September, Mr. George Ball, a very senior official from the State Department, paid a short but clearly significant visit to Pakistan. He met not only Ayub Khan and Zulfikar Ali Bhutto but also the chiefs of the armed forces. It is, however, just as clear that George Ball was convinced that Pakistan intended no fundamental change in foreign policy and on departure he declared that his mission had been fulfilled.

This was not, and is not, surprising. However much acid comment there might be in Pakistan concerning the United States, and however often Cabinet Ministers and other public men might talk of 'new looks', 'agonizing re-appraisals' and other current clichés, it is abundantly plain that Ayub Khan was careful to avoid any actual *démarche* which might permanently damage relations between Pakistan and the United States of America.

But whatever Ayub's personal reservations might have been, the feeling which prevailed in the country was a good deal sharper and its nature was accurately reflected by Mushtaq Ahmed: 'Pakistan was the main victim of the sinister competition between its own so-called allies, and enemies of its allies, to build India into an arsenal.'[57] (The word 'sinister' aptly discloses the sense of conspiracy that constantly appears

[55] *D*, 9 May 1963.   [56] *D*, 13 May 1963.
[57] Mushtaq Ahmed, op. cit., p. 39.

in Pakistan's thinking about itself and the world at large.) Then, 'an obsession with China determined the direction of American foreign policy in the rest of Asia, where the object was not to strengthen the new democracies but to sustain or sabotage governments to checkmate the expansion of communism'.[58] Mushtaq Ahmed goes on to say, 'It is from Washington that, time and again, sometimes clandestinely, and on other occasions openly, the idea of confederation is mooted as a permanent solution to the Indo-Pakistan problem. The confederate notion shows how much the Americans underestimate the historical strength of Pakistani nationalism and how much their thinking about the area is dominated by their domestic background and their international interests.'[59]

This very clearly states the view, widely held in Pakistan, that it was the policy of the United States, supported by the United Kingdom as well as of the Soviet Union, to bring Pakistan and India as closely together as possible. The ability of these countries to make this policy effective with respect to Pakistan has fluctuated with time and circumstance. So far as the U.S.A. is concerned, it reached its lowest point in September 1965, and at no time since has the U.S.A. been able to exert that kind of exclusive influence in Pakistan's affairs as existed before 1960. Nevertheless, American influence has certainly grown again, if not to the same extent.

In February 1966 the then American Vice-President, Humphrey, visited Pakistan and was received at the airport with hostile demonstration. Shortly after his departure, the United States Information Service published his statement, made in Canberra, that Pakistan was fully aware of communist China's threat to the sub-continent. This drew the prompt rejoinder from Zulfikar Ali Bhutto, that foreign policy cannot be dictated through economic aid.[60] Commenting in surprisingly mild terms, *Dawn*[61] said that the USIS handout was 'maladroit to say the least of it', as it undoubtedly was. Ayub Khan was not to be outdone by his Foreign Minister, and in his broadcast on 1 March 1966 he said that China offered no threat to the sub-continent and that friendship with China constituted no bar to ties with the United States. In the following month

[58] ibid., p. 35.   [59] ibid., p. 40.   [60] *D*, 21 February 1966.
[61] In its issue dated 22 February 1966.

Mrs. Indira Gandhi was reported as saying that China offered no military threat to India, only an economic and political one.

In April, Liu Shao-chi visited Pakistan and was given an ecstatic welcome. There were the customary mutual assurances of eternal friendship and sacred ties, but it was at about this time that Ayub Khan began to experience his sense of disenchantment with China and, by the middle of the year, it had become evident that the attachment with the United States was strengthening.[62] The Americans seemed to be satisfied that they had brought Pakistan to heel, India already being there, and that, given an official peace, trade and other useful regional developments would become possible.

Thus, in 1967, Mr. George Woods visited Pakistan bearing, as it then appeared, proposals of great significance and suggesting joint ventures between India and Pakistan, having special reference to the efficient utilization of natural resources such as river water in which their interests were mutual. George Woods' visit was also intended to encourage the implementation of some of the suggestions made in the Report to the World Bank of the Bell Mission to India, which had examined India's capital requirements for economic development. However, Woods' mission was not acceptable in Pakistan and he attracted the anger of Zulfikar Ali Bhutto, no longer Pakistan's Foreign Minister and pursuing, with even greater insistence than before, his pro-China policy.[63]

These shifts in the official attitude to its foreign relations and the apparent contradictions in policy and approach, are attributable to Pakistan's immense and long-continued dependence upon American economic assistance in cash and kind and to the fact that the point of view of each country is exclusive to itself. There is no common identity of interest and there cannot be.

In terms of money, the position at the end of 1969 a few months after Ayub Khan's fall from power, was that the total external indebtedness of Pakistan including such international financing institutions as the World Bank, was about U.S. $3·528 billion of which approximately $1·389 billion had

[62] *D*, 28 June 1966, contains an interesting and objective despatch on American policy in the sub-continent.
[63] The *Pakistan Times*, 13 May 1967.

been provided by the United States, a contribution equal to about nine times those made by China and the Soviet Union put together. Moreover, this does not include those amounts indirectly provided by the United States by reason of its participation in the World Bank, the Import-Export Bank and so on. In accepting this help, whether from the United States or any other source, Pakistan maintains its position that this is strictly subject to the condition that all financial help is given and accepted *without strings*. This comfortable but illusory gospel has been steadily nurtured and as late as December 1969, the Minister for Information and National Affairs, Major-General Sher Ali Khan, said at an orientation course held by the National Institute of Public Administration for some twenty-five foreign experts who had just come to Pakistan, that Pakistan would 'accept, with gratitude, foreign assistance from anywhere, but with the complete understanding that no strings are attached to it'. The fact that Pakistan (or any other recipient country) believes this cannot nullify the ascendant influence which the donor-country must acquire.

In some respects a more important factor is the commodity aid which Pakistan has been obliged to look for from the United States. The provision of American wheat to supplement inadequate harvests is well known, but other important requirements have been met from the same source in times of acute shortage, such as edible oils. But it is not only the risk of famine that has placed Pakistan in a position of dependence. It is probable that many industrial establishments would come to a standstill but for essential materials and spare parts which the United States Government has provided. Most of this commodity aid has been supplied under Public Law 480 which facilitates provision in so far as foreign exchange reserves are not depleted, but it leads nevertheless to the building up of huge rupee funds in the hands of the United States which creates other forms of obligation. The utilization of these rupee funds may be subject to agreed limitations; they may even become worthless, but their existence is indisputable.

This, then, is one of the major aspects of the problem of Pakistan-United States relationships. The other lies in the fact that the two countries view their relationship from irreconcilable standpoints in which the question of Indo-Pakistan co-operation is important. The United States would like to see the entire Indo-Pakistan sub-continent a politically stable and economically self-supporting, prosperous area. In these particular aspects it would like, also, close economic relations between itself and the sub-continent, recognizing, as Robert Mcnamara said, 'the common enemy to the north'. The achievement of such stability could reinforce and strengthen the impact of the immense sums of money made available over the years to both India and Pakistan by the United States.

Pakistan, on its side, is fully alive to all these considerations, but measures them against entirely different yardsticks. To begin with, for Pakistan, the enemy at the gate is not China but India. The possibility that communism of the Maoist or any other school may sweep the sub-continent is much less of a threat or reality than the prospect that India might seek to overwhelm or absorb a Pakistan greatly handicapped by the division of its territories into two Provinces separated by India itself. The development of the East Pakistan movement for autonomy served to intensify this concern.

This firm tenet of Pakistan's policy is founded upon a two-fold conception of India's intentions. There is the possibility of conquest by force of arms and there is the possibility of an economic, intellectual and cultural penetration which would make of Pakistan an empty shell and a client of India.

The possibility of India's aims at conquest has long been a popular theme in Pakistan, especially among the politicians, as we shall see in the chapter on Indo-Pakistan relations. Despite the professed ambitions of some extremist Hindu organizations seeking the restoration of *Akhand Bharat*,[64] (if such a thing ever really existed outside the ancient Sanskrit epics and the imaginations of these extremists) such conquest has become more and more unlikely,* especially since 1965, partly because Pakistan does not want to be drawn into fresh adventures in Kashmir and partly because India is too deeply concerned with internal political troubles which threaten its integrity as a single, sovereign state. Pakistan would add to this that India received an unpleasant surprise in September 1965 which she would not like to meet again and we will come to this side of it in the next chapter.

[64] Signifying *India Undivided*.   * Bear in mind the date of writing: 1970.

But the real reason that deters—or should deter—India from any actual conquest and annexation lies in the consequences to itself of such a policy, assuming it were possible. The absorption of Pakistan would alter the communal situation drastically and would reshape the nature of Indian politics. Taking the census figures for 1961 of both countries (which hold the census in the same year and have about the same rate of population growth in the principal religious communities), we find:

	India	Pakistan	(East Pakistan)	(West Pakistan)
		(in millions)		
Hindus	366·5	10·0	9·4	0·6
Muslims	46·9	92·6	40.9	41·7
Total (all religions)	439·2	93·7	50·8	42·9

From these figures it is evident that in India Hindus at present outnumber Muslims in the ratio of eight to one. If Pakistan were annexed or absorbed, not only would the ratio change to three to one, but the distribution of population in terms of religion would become much more uneven than it is at present, with an intense concentration of Muslims in the present territory of West Pakistan amounting to about 99 per cent in that area. Representatives in the Indian parliament of such a solid phalanx of Muslims would present a complete Islamic loyalty and would be highly sensitive to the interests of Muslims throughout the sub-continent. If East Pakistan alone were annexed, the ratio of Hindus to Muslims would then be four to one, with the undesirable possibility, arising from the well-known separatist tendencies of the Bengali-speaking people, that the late Hussain Shaheed Suhrawardy's united, sovereign Bengal might become a reality. Were this to happen, the new republic would, based on 1961 census figures, have rather less than forty-eight million Muslims and about thirty-eight million Hindus. One thing is very plain. West Pakistan would be a most indigestible morsel to swallow, and why should India deny itself the advantages of a West Pakistan obliged to deal with such irredentist problems as might crop up on its western and north-western frontiers?

It is surely evident that whatever danger India presents to Pakistan, it lies far less in any prospect of military conquest than in the possibility of economic and cultural penetration. This is a danger to which Pakistan has always been alive and with good reason. There has always been an understandable tendency for otherwise loyal Pakistanis to remember what they left behind in India at the time of partition. The danger springs from the fact that both countries belong to a single civilization area. It is simply not possible to throw aside, in a gesture of emancipation, that part of the cultural and intellectual inheritance acquired from the people and from the soil to which the first Muslims came. Still less can they cast aside that culture which evolved from the fusion of Muslim with Hindu over the centuries. To deny such a fusion is to deny the significance of the Muslim impact on the area which is now Pakistan. It must also be acknowledged that the majority of Muslims in the sub-continent are converts to Islam or are the descendants of more or less recent converts, though this fact has been overstressed. Much has often been said, for example, about the fact that Allama Iqbal's ancestors were Sapru Brahmins or that Jinnah's ancestors were Hindus belonging to a trading caste. All that can be inferred is that, with such an ancestry, these men were probably more intelligent than would have been the case had their ancestors been village scavengers. The essential fact is that Allama Iqbal and Jinnah were Muslims.

It is the fact of a shared cultural heritage that is important. Where a nation has strong cultural affinities with a neighbour, it will be exposed to such intellectual influences as that neighbour may be able to exert. With respect to Pakistan, India has the power to do this in several meaningful ways, beginning with the fact of a substantially larger population and a generally higher standard of intellectual endeavour. This kind of influence has specific and easily identified forms. The birthplace of Urdu —one of Pakistan's national languages—is not Pakistan but India. It is no unfair exaggeration to say that even today the Indian Institute of Islamic Studies produces, in a year, more and better work on Islam than has been produced in Pakistan these last twenty years. The work of Rabindranath Tagore, is as much cherished and prized in East Pakistan as it is in West Bengal. The present home of Bengal's greatest Muslim poet, Nazrul Islam, is not Pakistan but India. When the centenary of the death of Ghalib, quite probably the greatest poet who ever wrote in Urdu, was observed in 1969, the celebration in India was much more impressive than in Pakistan.[65] The poetry of Iqbal still receives as much attention and study in India as it does in Pakistan.

The matter does not end there. For more than half the population of Pakistan, the people of the eastern Province, the mother-tongue is of clear Sanskrit origin and is written not in Persian or Arabic characters, but in an adaptation of *devanagari* script. And why not? Surely it is possible to be a satisfactory Muslim even though one's language is derived from Sanskrit. It is possible for a French-speaking European to be a good Muslim if the teachings of that faith win his allegiance, but—and this well states the difficulty for Pakistan—he will still be attracted to the culture he has inherited and to which he was born.

All this being so, what Pakistan has to fear—and believes it has to fear—is the silent, invisible, inexorable penetration of Indian thought, ideas and influence, through both the cultural inheritance already mentioned and the lack of regeneration within Pakistan. The reasons why intellectual life has not adequately flowered are not creditable. This is why Indian newspapers, periodicals and books may not be imported into Pakistan. It is not so much that the Government of Pakistan fears the consequences of tendentious propaganda or the dissemination of uncomfortable truths, but rather the possibility that the generally superior quality of such work might lead people to an intellectual focus beyond that of the Pakistani concept and the Pakistani ideal. And so any means by which Indian influence can be exercised on the soil of Pakistan is unwelcome and this explains why Pakistan has been content not to trade with India for that, too, is a source of contact and influence.

The problems of identification and assimilation into some kind of unity in outlook and idea of the diverse influences which exist have not been solved. People have been content to debate such shallow and simplistic suggestions that East Pakistanis should learn Urdu as well as their own tongue and that West

---

[65] Some Pakistanis were invited to attend, but their Government did not provide the necessary facilities.

Pakistanis should learn Bengali. They have contented themselves with discussion as to what is Islamic and what is not, and whether Arabic script should replace *nastaliq*. The utility of Arabic script, as opposed to *nastaliq*, for example, is that a typewriter with Arabic characters is a simpler machine to make, but obviously such an issue occupies a subordinate place relative to the question of unification of the country in outlook and sentiment. This is not, in general, the sort of thing that can be done by politicians and legislators, although a few minds of the rare, statesmanlike type, are needed to help and encourage the intellectuals for whom the task is more appropriate. Those who can justly lay claim to such status have failed to provide this lead, though the reasons may be largely beyond their control.

I think that when a history of Pakistan, more definitive than is now possible, comes to be written, it will be found that this history provides as clear a case of the *trahison des clercs* as has been witnessed in this century. To this betrayal, the civil services, especially in the higher cadres, have contributed much, partly by their own failure to recognize the country's need for a sense of intellectual solidarity and partly by failing to contribute to the creation of a free and unfettered intellectual atmosphere.[66] All the same, it is fair to add that the atmosphere has never been totally stifling and either through want of comprehension, indolence, indifference, ignorance or craven-heartedness, the intellectuals of Pakistan have failed to provide solutions to the gravest single problem that has beset their country. As a result, Pakistan has remained as uncertain of itself as in those early days of newly won independence when, overshadowed by a hostile India and confronted with a succession of urgent and compelling difficulties, the country picked its hesitant, halting way.

I hope this lengthy digression will be condoned. It was neces-

---

[66] For example, the eminent Islamic scholar Dr. Fazlur Rahman was virtually driven out of Pakistan. His book *Islam* was banned in 1969 after having been freely sold in Pakistan since it was first published by Routledge and Kegan Paul, in 1967. There does not seem to have been a single Pakistani intellectual or civil servant who uttered a word in his defence or in protest, either publicly or privately. Unsavoury matters influenced the Government's decision, matters which had little to do with Quranic interpretation. It seems also that Dr. Rahman did not handle the matter as skilfully as he might. Still, a scholar is not expected to be a tactician in intrigue and Dr. Rahman was the undoubted victim of a shabby business which reflected no credit on his country.

sary to explain why Pakistan sees so very clearly for itself a range of purposes that does not differ so very much from that which the United States also envisages, but Pakistan sees them with reference to a different modulus and in a different order of priority. For the United States it is clear that Pakistan and India need to co-operate as much as possible, to accommodate each other's point of view and to share their resources as productively as they can. For Pakistan the validity of this thinking is also obvious, but it is just as obvious to Pakistan that there are some things that come before all this and one of them is to ensure, no matter what, that India will not be able to use its intellectual and economic *bulk* to lean on Pakistan and slowly wear it down.

Thus, although in 1958 Ayub Khan was firmly wedded to the American alliance and had often publicly expressed his disapproval of communism, he was urged by many of his countrymen to represent Pakistan's grievances to the United States.[67] In 1964 he published an article about those grievances in the authoritative American quarterly, *Foreign Affairs*.[68] It has not been possible to narrow the difference in outlook between the two countries and thus it was inevitable that in September 1965 Pakistan, bitterly disappointed by what it considered an American betrayal, should revile its ally in the language of harsh reproach,[69] and should conclude that its firmest, as well as its most powerful, friend was China.

[67] In October 1963 Zulfikar Ali Bhutto visited the United States and met President Kennedy. He returned to Pakistan where he expressed himself as being not fully satisfied with the outcome of his meeting. This view gained much publicity and approval in Pakistan.

[68] The article was entitled *Pakistan-American Alliance—Stresses and Strains* and appeared in the issue dated January 1964. There is a markedly interesting comparison between this and Ayub Khan's previous article in the same journal, dated July 1960. This was entitled *Pakistan Perspective—An analysis of Pakistan's ideology, problems and their solution*. It is this article which contains the much-quoted reference: 'As a student of war and strategy, I can see quite clearly the *inexorable* push of the north in the direction of the warm waters of the Indian Ocean. This push is bound to increase if India and Pakistan go on squabbling with each other.' (My italics.)

[69] Scurrilous pamphlets appeared after September 1965, which attacked the United States, often in abusive language. A fair example of this category of polemics, if the word can be justified in such a case, is *Americans are Villains and Enemies of Pakistan*. Authorship is ascribed to one Asadul Haq and it was published in Hyderabad, West Pakistan. It was banned by the Government of Pakistan under the Defence of Pakistan Rules in July 1967.

All that has been said concerning Pakistan's relations with the United States and the difficulties involved, may help to clarify also the difficulties that impede Pakistan's relations with the Soviet Union. In many respects the purposes of the Soviet Union and the United States in Asian affairs are not identical, but there are similarities. The reasons which lead both superpowers to seek a stable and tranquil sub-continent are more or less the same, and if the reasons which have created enmity between China and the Soviet Union are not precisely those which have created enmity between China and the United States, the consequences in Asia have so far proved similar, at any rate with respect to the sub-continent. To some extent, the Soviet Union has abandoned its attitude of complete identity with the Indian view of the Kashmir problem, but this has scarcely resulted in a more positive approach to the Pakistan case. Rather, it has led to a withdrawn, dispassionate, and even ambiguous attitude. This can hardly satisfy Pakistan despite Soviet offers of help in establishing a steel industry. So far as the United States is concerned, Pakistan is now convinced that American policy has been, and is, guided by purely selfish motives. This may be so, but it is no less true of the Soviet Union and, for that matter, of China.[70]

[70] I have not thought it necessary to elaborate on Pakistan's relations with countries apart from those discussed in this chapter, during the period 1962 to 1969. They tended to be conventional and determined by considerations of trade and the ever-present Kashmir question. Among other countries, the United Kingdom is conspicuous as Pakistan's second biggest trading partner, as third largest contributor of economic assistance and still the greatest single source of foreign private investment in Pakistan. All this is important but as a factor in the determination of Pakistan's foreign relations must be deemed to be of secondary significance.

VIII

Indo-Pakistan Relations: I

PAKISTAN'S relations with India play a very important part in the shaping of its relations with the world at large, and they are directly influenced by the condition of Pakistan's internal security and prosperity. At the beginning of his Martial Law administration in 1958, Ayub Khan sought to create an improved atmosphere between the two countries, but he over-simplified the issues by saying that only two problems clouded their mutual relations. The first was Kashmir and the second was the question of the Indus basin waters. It is on record that the latter problem was disposed of when the Treaty was signed by the two countries in 1960, but the problem of Kashmir remained, as intractable as ever. Even if Kashmir had been solved, there was no reason to suppose that fresh sources of difficulty might not have arisen. Indeed, that is precisely what happened when India set about constructing a barrage at Farrakha in West Bengal.[1] Further, Ayub Khan, in making his pronouncement, overlooked the abiding problem of communal strife.

In this chapter I do not propose to trace the course of events touching communal violence which is, in any case, a much more complicated matter than a simple conflict between Muslims and Hindus.[2] At various times between 1962 and 1969 Indo-Pakistan relations were disturbed by trouble of this kind, whether it were at Khulna in 1964 or at Jamshedpur and Ranchi in the same year. On the whole, to judge by such reports on Hindu-Muslim disturbance as are available, Pakistan had substantially more to complain about than India and, so far

---

[1] It was with respect to the barrage at Farrakha that Mr. George Woods sought collaboration between the two countries. See the previous chapter.

[2] In my 'Communal Problem in the Indo-Pakistan Sub-continent: Some Current Implications', *Pacific Affairs*, University of British Columbia, Vancouver, Summer 1969, I endeavoured to disentangle some of the threads of this difficult and sensitive subject.

as this is concerned, it is my firm belief that in Pakistan more Muslims have died at the hands of Muslims (that is, after the troubles which accompanied the migrations of 1947) than have Hindus or members of other communities. In stating this, I do not include all those Muslims who, at various times, have lost their lives in the course of official repressions.

Disgraceful as is the butchery which, at various times, takes place between religious communities in the sub-continent, I do not think this is the principal cause of disharmony between India and Pakistan. In spite of the scale of these conflicts, and their effect on these two countries' public image throughout the world, it is Pakistan's fear of absorption—political, intellectual and economic—by India which is probably the main cause of disharmony. It is, I believe, this fear which led to the suggestion that Pakistan *needs* India as an enemy.[3] Yet another persisting element is the pressure, in both countries, from people with a vested interest in disharmony, people who realize that were this disharmony to cease, so too would their influence in public affairs.[4] It is beyond doubt these people who have effectively frustrated those moments of genuine intention on both sides to find solutions to Indo-Pakistani disputes. However, such moments were infrequent, and although in the early days of his administration Ayub Khan seemed to hope for the possibility of a *rapprochement*, he soon discovered that the prospects were slender and that politically it might even be undesirable.

Whatever may be the apportionment of blame and responsibility, Pakistan's relations with India during the period 1962–9 were almost always bad although they oscillated between occasions of extreme repulsion to faint hopes of settlement. On the whole, both sides found it necessary to play this game coyly and the indications are that those occasions when they seemed to be coming together usually had their inspiration from outside the sub-continent.

On Pakistan's side, it is clear that the sense of hostility towards India was aggravated by the provision of arms by the United Kingdom and the United States in 1962 and 1963.

[3] See, for example, an article by Rawle Knox, the *Daily Telegraph*, London, 28 May 1965.
[4] *D*, 10 July 1965, referred in an editorial to sections in India which thrive on Indo-Pakistan tension. The remark was just in itself, but unjust in that it omitted reference to comparable sections in Pakistan.

But while Pakistan's apprehensions are understandable, it is difficult to believe that had there been no such supply of arms, feeling between the two countries would have been any better. Indeed, it can be argued, particularly by India, that an India disarmed and enfeebled by China, without succour from outside, would have presented to Pakistan a temptation difficult to resist—certainly so far as Kashmir was concerned.

As we know, things turned out differently. We have seen that from the beginning of Ayub Khan's administration under the presidential system, Pakistan had suffered two serious disappointments with respect to India. One was the supply of arms and the other was the Soviet veto in the Security Council relating to Kashmir. From this time onwards, the cry was constantly repeated in Pakistan that India was seeking to destroy Pakistan; that India was engaged in troop dispositions that gave cause for grave suspicion as to Indian intentions and that India's various professions of a desire to solve Indo-Pakistan problems were in no way sincere.

Within two months of the inception of his new Constitution, Ayub Khan was accusing India of aiming at Pakistan's destruction,[5] and this sense of disappointment with India expressed itself in repeated and sharper accusations of India's intended aggression. In 1963 Ayub Khan said that any attack by India on Pakistan would result in an unprecedented bloodbath[6] and thereafter he and members of his Government continued to remark in this spirit. Zulfikar Ali Bhutto accused India of neo-colonialism in its worst form and the western Powers were informed that arms aid to India had not only increased the tension between the two countries, but had led to a build-up of Indian forces on Pakistan's borders. It was said that this form of aid had emboldened India, which was seeking a show-down with Pakistan and was working up its aggressive intentions. Habibullah Khan, Pakistan's Minister for Home and Kashmir Affairs,[7] belligerently said that force would be met with force, while Ayub Khan complained in 1964 that the United States and the United Kingdom had let Pakistan down.

[5] *D*, 6 August 1962.
[6] This heated remark can be considered in the light of what happened in September 1965, when both sides agreed to an armistice after seventeen days.
[7] Not to be confused with Lieutenant-General Habibullah Khan Khattak.

Consonant with all this, the Indian Government was asked to close its reading rooms and libraries in Dacca and Rajshahi which, it was said, were being used as centres of subversion.[8]

There is no doubt that a good deal of all this was intended for home consumption. Chapter VI, which discussed the election of 1965, has shown how Ayub Khan presented himself as the only man who could save Pakistan from India's evil intent and much of the earlier declamation, during 1962–4, was part of a strategy to win election votes. But it would be an error to think that this was the sole reason for the attitude adopted in Pakistan because, in India, extremist Hindu organizations were openly propagating their doctrine of *Akhand Bharat* and urging the dissolution of Pakistan.

However, during these years, there was another kind of activity consisting of efforts, if they can so be called, to persuade the two countries to work together. In November 1962 Ayub Khan was in correspondence with Jawaharlal Nehru, with the purpose of arranging meetings between the two countries without other intervention in the hope of finding a solution to the problem of Kashmir. The proposal that such meetings should be held was hotly debated in Pakistan's National Assembly and it aroused much feeling in the country, where it was generally believed that nothing could possibly emerge that would be constructive or would conform to Pakistan's idea of a just settlement based on the principle of self-determination for and by the people of Kashmir. Despite this opposition, Ayub Khan pursued the idea of a meeting between representatives of the two countries and it seems probable that he, as well as Jawaharlal Nehru, was under extreme pressure to do so.

The grounds for suggesting this are convincing enough. So far as India was concerned, we have seen in the preceding chapter that a proposal made at the United Nations in May 1962 that the two nations should meet in order to solve their problems, was the object of a Soviet veto which, it must be presumed, was exercised with the prior knowledge and agreement of India. Yet six months later, in November 1962, we find Nehru and Ayub Khan exchanging letters whose purport was

---

[8] *D*, 25 October 1963. Eventually, the Indian Government was asked to close all such libraries and reading-rooms. Indian newspapers, periodicals and books are not now allowed into Pakistan at all.

that the two Governments should meet. We have also observed the part played by the United States and the United Kingdom in working for a settlement of the Kashmir question.

These moves will explain why Ayub Khan did not give way to the opposition in his own country to the idea of a meeting. Indeed, meetings began at a ministerial level in January 1963, when Zulfikar Ali Bhutto, at that time Minister for Fuel, Power and Natural Resources, led a delegation to Delhi to meet the Indian Foreign Minister, Swaran Singh. These talks did not make much headway and at their conclusion on 29 January Bhutto commented: 'Undoubtedly there has been considerable progress . . . but that does not mean we have come any closer to a settlement or that prospects of a settlement have improved,' a Delphic utterance that seems to have been designed to satisfy everyone. Nevertheless, it was arranged that, in the following month, Swaran Singh should visit Rawalpindi in order to continue the debate. This too yielded little and the third round was arranged for March 1963, in Calcutta. (The venue was convenient for the Pakistan delegation since, at that time, the National Assembly was in session in Dacca.) In April 1963, Swaran Singh went to Karachi for yet another attempt and this visit preceded by only a few days the CENTO Ministers' conference. At about the same time, the British and American newspapers were publishing maps showing a partition of Kashmir.

As we now know, none of this was fruitful and there were the usual recriminations and mutual accusations of insincerity. If it be true that both sides acted under severe external pressures, it may well be that in their secret thoughts both sides intended that there should be no positive results except on the basis of their respective points of view. Certainly, there was not a moment during the course of the negotiations when the outlook appeared promising, although there does seem to have been a time when Pakistan was in a mood to accept the partition principle for Kashmir. Instead, matters drifted, and in May 1964 Zulfikar Ali Bhutto permitted himself to remark that Soviet obstruction in the Security Council could lead nowhere.[9]

Surprisingly, this remark was made only two days before the arrival of Sheikh Abdullah at Chaklala Airport in West

[9] *D*, 22 May 1964.

Pakistan, where he was given a rousing reception. Not only was the idea that he should come very acceptable in itself to Pakistan, but it was believed that he did so armed with Jawaharlal Nehru's authority to reach a settlement, if he could, on Kashmir and, perhaps, other questions too. It appears that at this time Nehru had been much influenced by the writings of his old Congress colleague Jai Prakash Narayan, and wearying perhaps of the risks and intricacies of the Kashmir problem, was ready for a solution to which Sheikh Abdullah would also be a party.[10]

Unfortunately, what Sheikh Abdullah had to say did not prove to be at all congenial to Pakistan. Four days after his arrival the Pakistan press was recording disappointment with his statements. His reference to Indian secularism was disliked and his assertion that India was genuinely desirous of friendship with Pakistan caused surprise and was met with disbelief. However, it was reported that on the question of the plebiscite the Sheikh was firm and it was said that in consequence of his discussions in Rawalpindi Ayub Khan and Nehru might meet in the following month. But Pandit Nehru died suddenly and the negotiations were abruptly terminated by the immediate return to Delhi of Sheikh Abdullah. Thereafter, they were not renewed and under the succeeding Prime Ministers, Gulzarilal Nanda, who acted in a temporary capacity, followed by the late Lal Bahadur Shastri, the Indian attitude changed and became perceptibly stiffer.

So far as concerns Sheikh Abdullah and the disappointment with him displayed in Pakistan, one important reason for this is that in Pakistan his position seems never to have been properly understood. In the early days of independence, he was regarded in Pakistan as a mere puppet of the Indian National Congress and as a mouthpiece of Jawaharlal Nehru on Kashmir affairs. When he and Nehru fell out over political issues, the Pakistani attitude changed immediately and he came to be regarded as a great Kashmiri patriot who had suffered much in the cause of

---

[10] Alastair Lamb, *Crisis in Kashmir*, London, Routledge and Kegan Paul, 1966, p. 106. I have said nothing in this book about the pressures put on Nehru and the Indian Government by the United Kingdom and the United States at the time they were providing arms to India after the débâcle against the Chinese. Neville Maxwell has dealt with this aspect in *India's China War*, London, Jonathan Cape, 1970.

his Kashmiri countrymen. What does not seem to have been realized in Pakistan is that Sheikh Abdullah's differences with the Indian Government were of precisely the same nature as would have existed were he in similar relation with the Pakistan Government. His first long incarceration sprang from his opposition to India's efforts to erode the effect of Article 370 of the Indian Constitution which made *temporary provision* for the State of Jammu and Kashmir and limited the legislative powers of the Government of India with respect to that State. Abdullah, however, had seen the matter somewhat differently from the Indian Government, as indeed had everyone else. If the provisions of Article 370 were temporary, it was because the affair of Jammu and Kashmir stood very differently from the other princely states of India and was the subject of a dispute that lay before the United Nations.

The question of Article 370 need not be pursued just now. We are concerned here with Sheikh Abdullah's purposes which were, and doubtless will remain, to ensure the maximum measure of autonomy—if not actual independence[11]—for a united Kashmir. A partitioned Kashmir, or a Kashmir falling totally within the influence and power either of India or Pakistan, would mean the extinction of Sheikh Abdullah as an influential political figure. He had himself been imprisoned continuously for eleven years, and had witnessed the fate of Bakshi Ghulam Mohamed, at the hands of the Indian Government. He was also aware of the summary dismissal of two Presidents of Azad Kashmir, Sardar Ibrahim and M. H. Khurshid, at the hands of the Pakistan Government. These were all lessons he could not ignore and it has become very clear, as the years passed since 1947, that Sheikh Abdullah pursued a course of action which had as much to do with safeguarding his eminence in Kashmiri affairs as it had with the welfare of the people of the State.

[11] During the talks in May 1964 Sheikh Abdullah proposed to Ayub Khan that Kashmir should become independent. Ayub Khan rejected this idea on the ground that Kashmir would then become a hotbed of international intrigue. c.f. B. L. Sharma, *The Kashmir Story*, New Delhi, Asia Publishing House, 1967, p. 143. Mr. Sharma, a former Director-in-charge, Kashmir Affairs, in the Indian Ministry of External Affairs, knows the subject well. Unfortunately, the same violent feeling that colours his book *The Pakistan-China Axis* disfigures this book also and robs it of completeness and any pretence to impartiality. For this reason, both books, although well-documented and therefore useful, are not valuable.

Personal relationships stand somewhat differently. It is plain that, in this respect, Sheikh Abdullah was never very distant from Jawaharlal Nehru and never very close to the men of Pakistan. His prime concern, moreover, was always with Kashmir, and not with the sub-continent, and with his opposition to the autocratic rule of the previous Maharaja of Kashmir. In all this, Sheikh Abdullah was associated with, and to some extent relied upon, the Indian National Congress, not upon the All-India Muslim League. When in 1942 he was arrested by the then Government of Jammu and Kashmir, it was not Mohamed Ali Jinnah who rushed to Srinagar to conduct his defence, but Jawaharlal Nehru.[12] Yet it seems true that, as the years went by, and as his own ambitions seemed as distant as ever, Abdullah began to feel a sense of estrangement with respect to India and was no longer quite so antipathetic to Pakistan. Perhaps in Pakistan he saw an instrument leading to the realization of his objectives for Kashmir and for himself. The application, in December 1964, of Articles 356 and 357[13] of the Indian Constitution to Kashmir, was followed, in January 1965, by an extension of Indian control. These moves could only serve to convince Sheikh Abdullah that he was as far as ever from the attainment of his purposes.

Indeed, in Srinagar rioting and civil commotion took place and the crowds were fired on. Cries favouring accession to Pakistan were heard and an opinion was growing that more and more Kashmiri Muslims were in favour of a link with Pakistan.

This feeling appeared to be endorsed further when three months later Sheikh Abdullah himself made reference to the possibility of an accession by Kashmir to Pakistan.[14] However, a month afterwards, Sheikh Abdullah proceeded on pilgrimage and the Pakistan Government offered to provide him with a

[12] At the State border, Nehru was forbidden entry. In a fine and typical flourish, Nehru involved himself in a scuffle with the Kashmiri frontier guards and received a minor bayonet scratch. It was all good, dramatic publicity.

[13] These Articles relate to measures which may be taken by the President of the Indian Republic in the event of a failure of the constitutional provisions in any State of the Indian Union, and to the exercise of legislative powers by the President of India under a Proclamation of Emergency made pursuant to Article 356.

[14] Notable among the foreign journals endorsing this view was the *Economist*, London, 17 January 1965.

passport should the Indian Government not do so. In the course of his travels, which were not limited to the Holy City, Sheikh Abdullah made some noteworthy statements relating to the aspirations of the Kashmiri people and also highly critical of the Indian Government. In the Indian Parliament, the Opposition seized upon these circumstances to attack and embarrass the Government so that on his return Sheikh Abdullah was arrested. In the circumstances there seems to have been no alternative, but news of his arrest caused more disturbance in Srinagar and more firing on the crowd.[15] Sheikh Abdullah was first detained at Ootacamund in South India where the unauthorized visit of the British journalist Tom Stacey took place. For this enterprising endeavour Stacey was asked to leave India and not return, while Sheikh Abdullah was moved to Kodaicanal a couple of months later.

At this point in the narrative, it is necessary to turn to a significant incident which occurred in the spring of 1965—the affair of the Rann of Cutch. Measured against the momentous military operations that followed in September in the Punjab the confrontation between the two countries in the Rann was trifling. Nevertheless its meaning and consequences were significant and it is with these, rather than with detail of the petty skirmishing itself, that we are concerned.

That a dispute relative to the Rann existed between the two countries had been acknowledged by India some eight years before, although when the trouble began in 1965 India professed to have no knowledge of any such dispute. This profession of ignorance need not necessarily be ascribed to duplicity. It might equally well have arisen from departmental incompetence. In any case, as has been suggested, it is difficult to assess the respective purposes of the two countries when the trouble actually broke out.[16] At one time, it was suggested in India that that country's purpose was to safeguard any possible extension of oilfields which had already been discovered in the State of Gujarat of which the Indian territory in Cutch forms part. Apart from this idea, which seemed later to have been officially discouraged in India, it may be that this minor affair was a mutually conducted experiment in nerve-testing, in which each side was trying to determine how far the other would

[15] *D*, 11 April 1965.   [16] Lamb, op. cit., p. 116.

go in a confrontation of troops across the international border.

If we are to accept all the claims and counter-claims later put forward by Pakistan and India, we should be forced to conclude that:

(a) Both sides fired first.
(b) On the commencement of enemy firing, each side withdrew its troops as far as it dared, consistent with safety and national integrity.
(c) Each side did everything in its power to minimize the conflict and bring it to an early and peaceful conclusion.

With all this, we need not trouble ourselves. The first important aspect of the Cutch affair lies in the historic fact that the ceasefire and an agreement to arbitrate were brought about by the mediation of the British Government. This may prove to have been the last occasion on which Commonwealth ties were used to achieve settlement of a dispute between two of its members finding themselves in conflict.

Secondly, the fact that recourse was made to arbitration, which satisfied Pakistan considerably, pointed to the admissibility of arbitration as a means of settling *all* disputes between the two countries. This is made clear by Ayub Khan's statements at the time and particularly that dated 30 June 1965. It was indeed this creation of a precedent that made acceptance of arbitration far less welcome in India where the Prime Minister, the late Lal Bahadur Shastri, was heavily criticized in Parliament and out of it for agreeing to this course. What alternative was open to him in the case of so simple a boundary dispute it is difficult to understand, and his critics never suggested one, unless it were to continue the fighting. Perhaps they relied purely on the assertion that Pakistan had again committed aggression and presumably ought to be punished by the United Nations.[17]

---

[17] The result of the arbitration was also received in India with much outcry and resentment. In fact the arbitrators, an independent international tribunal, did no more than try to simplify the boundary on as fair a basis as possible and to rationalize it with respect to geographical features, particularly when measured from the military point of view. The effect was to give 350 square miles of territory to Pakistan, a trifling area in the circumstances. The veteran Indian lawyer and politician, Mr. Mohamed Currim Chagla, vehemently opposed the award and described it as 'political'. In a sense, he was right, but it has long been

Thirdly, although the scope of the operations in the Rann was extremely limited, what is known of them gives rise to some interesting conclusions relevant to the September 1965 war. It seems evident that in the Rann the Pakistani troops had the better of the fighting and captured a fair quantity of warlike stores, less perhaps through their own prowess than through India's mistake in placing its supply depots too far forward and with inadequate protection. The number of men involved, the duration of the operations, and the casualties sustained on each side, were too insignificant to lead to any reliable conclusions, but such advantage as Pakistan gained seemed to convince Ayub Khan that the Pakistani soldier had demonstrated a clear superiority over his Indian counterpart and that the Indian forces in the Rann had displayed a feebleness comparable with their performance against the Chinese in 1962. This conviction had its bearing on his thoughts when considering other decisions later that year.

The numbers of casualties inflicted helps to throw light on subsequent happenings. The Indian Government published official casualty figures as follows:[18]

	Killed	Wounded	Missing
Police	8	10	20
Army	7	31	17

The names of the casualties were listed and it is a point of some interest that no Muslim name appears among them, presumably because either no Muslims were employed by India in the Rann operations or the Muslims were sharp enough to keep out of the line of fire. The Pakistan Government, consonant with what appears to be its normal practice, did not publish any casualty figures. The Pakistani commander in the field, Major-General (afterwards Lieutenant-General) Tikka Khan, gave his own estimate of casualties on both sides and

accepted that the settlement of international disputes should look not only to the letter of the law, but also to the practical consequences of the decision reached. For a balanced Indian view, see R. P. Anand, 'The Kutch Award', *India Quarterly*, New Delhi, July–September 1968, p. 183.

[18] *Statesman*, Calcutta, 20 May 1965.

challenged the Indian Government to disprove them, an approach which was neither satisfactory nor convincing.[19]

From all this, there arises the material point that the figures officially published by the Indian Government were to some extent confirmed in Pakistan when the exchange of prisoners took place. As against five prisoners returned by India to Pakistan, Pakistan returned thirty-five Indian prisoners, a figure which is convincingly close to the official India figure of thirty-seven persons missing.[20] This was to have an important bearing on the question of casualties sustained by both sides in September 1965.

Following the cease-fire and the agreement to arbitrate, the mechanics of these arrangements had yet to be completed. The atmosphere continued to be heated despite Shastri's offer of a no-war pact made in June 1965. Even in Pakistan, which had welcomed the arbitration proposal, warlike feelings persisted and were reflected in Ayub Khan's broadcast on 1 June 1965. He said: 'We have made it clear, time and again, that we do not want war. . . . Our abhorrence of war does not, however, mean that we are not going to defend our country if attacked. I visited the troops on the *front*[21] and found them in high spirits. I am confident that if war is forced on us, the fighting forces of Pakistan will give an excellent account of themselves.'

Indeed, the prevailing sense of hostility led Ayub Khan to adopt other measures. In June 1965 ordinances were issued by which employers were obliged to release military reservists eligible for recall to the colours and to guarantee their re-employment on return to civil life. In the same month, also, a Mujahid Force[22] was set up and made part of the Regular

---

[19] *Evening Star*, Karachi, 29 April 1965. This feebleness does less than justice to General Tikka Khan who is generally recognized as an officer of considerable military ability. His estimate of 350 Indians killed in the Rann operations was given by him to journalists only after persistent questioning and with much reluctance. Clearly his questioners wanted something that would please their readers. Newspaper reports in Pakistan on the Rann operations were ludicrous. The *Evening Star*, in the issue referred to, carried the headline 'Indian Army Rout in Biar Bet Action' and proceeded to narrate the capture of vehicles, arms and *ten* prisoners. (My italics.)

[20] *D*, 17 August 1965.

[21] My italics.

[22] *Mujahid* signifies 'one who strives'. It comes from the same root as *jehad* and the relationship between the two, particularly in the sense that *jehad* can mean, and is often taken to mean, war in the cause of Islam, is obvious.

Army. However, it appears that only a few units of this Force have ever been established and they represent a negligible part of Pakistan's armed forces.

We are now on the threshold of the events which culminated in the hostilities of September 1965, a very difficult and delicate matter. To this brief campaign, along with its many-sided outcome, the next chapter is devoted.

IX

Indo-Pakistan Relations: II

RETURNING from a Conference of Non-aligned Nations at Cairo, the Indian Prime Minister, Lal Bahadur Shastri, broke journey at Karachi on 12 October 1964 for a brief meeting with President Ayub Khan. They lunched together at the airport and the outcome of their discussion appeared to be that they were in agreement over the need to settle outstanding disputes between their respective countries.

Obvious as this was, the meeting and discussion afforded ground for satisfaction, particularly as they followed Jai Prakash Narayan's unofficial goodwill visit. This encouraging atmosphere did not last long. By the beginning of 1965 it was evident that the prospects of a settlement over Kashmir had deteriorated substantially with the application of Articles 356 and 357 of the Indian Constitution and the extension of the Indian Government's control in the State. Moreover, by the middle of 1965, if not earlier, it had been made clear to Ayub Khan and his Government by the Indian Prime Minister and his Foreign Minister, that in any negotiations for a permanent settlement of the dispute, Pakistan must accept Jammu and Kashmir as a constituent State of the Indian Union. According to India, Pakistan had no claim whatsoever in or to Jammu and Kashmir.[1]

---

[1] B. L. Sharma, *The Kashmir Story*, op. cit., p. 189. As set forth by Mr. Sharma, the record of what the Indian Government is said to have made clear to Pakistan is all quite ambiguous, but the sentiments he expresses are obvious enough. Without venturing any opinion here as to the merits of the Kashmir dispute, it seems to me that the long-continued and complicated involvements of the problem have made it, in one respect at least, comparable with the Schleswig-Holstein question. Readers will remember that concerning the latter, Palmerston said: 'Only three people ever understood it. One is dead; the second is mad, and I, the third, have forgotten all about it.' There can be no doubt about the widening intricacies of the Kashmir dispute. It is, for example, an interesting fact that part of the Mangla Lake, created by Mangla Dam, feeding the great irrigation system which it commands, lies in Azad Kashmir. In the event of a plebiscite successful

It is not at all certain that Pakistan has ever laid claim to Jammu and Kashmir, although in more exalted moments Ayub Khan and others said that Kashmir was bound to go to Pakistan.[2] Be that as it may, after India had taken this stand, it appeared to the Government of Pakistan that five courses of action were open. Pakistan could, first, make a fresh reference to the United Nations with every prospect of a Soviet veto if the Security Council appeared to be acting in a manner unfavourable to India's interest. The second was to seek some other form of mediation, if India agreed to it. The third was to initiate direct negotiations with India, a prospect scarcely encouraged by the experience of 1963. The fourth was to forget all about Kashmir. The fifth was to adopt such other measures as Pakistan might select, irrespective of the United Nations or anyone else— in short, to go it alone.

For reasons which will be elaborated later, I hold it to be clear that out of these five choices Ayub Khan decided to embark upon an independent course of action, not excluding the use of Pakistan's armed forces should that become necessary. What has earlier been said concerning the intensification of Pakistan's diplomatic activity during the early part of 1965, and more particularly about the development of closer relations with China and Indonesia, supports the view that Ayub Khan was already preparing for a new approach to the solution of the Kashmir problem. This does not establish an intention to fight, but it does indicate an intention to press for a settlement.

Furthermore, it could be said that the affair in the Rann had removed a psychological barrier. It proved that an armed confrontation between India and Pakistan across an international boundary was possible. Moreover, this brief skirmish had enlivened people's interest and concern with the idea of war. In its issue dated 6 June 1965, the Karachi newspaper, *Dawn* carried a particularly significant middle-page article

---

for India, what would be the consequences so far as Mangla is concerned? It may be that Pakistan regards such a result as impossible. Or, perhaps, the principle of partition has been *de facto* accepted? Unfortunately, the terms of the Indus Basin Treaty are not accessible to the public.

After the Karachi airport meeting, Ayub Khan is said to have spoken disparagingly of the Indian Prime Minister. Perhaps he was unwise enough to have equated Shastri's diminutive stature with his power of determination.

[2] See *D*, 29 January 1960.

entitled 'Where are India's West-equipped Mountain Divisions?' written under the pseudonym 'Scanner'. The article bore all the marks of official inspiration and was accompanied by a map which purported to show the deployment by divisions of the Indian Army. It was there stated, among other things, that if India forced a war on Pakistan, the correct strategy for Pakistan would 'obviously be to go for a knock-out in the Mohamed Ali Clay style'.[3]

If we assume, therefore, that Ayub Khan decided on the fifth choice of action, the question also arises as to the extent to which this decision was the consequence of his independent judgement. It has often been said with hindsight that Ayub Khan was influenced by unwise counsellors—even if he never relied on them—concerning what India might, could, or would do. If this policy over Kashmir in 1965 was politically and economically disastrous for Pakistan, Ayub Khan cannot escape the major share of the blame.

The trend of events in Jammu and Kashmir in 1964 and 1965, and the disquiet generated in the State by the continued detention of Sheikh Abdullah, appeared to convince Ayub Khan and his advisers that an internal situation that could lead to open revolt against the Indian Government had developed. Clearly there was here a situation which, because of geographical contiguity, the ease of slipping in and out of Kashmir, and the identity of race, custom and language, could easily be fostered and encouraged.[4] If this came about, many advantages could accrue to Pakistan. The claims made by India with respect to Kashmir would be convincingly belied and would bear out the absolute need for a plebiscite. If, moreover, India undertook a state-wide suppression of revolt, civil rebellion could develop into civil war and outside intervention might become necessary, perhaps through the United Nations. In that case, the threat of a Soviet veto would be diminished considerably. Thus, in brief, a general uprising in Jammu

---

[3] I have referred to this in my article on the Indo-Pakistan communal problem already mentioned. See Ch. 8, fn. 2.

[4] The Indian Government has always complained of this kind of intervention in Kashmir by Pakistan. It would be surprising if it were otherwise. It is obvious that the situation in the sub-continent being what it is, intelligence work and subversive operations, one country against the other, could not be simpler. (See also *Raiders in Kashmir* by the former Major-General Akbar Khan (Karachi, 1970).)

and Kashmir offered highly promising possibilities for Pakistan.⁵

This theory depended on two assumptions. The first was that the Kashmiris would rise. The second was that Pakistan could, secretly and surreptitiously, stimulate and extend the uprising so that it would grow and spread. To this was linked the question of what action India might take against Pakistan if and when the presence of Pakistani agents or military formations became known. It would be necessary to train and prepare groups of men who could infiltrate and carry out the tasks of creating confusion, assist the rebels and carry the Pakistan message. With this object in view, military units were trained under the code-name *Force Gibraltar* at Murree in West Pakistan. Here, in July 1965, Ayub Khan addressed the officers of these formations and explained to them the tasks they would be required to perform.

Whatever assessment Ayub Khan and his advisers made of the probable or possible Indian reaction, it must have been evident to them that the greater the success of their plan, the more trenchantly might India react to it. What does not seem to have been seriously considered by them is the possibility that India might extend the operations in Kashmir relative to the success achieved by Pakistan. If this idea did occur, either Ayub Khan and his advisers discounted it altogether, or concluded that India would hesitate long before extending the area of conflict. In any case, they decided to risk it. Both during and after the September hostilities, Ayub Khan as well as the then Commander-in-Chief of the Pakistan Army, General Mohamed Musa, claimed that India's plans were known to Pakistan's General Staff before hostilities began in September 1965. This does not necessarily mean that they knew, earlier in the year, India's intended D-day and H-hour, but it does

⁵ Little has been published, in Pakistan, on these matters, although the truth is emerging bit by bit. The information contained in this chapter owes much to the Security Council debates which followed the September 1965 operations. For this reason, much must be attributed to Indian sources, but the information given at the Security Council is probably accurate, although Pakistan never conceded it. The reason for using the code-name *Gibraltar* is that this word is a corruption of Jebel (mountain) Tariq. Tariq was a famous Arab general. He crossed from North Africa into Spain and then burned his boats so that no retreat was possible for his force. Tariq, as he is usually known, is a great figure in the military annals of Islam.

indicate that they knew what India would do in certain eventualities.

At the beginning of August 1965 it became clear to the world that the situation in Kashmir was no longer normal. Unusual military activity was going on, including Indian operations in the Kargil area, in Azad Kashmir. It appeared that India considered that the Srinagar-Leh road, linking India to Ladakh, was threatened and had acted accordingly. The Secretary-General of the United Nations addressed a request to both countries to cease operations across the cease-fire line, a request which met with a negligible response from both. Military manœuvres continued on both sides, all of which were reported by the United Nations observers stationed there. On 9 August, it became known that a Revolutionary Council had been set up in Jammu and Kashmir[6] and on the following day this Council 'took over' by an announcement made from its secret radio station, *Sada-i-Kashmir*.[7]

In the ensuing days, disturbances broke out in Srinagar and Sheikh Tariq Abdullah, son of Sheikh Abdullah, then residing in London, wrote to the British newspapers claiming that the Kashmiri people had risen in order to free themselves. Rioting and civil commotion intensified and by the end of August the Indian Government admitted that its Army and police had sustained 153 deaths and that about 100 civilians had been killed. Two days later it became known that Azad Kashmir forces, supported by units of the Pakistan Army, had crossed the cease-fire line and were operating in Jammu and Kashmir against Indian troops.[8]

The situation speedily mounted to a crisis. Progress made by the attackers was considerable and rapid. In a very few days they had driven their way down to Akhnur and Chhamb, creating the serious threat of a break-out into the Punjab plain, thus building up the very situation about which Jawaharlal Nehru had once warned Liaqat Ali Khan. There was, as every strategist on both sides knew, a point at which India would be

[6] *D*, 9 August 1965.
[7] *D*, 10 August 1965. *Sada-i-Kashmir* means 'The Voice of Kashmir'. This threadbare dodge was a mistake on the part of Pakistan, on which country suspicion instantly fastened. The station was probably located in Murree or Rawalpindi.
[8] *D*, 31 August 1965.

compelled, in order to relieve these dangerously threatening pressures, to move against the boundary that divided the two Punjabs. That moment, in the opinion of the Indian General Staff, had evidently arrived, for on the morning of 6 September Ayub Khan announced to his countrymen by radio that Indian troops had advanced towards Lahore and had started to shell its outskirts.

I do not propose to attempt any narration of the hostilities which lasted until 22 September 1965, a period of seventeen days.[9] Both countries have been extremely secretive about them and while the fighting was in progress everything possible was done to deny foreign observers any chance of witnessing it. No official history of the operations has been produced by either side and it is improbable that any will ever appear. In the remarks which follow, I am less concerned with the course of the battle than with reasons for military and political actions, their consequences and implications.[10]

As in all armed conflict, the first casualty was truth. On both sides propaganda, accusation, and counter-accusation rose swiftly in pitch and exaggeration. In Pakistan the people responded strongly to the notion that at last India had set out to do what it had always desired, namely to destroy Pakistan and erase the partition boundaries from the map. Emotion, strongly fortified by bold claims of immense destruction inflicted on Indian forces, vastly superior in number but not in courage or fighting ability, swept the country. It was noted that India was issuing misleading explanations of the events that led up to the fighting and totally false reports of the course of the conflict itself. None other than the Prime Minister, Lal Bahadur Shastri, announced the fall of Lahore in the Lok Sabha.[11] Not only this. All-India Radio actually broadcast the statement that Pakistan's Foreign Minister, Zulfikar Ali Bhutto, was an Indian national. Amused or indignant, Pakistanis immediately pointed to this as positive proof of the reckless mendacity of Indian propaganda. The then Pakistan Government maintained

---

[9] India considers that its engagement with Pakistan began on 1 September and treats the hostilities as involving a period of twenty-two days.

[10] See Appendix C, p. 307, for an estimate of the forces at the disposal of India and Pakistan at the commencement of hostilities.

[11] Also broadcast by the B.B.C. on the strength of a statement issued by the Indian High Commission in London.

an attitude of silent contempt towards this impudent allegation (though such is the mutability of human affairs that, two years later, the same Government was saying the same thing about the same man).[12]

The fighting was determined and bitter but as to the generalship and state of training of the troops, misgiving was expressed by military attachés accredited to Pakistan and India. It is known that on the Pakistan side one general officer commanding on the Sialkot sector was removed summarily for incompetence, and at Khem Kharan Pakistan's armour was badly shot up. It is also known that on the Indian side the Army was afterwards considerably reorganized mostly among the ranks of brigadier and lieutenant-colonel. Of civilian officials posted in the areas where hostilities were in progress at least one Pakistani officer in the Sialkot sector appears to have abandoned his post at the approach of the Indian troops. On these matters there has been much reticence, particularly in Pakistan, and although a disinclination to wash this kind of dirty linen in public is understandable, it is always better to bring ugly truths to the surface.

When the cease-fire came into effect, Pakistan claimed to be in occupation of 1,616 square miles of Indian territory, but admittedly this included about 1,200 square miles of real estate in Rajasthan whose occupation looked good on the map and boosted morale, but was otherwise a waste of effort. The other areas occupied by Pakistan comprised:

340 square miles in the Chhamb area (Jammu and Kashmir)
 36 square miles in the Khem Kharan area (Punjab, India)
 46 square miles in the Fazilka area (Punjab, India)

India claimed to be in occupation of 740 square miles of Pakistani territory which included its foothold in the Sialkot sector. The total area was made up of:

180 square miles in the Sialkot area
140 square miles in the Lahore area
150 square miles in the Sind area
230 square miles in the Uri-Poonch area (Azad Kashmir)
 20 square miles in the Tithwal area (Azad Kashmir)
 20 square miles in the Kargil area (Azad Kashmir)

[12] This is no idle gibe. The action of Ayub Khan's Government in 1967 in this matter had material consequences, as will be seen in Appendix E, p. 313.

On the question of losses in men and material inflicted and sustained the two countries naturally had very different statements to make. Neither side has published its losses in material, but the Indian Government in November 1965 published its casualties in personnel from 6 September 1965 to 5 November 1965 and, in this way, masked to some extent the losses between 6 and 22 September. The losses as stated by the Indian Government were as follows:

Killed	2,212
Wounded	7,636
Missing	1,500

The Pakistan Government challenged these figures and claimed that the loss in men sustained by India were very much more than this. However, it made no precise statement and, significantly, has abstained from publishing official figures for its own losses. Later, in a Lok Sabha session, Mr. Frank Anthony, a member of the Indian Parliament, said that the Indian Government had published false figures concerning Indian casualties and that on the Lahore sector alone, the Indian Army had losses exceeding 400 officers and 10,000 men killed or wounded. In Pakistan, not surprisingly, this statement has been seized upon as evidence that supports Pakistan's claims to have inflicted greater losses than India has admitted, but on what basis Frank Anthony made his statement is not clear. In any case, the attitude of the Pakistan Government continues to be vague, and as late as 6 September 1969, in a Defence Day article, General Mohamed Musa, on the subject of comparative casualties in September 1965, could only aver: 'We reckoned six to one,' a statement which simply does not satisfy.

The only solid evidence on which both sides concur relates to prisoners of war. In December 1965 370 gift parcels for Indian prisoners in Pakistan and 360 gift parcels for Pakistani prisoners in India were exchanged through the Red Cross.[13] On 3 February 1966 there was an exchange. India sent back 15 Officers, 12 Junior Commissioned Officers and 525 Other Ranks. Pakistan returned 22 Officers, 20 Junior Commissioned Officers and 541 Other Ranks. On 11 February India returned 163 prisoners to Pakistan and on 24 February Pakistan returned

[13] *D*, 10 December 1965.

288 Indians, including 14 policemen, while India sent back 21 Pakistani prisoners. The only other published exchange was that of pilots shot down. Pakistan returned seven Indian pilots and India returned three Pakistani pilots. This could be taken to show that in the air battle Pakistan had the better of it in a ratio exceeding two to one, but the figures involved seem too slender to justify a firm conclusion to that effect. They do, however, throw some light on the probable number of aircraft lost by either side.

Before the Indian Government published its casualty figures, the Institute of Strategic Studies, London, had published an estimate of losses in men and material sustained by each of the belligerents as follows:

Pakistan
  Army: Casualties, 3,000–5,000 men. Over 250 tanks.
  Navy: Nil.
  Air Force: Up to 50 aircraft.
India
  Army: Casualties, 4,000–6,000 men. Up to 300 tanks.
  Navy: Nil.
  Air Force: About 50 aircraft.

To this I may add another estimate of losses, with respect to Pakistan only, prepared by an authoritative, non-Pakistani source whose anonymity I am obliged to respect. This states:

  Army: Casualties in men: 3,500 plus. Tanks 108 plus.
  Navy: Nil.
  Air Force: 21 aircraft, 20–30 personnel.

As for losses in men, therefore, from the confirmed data relating to prisoners of war, and if one bears in mind that in the Rann affair India's published casualties were confirmed by similar data, it could be inferred that India has probably stated its casualties for September 1965 correctly. In the September hostilities as a whole, losses in men and weaponry sustained by each side were probably quite close, with the edge in favour of Pakistan.[14]

---

[14] Claims made by both sides with respect to losses inflicted were undoubtedly exaggerated. As to their respective claims regarding enemy aircraft destroyed, grave doubt was cast on their magnitude by Charles Douglas-Home, Defence Correspondent of *The Times*, London, in a B.B.C. interview on 9 February

As to the tactical result on the battlefield, the speed of Pakistan's advance in Kashmir was striking. It may be—and on this point I am unable to offer a firm opinion—that the lie of the land and the communications favour an advance from the west, but however this may be, it has always appeared that in the Kashmir terrain, Indian troops have never been comfortable when engaged with Pakistani forces. This point has some bearing on those factors which led Ayub Khan into the Kashmir adventure, since he could look forward with confidence to military success there. To all these matters we shall return.

What is more important just now is the question of the strategic advantage and where it lay when the cease-fire sounded. On this vital point there can be no doubt that India got the better of it, and this very assertion raises the question of India's claim to have entered or captured Lahore.

Having been made to look rather foolish over this, India has since been at great pains to establish the point that it did not want or aim to capture Lahore, and would have regarded its capture as an unnecessary military liability. All this is acceptable in the sense that, as a means of relieving pressures in Kashmir and preventing a break-out into the Punjab plain, the capture of Lahore was not necessary. Once the Lahore front was opened, pressure in Kashmir was bound to be reduced and so long as India could keep the Pakistan Army engaged on other fronts, its purposes were bound to be served. Only two further possibilities could arise. The first, and more likely, was intervention by the United Nations backed by the Great Powers and the second was an extension of hostilities, with the chance that other countries would come in, thus complicating everything.

1968. Such overstatements are common and perhaps unavoidable. The case of R.A.F. claims during the Battle of Britain in 1940, is well known. Rear-Admiral S. E. Morison, in his history of the *United States Naval Operations during World War II*, Vol. VI, p. 288, cites the instance of General Kenney, who, after an air attack on the Japanese at Rabaul, claimed '85 planes definitely destroyed and 23 probables', and that in twelve minutes his attack had 'destroyed or damaged 114,000 tons of shipping'. The actual score was 20 planes destroyed, two small Marus, totalling 4,600 tons and a 500 ton minesweeper sunk, and doubtless some others damaged. For their part, the Japanese, 'out-Kenneyed Kenney' by claiming 22 B-25s and 79 P-58s as 'sure kills'. I spare General Kenney a repetition of Admiral Morison's mordant comment since the General was by no means alone. Here, it may be added that Pakistan also claimed to have sunk an Indian destroyer by submarine attack, but this claim has been tacitly abandoned.

This view has its support both in India and in Pakistan from those well qualified to comment. Mr. K. Subramanyam, in the authoritative Indian monthly *Seminar*, speaks correctly of India's limited objectives when advancing on the Lahore front and describes it as 'strategic bargaining' by India.[15] Yet it is worth noting that Mr. Subramanyam does not, in definite terms, ascribe this policy to the wisdom of the Indian Government and its military advisers. While the desired result was achieved, it appears doubtful to Mr. Subramanyam whether it was *intended*. Something like this could be said, perhaps, about many things done by governments which turn out well.

This is, of course, an Indian opinion and we should consider what Mr. Zulfikar Ali Bhutto has to say, bearing in mind his intimate association in Pakistan with these events. Deploring what he considers inadequate military expenditure by Pakistan prior to 1965, he goes on to add, 'One or two more divisions might have made the decisive difference between victory and defeat.'[16]

It cannot for one moment be supposed that Mr. Bhutto believes Pakistan's armed forces were defeated in the field, and his meaning can only be that a shortage of divisions with which to overcome Indian pressures at Sialkot, Lahore and further south, made it impossible to prevent India from securing its strategic object. On this issue he may well be right and it is certain that Pakistan was in no position to prevent India from securing this advantage whenever it sought to do so.

Indeed, the longer one considers Ayub Khan's choice of action over Kashmir in 1965 and his execution of that choice it becomes increasingly difficult to resist the conclusion that he gambled and lost. It must be remembered that the wager did not depend upon the answer to a simple question involving the possibility that India might advance against the international boundary in the Punjab, vital as that question was. We have said nothing yet of what Afghanistan might have done in such an eventuality, for it seems probable that had India broken into

[15] M. K. Subramanyam, 'The Defence Effort', *Seminar*, New Delhi, No. 110, October 1968. The reference to 'strategic bargaining' is reminiscent of von Clausewitz's well-known dictum: 'War is nothing other than the continuation of policy by other means.'
[16] Bhutto, op. cit., p. 98.

Lahore, fanning north, south and west, Afghanistan would have been in Peshawar first. But in that case pressures might then have been put on Afghanistan not to extend the conflict and add further complications to its international nature. This is possible, but what is very certain is the chance that Pakistan might have found itself fighting on two fronts.[17]

All that has been said so far is tantamount to an assertion that the hostilities in September 1965 sprang out of a situation for whose creation Ayub Khan and his closer advisers were responsible. At this point, it is worth summarizing the reasons which seem to have influenced Ayub Khan in planning for the creation of unrest in Kashmir, leading to an invasion with a view to acquisition. These seem to me to be as follows:

(a) He had every reason to suppose that such a policy would have the approval of Pakistan, and in particular of West Pakistan. His convincing victory in the presidential election of January 1965 appeared to have armed him with a clear mandate.
(b) The creation of the China-Indonesia-Pakistan Axis had involved India in a triangular containment.
(c) The poor performance of India's troops against China in 1962, and a belief that the short hostilities in the Rann of Cutch had demonstrated a definite superiority in Pakistan's troops over those of India.
(d) His extensive tours of foreign countries during the months preceding September 1965 had enabled him to present Pakistan's case on Kashmir and, perhaps, to discover a measure of sympathy. In particular, he was encouraged by China.[18]
(e) The failure of his talks with Sheikh Abdullah and the subsequent application of Articles 356 and 357 of the Indian Constitution to Kashmir, led to the conclusion that the issue could no longer be settled by negotiation and that if Sheikh Abdullah had his way the State would never accede to Pakistan at all.

---

[17] In January 1966, when explaining his Tashkent policy to a privately conducted meeting of businessmen in Karachi, Ayub Khan said that one reason for calling off the fight was that Afghanistan was preparing to attack.
[18] It must be explained that China's complicity in this respect is strongly asserted by India.

(f) The Hazratbal incident in Srinagar and the demonstrations in favour of Sheikh Abdullah against the Indian Government proved that the Kashmiris were far from being a cowed people and would rise against their Indian oppressors if encouraged or helped. In this belief he was no doubt fortified by certain Kashmiri leaders who later were to participate in the 'Provisional Government'.

(g) A belief that all the circumstances, including the respective past performances of Pakistani and Indian troops in Kashmir, favoured the possibility of a swift *fait accompli*.

(h) A belief that irrespective of the military pressures which Pakistan might exert in the territory of Jammu and Kashmir, the Indian Government would not, in order to relieve these pressures, undertake the various risks involved in an advance across the international boundary that divided India and Pakistan in the Punjab or elsewhere.

The conclusion to which these views lead, namely Ayub Khan's decision to take the initiative in Kashmir, is supported by some collateral evidence. Air Marshal Asghar Khan who, at the time with which we are presently concerned, was Commander-in-Chief of the Pakistan Air Force and must have been privy to much that was going on in connexion with the development of Ayub Khan's Kashmir policy, has stated that never again should it be possible for one man to lead the country into war. This statement was made four years later, when the Air Marshal had retired from the service, had entered political life and was bitterly opposed to Ayub Khan.[19] There is, no doubt, an element of ambiguity in the statement, but it is

[19] So far as I am aware, this statement did not appear in Pakistan's English language newspapers, but only in the vernacular press. It is worth noting that in an election speech made on the third anniversary of the Indian attack on the Lahore front, Zulfikar Ali Bhutto said that he was ready to own to the charge that he had engineered war in September 1965 and compared himself with Mohamed Ali Jinnah who had agreed to the entry of the Pathan tribesmen into Kashmir. The speech was made at the village of Burki, near the Indo-Pakistan border where fighting had taken place. Air Marshal Nur Khan refuted Bhutto's claim. He said: 'Mr. Bhutto is wrong when he says he wanted war with India. It is we who wanted war.' By 'we', he meant the officers of the armed forces. *D*, 22 September 1970. It seemed as if a point might have been reached when every prominent man in Pakistan was about to claim the merit of having organized war with India.

difficult to know what is meant if not the September hostilities. Other confirmatory, collateral evidence has appeared from time to time, notably in an article by a Pakistani journalist, Askar Ali Shah, who is very well informed on Kashmir affairs.[20] Finally, there was the reference to an anticipated national emergency in August 1965 at a session of the Pakistan Labour Conference, when it was suggested that there should be a truce between employers and workers leading to a suspension of strikes and lockouts.

In forming this assessment of Ayub Khan's intentions, no account has been taken of the various sabre-rattling, blood-curdling statements made at various times by public men on both sides. These irresponsible outbursts can be used to prove anything and they are, for that reason, worthless. No doubt they can be treated as symptomatic, but this apart they serve only to provide excellent material for undiscriminating publicists in both countries.

If the cogency of the foregoing reasoning be granted, it follows that on one major issue Ayub Khan's judgement was sound and on two, unsound. He was right in thinking that the Pakistan Army could secure a quick break-through in Kashmir. He was wrong in thinking that in Kashmir there would be a general rising and in view of the later consequences Ayub Khan's adventure in Kashmir has been described as his Bay of Pigs. He was wrong also in the belief that India would hesitate before extending the conflict in order to frustrate Pakistan's Kashmir operations.

[20] *PO*, 1 February 1969. This quotation comes from Askar Ali Shah's series of articles entitled *The Punjab Scene* which have a great deal to do with the upsurge that had started against Ayub Khan. The following is a fairly representative passage. 'The saga of sustained tension with India—Mr. Bhutto's own almost pathological hatred of that country had played no mean part in this—had culminated in flash, commando-type raids in Indian-held Kashmir which the Indians blamed on large-scale and systematic infiltration from our side during August 1965. To counter this activity, the Indian Command decided to cut the routes that . . . kept it [i.e. the infiltration] fed. . . . We countered the Indian action by attacking in the Chamb-Jaurian sector where we could put our superiority in armour to purpose and the Indians . . . decided on creating a powerful diversion by attacking in the Lahore sector.'

The author does not, of course, say that the infiltrators were Pakistani regular troops. They could have been Azad Kashmiris, but he was writing at a time when it was still not possible to be over-explicit in such matters.

THE POLITICAL IMPLICATIONS OF SEPTEMBER 1965

The cease-fire took place at 3 a.m. on 23 September 1965, both sides having intimated their agreement on the previous day. On the evening of 22 September Ayub Khan gave a broadcast address in which he expressed the nation's gratitude to China, Indonesia, Iran, Turkey, Saudi Arabia, Jordan, and Syria, in that order. He insisted that India had been guilty of 'blatant and unprovoked aggression' which had a 'history of eighteen years behind it'. He said: 'We have informed the Security Council that the United Nations are faced with a grave responsibility and are on trial. If they wish to bring about lasting peace in this area, they must address themselves urgently to the need of evolving an honourable solution of the Kashmir dispute. If they fail in this, this continent will be engulfed in a much wider conflict.'

The reasons which led him to give public thanks to the countries named were fairly well known. In the case of China, it was, to use his words, for their 'moral support' which earned Pakistan's gratitude. The form this took was that of a three-day ultimatum to India which India rejected but in conciliatory terms, and suggesting a Sino-Indian examination of all matters in dispute. On 19 September China extended the ultimatum by three more days and this spectacle of two big countries sparring at a safe distance evoked a certain amount of sardonic comment, notably by *The Economist* of 25 September 1965, in an article entitled 'Thanks for Muffing It'. The possibility that China might intervene undoubtedly existed, and at a very early stage of the hostilities the United States warned China that such a course would be dangerous. In 1966 Zulfikar Ali Bhutto informed the National Assembly that, in Warsaw, China's diplomatic representatives had informed their American counterparts that if India invaded East Pakistan China would enter the war.[21] In Pakistan it was believed that this warning had caused so much consternation in the United States that U Thant was required to proceed at once to the sub-continent and arrange a cease-fire.

---

[21] *NAD*, 15 March 1966. The effect in East Pakistan was not quite what was intended. There, the inference was drawn that *only* China could be relied upon to help defend the integrity of East Pakistan.

Indonesia, as I have already mentioned, sent its Navy into the Bay of Bengal, and some of its ships, believed to be submarines, to Karachi, where for some weeks Indonesian naval officers and ratings were to be seen. The other countries named lent material help in various ways and the aircraft of Pakistan International Airlines were garaged each night at Teheran. Indeed, so far as concerns the sinews of war, expressed in terms of weapons and ammunition, these countries did most to help Pakistan.

But before the cease-fire, and before Ayub Khan's acknowledgement of Pakistan's indebtedness to the friends he named, other events of great political significance had already occurred. One, though of no great weight, was the opportunity, seized by Malaysia, at that time a member of the Security Council, to pay off an obligation laid upon it at the Commonwealth Conference three months before, when Pakistan secured the omission of all reference to Indonesian aggression from the final communiqué. The Malaysian representative at the Security Council, a Hindu named Ramani, said to have been born in India, attacked Pakistan in terms of unpardonable virulence. No doubt he had been instructed to oppose the Pakistan case, but there is equally no doubt that his intemperate language was quite inappropriate to the purposes and intentions of the Security Council. For this reason, it made no effect and was injurious to Malaysia and its point of view.

In Pakistan this incident aroused much anger and relations with Malaysia were later broken off, though subsequently resumed. However, Zulfikar Ali Bhutto, for his part, never forgave Malaysia and, as late as 1969, he was describing Tengku Rahman as a tool of imperialism.[22] The affair, in itself, is of little importance, but it is an interesting instance of the way in which the snatching of apparent advantages, without reference to their broader implications and possible consequences, may earn a speedy and undesired requital.

In describing this incident as insubstantial, the point arises whether it is worth examining the tedious detail of the Security Council proceedings, which resulted in nothing. Pakistan's case started badly having been entrusted to its Law Minister S. M. Zafar, a mild-mannered young man prominent at the

[22] *D*, 30 August 1969.

Lahore Bar but with no previous experience whatsoever in conducting affairs before the Security Council. His performance made it transparently clear that a more forceful and experienced personality was immediately needed and the choice fell, not unnaturally, upon the Foreign Minister, Zulfikar Ali Bhutto.

It was strange that he was not initially sent to these vital meetings, but to those who commented upon this at the time, it was explained that he had more important things to do at home. What, in the circumstances, could have been more important than for the Foreign Minister to be present at the Security Council when his country's vital interests were under discussion, it is difficult to imagine. There is an air of unpleasant intrigue about the whole business and it was said that the Governor of West Pakistan, the late Nawab of Kalabagh, who did not like Bhutto and who favoured S. M. Zafar, was responsible for persuading Ayub Khan to agree to this arrangement. This may or may not be so, but S. M. Zafar was certainly an unfortunate choice. During his campaign speeches early in 1970 Bhutto indicated that he had not been sent because of American pressure and there is no doubt that top-level American opinion was adverse to him. If it be true that Kalabagh was responsible for persuading Ayub Khan to send Zafar, it may well be that Kalabagh used this very argument.

Eventually Bhutto did go, but whether he can be said to have achieved any more is difficult to decide, so fruitless was it all. Bhutto certainly spoke with very much more vigour, slapping the table and actually being accused of having abused the Indian people in the course of his address to the Council. His speech was described by a B.B.C. correspondent as one of the best ever heard at the Security Council, and if this be so, then the conclusion must be that the standard of oratory which prevails before that august body is hardly distinguished.[23] Bhutto's material was highly charged with emotional content; his threat that Pakistan would leave the United Nations if the Kashmir question were not solved by means of a self-executing agreement, was expressed so vaguely as to constitute no threat

---

[23] I listened to a broadcast of the tape-transcript. Mr. Bhutto's disadvantage is that although he is an eloquent and forceful speaker, the timbre of his voice tends to become shrill as his language acquires more emphasis or emotion.

at all. If, indeed, he made an impact, it sprang from the recognition of an evident sincerity, even if the basis of his argument was not always well-advised.

Meanwhile, the atmosphere in which the cease-fire was observed gave cause for much alarm. Under the terms of the arrangement, each side continued in battle positions until the arrival of United Nations Observers who would supervise the orderly withdrawal of both sides to their respective territories. In each country there was anger and resentment. Inflamed feeling, which the tortuous proceedings at the Security Council did nothing to assuage, threatened to bring about a resumption of fighting.

This, perhaps, was more the case in Pakistan, where the strongly-held conviction prevailed that India had irresponsibly launched a destructive attack across the Punjab boundary, only to be thrown back with heavy losses by Pakistan's intrepid Air Force and Army. It was firmly believed that Pakistan's armed forces had administered a severe drubbing to the Indians and that if the fighting had gone on for a few days more, the Indian forces would have retreated in total rout, with not another Indian aircraft able to take to the skies. It was for these very reasons that, with accumulating rumours of a cease-fire, crowds gathered in Karachi on 21 September, proceeding first to the Chinese Embassy, there to felicitate that country on its defiant stand in the face of American threats. They moved on to the American Embassy where the flag was hauled down by the mob and windows were broken by stone-throwing. A mile or so away the library of the United States Information Service was set on fire and gutted. The reading-room of the British Information Services, as befitted its subordinate position in the Anglo-American alliance, got off rather more lightly.

The tone of the Security Council proceedings was characteristic of most, if not all, debate on the Kashmir question. The parties to the dispute came with different premises, to which they resolutely adhered. The Indians said that, in conformity with the Security Council resolution, Pakistan must vacate Azad Kashmir first. Thereafter, the question of the plebiscite could be considered. Pakistan said that all this was out of date, technical and unsatisfactory, in that it offered no assurance that India would not then occupy Azad Kashmir and retain its grip on the entire State for all time. All that was necessary, according to Pakistan, was a plebiscite by the Kashmiris to decide what they themselves wanted to do with their future. This simple summary is, of course, embroidered by a thousand and one complications. Under the circumstances it is clear that the argument can, and may, continue interminably and it was evident that, as the last weeks of 1965 wore on, this was precisely what was happening.

Not until 6 December 1965 did General Marambio, U Thant's representative, arrive in Pakistan to arrange troop withdrawals, by which time Ayub Khan and Lal Bahadur Shastri had agreed to meet at Tashkent in the Soviet Union. It was widely said, at the time,[24] that in securing an agreement to a meeting the Soviet Government scored a notable diplomatic victory. But in relinquishing this particular negotiation to the Soviet Government, President Johnson was distinctly shrewd. It may be true that the conference at Tashkent underlined the Soviet presence in the sub-continent, added something to its stature as a world power and, perhaps, was intended also to increase Soviet influence in Pakistan to offset that of China. At the same time, it also placed upon the Soviet Union a kind of responsibility which, in all probability, it could never discharge satisfactorily. It led to an involvement in complications of policy that could easily become an embarrassment and it made necessary a re-appraisal of Soviet relations with, and attitude towards, India. Events since 1966 have certainly proved the substance of all this. Not only that. If there was one man at Tashkent who really needed a written agreement of some sort, signed by all concerned, for display to the world at large, that man was neither Ayub Khan nor Lal Bahadur Shastri. It was Kosygin.

On his way to the Tashkent talks, Ayub Khan paused at Kabul where he spent two days in meetings with King Zahir Shah. In Pakistan this was regarded as highly significant in view of the forthcoming Tashkent talks and in all probability Ayub Khan did explore Afghan intentions. However, the communiqué—issued after some delay—was vague and brief, conveying the impression that although there had been an exchange of views, nothing concrete had been achieved.

[24] E.g. by the *New York Times*, 7 December 1965.

The Tashkent meeting began with speeches by each of the three leaders and they were remarkable for their omission of any reference to Kashmir. Shastri was strong on renouncing war and the use of force. Ayub Khan emphasized the necessity of finding solutions for differences. Kosygin concentrated on what might be called *togetherness*. There were photographs of the usual three-way handshake, all participants smiling broadly. One pressman desired to know in what language Ayub Khan and Shastri conducted their talks and an Indian spokesman replied that the Pakistani President spoke in Urdu while the Indian Prime Minister spoke in Hindi, which diplomatic reply meant that they both spoke the same language.[25]

It is clear that during the five days' discussion both sides refused to yield any ground and until the last moment, rumour prevailed that no agreement had been reached and that, quite possibly, the three leaders would separate without even a communiqué being issued. It appears that Kosygin, well knowing how high can be the price of failure in the Soviet Union, insisted upon an agreement and his persuasions may have been reinforced by veiled threats.[26] But the people of Pakistan were little concerned with Kosygin's own political security and the announcement of the Tashkent Declaration surprised and dismayed them. The sudden death of Shastri in Tashkent a few hours after the Declaration was signed delayed the impact of Ayub Khan's apparent defeat and softened the expression of public resentment in Pakistan. As it was, the Government, and a well-tutored press, leant over backwards to prove that the Tashkent Declaration was a very satisfactory outcome, 'with Kashmir at the forefront'.[27]

This did not prevent public misgiving and protest, with disturbances in Lahore and Rawalpindi. In the latter city, the District Magistrate forbade demonstrations of any sort and proclaimed Section 144 of the Civil Procedure Code. Soon it

---

[25] Since Shastri was born in Allahabad, it is probable that his Urdu was more chaste than that of Ayub Khan.

[26] Harrison E. Salisbury (*The Siege of Leningrad*, London, Secker and Warburg, 1969, p. 579), writing of Stalin's political purge in Leningrad after World War II, says: 'The career of Aleksei Kosygin (later he became Premier of the Soviet Union), hung in the balance. For several years, no one, including himself, could say whether he would survive.'

[27] For the text of the Tashkent Declaration see Appendix J, p. 330.

became known that in Lahore three persons had been killed by police firing and that hundreds had been arrested. In Lyallpur there were riots and in Sialkot District Section 144 was also imposed. At 12.30 p.m. on 14 January 1966 Ayub Khan gave a special broadcast seeking to explain the background to the Tashkent Declaration and appealing for national unity. Zulfikar Ali Bhutto, disappointed and angry, went to his home town of Larkana and there, brooding over recent events, drafted and published a statement in which he said that the Tashkent Declaration was not an end in itself and that the slate would not be sponged clean until the people of Kashmir had exercised their right of self-determination. It was known even then that Bhutto had violently opposed the signing of the document and it was already being rumoured that he might leave the Government. His popularity increased, particularly among the students and the younger generation, and he was regarded as Pakistan's real champion against Indian aggression.

In order to understand the intensity of this feeling, it is necessary to realize that the people of Pakistan, especially those in the Punjabi-speaking areas of West Pakistan, held it as an article of faith that India had not the least intention of coming to a settlement over Kashmir; that the attack on Pakistan was simply the precursor to its destruction and that in the hostilities which followed that attack, the Pakistan Army and Air Force inflicted such destructive defeats on the Indian forces that they, the Pakistanis, were actually poised for the decisive advance. That Ayub Khan should, in such circumstances, have submitted tamely to the provisions of the Tashkent Declaration, appeared to them a miserable and quite unjustified surrender. Feeling against him was harsh, particularly in the armed forces and among those who had lost menfolk in the fighting.[28]

The injury caused to Ayub Khan's image by the Tashkent

---

[28] Resentment in the armed forces became explicit and some of those who dissented openly were punished. News of this was kept secret, but in 1969 it became known that fourteen officers (possibly petty officers) of the Pakistan Navy had been sentenced to life imprisonment in consequence of opposition to the Tashkent Declaration. This appeared in *D*, 23 March 1969, when certain political leaders of Sialkot appealed for the release of these men in view of the withdrawal of the Agartala Conspiracy Case in East Pakistan. It may be added that after the Tashkent Declaration was signed there were processions of bereaved mothers and wives in Lahore. Was it for this, they demanded to know, that they had sacrificed sons and husbands?

Declaration cannot be doubted. He was obliged to undertake a special, countrywide campaign in order to explain it, although it is unlikely that he ever gave the real reasons for signing it. Had it been true that the Pakistan Army was on the brink of a crushing advance into India, it would have been a simple matter for him to have carried on the parleys with U Thant until that defeat had been inflicted, but on the Punjab front, the war was settling down to a life-consuming process of attrition and it is possible that Pakistan was running short of ammunition and jet fuel. Zulfikar Ali Bhutto, who must have known a good deal of the actual situation even if his military judgement was untutored, was nevertheless opposed to the Tashkent Declaration, and a few months later he quarrelled with Ayub Khan over it and left the Government. Bhutto has always claimed since that the whole truth about Tashkent has never been stated and, at various times he has threatened to expose everything. Whether this relates to the military situation and to the possibility of carrying on the fight with prospects of success, or to the course of the negotiations themselves, has never been made clear, and will probably not be made clear unless and until Bhutto speaks.[29]

Ayub Khan was able to weather the storm of indignation that Tashkent brewed. He was still, in those days, very much master of the political situation and was able, through his propaganda machine, to preach the 'spirit of Tashkent'.[30] In East Pakistan his cause was furthered in this respect by Sheikh Mujibur Rahman who, for purposes of his own, supported the

[29] The *Sunday Telegraph*, London, 2 March 1969, published a report from its correspondent, Harold Sieve, then in Rawalpindi, that according to a very reliable source the Tashkent Declaration had a secret protocol preserving the *status quo* in Kashmir. This appeared to favour Zulfikar Ali Bhutto, then pursuing his campaign against Ayub Khan and the Pakistan Government issued a denial. For Bhutto, this denial meant little but the Soviet agency, Tass, also published a denial which placed Bhutto in difficulty because although he might contradict Ayub Khan's Government, he was unlikely to contradict Tass, and in fact he remained silent. This seems to have been a case of shrewd exploitation, on behalf of Ayub Khan, of a foreign correspondent because Bhutto disclosed nothing at the time and has disclosed nothing since. It has been suggested that what Bhutto has to say relates to Ayub Khan's personal conduct of the Tashkent negotiations and his undue readiness to capitulate on the terms of the Declaration.

[30] This included, in February 1966, banning the film *From Russia With Love*. Since this film had already enjoyed two prolonged runs in Pakistan, it cannot be said that James Bond's admirers were unduly deprived.

Tashkent Declaration. Nevertheless, opposition was not quietened easily. Schools and colleges were closed, several hundred students and others were arrested, including five opposition leaders. Speeches made at the All-Pakistan National Conference, an organization opposed to Ayub Khan, in its February 1966 session, were forbidden publication by the West Pakistan provincial Government. This evoked so much adverse comment[31] that the provincial Law Minister was obliged to attempt an explanation for this decision, but it was evident that anything critical of the Tashkent Declaration was the object of censorship.

It cannot be said that the spirit of Tashkent prevailed for long. Within three months, exchanges between Pakistan and India grew in acerbity. In particular, India was accused of holding on to three posts in Sialkot in clear breach of the Tashkent agreement, and the newspapers in Pakistan continued to comment upon the sly methods of the Indian Government. In a long editorial on 27 March, *Dawn* discussed the 'Drift from Tashkent' and foreign observers commented to similar effect.

On 26 March, a Chinese delegation led by the President, Liu Shao-chi, visited Pakistan. The delegates were given a rapturous welcome in Rawalpindi and Lahore, but in his banquet speech Liu Shao-chi's reference to Kashmir had a faint nuance of reserve and the final communiqué, issued on his departure, added nothing to China's earlier statements on the Kashmir question. Nevertheless, this visit seemed to encourage Ayub Khan and his broadcast on 1 April 1966 referred in firm language to India and the Tashkent Declaration.

It was not very long before the 'spirit of Tashkent' had become very small beer indeed and its place in Indo-Pakistan relations became purely historical. All the same, in any study of Pakistan's affairs, it cannot be lightly dismissed for it was one of the seeds of Ayub Khan's later destruction. It was the real and precipitating cause of his quarrel with Bhutto, one of the principal leaders in the movement resulting in Ayub Khan's fall from power and loss of office.

[31] The important Urdu newspaper *Jung*, 7 February 1966, contained an editorial highly critical of the provincial Government's action in this matter.

THE CONSEQUENCES OF SEPTEMBER 1965

In Pakistan, it was said that the Indian advance on the Punjab frontier inspired the Pakistani nation to discover itself. Certainly, a great wave of patriotism swept the country and there was no lack of readiness and will to fight.[32] All day Radio Pakistan broadcast patriotic songs, one of which included a musical rendering of the Sacred Creed—*La Illah Ha Il Allah, Muhammad al Rasul Allah*—sung to a very racy tune, and even if the country was united over no other issue, it was determined to resist India at any cost. In East Pakistan, the display of belligerence was not quite so intense, probably because it is impossible to experience the same sense of zeal when the fighting is a thousand miles away.

But because of the grave implications of the conflict, its most important consequence lay in the fact that it took place at all. The commitment of forces on both sides, including full divisions with armour and artillery, supported by air attack, made concrete the possibility of full-scale war between India and Pakistan. This kind of war had been talked about, even threatened, several times before, but it had always seemed as if the leaders on both sides were inhibited from the final decision to unleash their forces. However, if such inhibition ever existed, it was removed in September 1965. Fighting in Kashmir was one thing; brisk skirmishing in the Rann was another. But neither led to the specific conclusion that war on the scale of September 1965 was possible. Only the very fact of it could prove that.

Between the two countries, bad feeling crystallized into a sense of real enmity.[33] For Pakistan, India had finally and clearly emerged as an aggressor, bent on Pakistan's destruction. For India, Pakistan, led by Ayub Khan, had not only tried to wrest Kashmir by force of arms, but had forged links with China and would, when necessity or opportunity provided the occasion, collaborate with China in an assault on two, perhaps three, fronts.

In both countries spending on arms rose, although this was

[32] In Lahore crowds of students and young men, armed with shotguns, home-made pistols, staves, pitchforks, etc., advanced in the direction of the battlefield, and the authorities had a difficult job in restraining them.

[33] It is very close to the surface still. A mere mention of September 1965 is likely to evoke a very sharp response, whether from Indian or Pakistani.

more specifically the case in Pakistan, which was placed in the more difficult position by reason of the ban on arms supply instituted by the United States. At the same time the American Government announced the withdrawal of its Military Advisory Groups from the sub-continent. The loss of American resources struck Pakistan hard since India could still rely on the Soviet Union. Pakistan was obliged to turn to China which provided some MiG aircraft and, it is believed, about one hundred tanks as well as other ancillary equipment and small arms.

The American ban on arms supply accelerated the deterioration in relations between Pakistan and the United States and although Pakistan continued to be dependent on economic aid from America, relations from this time on were cool and Pakistani resentment towards the United States became bitter. It is this circumstance which has contributed much to the virtual abandonment, by Pakistan, of CENTO and SEATO.

The actual spending on arms since 1965, from data prepared by the Institute of Strategic Studies, illustrates well the financial impact of the war, although, if one bears in mind the rising Gross National Product in each country, the impact has been less than many might suppose. As to the cost of the hostilities themselves, Mr. Subramanyam, whose article in *Seminar* has already been quoted, gives figures to suggest that the cost to Pakistan was greater than to India and he appears to think that the continuing cost is relatively greater for Pakistan also. The annual expenditure, expressed quantitatively in millions of United States dollars, is as follows:

India				*Pakistan*			
Year	*Total*	*As % of GNP*	*As % of total Govt. Expenditure*	*Year*	*Total*	*As % of GNP*	*As % of total Govt. Expenditure*
1963–4	1,858	4·7	26	1963–4	255	3·2	18
1965–6	1,042	3·8	17	1965–6	295	3·1	19
1966–7	1,259	3·3	17	1966–7	473	3·6	19
1967	1,368	3·3	17	1967	468	3·6	19
1968	1,452	3·3	17	1968	514	3·6	19

The basis of estimating the annual expenditure on defence, adopted by the Institute, changed halfway through this period, but the pattern is evident.

Expressed as percentages of the Gross National Product, the Institute of Strategic Studies gives the following figures:

	1963–4	1965	1966	1967	1968
India	4·7	3·8	3·6	3·3	3·6
Pakistan	3·2	5·3	4·5	3·6	3·7

The noteworthy point about these groups of figures is the high expenditure by India in 1963–4, which could be interpreted as evidence of aggressive intentions towards Pakistan. The more likely explanation is that defence expenditure rose sharply by reason of the hostilities with China in 1962, the immediately preceding year.

In any case, these percentages are less than those which prevail among the Great Powers, particularly those in the United States (9·2 per cent in 1968) and the Soviet Union (9·3 per cent in 1968 but for declared defence expenditure only). Japan is a notable exception, where the figure is only 0·8 per cent, this will rise though as Japan's defence responsibilities grow.

In 1968, the expenditure on defence in India was U.S. $3·00 *per capita* and in Pakistan U.S. $5·00. These compare with Burma ($3), Indonesia ($2), Philippines ($3), Thailand ($4), Turkey ($14), Iran ($19), and U.A.R. ($22). It is, therefore, incorrect to suggest that both India and Pakistan have flung themselves headlong into expenditure on arms as a result of September 1965. Nevertheless, it is an unhappy fact that defence expenditure takes up about half the national budget in each country.

In considering all these figures, it is necessary to bear in mind that to some extent they are deceptive. For ease of comparison, all expenditures are converted into United States dollars on the basis of official rates of exchange. To the extent that countries buy arms abroad these rates can be treated as valid, because payment has to be made in foreign exchange. As regards internal defence expenditure, however, this is no longer the case since the purchasing power of the currency does not necessarily correspond to the value implied by the official exchange rate. For this purpose the free market value of the currency must be taken. This may not have much bearing on the issue of comparative defence expenditure as between India and Pakistan, but it does have a bearing on what each country is getting for the money it spends. Bearing in mind that in the free market both the Indian and the Pakistani rupees have always stood at heavy but varying discounts, it follows that the armed forces they are able to maintain do not correspond in unit cost.

In March 1966 the Indian Government conceded the partition of the Indian Punjab in order to create the Punjab Suba. This partition, so long resisted by Jawaharlal Nehru and those who succeeded him, was the price of Sikh loyalty during September 1965 and the promise of it had probably been extracted at that time. During the hostilities Pakistan tried, as best it could, to woo the Sikhs and, the circumstances being what they were, the Indian Government could scarcely have avoided yielding on an issue by which the Sikhs set so much store. It was yet another partition based on language and community, and it was one of the direct consequences of September 1965.

In Pakistan the conflict enabled Ayub Khan to declare an emergency under Article 30 of the Constitution and this armed him with many unusual powers of legislation by ordinance and also placed limitations on the exercise of the individual's fundamental rights as provided in the Constitution. This was too good an opportunity for Ayub Khan to miss and the emergency continued in Pakistan, year after year, until in 1969 he was compelled under intense public pressure to withdraw it.

The Kashmir issue went into cold storage. What other possibility existed it would be difficult to say and, for Pakistan it represents one of the most serious consequences to emerge from Ayub Khan's errors of judgement. Had he succeeded then, he would have become a popular hero, but he did not and failure invariably exacts its due price. He had gambled for high stakes in taking the country to war, and its negative outcome affected public morale in Pakistan. This is why Pakistan works so hard, particularly at the United Nations, to generate support which will make it possible to revive the Kashmir question effectively.[34]

As to the fighting itself, and the commentary that it provided on the competence of the armed forces and their higher command, one commentator remarked: '... western pressures and Russian mediation saved India and Pakistan from the extended humiliation of military inefficiency'.[35] This is a very severe judgement and it is not clear on the basis of what information the author has formed it. Unfortunately, there is very little information available about these operations. The *New York Times* of 12 October 1965, discussing the fighting in quite general terms, added: 'In the hands of the relatively uneducated Pakistani soldier, the highly complicated Patton tanks were virtually useless.' This could account for the shooting up of these tanks at Khem Kharan, but it could also be argued that the *New York Times* was seeking to exculpate the Patton tank at the expense of the Pakistani soldier's reputation.

Another interesting consequence is the number of small arms that went into unauthorized possession, especially among the Hur community of Sind, a sect which pays special devotion to the Pir of Pagaro. These bellicose men invaded Rajasthan, apparently bent on a private war of their own. The dangers and impropriety of such behaviour, since they were neither in uniform nor organized as soldiers, are obvious. It is certain that the Government of Pakistan did not encourage them, but it could not restrain them either, and the people of West Pakistan, unconscious of or ignoring the legal implications, received the news of the Hur entry in Rajasthan with gleeful satisfaction. The Hurs returned heavily armed, surrendering a good deal but keeping plenty for themselves. In both countries, the illegal possession of arms increased greatly because of the hostilities and much of this contraband armament was sold for profit. Much also fell into the hands of dissident groups with a disposition towards violence, and prompted perhaps by this knowledge, the Pakistani Martial Law Administration, in 1969,

[34] At Rawalpindi, on 9 March 1969, in the course of his political campaigning, Zulfikar Ali Bhutto said at a public meeting that he fought tooth and nail against the Tashkent Declaration and told the Indian delegates he would not discuss anything unless the Kashmir issue were also discussed. Thereafter, according to him, Ayub Khan took everything into his own hands. *PO*, 11 March 1969.
[35] Michael Edwardes, 'India, Pakistan and Nuclear Weapons', *International Affairs*, October 1967, p. 655.

required all persons in possession of firearms, legally or illegally, to deposit them with the police.

Both in India and in Pakistan fairly large numbers of people were detained for security reasons. In Pakistan it is highly significant that whereas the fighting was on the West Pakistan border, only 451 persons in that Province were detained, whereas in East Pakistan, where there was no fighting, 1,840 persons were detained.[36]

Ever since 1965 a generally militant attitude between the two countries has prevailed and it appears that a postal censorship has persisted, if this can be judged from the time it takes for a letter posted in one of them to be delivered in the other. It is notable that in West Pakistan the bridges over the Bombanwala–Ravi–Bedian Canal have not been fully reconstructed. This canal, flowing between Lahore and the Indo-Pakistan frontier, was dug after partition as a part of the newly organized irrigation system which partition rendered necessary. It was sited, also, to provide a military obstacle to any Indian attack and in September 1965 it certainly served this purpose. Without bridges, it forms a protective moat for Lahore and the adjacent countryside.

Lastly—and this is by no means the least of all the consequences of the September 1965 hostilities—the effect was to provide means by which the interest of the Soviet Union in the sub-continent increased and took on an important change of aspect.

[36] These persons were detained under the Defence of Pakistan Rules. The figures were given by the Parliamentary Secretary, Cabinet Secretariat, *NAD*, 22 June 1968.

to the Provinces and the division of the infrastructure between the two Provinces, placed much more executive power in the hands of the provincial Governments. But the question still remained to what extent this authority and this power could be used for economic and social growth. The fact that each provincial Government administered its own railway system, docks and harbours, development of water and power and of industry in the public sector, in no way ensured development and improvement in any of them and the same was just as true in the private sector. The Third Schedule of Ayub Khan's Constitution which set out those matters on which the Central Legislature had exclusive power to make laws included (as Item 6): 'National and economic planning and national economic co-ordination.' There was, furthermore, an Article 145 which provided for the constitution of a National Economic Council whose business it was to review the overall economic position of Pakistan and to formulate plans with respect to financial, commercial and economic policies. Thus, so far as growth and development were concerned, a great deal of power and overriding influence were retained at the Centre, despite the devolution of executive responsibility.

It is also true that Clause 4 of Article 145 stated that 'a primary object of the [National Economic] Council ... shall be to ensure that disparities between the two Provinces and between different areas within a Province, in relation to income *per capita* are removed ...', but it was felt in East Pakistan that prevailing circumstances were quite adverse to all such effort, however genuine. Of all the organizations set up to deal with development and growth, particularly from the point of view of financial resources and the allocation thereof, there was not one which maintained its Head Office in East Pakistan. These included the Pakistan Industrial Credit and Investment Corporation, the Investment Development Bank of Pakistan, the Housebuilding Finance Corporation, the Agricultural Development Bank of Pakistan and, later, the National Investment Trust Ltd. and the Investment Corporation of Pakistan. Why, it was asked, should *all* of these have their centres of gravity in the western Province and why should *all* be more immediately susceptible to West Pakistani influence?

The extent of this influence can be judged from the prominent place of West Pakistani personnel among Class I civil servants in the various ministries and departments of the Central Government. In 1966, the position was as follows:[2]

	East Pakistan %	West Pakistan %
President's Secretariat	19	81
President's personal section	nil	100
Commerce Ministry	36·4	63·6
Defence Ministry	8·4	91·6
Industries Divn.	25·6	74·4
National Resources Divn.	24·7	75·3
Rehabilitation and Works Divn.	17·4	82·6
Home and Kashmir Affairs Divn.	22·5	77·5
Education	33·3	66·7
Health, Labour and Social Welfare	19·0	81·0
Agriculture and Works	20·6	79·4
Foreign Ministry	22·2	77·8
Law and Parliamentary	35·0	65·0
Communications	17·8	82·2
Finance	24·4	75·6

The numerical distribution of all employees of the Central Government was:

East Pakistan		West Pakistan	
Gazetted	Non-gazetted	Gazetted	Non-gazetted
1,338	26,310	3,708	82,944

These, and other inequities, to which were added such charges as under-recruitment of East Pakistanis into the public services and, more particularly, into the Armed forces, had long been familiar topics and, by the time that Ayub Khan relinquished office in 1969, it was still maintained that nothing had been done to remove these reasonable causes of complaint. It was pointed out that the economic gap between the two Provinces was far from being closed, although the country's principal

[2] Information supplied by the Government in reply to a question in the National Assembly. *NAD*, 23 June 1966.

earner of foreign exchange since 1947 had always been East Pakistan. It was all very well for President Ayub Khan to boast of the rapid advance in the export of manufactured goods, thus vindicating his various policies in economic planning, but the value of exported jute goods from East Pakistan was greater than that of all other manufactured goods put together. It was probable that the total value of the raw jute and jute manufactures exported from East Pakistan was alone equal to about half of the country's export earnings. But did this money benefit East Pakistan? East Pakistanis did not think so.[3]

Much, if not all, of this was not new in 1962 and less so in 1969. Although the most important policy developments of the period stemmed from the Tashkent Declaration (January 1966) and the public reaction to it, the changing circumstances of political life, which started in the Province on the abrogation of Martial Law in June 1962 should be traced. But, in East Pakistan, it was significant that the disappearance of Martial Law was preceded by an event of great importance. Lieutenant-General Azam Khan had been replaced, in the month of May, by the appointment of Mr. Ghulam Faruque as Governor.

General Azam Khan was, with Ayub Khan, one of the military quadrumvirate which instituted Martial Law in 1958. His forceful personality earned for him a good deal of popularity buttressed, no doubt, by his own sense of public relations which gained him frequent appearances on the front pages of national newspapers. In April 1960 he was appointed Governor of East Pakistan where his zeal for the interests of that Province, as well as his brisk, genial manner, made him very popular. No one from West Pakistan, holding high office in the eastern Province, was ever before so highly regarded among the people

[3] It is probable that by the end of Ayub Khan's administration, the position of jute had become less favourable to East Pakistan's case. In 1957-8 the total export of manufactured and miscellaneous goods amounted to Rs.227·51 million, of which jute manufactures accounted for Rs.105·94 million. In 1966-7, the total had grown to Rs.1,429·43 million of which jute manufactures accounted for Rs.581·04 million, a relative decline from 46 per cent to 40 per cent. Comparing the value of the export of raw jute and jute goods combined against total exports for the same years, the results are even more revealing. In 1957-8 total exports amounted to Rs.1,421·65 million of which raw jute and jute goods provided Rs.959·50 million. In 1966-7 total exports amounted to Rs.2,871·00 million of which jute and jute goods provided Rs. 1,451·23 million, a relative decline from 67 per cent to 50·54 per cent. The outlook for jute continues to be unsatisfactory.

of that Province. On his departure in May 1962 he was the object of immense demonstrations of goodwill, but he did not relinquish office by reason of any official approval. On the contrary, it was evident that he and Ayub Khan had quarrelled seriously. Azam Khan was given no new appointment and rumour said that he was under house arrest.[4]

The choice of his successor proved to be an unhappy one and, as we shall see, Faruque lasted only five months. Underlying his appointment, the idea seems to have been that as he had been so closely identified with industrial growth in Pakistan, the people of the eastern Province would be encouraged to feel that this was the main reason for sending him. This interpretation was further strengthened when, about a month later, it was announced that the provincial Governments would take over development projects in their respective Provinces.[5]

But even so, the governorship of a Province has inescapable political implications and for these Ghulam Faruque had no talent and very little taste. In pre-partition days a senior railway official, Ghulam Faruque had come to Pakistan in unusual circumstances for, at the time of independence, he had elected to serve the new Government of India. This decision did not turn out well and some months later he migrated to Pakistan where he was given a top secretariat post. Even in this, however, he was not really at home and he was sent to East Pakistan as Chairman of the Jute Board. Later he became chairman-designate of the new Pakistan Industrial Development Corporation, a statutory company whose share capital was entirely owned by the Central Government. Its purpose was to stimulate industrial growth in those fields where private capital was shy and it was as Chairman of this new organization that Ghulam Faruque established his reputation as an industrial administrator of great energy and drive.

It was an appointment entirely suited to his executive flair and he was successful in promoting a considerable expansion in industry in both Provinces. 'Ghulam Faruque was a strong-

[4] The phrase *house arrest* is not known to Pakistan's Penal Code or Criminal Procedure Code, although Martial Law Regulation No. 78 promulgated by President Yahya Khan in 1971 seemed to create something very much like it. In General Azam Khan's case he was simply informed that, for a period of six months at least, he should not visit East Pakistan.

[5] *D*, 3 June 1962.

willed, powerful individual who made rapid decisions, saw them carried out and worried about government rules, procedures or approvals only afterwards, if at all. He was prepared to take substantial risks, smothered opposition by a combination of ability and ruthlessness.'[6] Not everything established by the Corporation under Faruque's direction was sound or successful and its privileged situation protected it from the adverse financial consequences that might have overtaken a private organization operating in the same way.[7] Still, a temperament such as his should not be underestimated and from the Pakistan Industrial Development Corporation, he proceeded to the West Pakistan Water and Power Development Authority, one of Ayub Khan's more important contributions to growth, which then stood in need of a more energetic and determined hand. From here, he was transferred in 1962 to East Pakistan to take the place of General Azam.

Ability and strength of personality such as Faruque possessed led him to thrust aside the querulous doubts of academically-minded civil servants or ride roughshod over Finance Ministry rituals and helped to get factories up and chimneys smoking. He was less successful, however, when confronted with politically-minded people for whom such issues as democracy, civil rights, electoral systems and student demands were of more fundamental importance than building jute mills. As Chairman of the Jute Board, Faruque had managed well enough with the people of East Pakistan, but that was a job he understood and could handle. Governorship of a Province called for qualities he neither possessed nor understood.

At an early stage of his governorship there were signs that he was uncomfortable. One of his immediate tasks was to form a cabinet of ministers and he found himself dealing with very flexible people whose mobility of ideas was equalled only by their vagueness. Unlike his master, Ayub Khan, who could be just as flexible and knew exactly how to deal with such men, Faruque found himself in a world he did not know and did not greatly care for. His discussions in Government House were very different from those across the Board Room table of the Industrial Development Corporation where, with feasability experts, engineers and finance men, the spirit of objectivity prevailed

[6] Papanek, op. cit., p. 95.   [7] ibid., p. 96 and passim.

and where the talk was less about high-minded principles and more about the end-product. As the weeks passed, it became clearer that he was uneasy and that his temper was ill-suited to this appointment.

His decisive misfortune was having to deal with student demonstrations against the Report on National Education which had recommended, among many other things, that the degree course should occupy three years instead of two. Both in Karachi and Dacca there were disturbances of increasing violence, followed by the externment from those cities of particularly troublesome student-leaders. This in turn caused about a dozen students in Karachi to undertake hunger-strikes. In Dacca Faruque endeavoured to deal with the situation in the way he knew best—to meet people, to discuss, to argue, to persuade, to evaluate merits and, if necessary, to disclose an inch or two of the big stick which authority placed in his pocket —but his way was not the way of politics. He was out of his depth and not really interested in the kind of political considerations that seemed to him so insubstantial and yet weighed so heavily with the people with whom he had to deal. The movement gathered force and on 17 September 1962 the students called for a nationwide strike. On 18 September there was police firing in Dacca. One person was killed, seventy-seven were injured, and the Army was called out.

But the students had their way and on 1 October 1962 it was announced that the three-year degree course had been put in abeyance. It was a defeat for Ayub Khan rather than for Faruque, but these events doubtless served to convince him that he had undertaken a job for which not only was he unfitted, but which was totally uncongenial. He resigned on 25 October 1962 and his letter of resignation, addressed to the President, gives clear enough indication of what he thought about the job and about himself in relation to it.[8]

[8] The letter is printed verbatim in *D*, 26 October 1962, with Ayub Khan's reply. This was not the end of Ghulam Faruque's career. Later he served as Minister of Commerce at the Centre and also, for a time, as Defence Adviser to the President. His qualifications for this latter appointment are not known. Eventually, in January 1968, he resigned office as Minister of Commerce in peremptory fashion and it appears that he and Ayub Khan had fallen out. In September 1969, six months after Ayub Khan's fall, Ghulam Faruque addressed a letter to the Minister of Industries in which he heavily criticized the policy pursued by Ayub Khan in the matter of establishing a steel mill in West Pakistan.

His successor, Abdul Monem Khan, was a very different kind of man. In addition to a long career in the Muslim League, he had practised, with no very great distinction, as a lawyer in Mymensingh, experience which taught him about the kind of men with whom, as Governor of the Province, he would have to deal. He continued in this appointment until March 1969 and during all that time he faithfully pursued the policies and purposes of Ayub, making himself the most execrated man in his Province, and perhaps in the whole of Pakistan. He was skilful in the use of patronage and he used the Basic Democracies system, and the Rural Works Programme which was so closely allied to it, as an apparatus for the distribution and employment of that patronage. Within his own party, the (Convention) Muslim League, he was, for most of the time, engaged in an obstinate feud with Sabur Khan (Minister of Communications at the Centre), Wahiduzzaman, a former Central Commerce Minister, and Qazi Abdul Qader, a former Minister in the East Pakistan Government. This situation seems to have fitted well into Ayub Khan's own method of dividing and ruling.

It may well be that the central fact of East Pakistani politics of those times was the death in March 1963 of Hussain Shahid Suhrawardy, which robbed the eastern Province, as well as the entire country, of one of its ablest men. Despite some flaws of character, injurious to his personal image, and despite a much-thwarted political career in Pakistan, Suhrawardy was a man of undoubted capacity and, notwithstanding his advancing years and his opposition to Ayub Khan, might well have made an important contribution towards the solution of the political conundrums that lay unresolved. His death left, among East Pakistan's political veterans, Khwaja Nazimuddin, respected more for the piety of his character than for his political ability. His brother, Khwaja Shahabuddin, was not really a part of the Pakistan political scene and Nurul Amin, also in opposition, had evidently lost much of his former vigour. Thus, in East Pakistan, political leadership fell more and more into the hands of men such as Maulana Bhashani (also in advancing years but possessing extraordinary vitality), Sheikh Mujibur Rahman (Suhrawardy's faithful lieutenant), and Mr. Farid Ahmed. Of the two last-mentioned, it seems fair to remark that the most distinctive aspect of their outlook lay in what might be called an East Pakistani nationalism. In politics, they were nothing if not East Pakistanis, but they did not belong to the same party. Mujibur Rahman belonged to the Awami League which Suhrawardy had founded and Farid Ahmed was a member of the Nizam-i-Islam Party of which, it is worth noticing, Choudhury Mohamed Ali of West Pakistan was the leader.

Maulana Bhashani had a party of his own—the National Awami Party—of which there was a corresponding version in West Pakistan. Of Maulana Bhashani it seems generally true to say that he is a law and a doctrine unto himself. Much that he has done in the course of Pakistan's political life is narrated in other chapters and his contribution—if such it can be described—is still difficult to assess. Of leftist views, he has always denied being a communist, but he has never concealed his sympathies for China and for Mao Tse-tung's Government. To what extent he has ever had a programme, or really sought office in order to implement a programme, remains an enigmatic feature of his political life. In the exercise of his particular skill in drawing and rousing the crowd, perhaps the most positive thing to be said of him is that he was moved by the visible miseries of the preponderating majority of his East Pakistani countrymen and, like the A. K. M. Fazlul Haq, was determined to do something about it. But this attitude, while commendable, is not a policy and, like the A. K. M. Fazlul Haq, Maulana Bhashani has constantly found himself involved in contradictions, a situation made more confused by the fact that his natural abilities fell far short of those possessed by the Sher-i-Bangla, as Haq was called. On the negative side, there is ground for supposing that Bhashani's interventions in politics have not always been inspired by the purest and most disinterested of motives and, for example, the part he played in the final act which saw the retirement of Ayub Khan, is open to discreditable interpretation.[9]

Of the men who became the dominating personalities in Pakistan between 1962 and 1969, the most important is Sheikh Mujibur Rahman, who, especially from 1966 onwards, was shunted from one jail to another, either as a political *détenu* or on various charges of making seditious speeches and other

[9] See pp. 323–4.

subversive activities, until he became East Pakistan's principal symbol of defiance against tyranny.[10]

Much of all that has so far been described was not new but what *was* new, when Ayub Khan launched his presidential system, was the expression, in East Pakistan, that the real trouble lay in Pakistan's political structure, which did not represent the intentions of the famous Pakistan Resolution proposed by Sheri-i-Bangla ('lion of Bengal') A. K. M. Fazlul Haq and passed at Lahore on 23 March 1940. This suggestion, which appeared to strike at the roots of the country's existence, was played down in West Pakistan, but even there it could not be totally suppressed, especially as Ayub Khan went on amending his Constitution and especially as other protests were heard. Ultimately, the issue had to be faced.

The Resolution of March 1940, referring to the political structure envisaged for Pakistan, contains these crucial words: '... areas in which Muslims are numerically in a majority ... should be grouped to constitute "Independent States" in which the constituent units shall be autonomous and sovereign'. The reference, it will be seen, is to *states* and not *state* and it is on this ground that certain political parties founded their entire doctrine of autonomy without, as they claim, departing from the idea of Pakistan.

Not surprisingly, this issue has been hotly debated and it has been claimed that the question of what was actually meant by the terms of the Lahore Resolution was resolved once and for all, in Jinnah's lifetime, by his (Jinnah's) own pronouncements and by the decisions of various Muslim League organizations.[11]

The debate seems likely to continue but it is all *ex post facto*. In 1940 neither Jinnah nor his colleagues had irrevocably committed themselves, explicitly or implicitly, to a political division of the sub-continent. In their own minds, it remained far from

[10] Sheikh Mujibur Rahman's own account of his experience was briefly stated to the Court at the Agartala Conspiracy Trial and is printed verbatim in *PO*, 29 January 1969.

[11] Syed Sharifuddin Pirzada, *The Pakistan Resolution and the Historic Lahore Session*, Pakistan Publications, Karachi, 1968. Mr. Pirzada is a former Foreign Minister of Pakistan and also Attorney-General. Pakistan Publications is a Central Government organization. See also the polemics exchanged in *D*, September 1969 by Mr. Z. H. Lari and Mr. Abdul Wahid Khan, both Muslim League veterans. For an interesting East Pakistan view, see Kamruddin Ahmed, *Social History of East Pakistan*, Dacca, 1967.

certain that such a division either would or could mature into a reality. It is therefore probably correct to say that the well-meditated consideration which Jinnah himself would have given to the drafting of the Pakistan Resolution, had he been convinced that he was committed to the kind of partition that 1947 actually witnessed, might have produced some very different language.[12]

However all this may be, it is these phrases, taken from the Lahore Resolution, that provided textual authority for the growing tendency in East Pakistan to call for autonomy. In West Pakistan, as we shall see, this word was equated with secession, but the proponents of autonomy denied this firmly and their line of argument suggested that, in their own minds, they felt they had come not to destroy the law but to fulfil it.

It was during Ayub Khan's administration that, despite his own efforts to meet some, if not all, of East Pakistan's grievances, this movement towards autonomy acquired firm shape. It was during his administration that the word *secession* became, in Pakistan, not only utterable, but printable. Eventually, it was Ayub Khan himself who expressed the liberal view that the only link between the two Provinces lay in the fact that the Governor of each of them was appointed by the Centre. 'Remove him [the Governor] and you have two countries straight away.'[13] Why then did the opposition to him and his Government become as determined, and eventually as irresistible, in the eastern Province as in the western?

Ayub Khan failed as explicitly in East Pakistan, as in West Pakistan, because his régime became more intolerable, more oppressive and more corrupt without providing any material benefits to the deprived masses. It is quite possible that these evils were felt more in East Pakistan than in West Pakistan, not only because greater poverty existed there, but by reason of the methods adopted by Monem Khan. He enlisted the support and loyalty of the Basic Democrats by entrusting them with such functions as the distribution of food grains, cloth and other necessities in times of shortage or disaster. The management of

---

[12] Some people even advanced the view that the word *states*, i.e. in the plural, was an inadvertent clerical error!

[13] Television interview at Rawalpindi on 14 August 1967, reported in *D*, 16 August 1967.

the Rural Works Programme was largely in their hands and many other forms of small patronage, allied to the exercise of minor administrative functions, enabled these people, especially in East Pakistan, to oppress the poor, to secure all kinds of unfair advantage, and, of course, to enrich themselves. It is for this reason that when in East Pakistan trouble became rife in the cold weather of 1968-9, violence took a specific turn against these village Caligulas, some of whom were brutally murdered.

It is not, I think, necessary to trace, month by month and year by year, the mounting grievances of East Pakistan. In earlier chapters, indications of their form and weight have been given and if the burden intensified as time passed, the form —political, economic and cultural—did not change. In terms of history, the movement towards drastic alteration can be said to have acquired its real and comprehensive shape early in 1966. Hitherto it had been a matter of variously stated, variously defined, sources of discontent and it was not until the early months of 1966 that this discontent, along with a movement founded upon the new interpretation of the Lahore Resolution, became forged into a political unity which represents, perhaps, the most momentous event in the history of the country since 1947. Briefly, it can be described as the Six-Point Movement and the launching of this campaign unified all the political, economic and cultural aspects of East Pakistan's claims into a clear-cut movement with a specific programme to offer and to urge. Whatever may be the future history of Pakistan and the sub-continent, this campaign left an indelible mark on those pages.

The opposition parties saw the Tashkent Declaration as a chance to embarrass Ayub Khan to a serious degree and a conference was called at the house of Choudhury Mohamed Ali, to which Mujibur Rahman was invited. Ostensibly, the purpose was to consider what might be done to press home the advantage over Ayub Khan which events had presented to them. Mujibur Rahman consequently went to Lahore with the apparent intention of collaborating, but he also raised the question of East Pakistan's grievances and produced the Six Points as they had been originally drafted and as they had come into his possession. This was waved aside on the ground that the only purpose of the conference was to discuss Tashkent. Mujibur Rahman's proposals could be discussed on another occasion. Sensing, in this, a repetition of the indifferent attitude to East Pakistan, Mujibur Rahman went back to his Province, announced his support for the Tashkent Declaration and proceeded to publish the Six Points which, he said, were essential if East Pakistan were to survive and prosper.

As originally drafted, this (four-point) programme read:

1. The constitution should provide for a Federation of Pakistan in its true sense on the basis of the Lahore Resolution and Parliamentary form of government with supremacy of the legislatures elected on the basis of universal adult franchise and direct voting.
2. Federal government shall deal with two subjects, defence and foreign affairs; all other residuary subjects shall vest in the federating states.
3. Regarding currency, either of the two following suggestions may be accepted:
   A. Two separate freely convertible currencies may be introduced, or
   B. One currency for the whole country may be maintained. In this case effective constitutional provisions are to be made in stopping the flight of capital from East to West Pakistan. A separate banking reserve is also to be made for East Pakistan.
4. Separate fiscal and monetary policy is to be adopted for East Pakistan.

Mujibur Rahman was not the author of these penetrating suggestions. He is no profound political thinker or theoretician. His ability lies in the direction of political organization for which talent Suhrawardy often spoke warmly in Mujib's praise.[14] Mujibur Rahman also possesses a gift for powerful oratory, with plenty of appeal to the emotions and, unfortunately

[14] An interesting instance of this gift occurred when Martial Law was declared in 1958 and when all political parties were abolished. At that time, Mujib was chief executive, in East Pakistan, of the Alpha Insurance Co. Ltd. He therefore recruited into that Company as many of his partymen as possible. In this way he not only provided them with incomes, but kept them together and provided a convenient cover for such meetings as they desired to hold. The trick is not new but it takes an organizer to think of it and execute it.

perhaps, with an undertone of violence. Armed with this programme, he now began to stump the countryside, preaching a new gospel of autonomy within the meaning of the Lahore Resolution and through the Six Points.

The original draft was the work of a group of East Pakistani intellectuals who were dissatisfied with the attitude of the Central Government towards East Pakistan and with the evident advantages that West Pakistan, justly or unjustly, enjoyed. The draft was first presented to the veteran leader Nurul Amin who realized that a demand for secession could be read into it. He delayed his reply and the authors showed the draft to Mujibur Rahman, then about to attend the conference on the Tashkent Declaration in Lahore. Seeing in the draft a crystallization of what he wanted but had not been able to enunciate so precisely, Mujib seized upon it and carried the proposals to Lahore. After their adoption by Mujib's party, the draft was amended and clarified so as to present six clear issues. They read as follows:

(a) A federal constitution for Pakistan.
(b) Central Government portfolios to be limited to Defence and Foreign Affairs only.
(c) The two Provinces to have separate currencies or, alternatively, there should be restrictions on the movement of capital funds from one Province to the other.
(d) All taxes to vest in the Province of collection.
(e) All foreign exchange earned by East Pakistan to be at the disposal of East Pakistan.
(f) An East Pakistan militia to be formed.

The movement gathered in pace and strength and Maulana Bhashani, sensing the change of atmosphere, decided to jump aboard the autonomy band-wagon. Following the example of Mujibur Rahman, he too made speeches declaring that full provincial autonomy was the only means of ensuring a viable, durable, united Pakistan. However, he did not speak in favour of the Six Point Programme and, significantly enough, incurred no visible, official displeasure. So far as Ayub Khan's Government went, Bhashani stayed out of trouble. For that matter his contribution was negligible and, as usual with him, enigmatic in character. In West Pakistan, in line with the customary practice of ignoring, or omitting to report, anything that had unpleasant or uncongenial implications, the situation in East Pakistan was vaguely reported and details of the Six Points were studiously kept out of newspaper columns. Instead, there was some writing about secession and secessionists and in March 1966 Ayub Khan made reference to the dangers of slogans about autonomy. At about the same time, Zulfikar Ali Bhutto, still Ayub Khan's Foreign Minister, challenged Mujib to a public debate on the Six Points. This contest in dialectics never took place, each intending disputant adroitly sidestepping the other without actually appearing to do so. This outcome must be regarded as fortunate since, had there been any public meeting for this purpose, the result must certainly have been uproar and possibly bloodshed.

Instead, in April, Mujib demanded a nationwide referendum on the Six Point issue and stepped up the intensity of his campaign with virulent attacks on those in power and on those who had been in power. He claimed that East Pakistan was being despoiled and robbed of its due share in the national product in order to feed West Pakistan. On 19 April he was arrested in Jessore under the Defence of Pakistan Rules and was promptly released on bail, which did not suit the Government. On 23 April he was again arrested under the Defence of Pakistan Rules and under the East Pakistan Safety Ordinance, but this time on a non-bailable warrant. He was removed to Sylhet, conveniently distant from Dacca, by train, and on the way was greeted by demonstrators at various stopping places. His trial began on 7 May, in Sylhet Jail, for making seditious speeches and other such offences. Thus began his two-year odyssey from one prison to another, terminating at the Cantonment where in 1968 he was among the accused at the Agartala Conspiracy Trial.

His arrest did nothing to sweeten the temper of East Pakistan and its people. The movement continued to gather strength and it was estimated, by competent observers of East Pakistan's affairs, that if an election had been held in July of that year, Mujibur Rahman's party would have swept the Province on the Six Point issue. It was known that many civil servants in East Pakistan, belonging to that Province by birth, shared the aspirations and resentment which Mujib and his programme expressed and symbolized; and some of those who displayed this sympathy too openly were disciplined by transfer, sometimes to West Pakistan. One of them, Ahmed Fazlur Rahman, whose name appears later in this chapter, went on long leave in order to avoid such a transfer and it is believed that he threatened resignation rather than accept such a transfer. Detentions and arrests continued and the Indian newspaper the *Statesman*, in its issue dated 3 August 1966, estimated that about 3,000 persons had been arrested or detained.

In August Ayub Khan visited the Province and, on the subject of the activities of Mujibur Rahman and his supporters, he made threatening reference to the idea of secession: 'If the trouble goes on, other measures will be necessary.' During this visit, he addressed a meeting of the members of the National and Provincial Assemblies in which he dealt with 'the secession issue', as he termed it, in undisguised language. In his words, there were discernible indications that West Pakistan was becoming weary of East Pakistan's constantly reiterated complaints, grievances and insinuations.[15]

Ayub Khan's visit led to a change of tactics, a change for which the visit itself may have had exploratory purposes. At all events, in the following month of September, the rumour spread that between Ayub Khan's representatives, and leaders of Mujib's party, the Awami League, secret negotiations were in train. A long, circumstantial, and seemingly accurate account of these parleys appeared in the Dacca weekly, *Holiday*, in its issue dated 12 September 1966 so that the reading public could not be unaware of some activity of this kind. In any case, the fact of these negotiations was no surprise when one remembers Ayub Khan's known preference for compromise and the question recurred: How long could the Six Point movement be contained merely by a process of detentions and arrests under the Defence of Pakistan Rules, the East Pakistan Safety Ordinance or the Pakistan Penal Code, along with censorship of the Press?[16] It was noteworthy that beyond the shores of Pakistan indignation was beginning to spread. At a meeting of the leaders of the Federation of Pakistan Associations in Great Britain, held in Birmingham, England, the Pakistan Govern-

[15] This speech is reported verbatim in *D*, 21 August 1966.
[16] See Chapter V, note 14.

ment was censured for these repeated arrests and detentions. A few weeks before this meeting took place, a former Secretary of a Pakistan Association in the United Kingdom had returned to East Pakistan and had been arrested in Sylhet where he had gone perhaps in the hope of meeting Mujibur Rahman. He was later released.

The attempt at negotiation did not succeed but some useful contact appeared to have been made and it seems that Ayub Khan had concluded that the time was ripening for other and, he hoped, more effectively persuasive measures. He may have concluded also that the arrest of Mujibur Rahman, an energetic and aggressive personality, had blunted the edge of the movement. In December 1966 he again visited East Pakistan where, it is said, he succeeded in weaning away some of Mujib's supporters and in cutting the Six Point movement down to manageable proportions by a lavish distribution of import licences and other money-spinning favours.

Despite this, the movement continued and, in the New Year of 1967, it was announced that on 13 February Six Point Programme Day would be observed. Encouraged by Ayub Khan's effective steps of the preceding December, the Press in Pakistan, notably *Dawn* in an editorial which appeared on the day itself, described the movement as a fiasco, but the Dacca weekly *Holiday*, in an issue dated 21 February, said that the popular observance of Six Point Programme Day amounted to an 'uprising'. Whatever it was, the event was significant enough to take Ayub Khan to East Pakistan yet again, in the following month of March.

On this occasion Tofazzal Hossain, editor of *Ittefaq*, who had been detained under the Defence of Pakistan Rules since 16 June 1966 for his part in the Six Point Movement, was released, but three members of the National Awami Party were arrested under Rule 47(5) of the same legislation. During this visit, Ayub Khan said that demands for autonomy would divide the country, involving dangers for East Pakistan. Later, on his return to Lahore, he also said that the autonomy demand was 'camouflage for separation'. It was evident at the time that this visit had not been so successful as the earlier one, but the official view claimed that the Six Point Movement was losing its appeal. On the other side, it was said that more and more

East Pakistanis were accepting this programme as minimal. So the wordy warfare went on until, some months afterwards, events took another and much more dramatic turn.

On 2 January 1968 the daily newspapers reported detail taken from a statement issued by the Government at Islamabad, that the activities of 'anti-national elements' had attracted notice and there was reference to arrests 'recently made'.[17] That evening All-India Radio broadcast news that a coup had been planned but had been forestalled. Gossip in Pakistan spread rapidly and, in the absence of precise detail, names of various people, including Zulfikar Ali Bhutto, by then at odds with Ayub Khan, were mentioned as being among the arrested persons. Meanwhile, All-India Radio continued to oblige with interesting details of bomb plots, attempts at the assassination of Ayub Khan and an estimated figure of 2,000 arrests.

On 7 January it became known that twenty-eight persons had been taken into custody on serious charges. All of them belonged to the eastern Province and they included officers and men of the armed forces as well as three members of the Civil Service of Pakistan.[18] It was also stated that the office of the Deputy High Commissioner for India was implicated and that the Pakistan Government had asked for Mr. P. N. Ojha, a First Secretary in that office, to be withdrawn. This request was complied with and the Indian Government retaliated by expelling Mr. M. M. Ahmed, Counsellor at the Pakistan High Commission in Delhi, it being alleged that he had distributed arms and money to subversive groups in India. In the Indian Press it was reported that about 600 persons had been arrested or detained,[19] and a few days later it was announced that Mujibur Rahman, at that time, of course, in jail, was involved and would stand trial along with those already under arrest.

[17] From petitions later presented to the High Court on behalf of some of the arrested men, it became known that some, if not all, had been taken into custody on or about 23 December 1967.

[18] One of them, Ahmed Fazlur Rahman, had been known to me when he was stationed in Karachi, and was very outspoken on the subject of East Pakistan's grievances. Although this has no bearing on the question of guilt or innocence with respect to the Agartala Trial, his indiscretions may have contributed something to his arrest.

[19] *Statesman*, Calcutta, 13 January 1968.

Excitement rose steadily with the news that some of the conspirators had visited Agartala, in India, to make plans by which, with Indian help, an independent East Bengal could be established.[20] In an issue dated 14 January 1968, *Holiday* published an article suggesting that the 'imperialists', meaning the United States, were involved. In fact, this article was a cleverly disguised attack on Ayub Khan's administration, criticizing the loss of civil liberties and referring to East Pakistan's poor economic situation.[21] But this suggestion of American involvement found ready ears and a rumour circulated that when Ayub Khan flew to Karachi on 24 December 1967 to meet President Lyndon Johnson during the latter's stop-over, an attempt on his (Ayub Khan's) life was intended but, fortunately, had been discovered in time.[22] Inevitably, the Central Intelligence Agency was associated with these tales and, in Karachi there were protest meetings, anti-American in character. Students of the Islamia College threatened to take out a procession and march on the American Embassy with incendiarism in mind. This commotion was firmly put down by the authorities and some student-leaders were arrested. Then, on 29 January, Ayub Khan fell seriously ill and attention was substantially diverted from Agartala, at any rate for a time.

Since the Agartala Conspiracy Case proved to be a total failure, there is little use now in examining its factual and legal merits. Its importance today lies in its consequences to Ayub Khan and to the history of the country. These matters we shall come to. The accused persons were among those East Pakistanis who were extremely dissatisfied with what they considered to be the unfair treatment of their Province. They were convinced that unless strenuous measures were pursued, little change could be expected. Whether they were actually planning dissociation from the existing constitutional structure of Pakistan or an armed uprising, assisted by the Indian Government, is quite another question. The evidence on these subjects given at the trial was not very clear and some of it, with respect to military preparation, as adduced by the prosecution, was laughable.

[20] And hence the *Agartala* Conspiracy Case.
[21] The title of this weekly is a wild misnomer. It is intensely political.
[22] Much talk went on about this meeting. It was said the Americans desired it to be kept secret whereas the Pakistan Government wanted publicity and hoped for a meeting longer than the one hour for which it in fact lasted.

X

East Pakistan

IN this chapter, the special problems of East Pakistan and its oft-expressed grievances, and their outcome during the years 1962–9, are considered. The contribution made by the Province in national development and the part played in national affairs and national politics will find their place elsewhere. Here we will be concerned with relations between the Province and the Central Government, with their particular bearing on the administration and career of Ayub Khan. As we shall see, it was in relation to the course of events in East Pakistan, and the measures that Ayub Khan was persuaded, or persuaded himself, to adopt, that he suffered his greatest, single, personal humiliation and defeat.

The specific measures which Ayub Khan employed during the Martial Law administration to meet the political and economic grievances expressed in East Pakistan did not prove sufficient. But this could only be judged afterwards, when the National Assembly had come into existence and the expression of public reaction became possible in the course of its debates.

The economic gap between the two Provinces was certainly closing but at a rate which did not satisfy the eastern Province, which continued to be heavily under-represented in the civil services and the armed forces. Although the continuing advantages which West Pakistan enjoyed could not be attributed, directly or indirectly, to anything Ayub Khan had initiated, there were still no signs that disparities were lessening in any substantial manner.[1] In East Pakistan it was felt that Ayub Khan was not prepared to do anything solid to create equivalent development opportunities.

It could be said to his credit that he had initiated the system by which a vast field of authority was delegated by the Centre

[1] These disparities are examined in an article by Mr. Rehman Sobhan entitled 'East Pakistan's Revolt Against Ayub Khan', *The Round Table*, London, July 1969.

After the arrests and the excitement associated therewith, little was heard of the matter until 22 April 1968, when an Ordinance appeared by which a Special Tribunal could be set up to try the conspirators. Entitled the Criminal Law Amendment (Special Tribunals) Ordinance 1968, it was promulgated by Ayub Khan under Article 30 of the Constitution, relating to the President's powers in an emergency (which had been declared in September 1965) and other provisions. The Ordinance is an interesting piece of legislation because it did not purport to set up a single, special tribunal to deal with the Agartala Case, but made it possible to set up a special tribunal, at any time, to try any case relating to offences concerned with conspiracy, mutiny in the armed forces, or inciting or seducing a member of the armed forces against or from his allegiance or duty. Thus, under this Ordinance, the Government could, whenever it chose, set up a special tribunal to deal with any such alleged offences. The Ordinance contained a section which said that it overrode all laws in effect for the time being in Pakistan including the Evidence Act, and the provisions of the Ordinance could not be questioned in any Court including the Supreme Court. What was actually meant by the omnibus clause to do with overriding effect is not clear. Mainly it was aimed at the Evidence Act so that the Tribunal should not be bound by the existing law on the subject which might make certain evidence inadmissible and so preclude the possibility of conviction. But the section apparently went further than this and could be interpreted to mean that the Tribunal could make its own law as it went along. There appeared to be no provision by which persons, convicted by any such tribunal, could appeal.

At the time, it seemed as if the Rawalpindi Conspiracy Case precedent might be followed, with plenty of sensation, total secrecy and, as indicated, with the law of evidence adjusted to suit the necessities of the occasion and of the prosecution. As it turned out there was sensation but no secrecy, since the trial was held in public and the existing law of evidence followed. In these last two respects the Government was obliged to submit to popular will, but although judicial rigour was preserved, it was impossible to conceal the political implications of the case. Its resemblance to the Rawalpindi affair was ominous and it proved up to a point to be prophetic.[23] It was clear that if, in particular, Sheikh Mujibur Rahman were convicted and sentenced to a substantial term of imprisonment, he could be safely silenced for a long time, without the constitutional complications inherent in any sole reliance upon the Defence of Pakistan Rules and without the legal difficulties involved in sedition cases before the ordinary courts.

On 19 June 1968, the trial opened and was conducted in Dacca Cantonment where the accused were kept in custody. Eleven persons associated with the affair had made full confessions and were pardoned. Four of the accused made judicial confessions. All these confessions formed, of course, the testimony of accomplices and even if these confessions corroborated one another, as accomplice-testimony this evidence was clearly tainted. These apart, the amount of direct evidence, as it came out in the Court, was limited. During the proceedings there was some confusion over identification and one prosecution witness was declared hostile and, therefore, made liable to cross-examination by the prosecution. The evidence was extensively reported and provided people with plenty to talk about and discuss, especially in East Pakistan where, in offices and factories, the day's work started with a thorough going-over of that morning's newspaper report. At any rate there was no want of publicity.

On behalf of Sheikh Mujibur Rahman, a British lawyer, Mr. T. Williams Q.C., appeared before the Dacca High Court

---

[23] Surely, it can now be stated publicly what in Pakistan has long been known privately, namely that when the Rawalpindi conspirators were arrested, they had already abandoned their ideas and the fact of this abandonment was within the knowledge of those in authority at G.H.Q. Concerning the eventual consequences of the Agartala trial, I noted on 16 June 1968, '... this case is now referred to as *The State versus Sheikh Mujibur Rahman and Others* which is a fair indication of the prominence given to Mujib in this matter. The plan is clear. If Sh. Mujib is convicted, he may get anything up to ten years. Thereafter, the question of securing his release in relation to the Defence of Pakistan Rules ceases. I still think this Agartala business may have serious repercussions.' (As also indicated in the text, the point is that at the time of the Agartala trial, Sheikh Mujibur Rahman was detained under the Defence of Pakistan Rules which, as they then stood, did not guarantee that he could not be released at any time. A conviction over the Agartala affair would have been a very different business.)

In these efforts at political prophecy, I was attempting, here as in other instances, to 'extrapolate the future from the present and recent past', to use Professor Richard Rose's apt and meaningful phrase in his *Politics and People*, London, Faber, 1970, p. 138.

with a petition that raised a number of weighty and pertinent constitutional issues relating to the validity of the Ordinance under which the trial was proceeding. The High Court heard Mr. Williams, but the petition was adjourned for further hearing, subject to the condition that the trial would meanwhile go on. As it turned out, the petition was rendered infructuous by the Government's own action in withdrawing the Agartala case and nothing more was heard of Mr. Williams' legal ingenuity.

The accused elected not to give sworn evidence in the witness-box. Instead each of them submitted a written and signed statement to the Court. The burden of all these statements, taken together, was that:

(a) None of them had conspired against the State.
(b) During interrogation, they had been subjected to inhuman treatment, including various specified forms of physical torture, in order to extract confessions.
(c) Those accused who were members of the armed forces or the Civil Services had taken no part in politics and did not know the political people implicated in the case.
(d) At least one of the accused, Ahmed Fazlur Rahman, said he had been falsely implicated out of spite. As a Deputy Secretary in the Ministry of Finance of the Central Government, he had made it his business to conduct his work equitably between the two Provinces and had opposed measures which were unfair to East Pakistan or wasteful of the nation's resources. For these reasons he claimed that he had incurred the dislike of his superiors who happened to belong to West Pakistan.
(e) Sheikh Mujibur Rahman put in a statement giving details of the preceding two years during which time he had been moved from one jail to another, the inference being that a man in jail will find it difficult to conspire with others outside in order to plan a revolution. He declared his total innocence and mentioned that he had supported the Tashkent Declaration.

And so the trial wore on. While touring East Pakistan in September 1968, Ayub Khan announced a four-point plan 'to thwart disruption'. It comprised propagation of the legacy of the Pakistan struggle; confirmation of Islamic ideology as the basis of Pakistan; projection of the urgency and benefits of a strong Centre and the forging of a common front everywhere against the forces of disruption. The implementation of this plan was not marked by any great show of vigour and if it was intended to bring the two Provinces closer together it cannot be said that it was pursued with any real determination. In fact it more or less died of lack of interest and, towards the end of the year, events took a very different turn.

This drastic change in the course of Pakistan's history and Ayub Khan's administration, is outlined in a later chapter, but its effect was to force Ayub Khan into a total withdrawal of the Agartala Case. The proceedings came to an abrupt end and all the accused were released. This outcome was marred by the death of one of the accused when he was shot and bayoneted 'attempting to escape' as the official version had it. Apart from this tragic incident, all the personnel of the armed forces were reinstated with arrears of pay. The three members of the C.S.P., however, were compulsorily retired, with pension rights, by an order made by Ayub Khan's successor, President Yahya Khan.

The withdrawal of the Agartala Case was a political event of great significance. Of all the reverses which Ayub Khan suffered in the course of his ten years' administration, this was the most serious and the most humiliating. It was inflicted by East Pakistan and it was the outcome of his duel with Mujibur Rahman and of his efforts to crush the Six Point Movement. The fact of withdrawal and the circumstances which compelled it bear implications of the most penetrating character. Either it was believed that the accused were guilty, that there was a true bill against them, in which case Ayub Khan was evidently bent on saving his own skin, irrespective of the nation's interests, or they were not believed guilty in which case the prosecution should never have been instituted. And what of the allegations against the Indian diplomat, Ojha? Had they too been withdrawn? If not, on what grounds were they permitted to remain? Such were the contradictions that sprang from conduct either misconceived in the first place, or wrongly pursued afterwards.

XI

West Pakistan

IN recording the course of politics in East Pakistan during the period from 1962 to 1969 I have laid special emphasis upon the Six Point Movement, and on the inability of Ayub Khan to stem or crush it, as the decisive political event in that Province. So too, in the political history of the western Province during the same period the development which had the most bearing upon its future, and the future of Pakistan, was the rising opposition to that important act of administrative consolidation known by the inept and clumsy title 'One Unit'. It is a highly significant comment on Ayub Khan's ultimate failure that not even in West Pakistan was he able to pursue and successfully maintain the retention of the One Unit and that retention must be considered as one of the most prominent among his political objectives. In East Pakistan, his failure could be explained, at any rate in part, by extenuating circumstances which undoubtedly exist and for which reason that Province has proved to be a rock on which the hopes of so many West Pakistani politicians have foundered. In West Pakistan, however, on home ground, so to say, and among people whose languages, culture and way of life he largely knew, the fact of Ayub Khan's failure was an incontrovertible demonstration of a limited power of political judgement, as distinct from a gift for political manipulation.

Elsewhere something has been said of the turn of political events, particularly in West Pakistan, and something, too, with special reference to the autocratic manner in which the western Province was administered by the late Nawab of Kalabagh. Those years comprised, among other things, a period of mounting violence, when atrocious crimes were committed and went unpunished, and when political murders multiplied, many of them unsolved or, at any rate, with the murderers untraced and never arrested. In January 1965 occurred the 'Mari Indus' murders, to be followed in the next month by the 'Sheikhupura murders'. These achieved special notoriety for their political implications and as the state of law and order continued to decline, public comment could not be totally silenced.

Some sense of the dark atmosphere of outrage and lawlessness that prevailed in the later years of Ayub Khan's administration is well conveyed by the circumstances which led to the death of a journalist, Zamir Qureishy, who was shot by assassins evidently aiming at someone else. This occurred in Lahore in January 1965—a fateful year for Ayub Khan—when Qureishy, a correspondent of some seniority, accompanied by Mir Baqi Baluch, a politician who had opposed Ayub Khan and had suffered detention for it, had paid an evening visit to Malik Ghulam Jilani, another opposition leader who had spoken with considerable vehemence against the Government and had likewise suffered for his trouble. At the end of the interview, the two visitors took their leave and were accompanied by Jilani to the door of his house. In Lahore, in the cold weather, the sun sets early and, while the three men stood in darkness, they were fired upon from the hedges. A bullet struck Qureishy and he died.

There is little doubt that he was an unintended victim. The shots were almost certainly meant for Baqi Baluch or, even more likely, for Jilani. Newspapers took the matter up vigorously and there was a considerable outburst of indignation. A fund was opened for the benefit of the dead man's widow and children, and six months later the Governor of West Pakistan, Kalabagh, sent a tardy cheque of Rs.5,000. This was published in the newspapers, the more servile of which quoted the official handout which said that the cheque had been sent following the death of Zamir Qureishy after 'a shooting incident'.

The detection and arrest of the murderer or murderers proved beyond the powers of the West Pakistan police. The subject was raised in the West Pakistan legislature towards the end of 1965 but, on behalf of the Government, a reply was given that it would not be 'in the public interest' to disclose details of the investigation. There the matter lay until in October 1966, after General Musa became Governor in place of Kalabagh, Qureishy's widow asked for the enquiry to be re-opened. The new Governor agreed and a month afterwards it was blandly given out that Qureishy had been shot by one Mohamed Khan, a proclaimed offender. Three members of his gang were said to have been arrested and other arrests were expected. Yet it was noted in Karachi's newspapers in 1968 that Zamir Qureishy's murderers were still at large.[1]

At this time violence lay heavy in the air and crime went unpunished but this, instead of silencing or erasing the undertone of opposition to the existing régime, served only to inflame it. It was with a firm belief that violence, and conniving at violence, had become an integral part of Ayub Khan's method of government that the public rose so vehemently against him, once the spark had been struck in November 1968. There is, moreover, another side to this grim tale. It is fully representative of the methods by which Ayub Khan and Kalabagh sought to keep together the constituent parts of the Province which together formed the One Unit, meaning the consolidation of the four Provinces of the western wing into one Province called West Pakistan. They failed, and this chapter is an account of that failure along with some remarks on its consequences for Pakistan.

Readers of Ayub Khan's book *Friends not Masters* will remember that he claimed much, if not most, of the credit for the One Unit conception and even its execution. The truth of the matter is that by the time Ayub Khan came to consider things of this sort, the essence of the idea was nearly a century old. As early as 1866 in a memorial addressed to the Secretary of State for India on the subject of railway and river traffic, the Committee of the Karachi Chamber of Commerce (now the Overseas Investors Chamber of Commerce and Industry) concluded with this remark: '... eventually Sind and Punjab must form one Government.' Again, in an address to the Governor-General in 1871, the Committee said by way of conclusion: 'It must however be admitted that the true

---

[1] The phrase 'shooting incident' is used in *D*, 10 June 1966. For the question raised in the West Pakistan Assembly see Assembly Debates for December 1965 and *D*, 7 December 1965. In October 1966 the Urdu newspapers carried stories that, as a result of this affair and the anxieties it created, two intelligence officers had had nervous breakdowns. See also *D*, 16 November 1966 and *Daily News*, September 1968.

interests of this Province (i.e. Sind) are much more closely allied with the Punjab than with the Bombay Presidency, Karachi being the natural channel through which the trade of the Punjab must eventually flow.'

Apart from this, it is also the case that very soon after partition the idea of consolidating West Pakistan was mentioned to Jinnah by his then adviser, the late Sir Archibald Rowlands, a senior British civil servant who had been lent by the Treasury.[2] It does not follow from this that Rowlands was the first or only man to think of an administrative reform of this kind, but it does follow that as early as 1947 top men in the administration were aware of the idea. Jinnah, naturally enough, saw the force of the suggestion but took the view that there were other and more important things to be attended to first. It is perfectly possible that had he lived, the country's first constitution would have included an administrative arrangement of this sort. In any case, it is likely that Rowlands discussed the idea with the Finance Minister, the late Ghulam Mohamed, and with the Secretary-General, Choudhury Mohamed Ali, since Rowlands worked with both of them in close contact. It is improbable that Ayub Khan, who at that time was outside this elevated circle, would have had any direct knowledge of these conversations and a few months after partition he was posted as General-Officer, Commanding-in-Chief, in East Pakistan.

It has long been recognized that one of Pakistan's great misfortunes lay in the prolonged delays that attended the preparation of a constitution and for this the late Liaquat Ali Khan has been rightly criticized. To be sure, after his death in 1951 there was little contribution that he could make, but it is no doubt true that in his time the matter proceeded in too dilatory a manner. His own position was not an easy one and there were good reasons that deterred him from hastening

---

[2] Feldman, *A Constitution for Pakistan*, Karachi, Oxford University Press, 1955, pp. 77–8. Further evidence is mentioned which shows at how early a stage the West Pakistan consolidation was being considered. It is fair to Ayub Khan to mention that, in 1955, his brother, Sardar Bahadur Khan, stated that as far back as 1948, Jinnah wanted to implement a One Unit scheme for West Pakistan. To this extent, therefore, Ayub Khan may have had early knowledge of what was being considered. The conversation between Sir Archibald Rowlands and myself took place in Karachi in September 1947.

with the constitutional problem, but it remains clear that had there been a constitution prepared with reasonable speed and diligence, while the country was united by the initial enthusiasm and excitement created by the simple fact of independence and Pakistan's existence, much that came later to its disadvantage might well have been avoided. It would then have been possible to have created an arrangement in the form of a One Unit consolidation which would have conferred all the advantages it had to offer without incurring the adverse consequences which were experienced when the One Unit consolidation actually took place in 1955.

What then became its territories comprised the Provinces of the North-West Frontier, the Punjab, and Sind. In addition Baluchistan was administered through an Agent to the Governor-General, an official possessing a status comparable with that of a provincial Governor. However, Baluchistan involves substantial differences with respect to administration, taxation and the law. It is peopled largely by tribes amenable to the jurisdiction of their own *sardars* or *tumandars*, hereditary chiefs who exercise a paternalistic authority and are expected to maintain the peace. It is a much criticized system being regarded, with a good deal of truth, as backward, out of date, obscurantist, and unprogressive.

This condition of quasi-independence was permitted to continue by the British who found little to interest them in Baluchistan. A wild, rugged land, it offered small promise of wealth and economic growth and the main concern of the British Government was to ensure tranquillity and to maintain these barriers against penetration by other powers. If this could be ensured by minimum interference with the exercise of authority by the tribal chiefs and if, with financial subventions where necessary, those chiefs could maintain law and order, what could be simpler and more convenient? In this way, the sardari system continued and, as might be said, flourished.

It can be argued that the system has not a great deal to commend it, but it has to be recognized that Baluchistan is a difficult country to administer and to develop. It comprises 126,000 square miles (out of West Pakistan's total of 310,000 square miles) of poor soil, mostly rocky desert, with inadequate water resources. The population, which numbered 1,161,000 in 1961, is scattered among villages many miles apart, circumstances all adverse to social advance and economic progress. In 1961, the literacy rate in the Quetta Division of Baluchistan, expressed as a percentage of the population five years and over, was 13·2, a figure mostly due to the surprisingly high rate of 22·9 per cent in the Quetta-Pishin District of that Division. In the Kalat Division the figure is a mere 3·9 per cent. It is these very circumstances which have helped, rather than hindered, the survival of the sardari system and they account in part, but only in part, for the fact that when this system was withdrawn in the case of certain chiefs—notably Mengal, Bugti and Marri—the bureaucracy did not serve the people any better.

Being strongly opposed to any form or suggestion of power-rivalry, the bureaucracy disliked the sardari system intensely and no opportunity was ever lost of withdrawing or clipping the powers of a sardar. Some members of the administration were greatly resistant to the idea of giving any financial or other help to Baluchistan so long as the sardari system continued, an attitude as obscurantist and as obstinate as the system they so heartily professed to condemn. Thus, when the sardari was restored to the chiefs I have named by President Yahya Khan in October 1969, no one suggested that the tribesmen felt that their lives and interests had suffered any setback.

Finally it must be added that the One Unit comprised not only the territories mentioned but could, in a sense, be said to include Bahawalpur, the four Baluchistan States, and the Frontier States, all of which had acceded to Pakistan after independence. Bahawalpur and the Baluchistan States were absorbed into West Pakistan years before, but the Frontier States were absorbed in 1969, after Ayub Khan's departure. At the time of accession, however, all these States bore the same relation to the Central Government of Pakistan as did the princely states in the time of the British administration.

Until the republican constitution was promulgated in 1956 Pakistan was administered within the provisions of the Government of India Act 1935, with such amendments as had been made by the Independence Act of 1947 and afterwards by the Government of Pakistan. For this reason the three Provinces of the North-West Frontier, the Punjab, and Sind not only had a Governor with all the legal authority and trappings which go with that high office, but also a legislature, ministers and parliamentary secretaries all enjoying the authority and trappings which go with those high offices. Along with this constitutional furniture inevitably went provincial elections, ministerial crises, changes of ministry, the scramble for office, perquisites, peculation, and nepotism, all in multiple form. In addition there went a clear duplication of effort in many departments of the public administration, as well as a great deal of unnecessary and even injurious political rivalry at an inter-provincial level. In those days, a lot was heard about provincialism in Pakistan.

The effect of such a situation was to nullify most efforts at procuring any real measure of administrative uniformity or collaboration in an otherwise compact territory lying astride the Indus which forms its geographical backbone as well as its principal source of life-giving water. The justification for preserving these provincial divisions was difficult to discover since none of this territory is markedly cut off from the rest although some is more remote than that which spans the Indus and the main road and railway communications.

The existence of several provincial legislatures with power to make laws on a wide variety of topics, as set forth in the Government of India Act 1935, was an evident source of administrative confusion. Obviously, what might be legal in Sind, could be illegal in the Punjab. What might be taxable in the Punjab could be free of all impost in the North-West Frontier. Such circumstances as these might well influence a man in locating his business or industry, and inter-provincial competition could develop in law-making aimed at attracting industrialists and others, with rivalries which could easily prove harmful.

A source of much trouble was the ability of each Province to place restrictions on the movement of goods and produce in and out of its jurisdiction. It was possible, in fact, for each of them to create what might be called 'customs barriers' between themselves, and they often did so. There could, furthermore, be a conflict of interests, injurious to the people as a whole, springing from purely local, political considerations. It is not difficult to see how this might adversely affect the promotion of irrigation schemes, the utilization of river water, and the development of plans for the generation and distribution of high voltage electric power. As to the duplication of effort, of taxes, of conflicts in jurisdiction and other forms of administrative incompatibility, little imagination is needed to visualize the scope.

Seen in this way, it is not surprising that Rowlands and others felt that the geography of their Provinces should pose no reasonable objection or insuperable difficulty in the way of their administrative consolidation. The disappearance of a multiplicity of governors, of ministers, of legislators, and of official secretariats, along with all the paraphernalia associated with these dignitaries, appeared to offer many advantages. In their place, so it seemed, could come a rationalized uniformity in the law, the possibility of extensive economies, and a more efficient system of government altogether.

That there were material arguments against the idea must be allowed. Why, for example, had not the British, generally thought to have administered the sub-continent rather well, done this very thing? Circumstances alter cases and the sub-continent administered by the British, as well as the form in which British rule rose and developed, gave rise to a series of situations, as British dominion in the sub-continent extended, that were far from identical with the situation that prevailed when independence and partition took effect in 1947. Until 1935 Sind was a part of the Bombay Presidency and was split off from it by the Government of India Act of that year only after considerable agitation and opposition to the proposal. The pre-partition Punjab was a very much larger unit than the Punjabi-speaking area of West Pakistan. The North-West Frontier and Baluchistan were, for political reasons, treated by the British as rather special cases.

There were, however, other and possibly more cogent arguments. One lay in the magnitude of the area to be administered, 366,000 square miles, and the problem of communication involved. It seemed, however, that the development of road and rail travel, especially the former, the growth of the internal air network and the increasing provision of telecommunication services, would mitigate the worst difficulties caused by mere distance. The wide variation in population densities was a more difficult problem. In the Lahore Division, 9,000 square miles in extent, the population density was 721 persons to the square mile. In Kalat Division, with an area of 73,000 square miles, the density was seven persons to the square mile.[3] In a fairly well-developed urbanized area such as Lahore Division, problems of administration tend to be minimized and although high concentrations of people create their own problems, they certainly reduce the difficulties of providing schools and hospitals. When people are widely scattered and the density is extremely thin, it becomes a real problem to know how to provide schools and hospitals at all. The result is that the administration, consciously or unconsciously tends to pay more attention to those places where the task is easier and to overlook those areas where it is more difficult and may even appear intractable. It was considered that in the event of a One Unit consolidation, areas such as Kalat would find themselves at even greater disadvantage than before.

The people of the projected new Province were not homogeneous in language, culture, or way of life. They were all Muslims and, for the most part, of the Sunni sect, but the language of the North-West Frontier, Pushto, is as different from Punjabi as is the language of East Pakistan, Bengali. Punjabi-speaking persons would experience real difficulty in understanding a Sindhi or a Baluchi and might well not understand him at all. Theoretically, of course, everyone in West Pakistan was to learn Urdu at school, but this assumed that everyone would be going to school and that ideal was far from realization.

A more significant objection, the dominant consideration in the minds of those who opposed the One Unit consolidation, was that more than half the population of the projected One Unit would be Punjabi-speaking and this group might well be expected to exercise the major influence in the new Province. They were not only more numerous but could reasonably claim to be better educated, harder working, and more enterprising than their provincial compatriots, apart

[3] 1961 Census.

from the small, well-known commercial communities (Memons, Khojas, Bohras, Hindus and Parsis) which are numerically tiny and politically insignificant. Again, by reason of numbers and a generally higher educational standard, the Punjabi-speakers dominated the armed forces and the public services, and although in the professions and in business they were less numerous, the Punjabis, particularly those from the Chiniot community, were well represented in industry and trade.

The implicit dangers were instantly recognized by the smaller linguistic groups and opposition to the One Unit consolidation was prompt and vigorous. No less than three provincial Chief Ministers fell from office because of it, but the consolidation was carried through with the help of leaders from these very same linguistic groups in anticipation, perhaps, of later reward. The late Ghulam Mohamed and Choudhury Mohamed Ali have, in the main, been praised or blamed—according to the point of view—for the construction of the One Unit. Choudhury Mohamed Ali's own attachment to it was made clear enough in a newspaper article appearing in the *Pakistan Times* dated 3 January 1969, when it became apparent that a dissolution of West Pakistan was in prospect.

It is often alleged that those who proposed the One Unit consolidation in 1955 were little concerned with the intrinsic merits of the idea and that their purposes were inconsistent with the need for a just distribution of its benefits. These allegations do not have to do with the administrative proposals first tentatively aired by Sir Archibald Rowlands and others, but with the actual implementation of the plan years later. Ayub Khan's claims, distinctively set out in his book, that *he* was the real architect of the One Unit plan have inevitably been interpreted to his disadvantage. It is plain enough now, as it should have been in 1955, that in the circumstances, the prime duty of those who organized the One Unit, and this really means the Punjabi-speaking community in particular, was to ensure that the new Province should possess an administration marked by an unswerving sense of equity.

The Punjabi-speaking community claimed that in so far as they bore this responsibility, they had discharged it and that it was not their fault if circumstances were, in some ways, more favourable to them than to others. They pointed out that in the newly created National Assembly, set up by the Constitution of 1956, they had yielded up some seats to which they were otherwise entitled on the basis of linguistic representation. This had been done partly in pursuance of the principle of parity as between the two Provinces of East and West Pakistan and partly as a concession to their other partners in the western Province. The importance of this can be overstated and the record since 1955 indicates clearly enough that the Punjabi-speaking community was guilty of a short-sightedness and a selfishness which, as the years went by, became more and more apparent. In particular, those in the public administration did not display a due sense of impartiality, and as time went on the very evils that the minority communities feared became more and more oppressive. They affected the choice of persons for desirable appointments; promotion and seniority; the allotment of permits to establish industries, and the award of valuable contracts. Ultimately, they gave rise to very sinister intrigues. These things had certainly taken root before Ayub Khan assumed power in 1958 and for this reason he cannot be entirely blamed for the eventual decision to dissolve the One Unit and revert to separate linguistic administrative units in West Pakistan.

Ayub Khan's particular failure lies in the fact that, armed as he was with exceptional powers, he did nothing to ameliorate a situation of whose existence he must certainly have been aware, in particular the sense of grievance that existed and was finding expression. Not only did he do nothing to satisfy this expression of grievance, but he adopted methods more repressive than had his predecessors. These methods ranged from hounding political rivals from one jail to another; the closure of all newspapers opposed to him; and the suppression of public discussion by the abuse of Section 144; down to police excesses which were never subject to enquiry notwithstanding promises that they would be. He appeared unable or unwilling to recognize that there might be a case for administrative reform which, while retaining the advantages that the One Unit offered, would redress the grievances of people living in those non-Punjabi-speaking areas which had been merged into the Province of West Pakistan.

It is not easy to comprehend either the thinking or the motive in his approach to the growing problem of opposition to the One Unit since he must have been aware, if only from the intelligence reports which lay on his table, that this opposition was expanding both in extent and in boldness. And even if his intelligence service betrayed him, he must have realized that men do not agitate, go to jail or incur the risk of punitive fines for amusement, and there are easier ways of procuring publicity. Moreover, the opposition did not only run the risk of legal consequences although these could be troublesome enough. Quite apart from the established processes of law, a man might be detained under the various forms of security legislation enacted by both the Central and the Provincial Governments or, as in the case of Sardar Ataullah Khan Mengal, could be charged with sedition under the Pakistan Penal Code and, as in this notorious instance, the case could drag on for five or six years.

There were other forms of harassment which might be used to induce a change of heart towards the Government, or, alternatively, to silence critical voices. The local administration, including the police, can trouble a man in many ways. He can, for example, be gratuitously involved in a criminal case, real or trumped up—the late Nawab of Kalabagh's favourite was said to be a murder charge, or a charge of complicity in murder and this, being a serious offence, ensured that the victim was detained in jail until it was felt that he had come to his senses. A man engaged in farming may discover extraordinary difficulties in the way of getting irrigation water and people may come forward with trumped-up lawsuits involving his property. Personal violence, as in the case of Zamir Qureishy, was not unknown, but the fact is that men like Hyder Baksh Jatoi, Ghaus Baksh Bizenjo, Ataullah Khan Mengal and Abdus Samad Khan Achakzai, to name but four, were prepared to suffer all these things in the pursuit of their anti-One Unit agitation.[4]

---

[4] I have referred elsewhere in this book to Ghaus Baksh Bizenjo. In 1968 he was sentenced to fourteen years imprisonment and to pay a fine of Rs.5,000, at a *jirga* trial held in Quetta Jail. (A *jirga* trial means trial by an assembly of tribal elders assisted by a magistrate or other official trained in the law. It was made legally applicable throughout West Pakistan by Ayub Khan and was undoubtedly a political instrument. After he fell from office it was abolished.) Bizenjo's crime consisted, principally, in circulating currency notes on which he had rubber-stamped anti-One Unit slogans.

It does not follow that because a man has launched an agitation against somebody or something, that he necessarily has anything valid to agitate about. He may be a mere crank prepared to endure much for meaningless ideals or hair-brained notions.[5] He may be a troublesome nuisance simply seeking self-advertisement, but in reaching such conclusions caution is necessary and good judgement must be applied. It is scarcely necessary to say how many of those deemed cranks have been accepted by later generations as prophets or as men of genius.

So far as concerns Ayub Khan, in relation to the One Unit and its ultimate fate, the truth and substance of the matter is that in his determination to preserve this structure he was right. His error lay in the obstinacy with which he ignored the possibility that all was not working out quite in the way that it should and that injustices were being perpetrated which could and ought to be put right. In saying this, I do not ignore the fact that some of those who opposed the One Unit did so less from a sense of the public good, or even of local patriotism, than from a sense of private interest. Neither side was wholly right or wholly wrong. The misfortune was that Ayub Khan, as the country's Chief Magistrate, could not see clearly where and how he should intervene.

It has been earlier said that opposition to the One Unit proposal persisted from the time it was first made and was never, at any moment, entirely dissipated. Indeed, evidence of reaction was by no means wanting, some of it in entirely legal and even commendable form. Of this the Sind Abadi (meaning *history*) Board is a good example. A scholarly organization with its headquarters at Hyderabad, it set about publishing books on the language, history and culture of Sind. This work had little about it that was political or controversial but the underlying motive was plain enough. In a different sphere and at a different level, pamphlets appeared in profusion setting forth the miseries, injustices, and oppressions suffered by the people in whose language these various polemics were written. They came out

---

[5] Thus in January 1970 the chairman of the Pakistan Socialist Party undertook a hunger-strike in protest against 'nude dances' in night-clubs. According to his posters, Martial Law 'never allowed' nude dances. It would indeed have been surprising if it had.

regularly and were just as regularly proscribed.⁶ Local newspapers also participated in this undercurrent of opposition and in July 1968 the West Pakistan Government issued an order to newspapers that they were not to publish news items that might create ill-feeling among Muslim sects.⁷

In view of the movement against the One Unit as a whole, it is possible that in Baluchistan there was more actual physical resistance to the integration than anywhere else and, at one time, it almost appeared as if Baluchistan had seceded *de facto* if not *de jure* so far as could be judged by the open defiance of authority which prevailed there. Nevertheless Sind, with which Karachi is for the present purpose included, was the greater problem and the Government was more concerned with the growth of opposition and unrest in Sind than elsewhere. There were three reasons for this. Sind, politically, was much more sophisticated, and in Karachi Ayub Khan lost the election of 1965. It was economically more important and its territory lay astride the vital communications—road and rail— that connected Karachi with the north.

A habit of the administration in Pakistan, which developed notably during the period of Ayub Khan's government, was that of ignoring unpleasant realities and, by not reporting them or by discouraging or suppressing all report of them, to create an illusion of their non-existence. This happened more than once, with the inevitable consequence that when, ultimately, truth could no longer be stifled or withheld, its effect upon the public mind was magnified so much more.

This attitude was very true of the opposition to the One Unit, but the fact of its existence could not be disguised totally and as early as 1965 we find the Governor of West Pakistan making speeches on the essential unity of the Province.⁸ The meaning was not lost on anyone, but not until 1967 did Ayub Khan's administration apparently realize that the movement

---

⁶ Examples are: *Disposal of Guddu Barrage State Lands*, to do with scandals relating to the allotment of land brought under irrigation with the opening of the Guddu Barrage, and *Baluchistan Zindabad*, in Sindhi, by Hyder Baksh Jatoi. The title means *Long Live Baluchistan* and speaks for itself. Both were proscribed.
⁷ This could also refer to ill-feeling between Sunnis, Shi'as, Ahmediyas, etc., especially at the time of Mohurram when Sunni-Shi'a antipathy is apt to heighten.
⁸ E.g. in *D*, 17 July 1965.

against continuation of the One Unit, at any rate in its existing form and as it was then being administered, had attained meaningful proportions. Ayub Khan's response to this discovery was to suggest that persons speaking against the One Unit would be well advised not to waste their breath. This airy dismissal implies that he and his advisers, while realizing that such a movement existed, were confident that it could be contained and whittled away. After all, to this end the jails were open, and amenable persons in dissentient areas could be won to the side of the Government by grants of land, and similar methods of persuasion which had proved very successful on other occasions.

If this be so, it was an error of judgement. By 1967 the agitation against the One Unit had assumed clear shape and fixed direction. More and more people were coming to support it or, at any rate, to recognize the need for reform. The causes of the agitation had crystallized and the grievances were being openly canvassed. Particularly among the Pathans, but also among the Punjabis, money-making favours were being distributed in the form of licences and permits for trade and for setting up industries. This was done openly and avowedly and was said to be in pursuit of Government's policy to ensure a more equitable distribution of wealth. Whether or not other people in West Pakistan were getting their share of these valuable advantages, the fact was that the permits and licences awarded were, as often as not, carried to Karachi and there farmed so that they found their way into the hands of established businessmen and industrialists in any case.

But, it was also said, with the cash thus acquired, these people—particularly Punjabi-speakers—were able to enter Sind and acquire agricultural land, to the disadvantage of Sindhis. The instance was commonly cited of Nawabshah District where, by 1967, Punjabi-speakers were supposed to be in a majority, and it is no doubt correct that a tendency for the Punjabi-speaking population to increase in Sind was traceable as far back as the Census of 1961.[9] The unfair distribution of barrage land,[10] a subject to which we shall return, caused much

[9] The Census is taken every ten years.
[10] Barrage land means land irrigated by water distributed from one or other of the barrages constructed across the Indus and its tributaries.

bitter condemnation. Land was distributed on the basis of political favour and members of the bureaucracy, even those with no ancestral roots in the area, helped themselves with great liberality. The claims of the local people, apart from political favourites and cheer-leaders, were ignored and the poor, uninfluential, landless peasants found themselves substantially excluded.

So, too, with other forms of livelihood. Baluchi truck-owners found it troublesome and difficult to procure permits for operating their vehicles while Pathans obtained them with surprising ease.[11] Their smuggling operations through Landi Kotal into Pakistan, via Quetta, became a flourishing business.[12] The distribution of public funds for purposes of education, public health, and development was said to be unfair and both Sind and Baluchistan claimed to have suffered greatly in this respect. In these, and in various other subtle ways, the progress of the people of these areas was hampered, and they even asserted that the clear object of the administration was, if it could, to mould them into Punjabi-speaking people. They were to be persuaded or forced into a sacrifice of their own language and culture, and become absorbed into the dominant, Punjabi-speaking community.

By the middle of 1967 it became known that in Baluchistan the state of law and order had degenerated to the stage where recourse to the armed forces was necessary and aerial bombing

[11] Baluchistan has a substantial Pathan community and this community was shown considerable favour as contrasted with the Baluch. It is true that in the North West Frontier, traditional home of the Pathans, there was agitation against the One Unit and favouring a proposal for the creation of an autonomous Pakhtunistan as proposed by Abdul Ghaffar Khan. This was not quite the same thing as the agitation in Sind and Baluchistan but, as events turned out, the agitators found much common ground in 1968 and 1969.

[12] Smuggling has long been a well-established activity in this area, complicated by the fact that in the tribal belt anti-smuggling laws do not apply. According to Qazi Isa, a lawyer, politician, and Pakistan's former Ambassador to Brazil, smuggling is no crime in Islam (*Daily News*, 12 May 1967). It has been said that if smuggling were effectively put down in these parts, people would starve for want of occupation. During Ayub Khan's time the Hazara Bazar in Quetta, which specialized in contraband merchandise, became very well known. The significance of the name is that both Ayub Khan and General Musa came from Hazara District. It is not suggested that either of them was involved in this illicit traffic but some members of their families undoubtedly were. It is an interesting commentary on the scope of this traffic in Pakistan that in 1967 Customs seizures of contraband were valued at Rs.50 million. *NAD*, 30 May 1968.

was resorted to. In some areas, the writ of the Government no longer ran but only that of the local sardar who, as like as not, was detained in jail, thus making confusion worse confounded. In particular, the method of distribution of Guddu Barrage land, guided as it was by political motives and bureaucratic greed, caused much ill-feeling not only against the Government but also between the Baluch tribes and it is even possible that by creating inter-tribal jealousies the Government hoped to break down their unity. At any rate, ill-feeling degenerated into violence in which small arms were used and regular skirmishing went on.

On or about 21 August 1967 Bugti tribesmen, in furtherance of a feud with the Jakrani tribesmen, breached the Pat Feeder Canal at the point R.D. 162 measured from the Guddu Barrage. The Bugtis' intention was to flood their rivals' land and ruin their crops. It must be said, at once, that breaching canals is not a pastime begun during Ayub Khan's régime. It used to happen during the British administration. Usually, the purpose was to cause injury to an enemy and at the same time embarrass or annoy the administration, a convenient and easy form of side-swipe. So it was in the case of the Pat Feeder except that, in the end, it appeared as if the side-swipe were the major purpose.

The Pat Feeder Canal, which replaced the old Desert Feeder, takes water from the Indus at Guddu and distributes it to Upper Sind, Jacobabad, Sibi and Kacchi Districts. It is a high level canal and as the breach was about 200 feet long, the area flooded by the waters so released was considerable. Since the canal would have to be closed in order to repair the bank, areas additional to those flooded would not receive water until the repairs were complete and it was reckoned that as much as 300,000 acres of land might be adversely affected in consequence of the breach.

Repair was complicated by the fact that when the Irrigation Department engineers arrived to execute it, they were fired upon by entrenched Bugtis. The situation was aggravated when the nearest Deputy Commissioner refused to involve himself in the problem since the breach was located 160 feet outside the boundary of his jurisdiction. Later it was also reported that the Deputy Commissioner, within whose jurisdiction the matter actually lay, had taken sides in the dispute, which inflamed feeling all the more.

News of the trouble was kept out of the newspapers until in May 1968 the sardar of the Bugti tribe, Akbar Khan Bugti, was detained under the Defence of Pakistan Rules.[13] Two paragraphs from the official handout explaining this action are illuminating. 'An idea of the manner in which Mr. Mohammad Akbar Khan has been acting can be had from the *allegations* which led to his present arrest. These include disturbance of public order in the Pat Feeder Canal area, under his direction, raising of a lashkar[14] and directing it to commit acts of lawlessness in which law-abiding citizens were killed, creating hatred, unrest and agitation against the Government and inciting tribesmen to launch full-fledged operations against the authorities established by law.' In short, the Bugtis had declared war on the Government of Pakistan.[15]

Or very nearly. There is no doubt that troops were continuously engaged in various operations—patrolling, rounding up dissidents, skirmishing. The task was not an easy one, for the Baluchistan terrain is formidable. The climate is extremely hot and dry in summer, very cold in winter. It is mountainous, with a myriad of tracks and paths known best to the tribesmen who managed, without much difficulty, to elude their pursuers. They are masters of hit-and-run tactics and their familiarity with the mountain ranges gave them immense advantages and, if necessary, they could disappear across the border into Iran whither the Pakistan troops could not officially go. In these operations, casualties were not only inflicted by the Pakistani troops but also suffered, and in December 1968, in the course of one of these encounters, it was reported that twenty Pakistani soldiers were killed.[16] The affair of the Pat Feeder drifted on as late as November 1969, when the new Governor of West Pakistan, Air Marshal Nur Khan, at a gathering of tribal sardars at Khazdar in the Kalat Division,

---

[13] *D*, 7 May 1968. The word *allegations* quoted below has been italicized by me.

[14] *Lashkar* means an army or an armed levy.

[15] The scale of the Pat Feeder affair can, perhaps, be gauged to some extent from the title of a pamphlet which appeared concerned with it. The title reads: *Baluchistan men Pat Feeder ka Khooni Drama* (*The Bloody Drama of the Pat Feeder in Baluchistan*). The pamphlet was banned.

[16] The *Statesman*, Calcutta, 27 December 1968.

gave an assurance that a tribunal would be set up to settle disputes relating to land irrigated from this canal.

The spirit of discontent spread to the townsfolk and inflamed sentiment there. In June 1968, serious rioting occurred in Quetta which had its origins in a minor but distasteful incident all too common during Ayub Khan's administration. A relation of the Governor, General Musa, was accused of having troubled a girl, who informed her father, an Army officer. The boy and *his* father were beaten up by indignant sympathizers of the girl and her family. In the heated atmosphere that prevailed the trouble spread instantly and at once took on a Baluch-versus-Punjabi aspect. It was yet another opportunity to beat the Government with the anti-One Unit stick.

But the problem was not confined to agitation in the countryside and tribal warfare. It found its way into the legislature also. In another chapter we shall have occasion to refer to the Eighth Amendment to Ayub Khan's Constitution which became law in December 1967. The effect of this Amendment was to restore to the Punjabi-speaking area its full representation in the National Assembly. The political implications of this, so far as the One Unit was concerned, were very plain and they were seized upon at once. The leader of the Opposition in the Assembly, Nurul Amin from East Pakistan, immediately declared that this change put the One Unit consolidation in danger. This proved to be a theme which other leaders from East Pakistan took up and when, late in 1968 and in 1969, Ayub Khan was in retreat, they pressed it with increasing vigour.

Nurul Amin's ominous words drew a prompt response. Yet it was apparent that, so far as the One Unit was concerned, Ayub Khan's habit of riding roughshod was missing, and the Government showed itself more and more to be on the defensive. It became both the price and the test of loyalty to the administration that leaders in West Pakistan should declare their support for the One Unit and expound its virtues. There were threatening hints directed towards those who persisted in the seditious notion of wanting to break it up. In March 1968 the Governor, General Musa, made what was evidently intended to be a major pronouncement on the subject, but the effort was distinctly poor. Reading what he had to say, one is left wondering whether he really grasped the issues involved and the remedies necessary for legitimate grievances.[17]

Until November 1968, when all restraint disappeared, debate on the One Unit tended to be reserved. The topic was still sacrosanct and any adverse mention of it might carry a charge of sedition, for sedition had come to signify any opinion which did not correspond with that held by Ayub Khan. After November 1968, however, all who disliked the One Unit cast aside their reserve and came out openly in their condemnation. As earlier indicated, among those who had much to say on this topic were leaders from East Pakistan, notably Sheikh Mujibur Rahman, who declared that the One Unit arrangement could not remain. Since the people of his Province could scarcely claim to have endured any of the misery or oppression which had fallen upon people in West Pakistan as a result of this consolidation, it is worth considering why Sheikh Mujibur Rahman and other East Pakistani leaders were so emphatic about its disappearance.

We can charitably assume that they were genuinely moved by the spectacle of gross injustice inflicted upon their Sindhi-speaking, Baluch-speaking, and Pushto-speaking countrymen, but it cannot be overlooked that out of the dissolution of the One Unit, valuable political advantages could accrue to East Pakistan. The reappearance of the old Provinces that later made up West Pakistan would greatly simplify the possibility of forming some kind of alliance with, for example, the Sindhi-speaking members of the National Assembly. Such an alliance would certainly make it possible for East Pakistan to dominate that chamber. The weight of this political fact is incontestable and has all along been a powerful element in the thinking of everyone concerned with the One Unit and its future.

All the problems associated with these matters belong to the future. With the departure of the One Unit, it remains to be seen to what extent a rigorous separation between the Provinces will operate. After Martial Law was declared in 1969 a Commission was set up by President Yahya Khan to investigate the question of de-centralization, a euphemism for enquiring into the need and method by which the One Unit

[17] This speech was deemed important enough to justify verbatim report in the newspapers. See *D*, 21 March 1968.

could be dissolved. The Report of the Commission was not published, but it is certain that a dissolution of West Pakistan into its constituent linguistic areas[18] was the minimal demand from those who gave evidence before the Commission. This, too, appears to have been the opinion expressed by political leaders who met President Yahya to discuss the country's political future.

Such, then, was the fate of West Pakistan after ten years of Ayub Khan's administration. It was yet another misfortune that accrued to the country springing from his faulty judgement, a megalomaniac unwillingness to consider facts and an apparent inability to listen to opinions which did not coincide with his own.

It is an undoubted disaster for West Pakistan that his period of administration led to these results. The One Unit consolidation had its political, financial, economic, and cultural difficulties but the logic of the idea can scarcely be contested. If so, the logic of those who led or rallied to the agitation against it must be conceded. But it was a case that pointed not to dissolution but to reform. It is difficult to see why, with a realizable scheme of regional councils, or bodies of that nature, it would not have been possible to remedy grievances and, at the same time, retain the advantages which a single provincial legislature and administration offered.

The attribution of purely selfish motives to those who sponsored and carried through the One Unit consolidation which, in any case, was achieved, and could only be achieved, with the help and collaboration of non-Punjabi leaders, later became commonplace in Pakistan. It is true that political conduct is rarely divorced from ulterior purposes, but it is equally untrue that only concealed purposes count or are intended to count. Were all political action thus guided, neither social nor economic progress would be possible. In West Pakistan, despite obvious sources of divisive feeling and purpose, both religious and secular, many people believed in and looked forward to the evolution of a solid, stable, political unit. With a population 99 per cent Muslim, there seemed to be the clear opportunity,

[18] The Baluch leader, Abdus Samad Khan Achakzai wanted new Provinces organized on a purely linguistic basis. This view is reported in *The Daily News*, 16 August 1969.

despite sectarian differences, of uniting around the banner of Islam and thus deriving inspiration sufficient to dissolve such causes of division as language, custom and local affinities, tribal or other. In the One Unit, many people believed the foundations were laid on which to construct a well-ordered Islamic community spared the disruptive agony of Hindu-Muslim antagonisms. To them it appeared that between the troubled Middle East on the one hand and a febrile India racked by communal discord on the other, West Pakistan could provide a bastion, both powerful and tranquil, undisturbed by religious and political turmoil. It seems this was an erroneous judgement. Perhaps, as the Arab states have long demonstrated, Islam is not enough.

It appears certain—at any rate President Yahya Khan was evidently convinced of its truth—that by the time the agitation against the One Unit had become fully explicit, public feeling had gone far beyond the point where anything less than total dissolution would be acceptable. This does not in the least mean that total dissolution was desirable, but the inflexible public demand for it simply underlined the destructive consequences of Ayub Khan's period of rule. In justice, it should be said again that the blame does not lie on his shoulders alone. Many among the Punjabi-speaking majority of West Pakistan shared it.

It is not necessary to dwell further on this point. The important question changed to something different. Those among the linguistic groups who comprised the One Unit and sought dissolution had their way. In their own respective territories they became masters with the certain belief that this was well. But they had yet to show that they could manage and administer what they had regained and could do so without inter-provincial rivalry and conflict of aim. Could the North West Frontier or Baluchistan manage their affairs without other help, including that of the Punjabi-speakers? Would each Province erect ever-rising barriers around itself so that only a Sindhi-born, Sindhi-speaking person could expect to thrive in Sind? And likewise in other Provinces? What would be the fate of *muhajirs* (refugees) who had come from India in 1947 and had settled themselves in the towns and countryside of these Provinces? Could the energetic and enterprising Punjabi be successfully restrained from applying his talent and determination where he would? And, if so, how?

The men of the old Provinces got what they wanted—no doubt of that—and the problem of Pakistan's western wing assumed new shape. In its new form, the problem could be very simply stated: What would they do with it?

XII

Constitutional Change after September 1965

As discussed in this chapter, constitutional change means a great deal more than the four further amendments introduced by Ayub Khan between November 1965 and December 1967. It includes consideration of the ultimate fate of his constitutional structure and the reasons that led the nation to reject it with so much emphasis that Ayub Khan himself was obliged to propose its dismantling. Moreover, we have to consider the merits of the claim, so often made on his behalf, both in Pakistan and abroad, that whatever else might be said of his administration and the Constitution he had devised, he had, at any rate, succeeded in giving to the country a structure that brought with it a sense of calm and stability that made other progress possible.

These four Amendments were facilitated by the fact that, as we know, the hostilities of September 1965 had enabled Ayub Khan to declare an emergency under Article 30 by which he was armed with very much more power, particularly with reference to the power of legislation by ordinance. Indeed, as we shall see, some of the amendments themselves were the product of those restrictions imposed by Article 30 because, as time passed and as the state of emergency continued, people became more and more impatient of the restrictions and constitutional amendment proved to be the only solution.

The easiest way to deal with these Amendments is to assimilate them under the subjects with which they dealt, namely:

(a) Terms and conditions of public service with special reference to the age of retirement and the power of the President to direct the retirement of individuals.
(b) Other minor changes in terms of service[1] and changes of definition of certain categories of public servant.

[1] Clause 2 of one of the Articles affected by the Fourth Amendment was described as being 'not very complimentary to the higher judiciary of the country and not worth incorporation in the Constitution.' Munir, op. cit., p. 439.

(c) Changes in the enforcibility of fundamental rights as set out in the Constitution.
(d) Changes in Article 30 with respect to the President's power of legislating by ordinance.
(e) Increase in the number of seats in the National and Provincial Assemblies.

Of all these, the most important group, so far as concerned its practical effect and the power it gave to Ayub Khan to manipulate the public administration, belonged to the first category listed above. Ayub Khan's intention was to empower himself to get rid of public officials whom he did not like, and to retain those whom he did like for as long after the prescribed age of retirement as he might wish.

It may be said that these were very necessary powers. It should and must be possible for any public administration to disembarrass itself of incompetent or otherwise undesirable public servants. No one will contest these arguments, but there are one or two remarks to be made concerning them. The first is that, like all other public administrations, the Government of Pakistan has set up machinery for recruitment that is intended to ensure that persons taken into service are likely to possess the qualifications—ability and integrity—which the public service requires. The second is that at no time has it ever appeared that the administration in Pakistan lacked the power to get rid of public servants who did not measure up to the standards required although, admittedly, there may be legal difficulties, especially when misconduct is alleged. Moreover, after prerogative writs were introduced in Pakistan, the Courts were flooded with petitions for them, the majority originating with government servants who considered themselves aggrieved, usually over matters of promotion, seniority, dismissal, and other such problems of service life. However, the important question in the present context is whether Ayub Khan exercised the powers which these amendments conferred on him solely in the public interest or, on occasion, in his own.

The answer to this question has two forms. The first—which will be discussed here—lies in the manner in which the Constitution was amended with respect to the subject. In short, was the method of amendment such as to lead to the conclusion that his motives were entirely pure? (Elsewhere in this book, factual evidence has been adduced which gives rise to the suspicion inherent in this question.) The attempt to change the Constitution, in a material respect, within ninety-six hours of its coming into effect; the numerous amendments made in a brief period of five and a half years; the repression of criticism and the victimization of critics—all these are some of the circumstances which cast doubt upon the innocence of Ayub Khan's purposes.

Secondly, how were these powers used? Were the men retained by Ayub Khan of such loftiness of character, good reputation, and ability that their retention was in the national interest? As a corollary, it must be asked whether the continued presence of some of those he dismissed after the Constitution was amended would necessarily have been detrimental to the nation? It is by no means certain that the answers to these two questions are favourable to Ayub Khan.

We are here concerned with the Sixth Amendment, enacted on 31 March 1966, which was an elaboration of the Fourth Amendment, enacted on 11 August 1965, seven months earlier. The Fourth Amendment, it will be recalled, made it possible to direct the retirement of civil servants in the Central and provincial Governments at the age of fifty-five instead of at the age of sixty, as had been established by Ayub Khan from December 1962 onwards. The reasons for adopting a retirement age of sixty have been explained,[2] but thirty-four months after giving effect to this policy, Ayub Khan evidently concluded that fifty-five was the right age, after all. The Fourth Amendment gave effect to this conclusion, as we have seen, but the manner in which it did so apparently did not suffice and, seven months later, it was decided that this arrangement required elaboration so that the President (or a Governor) could not only direct retirement at the age of fifty-five, or after completion of twenty-five years of pension-qualifying service, but could also allow extensions of service beyond the official retirement age, at his discretion, on such terms as he might decide.

With respect to all this, a number of interesting questions arise. The advancement of the age of retirement to sixty was provided for by a simple Finance Ministry notification. Why

[2] See pp. 31-2.

could not the new arrangement for retirement at fifty-five with possible retention after that age have been made in precisely the same way? Why was it necessary to import the new arrangements into the Constitution, when the previous arrangement in respect of a retirement age of sixty had been carried out by a simple administrative act? I do not pretend to know the answer to these questions, but it could well be that having decided on the new arrangements, Ayub Khan wanted to make them as unchallengeable as possible.

It may further be asked why the elaboration contained in the Sixth Amendment was thought necessary so soon after the Fourth Amendment was enacted. Why was the entire change—lowering of retirement age and the right to retain persons after reaching retirement age—not made in one amendment? Why two bites at the cherry? Two explanations are possible. Either, when preparing the Fourth Amendment, the clause authorizing retention after retirement age was not thought about, or it was thought about but it was also considered that the public—and more particularly the civil services—should not be asked to swallow too much at once. It must be remembered that these changes affected many men's lives, favourably or unfavourably as the dice might fall, and the reduction of the retirement age, so soon after its advancement to sixty, was far from being a universally popular measure.

In the absence of very clear evidence it is impossible to say which of the explanations suggested is the more probable. There are ample, collateral indications that Ayub Khan's advisers were often lackadaisical in their thinking and much half-baked advice was given. There are, however, equally cogent indications that Ayub Khan, in his various and successful efforts at manipulating the Constitution to serve his purposes, adopted devious and carefully planned methods to disguise his intentions. In the present case, it could well be that he decided at the outset that he would not only return to a retirement age of fifty-five, but retain power to keep any man over that age if he so chose. Having made this decision, he deemed it wiser to achieve these purposes in two stages. The brief period of seven months which separated the Fourth and Sixth Amendments lends weight to either argument.

The outcome of all this was to blight many men's prospects

and to throw the careers of many others into the melting pot. The Sixth Amendment was mostly used to retain at pleasure those men who had proved, since 1958, to be Ayub Khan's most amenable creatures. It is not difficult to see how rules of this kind, by which a civil servant's retirement or retention becomes almost a matter for one man's discretion, can be used or abused to ensure the advancement of some men and to impede the advancement of others. It could be argued in favour of the reduction of the retirement age to fifty-five, that it had been shown by experience—thirty-four months' experience!— to be in the better public interest, and that the old administrators were right, after all. What could not be shown was that the public interest would be better served because some men might, purely as a matter of unregulated choice, be retained in the service after retirement age, for as long as any President might care to keep them.

Changes in the power of the individual to enforce the fundamental rights prescribed by and defined in the Constitution were the product of the Fifth Amendment dated 30 November 1965. This Amendment was enacted at a time when relations with India were still considerably heated and when a resumption of the September fighting seemed possible. For this reason Ayub Khan reinforced the operation of Article 30, which defined the power of the President to declare a state of emergency, and the consequences that flowed from such a declaration. The Amendment provided that after an emergency had been declared, the restriction, as provided elsewhere in the Constitution, on making laws or taking executive action in contravention of certain fundamental rights, would be automatically removed. The fundamental rights so affected comprised freedom of movement, of assembly, of association, of trade, freedom of speech and the right to hold property. The Amendment also empowered the President, with respect to other fundamental rights provided by the Constitution, to declare that the right to enforce them in the Courts should remain suspended during the period of the emergency.

It can readily be conceded that the power of the Government to act in contravention of some of these fundamental rights was consistent with the necessities of a nation at war or with partially severed relations with another country. An obvious instance of the latter case is that in which a country, by reason of its obligations under the United Nations charter, finds itself compelled to make laws, within its own jurisdiction, restraining trade with another country on which sanctions have been imposed. With equal reason the Pakistan Government was entitled to deny its citizens the right to trade with India because certain relationships with that country had been broken and remained so for some time after actual hostilities came to an end. Denial of the right to hold property was consistent with the appointment of Custodians of Enemy Property when hostilities began in September 1965, and property which came into the hands of those officials was not restored afterwards.

Objection to and suspicion of constitutional changes such as the Fifth Amendment did not so much lie in their actual provisions but rather in the retention of the state of emergency for years after the hostilities which had given rise to it, were over, and it continued to be retained even after relations between India and Pakistan had taken clear shape. The root of the objection was not that the Amendment had withdrawn any fundamental rights, but that it had rendered them ineffectual and enabled the Government to contravene them as it chose, and without risk of challenge. Furthermore, this remained the position for more than three years.

It was this very continuance of the state of emergency, and the power that it placed in Ayub Khan's hands, which created so much discontent, and in the years that followed he was frequently taxed with it. An attempt was made in the National Assembly to have the declaration of emergency withdrawn or, at any rate, its continuance condemned, but this was easily and successfully resisted. To all suggestions that the time had come for withdrawal, Ayub Khan's answer was invariably the same. It amounted to an assertion that there *was* an emergency. The country was threatened by external foes and by internal dissensions and the implication was that the best judge as to whether or not an emergency existed was Ayub Khan himself.

However, he could not totally ignore the growing opposition to the continued application of Article 30. It was therefore changed, in the Seventh Amendment dated 19 December 1965, so as to extend, very slightly, the power of the National Assembly to participate in legislation by ordinance which itself was part of the presidential prerogative. Thus this Amendment was principally concerned with Clause 6 of Article 30.

As originally drafted, Clause 6 provided that the National Assembly had no power to disapprove of any ordinance promulgated under Article 30 but that it could, by resolution, approve of it, in which case the Ordinance would be deemed to have become an Act of the National Assembly. If the Assembly did not confer its formal approval in this way, the Ordinance would cease to have effect if and when the state of emergency ended. This arrangement was changed by the Seventh Amendment which replaced the existing Clause 6 by Clauses 6 and 6(A). While disapproval of an ordinance promulgated under Article 30 would still remain outside the authority of the National Assembly, the Assembly could, by resolution, approve of the ordinance with, or without, amendment. The power to amend was thus introduced and under the new arrangement an ordinance approved by the Assembly would become an act of the Central Legislature provided the amendments it had proposed received presidential assent. This extension of the Assembly's authority was clearly minimal and did nothing to moderate or clip the powers which Ayub Khan exercised for so long after the emergency was first proclaimed. Nevertheless, a dutiful chorus hailed these changes as a great and important addition to the Assembly's powers.

The eighth and last of these Amendments, dated 19 December 1967, has, to some extent, been noticed in earlier chapters. It was this Amendment which changed the Constitution by increasing the number of seats in the National Assembly from 156 to 218 and in the case of Provincial Assemblies from 150 to 200. The number of seats reserved for women was increased by two in each instance and there was a reservation of seats for persons who had distinguished themselves in certain walks of life as defined by the Amendment.

Whatever else may be said of these Amendments, there was nothing in them to lead anyone to suppose that they or Ayub Khan had the intention of reducing or limiting the power that he had gathered into his hands. Moreover, the nature of some of them indicated that he had no intention either of withdrawing the state of emergency, and so long as that continued such legislative powers as the National and Provincial Assemblies possessed were rendered null. Therefore dissatisfaction remained and this group of Amendments laid the foundation for fresh discontent. A number of senior and, in some cases, very capable civil servants were compulsorily retired from the service and a number of others were rapidly advanced to high place in the bureaucracy. Nor can it be said that all of these fortunate men, including those remaining on a contract basis after reaching retirement age, justified the confidence thus placed in them and some figured in the notorious list of 303 Class I officers suspended in December 1969 on various charges of misconduct including corruption.[3] As for those who had been compulsorily retired, it will cause no surprise to learn that some of them became active political opponents of Ayub Khan.

For all these reasons, therefore, the constitutional issue remained as important as ever. People concluded that Ayub Khan had no intention of meeting the objections and criticisms that were being made of the constitutional structure and of the vast personal power that he wielded. It was true that Ayub Khan had declared more than once that the Constitution could be changed and he went so far as to declare: 'Any change which is in the interest of the people and will help to maintain the unity and solidarity of the country will have my support.'[4] This sounded all very well but whose was the best judgement of what was in the interest of the people and would help to maintain unity and solidarity? Moreover, he qualified these encouraging remarks by making it clear that he did not contemplate any change that would lead to a return to a parliamentary form of government for this would 'open the floodgates of political instability which, as our experience has shown, will imperil not only our progress but also our security'.[5]

The fact that eventually it fell to Ayub Khan to propose a return to the parliamentary system—which he had so often condemned—based on elections by direct, universal adult

[3] Known popularly as 'Operation 303'. (A great deal of sardonic humour turned on the coincidence between this number and the bore (0·303 inches) of the famous Lee-Enfield rifle with which the Armed Forces of the sub-continent had long been equipped). Some of the suspended officers were subsequently exonerated and they returned to their duties.
[4] Speech at the Dacca Session of the National Assembly, 8 March 1966.
[5] ibid.

suffrage, is in some respects the greatest measure of his failure, and a measure, too, of his want of principle.

As we have seen, many people in Pakistan were, from the outset, suspicious of Ayub Khan's Constitution and they disliked the mechanics of its operation. The fact that these feelings persisted is significant and they could not be dismissed simply by saying that those who retained them were all wrong-headed, or selfish traitors bent on destroying Pakistan. On the other hand, not all of those who remained in opposition to Ayub Khan, and sought the end of his administration and Constitution, were, to a man, noble, high-minded fellows engaged in a valiant crusade to overcome tyranny. When it came to a comparison of that sort, were anyone unwise enough to embark upon it, Ayub Khan had plenty of cards to play, as he well knew. It may appear to be an over-simplification but the truth seems to be that both Ayub Khan and his Constitution had to go because both had failed and the various chapters of this book are studies of the varying aspects of that failure.

Thus, considered as an instrument of political stability, there is little to prove that the Constitution of 1962 was more effective than any which had preceded it, including the Government of India Act of 1935. The liberal application of Section 144, along with the frequent use of the Defence of Pakistan Rules and other security legislation, probably contributed as much to the maintenance of national unity as did Ayub Khan's Constitution, which he liked to regard as the expression of the 'genius and requirements of the people'.[6]

These remarks apply particularly to Section 144 which is very familiar both in Pakistan and India, as, for that matter, is its use.[7] The product of British rule, this stroke of administrative genius was inherited by two grateful independent governments and seems likely to endure in utility, as well as in popularity with the civil administrators of each. Its main purpose is to make it possible for a District Magistrate in times of civil commotion or tension to prohibit the gathering of people and to enforce restrictions as prohibition on the carrying of arms and matters of that kind. However, the terms of the Section are so wide that it can be used for an infinite variety of purposes.

[6] ibid.
[7] Section 144 of the Criminal Procedure Code is reproduced in Appendix F.

Interesting applications of this Section in Pakistan include a prohibition on tenants from removing grain from the threshing-floor before the landlord had received his share;[8] a prohibition on the use of firewood for brick-burning;[9] a prohibition on the export of wheat from a district affected by famine;[10] a prohibition on the entry of non-students and others within a radius of twenty-five yards of intermediate examination centres;[11] and a prohibition on 'all processions by members of a local Bar Association'.[12]

According to the Section, such orders can be made for a maximum period of two months, but there is power to extend this. In Dacca, on 31 March 1968, Section 144 was imposed for 'an indefinite period' and, shortly afterwards, in Chittagong also, as it appeared, indefinitely. Early in March 1968 it was accurately pointed out that Section 144, prohibiting meetings and assemblies, had been in almost continuous operation in Karachi for some three years, often for no reason more specific than that 'there exists a situation likely to disturb public peace and tranquillity'.[13]

There is no doubt about the usefulness of the Section in placing restraints during times of public disorder and the effect of imposing it is to aggravate any offence against law and order. In this sense, imposition is akin to reading the Riot Act. Quite apart from problems of law and order, it is useful in preventing or abating nuisances, e.g. improper use of loud-speakers. However, if the Section has to be invoked continually, or is retained year after year, it can hardly be said that it is the constitutional structure which is providing the basis of order and civic stability. If, in the circumstances mentioned, the life of Karachi appeared tranquil and undisturbed, it can scarcely be inferred from this that the people remained so by virtue of a Constitution so wisely conceived that they were content with the method of government and had nothing to complain about.

It would be false to suggest that the use of Section 144 prior

[8] In Gujarat, May 1967.
[9] In Dera Ismail Khan, May 1969.
[10] In Sibi, August 1969.
[11] In Gujranwala, August 1969.
[12] In Sahiwal, November 1969. This order under the Section was, however, suspended by the High Court on the ground that it was a fraud upon the statute.
[13] *Daily News*, Karachi, 6 March 1968.

to the advent of Ayub Khan's administration was rare, but it would be difficult to find an instance comparable with Karachi's experience during the years that he was President. Further, it would not be correct to suggest that even in his time Section 144 was used, and used exclusively, to restrict political activity adverse to himself. With the onset of the mourning month of Mohurram, for example, it has long been necessary, especially in some parts of West Pakistan, to impose Section 144 in order to prevent quarrels, and even bloodshed, between the Sunni and Shi'a sects.[14] And, as has been seen from the instances cited, there were many other occasions when the Section was invoked that had little or nothing to do with muzzling public outcry against Ayub Khan.

Although before his administration Section 144 was employed as often as appeared necessary, during Ayub Khan's rule it was used for political purposes and for political repression more than at any previous time. Indeed, during his administration, its use had become habitual and the constant application of the Section, especially in urban areas, had the disastrous consequence of numbing the civil administration to any sense of failure or even disquiet. It never seemed to occur to Ayub Khan or to any of his administrators that repeated recourse to Section 144 did not merely prove that the public had an incurable, insatiable hunger for violence. The readiness of many sections of the people to create commotion and disturbance at the least provocation or excuse can easily be admitted. The misfortune was that at no time did it ever seem to have occurred to the administration that this readiness might be due, in some part, to the inability of the Government to remove the causes that led people to go out into the streets looking for trouble.

The use of the Defence of Pakistan Rules and existing

[14] During the first ten days of Mohurram, Muslims mourn the martyrdom of Hussain, son of Ali and grandson of the Prophet. Since the Shi'as attach special importance to Ali and consider he should have been raised to the Caliphate on the Prophet's death, they lay special stress on mourning for Ali's son, martyred at Karbela. The Sunnis take a different view concerning the succession and this difference between the two sects has widened into a considerable conflict of attitude on many important questions of doctrine and law. It is during such times as the first ten days of Mohurram that it even becomes necessary for the administration to restrain certain individual *moulvis* and *maulanas* (religious teachers) from proceeding to places where their presence is likely to arouse violent sentiments.

security legislation speaks for itself and it is indisputable that Ayub Khan used these Rules and this legislation for political purposes. The case of Sheikh Mujibur Rahman has already been mentioned. The Defence of Pakistan Rules were part of the immediate product of hostilities with India and it can readily be conceded that regulations of this sort are admissible when a country is at war and even during the period of armistice that usually follows a war. The argument against the Defence of Pakistan Rules did not lie in the fact of their introduction, or even of their retention during the months of stress and uncertainty that followed the cease-fire in September 1965. The objection was to their retention for years afterwards and to their utilization for purely political purposes.

The same was true with such statutes as the security acts and the security ordinances of the Central Government and the provincial Governments. These statutes, it is fair to explain, were by no means all the work of Ayub Khan's administration. Some had been enacted years before; the sections of the Pakistan Penal Code which dealt with sedition and were rather well favoured by Ayub Khan and his administration, were the product of British rule. One of the more serious dangers of legislation of this kind is the ease with which it becomes an instrument of repression and for limiting the freedom of the individual in his right to make a choice. Thus Mir Ghaus Baksh Bizenjo, whose case has already been mentioned, was a Baluch who did not like the One Unit consolidation. He considered it had proved injurious to the people of Baluchistan and desired to see the end of it. The question here is not whether he was right in this opinion, but how, and in what way, this opinion and the propagation of this opinion could be deemed seditious? Yet it was on such a charge, founded upon such facts, that he was sentenced to a long term of imprisonment and a heavy fine. Indeed, during Ayub Khan's time, the utilization of Section 144 and the Defence of Pakistan Rules to limit political activity and to keep people in jail and the prosecution of others by appeal to security and sedition laws, became unrestrained. Officialdom lost all sense of balance and for this Ayub Khan had to answer.

The suggestion, therefore, that Ayub Khan introduced a Constitution which brought stability and a sense of ordered calm to the nation has very little foundation. If the political temperature seemed normal, if crowds and processions were rarely seen on the streets, if tumult and riot rarely irrupted upon the citizen's daily life, this had far less to do with the sagacious, far-sighted framing of a constitution, the principles and mechanics of which had evolved from the long-continued meditation of a profound mind, than with the plentiful use of rules authorizing detention, laws against sedition and, of course, the many-sided versatility of Section 144.

XIII

The Great Decade

28 October 1967 witnessed the inception of the tenth year of Ayub Khan's Great Decade of Development and Reform. During the months that followed a great deal of money, material, and effort was expended in eulogizing and publicizing its achievements. However, the central theme of this campaign was not so much the visible product of Ayub Khan's exertions as the tribute to be paid to his personality and genius. For this reason the correct and acceptable clichés of those times included *beloved President, dynamic leadership, soldier-statesman, pragmatic outlook*, and such other adulation as the alliance of wit and flattery could devise.

Since this period of rejoicing was to continue until October 1968, there was ample time in which to develop the image of towering ability and inflexible strength of character, indispensable attributes of a man in whom Pakistan could safely repose its hopes. The development of such an image was not, however, intended merely for the idle nourishing of Ayub Khan's personal egotism, but had deeper and more practical purposes to serve. It was designed to satisfy the prior requisite of his election strategy since, in 1969, elections for a new Electoral College would be held, followed by an election for the office of President in January 1970. This early move, it may be said in passing, faithfully reflected the care and forethought which Ayub Khan always devoted to projects in which he was personally interested and in this respect was the echo of his preparations in 1964.

As it happened, the tenth and final year of the Great Decade opened badly for Ayub Khan. About 29 January 1968, the news was published that he had a touch of influenza and had been advised rest for two or three days. On 6 February newspapers stated that he had developed virus pneumonia in the right lung and was running a temperature. His personal physician had advised rest 'for a few weeks'. Naturally, rumour spread quickly that the illness was a good deal more serious than the bulletins suggested and people noted a disparity between an attack of virus pneumonia and the necessity of rest 'for a few weeks'. On 18 February pictures appeared showing Ayub Khan in a dressing gown, talking to General Musa. Afterwards, the General gave a fulsome account of his conversation with Ayub Khan who had expressed a good deal of concern for the nation and also about other matters, including General Musa's ailing father. However, it appeared that General Musa was, apart from Ayub Khan's immediate family, the only person to have seen him on his legs at this particular time and to have spoken with him. The rumours still went round and eventually it was stated that Ayub Khan had suffered an embolism of the lung restricting the flow of blood to the heart and with this medical circumlocution the public had to rest content.

By 1 March 1968 Ayub Khan had recovered sufficiently to deliver his first-of-the-month broadcast, but it was obvious he was still convalescent. He spoke in Urdu for about five minutes, his voice firm but with the trace of weariness that always appeared in his formal broadcasts irrespective of his state of health. He was also seen on television and appeared to have aged and weakened in health. Still, as the weeks passed, it became evident he had made a good recovery and although certainly advised not to undertake undue strain, he resumed much, if not all, of his former activity.

Ayub Khan's illness had at least two important consequences of which one was a constitutional issue and the other related to the use of television in Pakistan. Neither of these was much commented on at the time since, by 1968, comment that had any undertone of criticism of Ayub Khan and of any course of action he might choose to adopt was not generally welcome. Later, both matters referred to here were adversely criticized, especially with respect to the Constitution.

This point had to do with Article 16 which provided, among other things, that when at any time the President was unable to perform the functions of his office because of illness or some other cause, the Speaker of the National Assembly should perform the presidential duties. The same Article placed some limitations on the powers of the acting President, but was clear enough on what was to happen if the President were incapacitated by illness.

It is a curious point that Article 14, which provided for the removal of the President in the event of physical or mental incapacity, on the motion of the National Assembly, also provided that in the event of such a motion being passed, the President would then be required to submit himself to a Medical Board whose membership was defined in Article 15. In this case, therefore, the mechanics were clearly stated and the question of incapacity would be specifically determined by a Medical Board constituted within the terms of Article 15.

In the case of inability of the President to perform his functions due to illness 'or some other cause', as Article 16 vaguely and clumsily had it, no provision was made whereby incapacity due to illness could or had to be professionally determined. So far as this went, under Article 16, the President might simply feign illness to avoid taking a decision which he did not like, or did not care to be associated with, using the excuse of illness for ulterior purposes of his own. There was no way by which he could be compelled to submit to medical examination for the purpose of determining whether he was fit for his job or not. But in either case, under Article 16, whether he was really a sick man or merely pretending sickness to escape some awkward responsibility, the fact remained that the Speaker of the National Assembly should then act as President.

When Ayub Khan fell ill in January 1968 nothing of the sort happened. It is a reasonably safe assumption that Ayub Khan was not then malingering and that he was, indeed, a very sick man. How, then, did it come about that the Speaker did not assume the office of President and that, during those weeks, Pakistan was without a President in any effective sense?

When these matters came to be discussed in later months, Ayub Khan was much criticized for his unconstitutional behaviour and was accused of flouting the Constitution that he himself had given to the nation. The inference was that having done this once, he could do it again, but it is difficult to understand how Ayub Khan was at fault. If, in January and February, he was as sick as appears from all that is known of his illness, then it follows that he was hardly in a position to say whether the Speaker, Mr. Abdul Jabbar Khan, should undertake the presidential duties or not. A man suffering from a restricted flow of blood to the heart is unlikely to be applying himself seriously to the terms of the Constitution and it is even more unlikely that his medical advisers would allow him even to be taxed with such things. The probable explanation is that the appointment of an acting President was quietly overlooked in order that the nation should not start guessing at the gravity of his illness or indulging in other speculation. At any rate, it is far from clear that this was a decision taken at the instance of Ayub Khan, although later, when he was convalescing, he may have approved it. Whatever the case, it is an interesting instance of the shortsighted, even lackadaisical, manner in which decisions of far-reaching implication were made and is another illustration of the error involved in seizing short-term advantage to the detriment of long-term interests.

The second direct consequence was the emphasis laid upon television which had been introduced a few years before. This highly controversial expenditure of foreign exchange had been justified on various grounds such as the educational value of audio-visual methods of instruction among a people largely illiterate. It was said that television made it possible to bring closer to the people an idea of what was going on in their own country, so that the man in Dacca could see for himself the magnitude of such immense undertakings as Mangla Dam and the man in Hyderabad could see for himself the developments at Kaptai or Chittagong. This would generate a sense of achievement and pride in the nation and in this way the spirit of patriotism could be nourished and strengthened. All this was obvious enough and it is not now necessary to analyse the applicability of these arguments to a country in Pakistan's situation with limited money to spend on such sophisticated equipment as television. Nor need it be asked how television could be carried throughout the vast spaces of the western Province. Certainly, it cannot be claimed that many of its programmes were of educational value; they were heavily criticized on this and other grounds in the newspapers.[1]

---

[1] And still are. This criticism is not entirely unmotivated. In Pakistan television offers advertising time and invites sponsored programmes. As a result, money that would otherwise have gone into press advertising was diverted to television.

The most important immediate purpose served by the introduction of television was the provision of a medium of closer communication between Ayub Khan and such urban centres as Dacca, Hyderabad, Karachi, Lahore, and Rawalpindi. His personality could be more easily projected to these important, articulate and influential audiences and he could do this in comfort, with a minimum of inconvenience. After his illness and the consequent need for caution, his reliance on television was certain to increase, particularly when fighting the election of 1969–70.[2]

This raised the question of Ayub Khan's future, in the light of the illness he had sustained and the strain imposed by high office. The possibility that the office of Vice-President might be created was frequently canvassed and at one time was treated as a certainty.[3] The idea that he might well need to be relieved of some of the many tasks that fell upon him undoubtedly inspired this much discussed suggestion, but as time passed the possibility faded and it seemed that Ayub Khan was as firmly opposed to the creation of such a post as when the Constitution was first drafted. No such office was created, therefore, and, in July 1968 Ayub Khan went to London for a medical check. The doctors appeared satisfied and, as the Karachi newspapers somewhat ambiguously put it, Ayub Khan was given 'a clean bill of health'. Encouraged by this, he was politically active again by September 1968 and had started to make speeches with electioneering implications. The inference strengthened belief in his intention to offer himself once more as a candidate for the presidency.

The Great Decade campaign was intended to illuminate the personality of Ayub Khan in a continuous glow of publicity. To the theme of the Great Decade was linked all advertising and publicity of an official nature or otherwise in the public sector. In the private sector, every inducement was provided, and sometimes firm pressures were exerted, to encourage pursuit of the same theme. The money spent was considerable and although it may be true that specific advertising on the

[2] Whether he really intended to fight this election has never become clear. It was widely thought in Pakistan that after his illness he would not be able to run the risk.

[3] In the middle of April 1968 newspapers were reporting on this as if it were a settled matter.

theme of the Great Decade may have been at the expense of other publicity, so that advertising budgets were not usually increased, substantial additional sums seem to have been spent in one way or another. One of the most popular forms of this publicity was the bringing out of newspaper supplements. There were supplements about the railways, shipping, banking, agriculture, irrigation, communications, textiles in endless series. While intended to expound the achievements of these various branches of the national activities, they prominently featured the development and growth during the ten years from 1958 to 1968.

It may be unfair to read too much meaning into all this, but there is no doubt that there was a deliberate cult of Ayub Khan's personality.[4] Similar things have been done elsewhere and, for that matter, with very much more skill than was always apparent in the campaign conducted in Pakistan on Ayub Khan. Above all, it is important that the object of this kind of projection should possess a balanced personality and a mature understanding if he is not to be spoiled by it. Ayub Khan's misfortune was that in these respects he was not very well equipped. As the Great Decade wore on, it became more and more apparent that he had come to believe in the truth of his publicity and the indications of his megalomania were increasing.

As a nationwide exercise in public relations, the Great Decade can be considered in two ways. The first refers to the ultimate outcome of Ayub Khan's administration. The second relates to its effect upon the public as the campaign proceeded.

Judged by the test of the ultimate fate of Ayub Khan, the Great Decade publicity campaign must be deemed to have failed totally. It did nothing to dispel the adverse image, which had taken hold of the public mind, of a man with an appetite for power and the firm intention of retaining it; of a man whose integrity in the conduct of his office had become doubted and whose administration was known to be highly corrupt. The campaign did little to remove the impact of rising prices and the knowledge that the economic miracle for which Ayub Khan had made so many claims was not quite the miracle that people had been persuaded to believe.

[4] See Ch. XV.

If, in this sense, the campaign failed, there could be two causes. The first was that grievances which were increasing in intensity could not easily be removed by a public relations effort. Pangs of hunger are not assuaged by warmly worded and widely circulated reports of a break-through in agriculture. The anxieties felt for fathers and sons detained in jail under the Defence of Pakistan Rules, or threatened with long terms of imprisonment by reason of criminal proceedings for sedition, were in no way decreased because the rising stature of Pakistan in the world was one of the triumphs of the Great Decade.

The second cause is that those who planned and executed the campaign had no true realization of the depth of public discontent, for they, like Ayub Khan, had come to believe in the publicity with which the country was flooded. It is certain that not until the very last moment did it occur to them that anger and dislike for Ayub Khan might be smouldering beneath an apparent acquiescence. When the flame of rebellion finally surged forth, their startled surprise was perfectly genuine, but much too late.

The effect of the campaign upon the public can also be considered in two ways. To begin with, it was conceived, managed and executed by the Ministry of Information and Broadcasting, under the leadership and guidance of the Minister, Khwaja Shahabuddin, a political veteran from East Pakistan with a considerable reputation for shrewdness allied to a marked capacity for intrigue. The civil service head of this Ministry was Altaf Gauhar[5] who had made a considerable name for himself as a highly intelligent and energetic man, and as one who enjoyed the special confidence of Ayub Khan. With Altaf Gauhar there went a team of officials of whom some could definitely be considered as possessing ability above the average.

The personnel of this organization could, with good reason, be regarded by civil service standards as sufficiently able for the work they had to do. This, of course, does not mean they could create and execute a public relations campaign of any sort. Men trained as civil servants, or long engaged in the sterile atmosphere of public administration, cannot be expected

[5] See Appendix A.

to possess the creative skill essential to success in a difficult and subtle art. A government department can no more be expected to produce such expertise at will than it can be expected to produce civil servants who paint fine pictures or write great novels.[6] The result was that the campaign, at its very best, was never more than moderate in quality. Its approach was pedestrian and the result lacked life and sparkle. The constant appearance of newspaper supplements, financed by more or less compulsory advertising, became the object, in the end, of ironic comment, and the sheer obviousness of it all ensured boredom. It can justly be said that the thing went on too long and that a first-class firm of public relations experts would have done a lot better for less money.

That is one side of the subject. There is another and more important aspect now to be considered.

While all this trumpeting was in progress, other, less agreeable things were in train. I have referred elsewhere to the impact of steadily rising prices upon the life of the people. This process continued during 1968 when the Great Decade campaign was promoting the claim that Pakistan had made great economic progress. It had long been apparent that the steady advance in the cost of ordinary consumer goods, particularly food, was bearing with ever-increasing weight on the ordinary man's budget and was a source of much discontent.[7] Nor was there the least indication that this inexorably rising graph would ever change direction. At the beginning of 1968 the price of Export Bonus Vouchers stood at Rs.167·50. The price fell to Rs.157·75 at the end of March and thereafter rose steadily to Rs.172 at the end of October and to Rs.180 by the end of the year. Nothing could better illustrate the generally rising tendency, not only in the price of food, but in the price of *everything*. Precisely the same situation was reflected in the free market value of the Pakistani rupee which stood at Rs.8·50 to the U.S. dollar in February 1968 and had fallen to Rs.8·85 by the end of October.

In November 1966 the price in Karachi of best quality,

[6] In saying this, I do not overlook the fact that Milton was a civil servant, Rimsky-Korsakov a naval officer, and that Gauguin had been in banking. I do not think these occupations bore any relation to their genius.

[7] I referred to rising prices as the most telling threat to Ayub Khan's administration in my 'Aid as Imperialism', *International Affairs*, April 1967.

unmilled, Punjab wheat stood at the unprecedented figure of Rs.32·50 a maund.[8] In other parts of the Province, the high price of whole-wheat flour had caused public commotion. But even if, in those days, the price was high, at any rate the commodity was available. In May 1968, however, the price of white flour rose to such levels in Karachi that bakers refused to buy and bakeries closed. On 26 May no bread was available in the city at all. The reason for this extraordinary breakdown in the supply of a common article of daily diet seems to have been that the provincial Government had fixed a high procurement price in order to satisfy the farmers and the official resale price was probably excessive. The Government, as was so often the case in state trading, was seeking to make good profits. Inevitably, the flour millers were accused of holding the public to ransom in order to make money. This, of course, was possible, but there is no doubt that the provincial Government mishandled the situation so that there was a closure of bakeries at the very time that Ayub Khan was claiming credit for a bumper wheat crop.

Similarly with other ordinary foodstuffs. Notwithstanding the number of new sugar mills set up in West Pakistan, the price of white refined sugar rose steadily and in May 1968 it was being sold in Karachi at a price higher than had ever been experienced in the history of Pakistan.[9] The price of *basmati* rice[10] rose to Rs.3·50 a seer, equal to about thirty-six United States cents a pound. Eggs and meat became consistently more expensive and so, also, such sources of nutrition for the poor as broken rice and pulses.

In East Pakistan, likewise, the price of food was making it difficult for most people to nourish themselves, even when it is remembered that most of them live in circumstances of extreme poverty. The political situation has already been discussed and, during the year of the Great Decade when the Agartala Conspiracy trial was in progress, newspaper readers were regaled with accounts of torture, maltreatment, and efforts to procure forced confessions. These accounts were used in

[8] One maund is equal to 82·236 lbs.
[9] See p. 240.
[10] *Basmati* is a highly prized quality. Most of what is grown in Pakistan is exported and cheaper qualities are purchased from abroad for sale to the public.

justification of the strongly worded speeches which Ayub Khan's Ministers were then making in condemnation of those 'disruptionists' who would destroy Pakistan by secession were Ayub Khan not there to preserve it. In West Pakistan, the political situation was not quite so explicit. That opposition to the One Unit consolidation was growing and that agitation against it was increasing in intensity and extent, was clear, but it was just as clear that Ayub Khan thought this opposition could be contained. All was not well even in the western Province, to which Ayub Khan belonged.

Thus, whatever the quality of the Great Decade campaign, whatever the objective truth on which it relied, there was plenty to diminish its impact. There were long nurtured discontents springing from genuine public grievances born of the conduct of a bureaucracy intoxicated with the exercise of more power than it had ever known; from the increasingly oppressive burden of the rising cost of living; from the growing sense, especially among the educated classes, of political exclusion; and from the brazen parade of relations and favourites who made money and flouted the law. None of these could be dispelled by the sorcery of an advertising campaign which had rather unimaginatively declaimed the virtues and achievements of President Ayub Khan.

Nevertheless, when the Great Decade came to its end on 27 October 1968, Ayub Khan was unanimously regarded as being as firmly installed in power as at any time since October 1958. It would have been a bold, not to say perverse, man who suggested to the contrary. Even if the grievances were pointed to and admitted, there remained at least one other argument which seemed unanswerable. Who was there to challenge, much less replace him? Miss Jinnah was dead; Lieutenant-General Azam Khan had retired to obscurity; Mujibur Rahman was evidently destined for a long term of imprisonment upon the closure of the Agartala trial, and Zulfikar Ali Bhutto, according to one unwise writer of editorials, was 'finished'.[11] As to the rest—Nurul Amin, Choudhury Mohamed Ali, Maulana Bhashani, and some others—there was not a statesmanlike personality among them.

Provided, therefore, that Ayub Khan could maintain an

---

[11] The *Pakistan Times*, 4 July 1967.

adequately robust state of health and carry on as he had been doing since his recovery from illness, the outlook for him was good and his chances of winning the next presidential election pretty certain. The Great Decade ended with a widely felt sense of optimism among Ayub Khan's supporters, but for careful observers there were other portents not quite so satisfactory. Two days before the Great Decade came to its close, it was announced that on 15 November, statutory sugar rationing would be introduced throughout West Pakistan.[12]

[12] In Karachi, sugar rationing was introduced on 22 October 1968 and in Lahore on 25 October 1968. The need for rationing was widely attributed to some very sinister designs in which the then Minister of Commerce was said to be deeply involved. Basically, there appeared to be three main reasons for the acute shortage in the Province: (a) the sugar factories in West Pakistan could not meet the demand; (b) the Trading Corporation of Pakistan, a Government-owned import and export company, mismanaged its sugar import programme and (c) a shortage of foreign exchange compelled Government to limit sugar imports. Although high hopes have often been expressed for the sugar manufacturing industry in Pakistan, based on indigenously grown cane, there are difficulties. The sucrose content of the cane has so far proved inadequate, and the cost of irrigation water—particularly in West Pakistan—and the price of fertilizer tend to raise the price which growers charge for cane.

XIV

The Last Phase

On 21 September 1968 Bhutto addressed a well-attended meeting at Hyderabad, in West Pakistan.[1] Because the District Magistrate did not give permission for the meeting to be held in public, the audience gathered on privately owned property. In the course of his speech, Bhutto made many personal and hostile references to Ayub Khan with particular emphasis on nepotism, favouritism, wrongful distribution of import licences, and other money-making favours. Bhutto said that Ayub Khan was a dishonest man, accused him of cowardice and declared he would not rest until he had toppled him. At this time, Ayub Khan was touring East Pakistan where, according to the newspapers, his visit was going extremely well. In no way dismayed by this triumphant progress, the Pakistan Democratic Movement, an alliance of opposition parties which had been formed in May 1967, took advantage of the occasion to hold its convention in Dacca, though naturally without attracting the same publicity as Ayub Khan.[2]

In response to Bhutto's increasingly vehement attack on the personality of Ayub Khan, the Government launched fresh enquiries into Bhutto's alleged misconduct while in office. Substantially, these related to wrongful utilization of Government-owned tractors for the cultivation of land owned by Bhutto and to the tampering with land-registration documents, including maps, so that a piece of agricultural property belonging to Bhutto and said to be 284 acres in extent mysteriously increased to some 584 acres. It was further said that, at Bhutto's instance, records were destroyed in order to

---

[1] Reference should be made to Appendix E.
[2] The Pakistan Democratic Movement was a fair reflection of the Combined Opposition Parties which fought the election in 1964–5. Some detail of its components and of its 8-point programme are contained in Appendix G.

evade payment of land revenue. At the beginning of October the then Home Minister of the West Pakistan Government, Kazi Fazlullah, gave details of these charges in the course of a press interview and said that cases against Bhutto were about to be filed. It was also noted that Bhutto had been interrogated by the police who declined to give any information to newspapermen. In some newspapers it was also reported that the Home Minister had said that Bhutto would be detained under the Defence of Pakistan Rules, but later Fazlullah denied having made any such statement.[3] However, despite these threats Bhutto was able to remain at large until his arrest on 13 November 1968, under the Defence of Pakistan Rules.

The Governor of West Pakistan also visited Hyderabad and on 13 October addressed a public meeting at which he referred to *someone* who had drafted the communiqué relating to the Tashkent Declaration and, in the National Assembly, had claimed credit for this very document. Now that *someone* was referring to the Tashkent affair in highly critical language and was threatening to make all kinds of disclosures about it. The *someone* was not named in the speech but few people doubted that Bhutto was meant. It now began to appear that Musa had been charged with the task of replying to critics in West Pakistan for he continued to make speeches against opposition leaders who, in general, were referred to as 'disruptionists'.[4] Largely for this reason Bhutto now became the centre of a controversy substantially between himself and General Musa and it was this controversy that underlined a clearly discernible change of attitude on the part of the Government towards newspaper reporting of opposition speeches. A marked liberalization made it possible for the press to give much more coverage to opposition speakers, and it was the newspapers owned by the National Press Trust[5] which took most advantage of this.

Two reasons appear to have inspired this change of policy.

---

[3] *D*, 5 October 1968.
[4] By this time, the word *disruptionist* had become part of Ayub Khan's standard political vocabulary. As with most words of condemnation in political language, it meant people who did not agree.
[5] A much criticized organization established during Ayub Khan's administration and intended, according to its critics, to serve Ayub Khan's political purposes. See pp. 60-1.

The first may have been a realization that restrictions on political reporting were lending credence to the claim that too many people were politically excluded and unable to make their due contribution to the solution of political problems. Secondly, unless the public knew what opposition leaders were saying, the spirited rejoinders made on behalf of the Government must fall flat. Whatever the case, the limitations on political news, explicit or implicit, were considerably relaxed.

At the same time policy-makers did not intend to throw caution to the winds. In West Pakistan an Ordinance was issued which defined twenty-six classes of person who could be declared to be a *goonda* within the meaning of the West Pakistan Control of Goondas Ordinance 1959. This word, of Hindi origin, signifies a rogue, a rake, or a dissolute individual. Legislation to control such people, who usually comprise the town pimps and bully-boys, has long existed and a person declared to be a *goonda* may have to submit to various forms of supervision, including the duty to present himself regularly at the police-station. The new Ordinance enabled the Government to declare new categories to fall within the definition of *goonda* and these were so worded as to spread the net very widely indeed. As a result it became possible to apply this opprobrious expression to persons of good character and thus injure or menace both liberty and reputation. A person who spread false reports or alarming rumours could be declared to be a *goonda*, as could those associated with him. A journalist who, for example, attended the press conference of a man criticizing the Government and drawing attention to reverses which Pakistan may have suffered, might find his name on the list of declared goondas maintained by the police.

More specific than this was the action taken at the beginning of November 1968 against Bhutto, whose invective against the Government was certainly reported in more liberal fashion. Although afforded this opportunity of making his case known, he was also the subject of police complaint in the Court of the Special Judge, Anti-corruption, at Sukkhur. The complaint charged Bhutto with conspiracy to cheat, forgery, and abuse of official position. A Superintending Engineer of the Department of Agriculture, was also associated with these charges. With this evident attempt to silence Bhutto, it could now be said that battle was really joined between the Government and himself and the political temperature was notably rising.

However, the spreading sense of public disquiet was not so much accentuated by Bhutto's fierce public attacks on Ayub Khan and his administration, or even by the seeming effort to victimize him through the criminal courts, as by other events which touched people a good deal more closely in their daily lives. Notwithstanding the introduction of sugar rationing in Karachi and the issue of ration cards after some delay, no sugar was available to supply even the ration. At the end of the first week of November sugar could only be obtained by surreptitious means, by those who could afford it, at a price which ranged between five and six rupees a seer.[6] The price continued to rise during the month until eventually it was double this.

Much more important than this was the continued violence by students, which caused the authorities to close all schools and colleges indefinitely. To calculate the loss of student-time throughout the country from the middle of 1968 to 25 March 1969 would be an intricate and laborious problem, but it would be fair to suggest that during this period half of the actual number of hours during which students and schoolchildren should have attended college or school was lost by enforced closure owing to disturbance of one sort or another. The effect on education is easily appreciated and the adverse consequences to the careers of those students who were in the final year is just as apparent, but it was not only they who suffered. Teachers, especially those employed in privately managed educational establishments of which there are many in Pakistan, did not receive their salaries and immense hardship was caused to a section of the community that is by no means prosperous.

The problem for the authorities was indeed a difficult and serious one. If the schools and colleges had been opened, no doubt bands of students, reinforced often enough by hooligans, would have appeared, throwing stones, breaking windows, entering class-rooms, and offering violence to teachers and children. In such circumstances, many parents would not have sent their children to school in any case. As it was, during the

[6] Equal to fifty to sixty U.S. cents a pound.

periods of closure, many parents got together to organize classes at home so that injury to educational progress should be minimized and to keep idle children out of mischief. At the same time, the fact that colleges were closed provided ample time and opportunity for politically-minded students to go out on the streets, and encourage their fellow-students to do so, in order to demonstrate, which usually meant smashing windows and traffic-light lenses, burning a bus or two and indulgence in similar pastimes.

This initial period of discontent and agitation culminated in a wild outburst of student trouble at Rawalpindi where, in the course of firing by the police near the Polytechnic Institute, a seventeen-year-old student, Abdul Hamid by name, was killed. The response to this was more violence and on 8 November the Army was called in to aid the civil power. A dusk-to-dawn curfew was imposed and the atmosphere in the city became extremely tense. Seizing the advantage offered by the occasion, Zulfikar Ali Bhutto attended the funeral of the unfortunate student who was buried at his home town of Pindi Ghaib, some sixty miles distant from Rawalpindi itself. The passage of the bier to the body's last resting-place provided yet another opportunity for demonstration, thus carrying the ferment through the countryside. It was this preliminary period of agitation and conflict, ending with loss of life, which marked the inception of a movement which began spontaneously but soon, as we shall see, acquired a more organized character. It was brought to a close only on 25 March 1969, when Ayub Khan relinquished office. From 9 November 1968 to 25 March of the following year, not a day passed in Pakistan without some kind of civil disturbance, riot, strike, bloodshed, or demonstration.

There could be no doubt that Bhutto's presence in Rawalpindi was complicating the situation and was providing further encouragement for trouble as, doubtless, Bhutto fully intended. Moreover, it was just as clear that the flame had taken hold. In the principal cities of West Pakistan, conflict with authority was spreading and in Rawalpindi two more people were killed by police firing. The curfew in force there was extended for a week. Section 144 was imposed, but people assembled in defiance of it to hear Bhutto speak. Excitement grew when, on

11 November, while Ayub Khan was addressing a meeting at Peshawar, a young man named Hashim fired two shots from a pistol, whether at Ayub Khan or in the air is uncertain.[7] The event was treated in some places as a serious attempt on Ayub Khan's life and a number of telegrams reached him from Heads of State and others congratulating him on his escape.

On 13 November what had long appeared inevitable to many actually occurred. Zulfikar Ali Bhutto, Wali Khan and ten others were arrested under the Defence of Pakistan Rules and sent to different prisons in Pakistan. These twelve individuals comprised seven from Bhutto's Pakistan Peoples' Party, five from Wali Khan's section of the National Awami Party, and one non-party man. Wali Khan was arrested for making speeches in which he advocated the dissolution of the One Unit and the creation of a North-West Frontier Province of Pakhtunistan. The precise reasons for Bhutto's arrest were not so explicit although on general grounds he had done enough by way of incitement to make his arrest at any time probable. It appears that the decisive reason for arresting Bhutto lay in the impending visit of Robert McNamara, President of the World Bank, on 14 November. It was feared that Bhutto, who had been declaiming violently against American influence in Pakistan and more particularly against Pakistan's membership of CENTO and SEATO, might organize a demonstration against McNamara's visit which, in the prevailing temper, could easily become violent.

These arrests were at once followed by a broadcast statement from General Musa, the Governor of West Pakistan. His tone was threatening rather than conciliatory, and arrests continued, particularly among members of Bhutto's Peoples' Party and the National Awami Party. The press claimed that after the arrest of Bhutto, Wali Khan and others, calm prevailed in the Province, but this was belied by demonstrations in Multan, Mardan, Mianwali, Jhelum, Charsadda and Abbottabad where protests against the arrests were noisy and threatened trouble. It was, furthermore, in Abbottabad, a

[7] A curious incident arose out of this. The Associated Press of Pakistan issued a report that when the shots were fired, Ayub Khan hurried behind the bulletproof rostrum. Later, this report was withdrawn. Hashim was overpowered by a retired Army subedar, who was rewarded with a purse of Rs.10,000. Hashim was later tried and sentenced to a period of imprisonment.

pleasant residential station in the foothills of the Himalayas, that a significant incident had taken place on 9 November which became public knowledge a few days afterwards.

House No. 71, Sherwan Road, Abbottabad, which was occupied by a lieutenant-colonel of the Army, his wife and two children, was raided by a mob, damaged and ransacked. The officer was absent at the time, but his belongings were destroyed or stolen and his family roughly treated. Since this officer was known to have behaved with much gallantry during the hostilities of September 1965 and had been decorated for courage, and since it did not appear that anything detrimental to his character or conduct was known, this unprovoked attack on his family and property was not only senseless, but spoke of an extraordinary ingratitude, quite apart from the illegality of the behaviour. The fact of the matter was that the house was the property of President Ayub Khan and it was the misfortune of this officer and his family to be living in it.

This event can only be interpreted as an expression of the resentment that was steadily spreading with reference to Ayub Khan, his family, and his administration. It was the absence of any true awareness of this which probably explains why, at the time, the tendency of the foreign press was to condemn the opposition, particularly Bhutto, and to speak well of Ayub Khan. It appeared to be thought that the opposition to Ayub Khan was all being worked up quite gratuitously, which was far from the case. The public had ample cause for dissatisfaction on many grounds and the opposition leaders were there to guide and canalize it.

Admittedly Ayub Khan's conduct provided no justification for Bhutto's promotion of violence, but it must be remembered —and we shall have further cause to realize it—that violence was by no means all on one side. There is sufficient evidence in this book to suggest that the utilization of violence had deeply penetrated Ayub Khan's administration and there can be no doubt that in both Provinces his henchmen frequently had recourse to it, always with impunity. It applied not only to youthful, well-connected blackguards who went about armed, creating trouble in hotels and restaurants and threatening anyone who appeared to object. It applied also to those

Basic Democrats and Chairmen of Union Councils, for example, who had settled themselves to the task of personal enrichment and the extension of their influence in the locality, as well as to party men who, in some cases, actually set up protection rackets. For a long time, the spirit and practice of violence had contaminated the life of Pakistan and for this Ayub Khan cannot evade a substantial share of responsibility.

By the middle of November, the state of law and order had gravely deteriorated and it was said that the number of people arrested in West Pakistan exceeded the total number of arrests in the Province when Martial Law was declared in 1958. In the middle of this month there also occurred two events of considerable importance. Opposition demonstrations began in East Pakistan and Air-Marshal Asghar Khan, a former Commander-in-Chief of the Pakistan Air Force, announced his intention to enter the political arena. This announcement was made in Lahore when the Air-Marshal issued a brief statement setting out his position. His entry into politics caused no surprise. Since his sudden resignation a few months earlier from Pakistan International Airlines, of which he had been President, said to be due to serious differences with Ayub Khan, he had been publishing newspaper articles on Pakistan's defence problems. At the outset it appeared that he was associating himself with Bhutto, his first purpose being to unseat Ayub Khan. It was Asghar Khan who made the strongly worded statement, quoted in the Foreword to this book, to the effect that Ayub Khan had come to represent all that was evil in Pakistan. It was he, too, who initiated the practice, afterwards sporadically observed, of returning the decorations which had been awarded to him during Ayub Khan's period of office as President.

At the end of November, the ranks of the opposition were further strengthened when S. M. Morshed, a former Chief Justice of East Pakistan, also entered the political field. He, too, had reason to dislike Ayub Khan for it was his independent attitude, when Chief Justice of the eastern Province, which led to his abrupt departure from the Bench.

The entry into public life of these two men, previously apolitical, marks the end of the second phase in the history of Ayub Khan's fall. Their appearance not only lent fresh meaning to the opposition to Ayub Khan, but encouraged others like themselves, who had hitherto abstained from political activity, to strengthen the opposition. This not only extended the struggle, but nullified, or weakened the effect of Ayub Khan's frequent charge that the people opposing him came from the ranks of the 'old politicians' who wanted to go back to the bad old days of the parliamentary system, disrupt the country, and regain the power they had abused and so lost. When people like Asghar Khan entered the field, this argument lost much of its force. No one supposed for a moment that the Air-Marshal wanted to disrupt anything.[8]

It could now be said that the stage was fully set and it remained only to act out the play. Rather than recite the continuous sequence of riots, disturbances, and strikes, we must now study the principal aspects of that extremely unsettled time. In this way we can understand how it came about that early in 1969 Ayub Khan was plainly retreating and was eventually compelled to ask the opposition to meet him at a Round Table conference. There he was obliged to make proposals for undoing so much that for ten years he had treated as sancrosanct articles of faith.

In analysing the broad impact on the public mind, produced by 132 days of uninterrupted disturbance, several aspects of the situation must be considered.

(a) The extent and nature of the period.
(b) The conduct of the police.
(c) The extensive role of the Armed Forces in assisting the civil power.
(d) The irruption of local feuds and fighting between factions.
(e) Disaffection in the civil services with special reference to a comprehensive attack on the top-ranking administrative cadre known as the Civil Service of Pakistan.
(f) The appearance of widespread unrest, particularly among the urban labouring classes.

---

[8] The somewhat unwelcome consequence has been a procession of retired generals announcing their entry into politics. What advantage to the progress of Pakistan is likely to be contributed by the combined wisdom of these superannuated officers appears most uncertain.

(g) A clear polarity between Right and Left emerged throughout the nation.
(h) The behaviour of political leaders, satisfactory or otherwise.

The extent and nature of the period of disturbance is a very broad subject. It had to do with a great deal more than the number of riots, the number of people killed and injured and the value of property damaged, destroyed, and looted. In any case, it is improbable that any accurate assessment of these matters could ever be made. The subject is by no means restricted to loss of life and property. It must include, as we have already noted, the effect on the education of the young when, because of disturbance or threat of disturbance, colleges and schools remain closed for months. It would include, further, the loss of wages, salaries and other earnings, caused not only by strikes in factories and offices, but by curfews and the enforced closure of shops and workshops during a hartal[9] called in a particular city, or throughout a Province, or even the entire country. All this must affect the smooth continuance of daily life and—very important—the impression, created abroad, among nations friendly or hostile to Pakistan. To this must be added the question of Pakistan's credit-worthiness and also of the effect on foreign private investment.

It is impossible to estimate confidently the number of persons killed or injured during this period. From all that is known, those killed by police or army rifle-fire (or even from the use of the bayonet), or in the course of faction fights, could not number less than 150, but the figure may well have been much more. The authorities, as usual, were always reticent in publishing details and it can be assumed safely that official figures were always minimal and, quite possibly, falsified. All this seems certain in the case of Dacca where a curfew imposed by military authority was defied. The people came on to the streets and were fired on. A twenty-four-hour curfew was then imposed and people alleged that this was to make it possible to dispose of the bodies without the public learning how many had actually died. It may well be that this was an exaggerated attempt to denigrate the authorities. In such affairs only specu-

---

[9] The word means 'strike'.

lation is possible, particularly so in Pakistan where a habit prevails of avoiding, as much as possible, the publication of ugly news in so far as it may reflect upon the administration and its conduct of affairs. It is a fair assumption, in any case, particularly in countries such as Pakistan, that when rifle-fire is resorted to in the course of rioting, more people are killed and injured than even the authorities truly know about.[10]

In any event, even if it be supposed that the official figures published in respect of killed and injured were absolutely accurate, the matter does not end there so far as concerns these unfortunate people and their families. There is the question of the loss of a bread-winner, or of a brilliant young man with the promise of a great career before him. There is the further question of the kind of injury sustained. It is possible that a person injured in a riot may be incapacitated for life. A blow on the head from an iron-shod bamboo stave could easily do serious brain-damage and there is simply no information available as to the number of people whose wounds have been so serious as to render them incapable of useful work.

Of the real extent of injury, fatal or otherwise, all that can be said is that the consequences go much further than the few hours of disturbance, of the passions then displayed, and the death or injury inflicted. Quite apart from the consequences to individuals, when rioting ends and order is restored, old antagonisms may have been sharpened and new enmities created while the embers of recently inflamed tempers continue to smoulder. Thus, it often happens that a period of civil commotion is followed by a period of unquiet marked by suspicion and a carefully masked spirit of revenge. It is during such a time as this that stray stabbings occur—a solitary policeman on his way home at night, or a member of a rival party seen alone in the dusk—the well-concealed knife is ready to hand and the unfortunate man falls dying while his assailant slips unnoticed away. Sometimes these sporadic murders lack even that measure of diabolic objectivity. In such an atmosphere, innocent persons may be surreptitiously stabbed in the bazaar or in a crowded street for no other purpose than to prolong the sense of civic

---

[10] I have dealt with this grave subject in my article 'The communal problem in the Indo-Pakistan sub-continent', *Pacific Affairs*, Vol. XLII, No. 2, Summer 1969, p. 145.

insecurity and to intensify further the mood of intense hatred.

Thus riot and commotion affect the life of the community far more extensively than their intermittent occurrence implies. The economic consequences may inflict serious injury to the nation, but these will be considered together with the labour troubles that became so marked a feature of the last phase of Ayub Khan's administration.

An allied question is the attitude and behaviour of the authorities. Assuming the best will in the world and the coolest, most refined powers of judgement, theirs is a difficult task. When these qualities are lacking, authority may well succumb to the weight of the problems that confront it and be overthrown. It might be said that this is what happened to Ayub Khan.

In a situation of countryside agitation and disturbance, the man presiding over national affairs will depend largely on the information and appreciations that he receives from others. He can, to some extent, see for himself, but he cannot see everything and if rioting is in train in half a dozen cities, some in one Province and some in another, there is no hope of seeing even the larger part of it. Whatever appreciations and advice were given to Ayub Khan, it seems that in the initial stages of the movement it was his belief, and the belief of his advisers, that the movement should from the first be firmly dealt with. Later, when charges of police brutality became so common that public opinion changed to public certainty, the attitude altered. Police remained on duty but to protect public buildings and public utilities while processions and crowds were not interfered with nor actively resisted unless showing clear intention to storm some building. In East Pakistan the defiance offered to authority was of a much more intransigent and perhaps more violent nature than in West Pakistan. A story was circulated that students in East Pakistan sent bracelets for the male students of West Pakistan, the implication being that the latter were womanish in their ready submission to authority. It was in East Pakistan that the Army was defied when the decision was made to call in the troops, and it was this defiance, had the troops sought to enforce their will by use of arms, that created a tangible threat of civil war.

Allegations of police excess in the conduct of their duty tend everywhere to be an automatic opposition ploy in times of

THE LAST PHASE

civil disturbance. Obviously, when rioters are running wild—smashing, burning, looting, killing—it is necessary for the police to interfere and interference is not likely to be effective if it is confined to a polite request to 'move along'. The only way to disperse a riotous, frenzied mob is to bring out the *lathis*[11] and if the retaliation is determined or the crowd threatens to overwhelm the police, the rifles and tear-gas afterwards. It is not a kid-glove business and anyone who dislikes the thought of a broken head or the risk of a bullet should stay away.

Moreover, policemen are human, subject to emotional stress and their energies are not inexhaustible. They, too, can lose their tempers and are more likely to do so after long periods of duty, without adequate arrangements for meals, insufficient sleep, and continuous periods of alert. It is not surprising if the Pakistani policeman easily became exasperated when it is remembered that a foot-constable's monthly pay, at that time, was about Rs.100 all told (U.S.$23 approximately).

Still, there are solid grounds for saying that during this period the police drew down upon themselves justifiable accusations which could have been avoided. It was common knowledge that some police officers had identified themselves far too closely with Ayub Khan and his régime. Some of them were known to be thoroughly corrupt.[12] During the disturbances, some police officers were apt to express their opinions of various opposition leaders and among those of whom they disapproved were religious leaders with substantial followings. Such expressions of opinion did not add anything to the reputation of the police for impartiality. There were, furthermore, acts of quite unnecessary folly. The police did not even try to discriminate between rioters and journalists who were covering the disturbances.[13] Journalists were injured and cameras smashed up. Protest went unheeded except, perhaps, to provoke another blow. Not only this. Some demonstrations became the object of the most foolish violence and the use of unnecessary force was undoubtedly the consequence of the initial determination to

---

[11] The iron-shod, bamboo staves, about six feet long, which are the first weapon used to disperse troublesome crowds.

[12] Included among the 303 officials suspended during 1969 were some very senior police officers.

[13] The case of the U.S. Democratic Convention at Chicago in 1968, is recalled here.

crush all opposition.[14] This determination led the police into even graver errors such as pursuing rioters who had taken refuge in mosques. One such incident occurred at the Arambagh mosque in Karachi and there the rioters who had found sanctuary were set upon with *lathis* until blood stained the floor. This affair attracted much notoriety. It aroused considerable anger and was regarded as a very serious desecration. It is not difficult to understand that among highly emotional people, with a deep sense of religion, the sight of a torn or blood-spattered Quran will generate much resentment. The utility of such events to the rabble-rousers is obvious.

To all this must be allied the possibility of using *agents-provocateurs* in order to set the crowds moving and so provide opportunity for the police to show their mettle. There were undoubted indications that such agents were employed, but it has to be admitted that this is mostly inference from observations. The raising of anti-Islamic slogans, for instance, was guaranteed to provoke violence and yet nothing could come less readily to the Muslim mind. It would be much the same thing as a Christian priest shouting blasphemies in public in order to make people indignant and angry. Yet there is no doubt that such slogans were raised and did lead to trouble. This could well have been an instance of the employment of planned provocation on the part of the administration.

Nevertheless, the rift between police and public continued to widen until, at Kharian police station, in West Pakistan, there occurred an atrocious crime in which policemen were exclusively involved. For those who take note of such things, it must have seemed that Ayub Khan's luck was truly running out with the news, on 23 January 1969, of the death of a girl named Khanum, aged about sixteen, at Kharian. The circumstances were that this girl, with her parents and younger brother, was detained on charges involving complicity in murder. Later that day, she was separated from her family and kept alone in a room from which, during the night, her screams

[14] On this there is a good deal of quite independent and reliable testimony, particularly from foreigners who were witnesses and had no side to take. One such incident may be mentioned of a procession of about thirty schoolboys in Lahore, carrying placards and shouting slogans. They were set upon by the police, using *lathis*. The insensible lads were then dragged to a lorry and flung in. This incident was witnessed by two reliable foreign witnesses.

THE LAST PHASE 251

and supplications were heard. Next morning she was found dead having, it appeared, committed suicide by hanging. Medical examination showed, however, that she had died by manual strangling and vaginal swabs revealed the presence of male sperms. The conclusion appeared to be that, while in the custody of the police at Kharian, she had been the victim of multiple rape and afterwards murdered on the sound principle that dead girls, like dead men, tell no tales. The entire police staff was suspended and held in custody except for one foot-constable who absconded. Throughout the country there swept a fearful sense of outrage and the reputation of the police became totally discredited.[15] In the public mind the case of the girl Khanum proved conclusively everything that had ever been said to the disadvantage of the police and it established just as conclusively every accusation that had been made, justifiably or unjustifiably, about the brutal and inhuman attitude of the police in the course of their duties.

Without wishing to dwell at unnecessary length upon these ugly matters, it is important to make reference to two other instances which occurred in East Pakistan and which intensified

[15] The case was tried by a Special Military Court after Martial Law was declared in March 1969. Two Assistant Sub-inspectors and three constables were given life sentences. The Station House Officer was sentenced to seven years' rigorous imprisonment and a fine of Rs.1,000 for having tampered with the evidence. Three constables were acquitted.

Khanum's case is, unfortunately, by no means unique in the annals of Pakistan's police. Equally vicious, although perhaps less tragic in their ultimate outcome, were the enormities committed upon the person of a young school-mistress, Riaz Akhtar, in Lyallpur District. This vile crime was committed in 1967 when the entire public administration lay within the all-embracing protection of Ayub Khan and his Constitution. As we shall shortly see, it is not too much to say that, but for the huge public outcry, there might have been no prosecution at all in Riaz Akhtar's case. As it was, the case was mismanaged to the advantage of the three accused, a police officer named Abdul Ghani and his two accomplices, who were each sentenced by a First Class Magistrate to terms of three years. These men filed revision petitions but this unwise audacity met with the consequence, in May 1970, that the appellate Judge, Mr. Justice Ataullah Sajjad, enhanced the sentence in each case by doubling it. He also ordered an enquiry into the circumstances in which evidence was suppressed during the earlier trial proceedings. The learned Judge said it appeared to him 'as if the police force of the District as a whole was interested in shielding its colleagues and subordinates'. Professor Bayley's dictum: 'It is generally accepted that the nature of police activities provides an important clue to the character of a political régime,' is especially relevant to Pakistan as, indeed, is his entire book. David H. Bayley, *The Police and Political Development in India*, Princeton University Press, 1969, p. 11.

the public conviction that Ayub Khan would, if it came to the point, declare war upon his own people in order to remain in power. Both of these incidents were marked by a common feature which had become a disturbing element in anti-riot methods of those days. This was the use of the bayonet, as well as rifle-fire, to resist and quell violent crowds. It is, moreover, quite clear that the bayonet was not simply used as a desperate measure of self-defence when the crowd was at close quarters, but that it was aggressively used. It must be borne in mind that both of these incidents happened at about the same time, in February 1969, less than a month after the news of Khanum's case was first published and while the newspapers were urging the most extreme punishment for those guilty of the Kharian outrage. Thus, there was an accumulation of events which nourished public anger not in arithmetic, but in geometric, progression.

The first of these two East Pakistani cases was that of Flight-Sergeant Zahurul Haq, one of the accused at the Agartala trial, still in progress. It was announced that he had been shot while trying to escape—very familiar official terminology. Here was a man who had already borne months of interrogation and appearances in Court, admittedly with little hope of acquittal, of whom it was now claimed he had suddenly attempted to escape from a thickly wired-in compound and from the custody of an armed guard. The case actually appeared to be that in the early morning Haq wished to use the latrine but the guard commander refused permission on the ground that it was not yet 7 a.m. This led to an argument and possibly a quarrel. It is feasible that Haq became angry and abusive, causing the guard commander to lose his temper and shoot him. It then appears that, while prostrate on the ground, Haq was bayoneted and suffered evisceration.[16]

---

[16] In *PO*, 6 March 1969, is an account, prepared by a lawyer, who made his own enquiries. Another of the accused, Fazlul Haq, was involved in this affair and was also shot, but survived the wound. Another accused, Lance-Havildar Mujibur Rahman, was present when the incident occurred. Since these two men were released after the Agartala Case was withdrawn, it would not have been difficult for this enquiring lawyer to obtain their testimony.

Zahurul Haq seemed to have become another of East Pakistan's martyrs. On 15 February 1970, the anniversary of his death was observed by a procession to his grave at Azampur Cemetery at Dacca where prayers were offered. A symposium on his life was held and the public was invited to hoist black flags as a mark of respect. Thus are created symbols by which resistance achieves both pattern and direction.

Feeling in East Pakistan towards the Agartala trial being what it was, no one believed the escape story, and the death of Flight-Sergeant Haq triggered off very severe riots in Dacca. Two Ministers' houses were set upon, damaged and fired. The State Guest House where Mr. Justice S. A. Rahman, Chief Judge of the Agartala Tribunal, was staying, suffered similar treatment. In Khulna, the house of the Central Government Minister for Communication, Sabur Khan, was attacked and set on fire.

Haq's death, and the manner of it, were bad enough, but there was worse to come. A few days later, a lecturer and proctor at Rajshahi University, Dr. Shamsuzzoha, while trying to restrain students leaving the campus, which they had been forbidden to do by the Government, was bayoneted by soldiers and died beside the gates of the university. He was a person of considerable academic distinction and very popular, and his death was a great blow to hopes of restoring civic calm. Since there was no ground for supposing that he was instigating or leading trouble-makers, it followed that he died simply from a want of discrimination and of good sense, not to speak of unnecessary brutality. His death provoked further animosities in East Pakistan and a donation, from the public purse, of Rs.1 lakh to Shamsuzzoha's widow. Neither compensated her for the loss of a husband nor her children for the loss of a father, nor did it dispel, from the public mind the rapidly growing determination to have done with Ayub Khan.[17] In the Province that year Martyrs' Day was marked by unusual fervour.[18]

The inability of the police, whether in an active or a passive role, to control the disturbances, led to an ever-growing reliance

[17] It is quite possible that Shamsuzzoha had become a marked man. On the previous day a students' procession which he was accompanying in his role as a university proctor, was halted by the District Officer, a West Pakistani, accompanied by a police party. This official rebuked the processionists in strong language and publicly abused Shamsuzzoha who, protesting, explained his position and the capacity in which he was then acting. It was for the same reason that on the following day he offered to negotiate for the students. Walking into the prohibited area, outside the university boundary, he was killed. Immediately after his death became known, the District official was transferred back to West Pakistan and he left Rajshahi as soon as possible.

[18] Each year on 21 February East Pakistan observes the memory of the students who lost their lives in 1952 when demonstrating against the proposal to make Urdu the sole national language of Pakistan. Both Zahurul Haq and Shamsuzzoha have become East Pakistan martyrs.

on the Army, with all the dangerous possibilities that this involved. It is well known that soldiers do not like the job of enforcing law and order in their own countries because, for one thing, it smacks of waging war on one's own people. It is the admitted business of soldiers to use force, but in an entirely different context and against external enemies. Although, with the declaration of Martial Law in 1958, the armed forces had become accustomed to the idea of a political role, they still held the traditional opinion that where politics were concerned, they should remain aloof. The danger of the armed forces becoming riven by politics is only too familiar and although in Pakistan they had become the instrument of politics, it remained the policy and the intention to keep them apart as much as possible.

Despite this, nothing was more likely to promote political awareness, particularly in the Army, than the constant employment of the armed forces in controlling civil disturbance and this is precisely what went on during the last months of Ayub Khan's administration. This growing awareness was not altogether an advantage to him. Soldiers asked themselves the reasons which imposed on them a task they so much disliked and they did not necessarily absolve Ayub Khan from blame. Secondly, the use of the Army in East Pakistan was regarded less as a necessary measure to maintain law and order than as a ruse by the Central Government to retain a hold on East Pakistan and to prevent the people of that Province from securing their just demands. In short, the troops were regarded as an army of occupation. Thirdly, the continued use of the armed forces could lead to a situation in which familiarity bred contempt. In other words, men would learn to dislike soldiers and then to defy them as they had the police.[19] Fourthly, there was the danger that if dislike for Ayub Khan grew in the armed forces, the troops might refuse to obey orders to fire on their own countrymen.[20]

Springing from all this were two possibilities. The armed

[19] I was in Dacca in February 1969 and noted the widespread defiance of the curfew and the sense of hostility to the Army.

[20] It appears, although no authoritative evidence is available, that such a stage was reached in Rawalpindi when some officers refused to carry out orders to fire on civilian mobs. In discussing this subject, it will be remembered that we are not now concerned with the events in East Pakistan of 1971.

forces might lose the confidence of the people and Ayub Khan might lose the confidence of the armed forces. Of these, it was the latter which came about and it is a fair conclusion that one, if not the only one, of the reasons that led Ayub Khan to relinquish office was the knowledge that he had lost the armed forces' support. It does not seem that there has been any marked divorce in feeling between them and the people, but the decision to impose Martial Law for a second time undoubtedly placed great strain on the links which ought to keep the people, the administration and the armed forces in well-ordered relation.

One of the uglier aspects which developed out of this period of civil commotion was the violence between rival gangs committed under the cover of political demonstration. Much, indeed, of the rioting that went on in those days had more to do with local feuds than with the broader issues on which opposition to Ayub Khan was based. Much of this localized rivalry sprang directly from his system and more particularly from his Basic Democracy system with its Union Committees whose members and chairmen frequently became petty tyrants, lining their pockets and oppressing the public they were supposed to represent. Eventually, greed created factions within the system, bearing similarity to Chicago's gang-warfare even if the stakes were much lower. This was the lateral aspect, internecine war. In East Pakistan, however, particular opportunity was taken, when disorder became general, to launch attacks on the Basic Democrats and several lost their lives or their property, or both.[21] This was the vertical aspect, the ruled assaulting the rulers.

As will be realized, some of this feuding and faction-fighting bore no relation at all to the causes of the riots and there is no doubt that the opportunity was sometimes seized to exact a private and murderous revenge. The fever which had gripped the nation provided opportunity for every kind of *malaise* previously concealed beneath oppressive government.

---

[21] Similar incidents occurred in West Pakistan, also. In Karachi, the case of Ali Kausar became notorious. This man's house and property in Liaquatabad were ferociously attacked, lives were lost, and the house was gutted. Had the mob had its way, it would probably have been razed to the ground there and then (actually this came later as will be seen), and Ali Kausar and his family probably murdered. This was fully reported in the newspapers of January and February 1969.

This was particularly so in the case of the civil administration which found opportunity to voice its dislike of, and its grievances with respect to, the seniormost cadre of the civil service known as the Civil Service of Pakistan.[22] In this case, the other branches of the civil service had the support and sympathy of the public because the members of the C.S.P, or some of them, had created for themselves a nationwide dislike. This might well have been founded upon envy for their privileged situation, but was certainly related to an undisguised hunger for power and an unrestrained urge to monopolize all the best jobs in the civil administration. There was, further, an attitude of contemptuous arrogance towards the rest of the community, founded upon a conviction of absolute superiority over everyone with the possible exception of Ayub Khan himself. To this, in many cases, was allied the exercise of a grossly corrupt avarice. It is not suggested that these repulsive qualifications should be attributed to the C.S.P alone. They were widely shared throughout all branches of the civil service, but it happened that the C.S.P was better placed to follow these base purposes and did so. In saying this, it is necessary and only just to add that there were many honourable exceptions.

This highly unpopular service became the object of criticism and attack not only by the public but also by other branches of the civil administration. This led to a widespread demand for publication of what was known as the Cornelius Report. This document was the outcome of the work of a Commission of Inquiry, set up during Ayub Khan's Martial Law administration, to examine problems of pay and service in the civil administration, and presided over by a former Chief Justice of Pakistan, Mr. A. R. Cornelius. The Report of this Commission proposed some far-reaching changes in the civil service structure and some of these changes would have affected the privileged status of the C.S.P substantially. Members of the C.S.P, who happened also to be members of the Commission, dissented strongly. For this reason and also, perhaps, because of other proposals affecting scales of pay and other terms of service, Ayub Khan withheld the Report from publication.

[22] This cadre is usually referred to as the 'C.S.P' and will be so designated in this text.

Naturally enough, the public, as well as other branches of the civil service, became aware of what the Report contained and the opportunity was now seized to call for the Report to be made public.[23]

There followed the extraordinary spectacle of various branches and cadres of the civil administration,[24] each of which had its own association, holding meetings at which demands were made for the publication of the Cornelius Report, for the abolition of the C.S.P and the assimilation of the civil service into five categories in which merit would be the prime consideration for advancement and in the selection for appointment. In the case of the lower grades, there were demands for better terms and conditions of service. In these respects, therefore, it could be said that even the civil administration[25] was helping to inflame opinion against Ayub Khan and the manner in which he had conducted the country's affairs. Thus, the civil services, which had prospered greatly during the days when they were securely entrenched behind Ayub Khan, now turned on him, not necessarily on grounds of principle but with the realization that civil servants in general, and the C.S.P in particular, had earned a widespread detestation in the public mind. In return, there followed the extraordinary business of members of Ayub Khan's family turning on the civil servants when his eldest son, Captain Akhtar Ayub, referred to members of the C.S.P as 'black sahibs created by the British'.[26]

By the beginning of March 1969 it seemed possible that this ferment about and among members of the public administration might lead to an administrative breakdown. In its issue dated 3 March 1969, the weekly paper *Chatan* printed a merciless attack on Altaf Gauhar in which the writer hurled at him every accusation he could suggest and concluded with an appeal to Ayub Khan to get rid of him before more harm

---

[23] On 20 March 1969, five days before his abdication, Ayub Khan's Government announced publication of the Cornelius Report.

[24] There were four categories: Class I and Class II (gazetted officials); Class III (clerical) and Class IV (doormen, messengers and the like.) These were also divided horizontally according to the kind of work performed, e.g. Audit and Accounts Service, Customs Service, Taxation Service, etc.

[25] Here, we speak primarily of the Central Government but the provincial administrations were also affected.

[26] The *Leader*, Karachi, 10 February 1969.

was done. This intemperate onslaught showed how far things had moved since the days when writers thought long and carefully before publishing mild suggestions that perhaps not quite *everything* was for the best in Ayub Khan's splendidly conducted system of government.

But there was other and far more convincing evidence of the way things were drifting within the public services. On 6 March, it was recorded that in West Pakistan alone doctors employed by the Government were on strike; so were teachers, so were postal workers, so were dock workers. Other strikes were threatened and, in some instances, lower-paid groups of government employees were having recourse to the *gherao*,[27] in order to extract better pay and other terms. To placate these agitators, Ayub Khan's Government began the practice of granting what was called 'ad hoc relief', and by March 1969 it was reckoned that the cost to the public purse of this relief was Rs.400 million a year.

This figure throws some light on the cost, to Pakistan's economy, of the disruption of industry and commerce during the last phase of Ayub Khan's administration. The total has been variously computed and there is no doubt that some of the figures suggested, particularly on the side of the private sector, were much exaggerated. But, whatever it was, the country suffered considerable loss, not only through a decline in production generally, but in exports resulting in a loss of foreign exchange which it could ill afford, and also in damage to factory buildings, machinery and equipment. Strikes and riots in industrial areas became commonplace and eventually factory-owners were appealing to the Government, weeks before Martial Law was declared, to send troops to patrol areas where industry was concentrated. The police were unable to maintain order and the danger that the strikers would storm the factories appeared probable. No doubt these appeals helped in encouraging the decision to resort to Martial Law.

That the labouring classes had ample ground for discontent is evident from what has been written in this book. Rising

---

[27] The word means 'siege'. Discontented employees lock their superior officers or company directors or managers in their offices and will not permit them to leave until demands are acceded to.

prices, the knowledge of corruption in high places and throughout the administration, the gross inequalities between rich and poor, the insecurity of life, the inadequacies in almost everything one could name—food, clothing, shelter, medical attention, education for children—provided sufficient cause for seeking change. Ayub Khan had expressed occasional sympathy for the labouring poor, but it tended to be lukewarm and became even more tepid as time passed. In December 1958 he declared that Pakistan aimed at building a welfare state where men should enjoy to the utmost economic, social and cultural amenities.[28] Shortly after this he further declared that management must realize it is dealing with human material, not machines, and must provide all comfort, convenience and dignity due to honest, hard-working and self-respecting human beings.[29] Four years later, his tone had changed considerably and labour had to be content with this frigid statement: '... present labour policies represent a very carefully worked out balance between the interests of the employers on the one hand and the interests of labour on the other.'[30] A very carefully worked out balance there may have been, but no one doubted which way the scales were really tipped.

As with so much else, labour unrest was not the product of the last phase, but it fiercely erupted because the opportunity was provided. Indeed, so greatly did this opportunity inspire the move to action that the stage was very soon reached at which labour was totally out of hand. By means of the *gherao* and other violence, it demanded and secured promises of increased wages and other amenities which, had they materialized, would have incurred ruinous production costs and thrown the national economy into devastating inflation. The time came when scarcely a factory, commercial establishment or workshop (and these include such publicly owned institutions as the two Industrial Development Corporations and the National Bank of Pakistan) was not aflame with meetings, demands, agitation, and threats of violence and strikes. It is not an exaggeration to say that there was a point at which it

[28] Message to the nation on Human Rights Day, 1958.
[29] Inaugural speech at the Conference on Labour–Management Co-operation, Karachi, 19 December 1958.
[30] Speech at the Annual Dinner of the Federation of Pakistan Chambers of Commerce and Industry, Karachi, 13 November 1962.

seemed possible that economic breakdown might become complete.

As it happened, this was averted by Ayub Khan's departure and by recourse to Martial Law. Quiet followed and labour returned to office and factory without further protest, but three things could not be obscured. The first was that labour, familiar enough with the idea of protecting its rights through trade unions, and of enforcing them by means of strikes, had now discovered within itself a greater potential. It was possible, by means of violence and *gherao*, to make employers capitulate and even the government might hesitate to create a situation in which the flames of riot threatened to spread. It cannot be doubted that after this period of disturbance from November 1968 to March 1969, the resort to violence became very much less restrained and not only among the working poor. Secondly, a philosophy had been discovered. The approach to the causes of discontent—low wages, long hours, bad housing, bad working conditions—became less empirical and more doctrinal. Instead of a demand for higher pay, improved working conditions and other amenities, the appeal was now, in effect, to the *right* of the worker to these things. This right was founded upon the argument that because the factories and the offices were the product of the workers' labour, they were their property. In short, labour leaders were preaching Marxism and the theory of surplus value was becoming readily accessible scripture. Thirdly, the question of a minimum wage acquired fresh prominence and even a measure of official acceptance. The idea was that some tangible help to relieve the working poor of some of the miseries that oppressed them would have to be given,[31] though this left open the question of the economic consequences of such a policy.

However all this may be, the fact was that the movement for better conditions for the working classes had undergone a transformation of outlook and it was this transformation that led to the appearance of a sharply defined polarity between Right and Left. Thenceforward, much was to be heard about socialism and Islam, and whether they are compatible or not.

---

[31] This was the reason for Air-Marshal Nur Khan's untimely statement on labour policy, made in July 1969 when he was a Deputy Chief Martial Law Administrator.

Political parties began to be identified in this way—some were rightist and others were leftist. Some declared that Islam had no need of socialism. It was a complete code in itself which, rightly applied, would find solutions for every problem. Others argued that socialism and Islam were mutually consistent and this harmony provided the doctrine known as 'Islamic socialism'. On all this no comment is offered. The principal point is that from the last phase of Ayub Khan's administration emerged for the first time in Pakistan a clear antithesis of Right and Left. From that time on, this would play a very important part in the country's politics.

There remains the question of the behaviour of the country's political leaders and the promise this behaviour offered of a better political order in Pakistan. To understand this, it will perhaps suffice to glance at the course of events from the time that Ayub Khan came to realize that he could no longer withstand popular clamour and that he would have to come to terms with the people, now plainly in revolt against his system and method of government.

In January 1969 the Pakistan Democratic Movement set up a Democratic Action Committee under the chairmanship of Nawabzada Nasrullah Khan. With Bhutto, Mujibur Rahman, and Wali Khan in jail, this organization not only became prominent but, apart from that inexplicable Savonarola, Maulana Bhashani, had the field to itself. Based on the eight-point programme, the Committee organized a number of successful protest demonstrations and it soon appeared probable that Ayub Khan would find himself compelled to concede to popular demands. This is not to suggest, however, that within the Committee there lay the germ of a political party that could successfully take over the reins of government. The Democratic Action Committee was the product of several parties whose aims and interests by no means coincided. Like its forerunner, the Combined Opposition Parties, the only issue on which the Democratic Action Committee was unanimous was the departure of Ayub Khan and this, as has been said earlier, was not a political programme of any sort.

It is necessary at this point to consider Ayub Khan's position in relation to the upsurge that had continued, without any sign of abatement, for nearly three months. By the end of January it was evident that some people regarded the ship as sinking and were abandoning it. Numerous resignations among Basic Democrats were reported and it may well be that these resignations were encouraged by knowledge of the fate that had overtaken others. In East Pakistan Ayub Khan's party, the (Convention) Muslim League, was split down the middle and had been so for a considerable time.[32] At the beginning of February 1969 prominent members of this party, in East Pakistan, issued a statement in which the conduct of affairs in the Province was condemned and the same group sent a telegram to Ayub Khan asking him to intervene.[33] It is, furthermore, evident that by now Ayub Khan was becoming aware that mere resistance to protest, opposition and criticism would not satisfy, and he began to fall back on apologetics. An article entitled *What went Wrong?* appeared from the pen of a well-known Pakistani political writer, Z. A. Suleri, generally considered to be a mouthpiece of Ayub Khan and a political confidant.[34] This article was an attempt to explain the upsurge against Ayub Khan and listed, for what they were worth, three reasons. First, the late Nawab of Kalabagh was chiefly to blame by reason of his harsh and oppressive conduct of affairs in West Pakistan. Secondly, civil servants were arrogant and troublesome to the public. Thirdly, Ayub Khan had been misled, misinformed, etc. As apologetics this did not really amount to much and, if written with the prior knowledge and sanction of Ayub Khan, it reflected badly upon his probity and strength of character.

Events now began to move faster. A petition for Bhutto's release was entered by his wife and the hearing began. This provided an opportunity to present Bhutto's voluminous affidavit in which he recounted much detail of his association with Ayub Khan and of events immediately prior to his dismissal. It was a piece of floridly written polemic, ringing with a good deal of truth and addressed to the younger generation

[32] See editorial in *PO*, 20 December 1968 entitled 'Deepening Discord'.
[33] According to the East Pakistan opposition leader, Nurul Amin, newspapers in Dacca were served with notices, under Rule 52(b) of the Defence of Pakistan Regulations, prohibiting the publication of joint or individual statements made by members of Ayub Khan's party expressing disapproval of the East Pakistan Government's conduct of affairs in the Province.
[34] The *Pakistan Times*, 2 February 1969.

rather than to the Court. Except for two paragraphs concerning the Tashkent Declaration, this affidavit was published in full in most newspapers. Both Ayub Khan and General Musa felt its sting sufficiently to write to the Attorney-General denying the contents of the document in so far as it contained allegations and insinuations about themselves.[35] Simultaneously with this, Bhutto announced that he would go on hunger-strike to force the Government to lift the emergency.[36]

In the meantime Ayub Khan invited the chairman of the Democratic Action Committee, Nasrullah Khan, to meet him on 17 February 1969, bringing with him any colleagues whom he cared to ask, in order to discuss the situation. The response to this was a declaration by the Committee that five points must be conceded in order to create a suitable atmosphere for political discussion. These were:

(a) The emergency to be lifted and the Defence of Pakistan Rules to be repealed *in toto*.
(b) All arrested students and political workers to be released.
(c) Section 144 to be lifted and processions, meetings, etc. to be permitted.
(d) Government proceedings under the Maintenance of Public Order Ordinance and the Press Ordinance to be withdrawn.
(e) *Lathi*-charging of students by the police to be stopped.

In fact, Ayub Khan had to some extent anticipated these demands by issuing orders that no further proceedings were to be initiated under the Defence of Pakistan Ordinance or under the Defence of Pakistan Rules. He had also said that there was no particular difficulty about lifting the state of emergency, although some legal points would have to be cleared up first. These had to do with providing legal sanction for questions relating to enemy property, war risk insurance, compulsory service in the armed forces and pending espionage cases, said to number between 100 and 200.[37]

Bhutto, still in jail, now had recourse to some clever tactics.

---

[35] *D*, 6 and 7 February 1969.
[36] Imposed, as the reader will remember, on 6 September 1965 under Article 30 of the Constitution.
[37] All these things, it will be appreciated, stemmed from September 1965.

He submitted a prayer to the Court, asking that the petition for release, which had been made by his wife, should be withdrawn. As the petition was made under Article 98 of the Constitution, it would fall upon the Court to consider the merits of this application, although it was difficult to imagine that the Court would do other than grant Bhutto's prayer since he would then remain in prison. It was a neat manœuvre. To begin with, Bhutto had already made his point. His long, polemical affidavit had been published all over Pakistan and he aimed now at humiliating Ayub Khan by forcing an unconditional release as opposed to a release ordered by the Court on mere legal grounds, should that be the view taken by the judges. Then, having submitted his prayer, Bhutto announced that if the emergency were not lifted by 14 February, he would begin a fast unto death. The implication here was that if, at any time in the near future, Ayub Khan *did* withdraw the emergency, it would be said that he did so under threat of Bhutto's intended fast.

It was by now clear that Ayub Khan was backtracking as fast as he could without actually subverting his own constitution or abdicating power. Addressing a meeting of his party, of which he had just been re-elected President, Ayub Khan said that 'the constitution must reflect the people's will', and that 'East Pakistan must have a sense of participation'. He also laid emphasis on the point that the Constitution could be amended.[38] Even more significant was the fact that facilities were given for Nasrullah Khan to visit Mujibur Rahman, still in confinement as an accused in the Agartala Case. The order, made in 1966, forfeiting the *Ittefaq* press, was rescinded.

It certainly seemed to Ayub Khan's opponents to be a case of capitulation all round and they had but to maintain the pressure in order to bring Ayub Khan down. However, this was not the end of his process of withdrawal. In East Pakistan 141 persons held under the Defence of Pakistan Rules, including eleven members of the Opposition, were released. In Lahore, Section 144 was withdrawn and, at a meeting of the Pakistan (Convention) Muslim League Council, presided over by Ayub Khan in Dacca, the release of detained students was recommended. On top of all this, a Government spokesman said that

[38] *D*, 9 and 10 February 1969.

the state of emergency was likely to be lifted in a couple of days.

But it would be a mistake to suppose that Ayub Khan's hand had lost all its cunning. By an order of the Court, Bhutto was to be removed to his home at Larkana, there to remain in confinement pending the decision of the Court with respect to the withdrawal of his wife's petition. The idea seemed to be that if the petition were withdrawn and if Bhutto consequently remained in jail in Lahore where he then was, and if, further, the emergency were lifted, then Bhutto would automatically be released in Lahore where he enjoyed the special regard of the younger people, particularly the students. He could then rely on getting a vast hero's welcome at the jail-gate and this celebration Ayub Khan was not prepared to allow him.

But notwithstanding these comparatively minor tactical manœuvres and the concessions that Ayub Khan was making almost daily to placate the public, rioting continued without diminution. At Peshawar on 10 February students and others burnt down the Family Planning Centre on the ground, perhaps, that it was an offence in the eyes of Islam. On 14 February, the entire country observed a *hartal* (strike). Every shop, tea-shop, restaurant, and cinema was closed and those hardy spirits who wanted to open their establishments were *ordered* by the police to close on the ground that to remain open would merely provoke trouble. Most cars, trucks and motor-cycles carried a black flag or black ribbon, not necessarily because the driver sympathized with the opposition, but because it was wiser to do so. Even officially-owned vehicles, such as municipal dust-carts, carried black flags. In any case, by noon there was very little traffic on the roads.

Notwithstanding the success of the *hartal*,[39] there was trouble in some cities, notably Karachi, Lahore and Hyderabad, where the troops were called out. Firearms were used in mob-clashes and there was further evidence of the use of *agents-provocateurs* by Ayub Khan's party. In Karachi, the remains of Ali Kausar's house as well as some retail-shop buildings which he owned, were finally demolished by the mob. Altogether, in West Pakistan, four persons were officially stated to have been killed and many were injured.

In this atmosphere of unabated turmoil, the central question

[39] Of all the *hartals* I have witnessed this was the most complete.

now turned on Ayub Khan's invitation to various parties and prominent men to confer with him. If a conference took place, what would Ayub Khan propose or do? And what could or would be the outcome? The Democratic Action Committee accepted the invitation, but desired that the talks should begin on 19 February instead of 17 February as Ayub Khan had proposed. Maulana Bhashani announced that he was opposed to any talks with Ayub Khan and on 19 February, the day on which the Conference was supposed to begin, it became known that Bhutto, Mujibur Rahman, Lieutenant-General Azam Khan, Air-Marshal Asghar Khan, and S. M. Morshed had all declined to join the conference.[40] Evidently, these men realized that Ayub Khan was in full retreat on all sectors and it remained only to continue pressing him without respite. But there was more to it than simply that. The question still remained as to the circumstances in which Mujibur Rahman could attend. As an accused prisoner, conducted from Dacca Cantonment under escort? As an accused on parole? As a free man? To attend as an accused under escort was plainly unthinkable. Mujibur Rahman declared he would not go as a prisoner on parole. And if he were to attend as a free man, that must imply unconditional discharge before the trial ended. Was this possible and what, in that circumstance, would be the fate of all other accused? The answer to all these perplexities lay in the famous broadcast by Ayub Khan on 21 February 1969, at 5.30 p.m.

Speaking in the faintly wearied tone, characteristic of his formal broadcasting manner, Ayub Khan said that the people could have whatever constitutional arrangements they desired. He indicated that he was not a candidate for the next presidential election and he suggested that the nation should 'forgive and forget'. He said, further, that if, 'God forbid', the Round Table Conference should break down, he had a solution to offer. This contrite address was followed shortly afterwards by the ultimate humiliation—withdrawal of the Agartala Case and the immediate release of all the accused, including Mujibur Rahman, now free to attend the Conference or not, as he chose.

[40] On this day also it was announced that the case against Bhutto, regarding the alleged wrongful use of Government-owned agricultural equipment, would be withdrawn. Such indecision invites immediate ridicule.

Curiously, at about this time Chittagong radio station resumed broadcasting the songs of Rabindranath Tagore, which had been banned since 1965. With that capacity for refined insult, so long and so well practised in the East, the first song in these resumed broadcasts was a recording of Afsari Khanum, wife of K. M. Shamsur Rahman, C.S.P, an accused in the Agartala Case and one of those whom Ayub Khan had been compelled to release unconditionally. Bhutto also made a contribution. He renounced the award of Hilal-i-Pakistan which he had received from Ayub Khan when serving as Foreign Minister.

Having brought Ayub Khan to his knees, the independent opposition men and Mujibur Rahman agreed to attend the Round Table Conference and on 26 February the first session was held. Present were Ayub Khan and three of his Ministers, leaders of the Democratic Action Committee, Mujibur Rahman and Air-Marshal Asghar Khan. Bhutto and Maulana Bhashani were conspicuous by their absence and this, in some measure, contributed to the emergence of Mujib and Asghar Khan as the dominating personalities on the opposition side. The first session was a purely formal gathering and it adjourned the same day until 10 March. Simultaneously with this, Bhutto and Bhashani signed an agreement that they would work together on the basis of (a) the establishment of democracy in Pakistan, recognizing the demands of the people of both Provinces; (b) the establishment of socialism in conformity with the ideology of Pakistan; and (c) the elimination of foreign interference and withdrawal from CENTO, SEATO and all military commitments; opposition to colonialism, neo-colonialism, and imperialism; and the liquidation of India's base in the Rann of Cutch at Biar Bet.

In May 1969 Nawabzada Nasrullah Khan, chairman of the Democratic Action Committee and a prominent figure prior to and during the Round Table Conference, made a long, rambling but nevertheless important statement.[41] The substance of this somewhat incoherent account of what actually happened before and during the Conference amounted to an admission that the Conference failed. It asserted further that this

---

[41] See the *Leader*, Karachi, 17 and 19 May 1969. The report is based on an account of an interview given by Nasrullah Khan to the editor of the weekly *Chatan*, where it was reported in Urdu.

failure was due to Mujibur Rahman's insistence on the Six Point Programme and because of the tactics adopted by people present at the Conference who had left-wing sympathies. No doubt the Conference was a failure although, as Ayub Khan himself stated when summarizing its results, there was clear consensus on a return to the parliamentary system of government and direct elections through universal adult suffrage. Although substantial, this was far from sufficient and a great many questions still called for answer. To complicate matters further, Mujib declared immediately after his return to Dacca that consensus on the issues of the parliamentary system and direct elections would not meet the aspirations of the people of East Pakistan. He again reiterated the need for the Six Point Programme.

As for the Conference itself, it seems that Ayub Khan, having lost his nerve for a time, then professed all willingness to meet the opposition in the belief that he could outmanœuvre them politically and show to Pakistan and to the world what an inept lot they were.[42] In this respect, the proceedings of the Conference itself amply justified that opinion. The speeches made on behalf of the opposition constituted very familiar fustian. Scarcely a word was uttered that did not evoke memory of all the old, well-worn controversies about parity, joint or separate electorates, provincial autonomy and so on. It was dreary reading and pointed to only two real conclusions. The first was that the opposition leaders were united on nothing except the determination to get rid of Ayub Khan, recourse to the parliamentary system and a reversion to direct elections. The second obvious inference was that, in ten years, these men had learned little.

The outlook was now indeed gloomy. Not merely the failure of the Round Table Conference, but also the circumstances of its failure, seemed to speak of immense political difficulties ahead. How, with such leaders, could the country find solutions to those grand issues, so long quietly ripening, which had emerged from the welter of protest, agitation, destruction, and killing? Who was there to come forward with some acceptable formula or proposals that would make it possible, not simply to

---

[42] See my article 'The Toppling of Ayub Khan', *Round Table*, London, July 1969.

bring about the desired constitutional changes on paper, but to make those changes work, at the same time providing amelioration of the great economic and social hardships against which the poor were clamouring?

But it was not so much the failure of the Round Table Conference that aroused disquiet at that time as the fast deterioration in law and order. On 6 March 1969 in Karachi, Pakistan experienced its first significant *gherao* when the clerical staff at the Head Office of the National Bank of Pakistan confined the President of the Bank and the Managing Director in their offices until midnight, when their demands were accepted. Two days later, a dissatisfied crowd at the Karachi Racecourse threw stones, smashed up everything they could lay hands on and threatened to burn down the grandstand, for which purpose twenty two-gallon tins of petrol were produced.[43] On 12 March the Adamjee Jute Mill at Dacca, the biggest in the world, had a ten-hour *gherao* and the management was obliged to accept seven demands. An interesting aspect of these negotiations lay in the presence of the Students Action Committee which appeared as a third party, in addition to representatives of the management and the workers. Three days later the Pakistan Tobacco Company's factory in Dacca experienced a *gherao* accompanied by threats to burn down the factory if pay increases, which amounted to 275 per cent of existing rates, were not agreed to. Strikes and *gheraos* were multiplying rapidly and the effect on the economy of the country was now being felt or, at any rate, anticipated. The Karachi Stock Exchange experienced a serious fall in prices and, on 13 March, the Exchange was closed owing to the failure of a prominent operator.

The flames of agitation and discontent were being actively fanned by Bhashani, now touring West Pakistan instead of his own Province. Making characteristically inflammatory speeches, he declared that no elections would be permitted until the demands of the people and of the students were met. He said that people who filed nomination papers, after being

---

[43] It must be admitted that it does not require a state of political unrest to agitate the Karachi Racecourse crowd, which often has good cause for dissatisfaction considering the number of favourites that somehow do not get anywhere near the winning-post.

requested not to do so, would have their houses burnt down. Largely as a result of his oratory a general strike was held in West Pakistan on 18 March. It was largely a success. Public transport did not appear on the streets, all factories and most shops and offices were closed. Not content with this, Bhashani was reported as having declared himself ready for civil war, should it be necessary, and that if the workers' demands were not accepted within two months, they would occupy and take over the mills and factories.

Notwithstanding Bhashani's absence from his own Province, East Pakistan in no way lagged behind and there the rioting was, if anything, worse than in West Pakistan. It was, indeed, assuming a thoroughly menacing aspect for the violence was not merely directed against the Government, but different sectarian groups were using it against each other and the old trouble of Bengali-versus-refugee[44] soon reappeared. Attacks on the police increased and there were at least two instances of policemen beaten to death by mobs. It was officially estimated that between 7 and 21 March, thirty-nine people were killed in Dacca alone, in the course of various affrays and clashes.

It was now that Ayub Khan made his last attempt to salvage his position. Monem Khan, in East Pakistan, vacated the governorship and, with his family, slipped quietly out of Dacca to the comparative security of West Pakistan. He was replaced by Dr. M. N. Huda, previously Finance Minister in the Province and a thoroughly acceptable and worthy selection. In West Pakistan General Musa relinquished the governorship in favour of Yusuf Haroon, a well-known political leader for whom it could be said that he had fallen out with Ayub Khan and had been more or less exiled from the country because of it. These two men endeavoured to restore confidence, particularly among the agitating students and working classes, by assurance of all sympathy and readiness to help. But the mood was ugly and uncompromising. In Karachi, the students informed Yusuf Haroon that if demands were not accepted within ten days, they would stage a *gherao* at Government House.[45] In short,

---

[44] Mostly comprising people who had migrated from Bihar. It was an old and persistent problem.
[45] *D*, 23 March 1969.

THE LAST PHASE

Ayub Khan's moves were much too little and much too late.[46]

On the evening of 25 March, Ayub Khan addressed the nation in a broadcast. He said it would be the last occasion on which he would do so as President of Pakistan. He said that the situation in the country had deteriorated to a point at which 'Self-aggrandisement is the order of the day. The mobs are resorting to *gheraos* at will and get their demands accepted under duress. And no one has the courage to proclaim the truth. . . . There is no one who can challenge this frenzy. The economy of the country has been crippled, factories are closing down and production is dwindling every day.' He added: 'The security of the country demands that no impediment be placed in the way of the Defence Forces. . . . In view of this, I have decided to relinquish today the office of President.' He expressed gratitude to the country and to all who had served the nation during his period of office. In a letter to General Yahya Khan, he said: 'I am left with no option but to step aside and leave it to the Defence Forces of Pakistan which today represent the only effective and legal instrument to take over full control of the affairs of this country.' Accordingly, Martial Law was declared at 7.15 that evening and, for the second time since independence, the people of Pakistan witnessed, in every city of their country, troops in battle order, patrolling the streets as sole repository of the duty to maintain law and order in the much troubled Republic of Pakistan.[47]

---

[46] By this time also, it is probable that recourse to Martial Law was being considered. See Appendix H.

[47] The verbatim text of Ayub Khan's speech and letter to General Yahya Khan, along with the first Martial Law Regulations are in *D*, 26 March 1969.

XV

Field-Marshal Mohammad Ayub Khan—An Assessment [1]

WHEN forming the judgement of a man, his quality, and his work, considerations are involved which it is both wise and charitable to keep in mind. As La Rochefoucauld once said, there may be merit without advancement, but there can be no advancement without merit. It is an ill-advised critic who treats as negligible the man who rises to high place only to meet his Waterloo at last. Secondly, there is all the difference in the world between doing the job, making the decision and bearing the burden of responsibility on the one hand, and simply writing or talking about it on the other. What Bradley has luminously described as 'encounter' defines the grand abyss that separates the man who fought the battle, ran the race, or made the journey to the moon, from the man who comes afterwards to describe, to criticize or, for that matter, to praise. Thirdly, a man and his achievements are entitled to receive judgement in the context and the ambiance in which they found themselves since '. . . a statesman must work with the material in hand. If the sweep of his conceptions exceeds the capacity of his environment to absorb them, he will fail, regardless of the validity of his insights.'[2] Field-Marshal Ayub Khan is entitled to be judged within such parameters as these, but although they may work fairly, they may also work unsparingly since justice is sad-eyed.

[1] It is fair to tell the reader, at the outset, that I have not met Field-Marshal Ayub Khan, although I have had various opportunities of observing him fairly closely. My personal associations with Pakistan, and more particularly with the Punjab, however, are not only long, but they are a good deal more intimate than those enjoyed by most foreigners. This may perhaps confer a deeper and more penetrating insight than might otherwise be possible, into the character and background of the Field-Marshal and into the circumstances in which he was born, lived and worked. I have written this assessment in the past tense because it relates to Ayub Khan as he revealed himself when holding the office of President. I may add here that the word 'encounter' is used in the sense defined by F. H. Bradley, as quoted by William James in the *Principles of Psychology*, Dover Publications, Vol. II, p. 7.

[2] Kissinger, op. cit., p. 64.

While it seems probable that Ayub Khan did not expect to find his book, *Friends not Masters*, taking rank with the great classics of English prose, it stands, even at its most modest estimation, exposed to several fair and serious criticisms. One of them is that although he described it as *A Political Autobiography*, what he tells us of the development of his political ideas or of the earlier foundations upon which his later concepts were built, is negligible. There is nothing to show what he read, or studied, or mused upon; not a scrap of correspondence exchanged with a relative, a friend or even a professional colleague from which it might be possible to deduce the sources and the directions of his thinking. In this autobiography the first forty-one years of the author's life are disposed of in the first twenty-one pages.

Despite our ignorance about his political maturation, it is clear that he was no upstart flung into high position by some irrational combination of force and circumstance. A genuine measure of capacity is proved by the fact of his appointment as the first among his countrymen to be Commander-in-Chief of the Pakistan Army. In securing this enviable distinction there was, to be sure, an undoubted element of good fortune, although in the circumstances the propriety of this expression might be questioned. Had Lieutenant-General Iftikhar not been killed earlier in an air accident, it is virtually certain that he, and not Ayub Khan, would have received this promotion. So long as General Iftikhar was alive and fit, the possibility of any other appointee remained remote. After his death Ayub Khan became a short-list candidate and was, in due course, appointed. His selection depended in part upon the advice of the previous Commander-in-Chief, the late General Sir Douglas Gracey, a circumstance which reduces the possibility that Ayub Khan's promotion was made with considerations in mind other than those of suitability and competence. For Ayub Khan it was an accident that opened the door to his advancement, but the significance of this need not be exaggerated to his disadvantage. Such propitious chances have favourably influenced the careers of men both abler and less able than he, and those who saw, in the manner of his advancement, some slur on his capacity, were much deceived.

Moreover, it is clear from his earlier record that he had ability and was prepared to work in order to get on. At the Royal Military College he passed out, as he himself has told us, about sixtieth in a class of 123 cadets and first among the Indian contingent. His later selection as A.D.C. to the British Resident at Hyderabad indicates that he had been noticed, but such an appointment does not establish exceptional promise in the profession of arms, however much it may pay tribute to personality and capacity in general. Indeed there is little doubt that an impressive appearance and a winning personality have done a great deal to sustain Ayub Khan in life and to advance his prospects. Much of his success abroad, when President of Pakistan, was due to this personal ability to impress. Such qualities by themselves are no evidence of talent, but they have their own worth and often compensate for the want of more solid gifts. This may not seem fair to those whose talent outweighs their charm, but it cannot be helped. The power of personality, as Conrad sagely tells us, is part of the naked truth of things,[3] and this applies to all those dominating people who have made their mark in life, be they a Churchill or even an Ayub Khan.

To a good appearance and an effective personality he allied a genuine talent for public speaking. His delivery was clear and firm and the timbre of his voice fell congenially upon the ear. He had the power of establishing, quickly, a rapport between his audience and himself and he was good, too, as an extempore speaker, having what he desired to say clear in his mind and the power to clothe his thoughts in agreeable and sometimes striking language. As a broadcaster he was less effective. His first-of-the-month radio broadcasts to the nation, for example, were never quite as good as his addresses to a live audience present before him. On the radio his voice seemed to betray an element of weariness or the sense that he was bored by the whole business.

His ability to speak well and persuasively in public had been noticed long before his entry into political life. Officers somewhat junior to him still remember him on the staff of the Infantry Training School at Bangalore during World War II, when he made a considerable impression on younger British-Indian Army officers attending courses there. It was then that he spoke of post-war India and of the probability of important

[3] *The Rescue*, London, Penguin, p. 239.

political change, although it does not appear that the prospect of Pakistan figured prominently in his remarks. His theme appears to have been the greatly increasing responsibilities that would fall on Indian Army officers when political changes came about, a legitimate and proper subject for discussion which he appears to have handled discreetly and sensibly.

His personal record during World War II was undistinguished, notwithstanding an effort, made later when he was President, to establish for him the reputation of a keen, fighting soldier who spent gruelling times in the Burmese jungles. There is no intention, now, to suggest by implication that he did not do his duty or that he sought to avoid it, but it is plain that his ability as a soldier lay in the direction of organization and administration rather than as a commander in battle. He belonged to the school of Carnot rather than that of Napoleon.

As Commander-in-Chief he is generally reckoned to have done a sound job in re-organizing and re-arming the Pakistan Army so as to make of it a modern, efficient fighting force, capable of carrying out the tasks which it might be required to perform and, in all respects, fit to be entrusted with the ground defence of the country.

His relations with his military subordinates were in general good. He was loyal to them and supported them in the manner that they deserved. It would not be easy to find an officer with any reasonably founded complaint of injustice or even of unkindness at the hands of Ayub Khan when he was Commander-in-Chief. He observed the norms of conduct and the spirit of brotherly comradeship usually associated with the profession of arms. This attitude to subordinates continued after he became President, then embracing officials of the civil services. He knew how to elicit their confidence and loyalty and even if this process was encouraged by rewards, including the conferment of such petty distinctions as flags on the motor-cars of senior officials, the fact remains that in this he was successful to the last.

I have said of him that, as a soldier, he was an organizer rather than a commander and his limitations have been suggested by himself, in the manner that such things are often brought to light—in curious and generally unnoticed ways. To be sure, he had little opportunity to prove his mastery in the art of waging war for the operations of September 1965 proved little test and, as we have already seen, the order of generalship displayed on both sides during those seventeen days has never been rated high.

It is doubtful whether he was deeply read in his profession for, in a television interview given to a team from West Germany in 1966,[4] he expressed his admiration for the German military tradition and proceeded to say: 'It was people like von Schlieffen and so on, who taught one soldiering.'[5] It is a curious choice of name because any soldier well acquainted with the literature of his profession, whose admiration was directed towards German prowess in land warfare, would almost certainly have thought first of von Clausewitz and then of the elder von Moltke, whose triumphs of 1866 and 1870 provided the pattern for later generations of the German General Staff. Moreover, for a Pakistani officer, von Moltke offers special interest in that it was he who played such an important part in the creation of a modern army for another Muslim country, Turkey. So far as von Schlieffen can be considered a representative figure of the German General Staff, he carried on where von Moltke left off and such measure of public fame as von Schlieffen enjoys owes itself to his association with the plan for the invasion of France rather than to the creation of new doctrine. It does no injustice to von Schlieffen to say that he simply continued all that von Moltke had so carefully, so industriously, and so successfully initiated and for which he laid all the necessary foundations.[6]

If I appear to have laboured this point, it is perhaps because Ayub Khan was almost always unfortunate in his literary references, professional or other. Early in the days of his Martial Law administration, he ventured to recommend, in warm terms,

---

[4] Reported in *D*, 15 and 16 November 1966.
[5] Field-Marshal Count Alfred von Schlieffen, 1833–1913. His *Collected Writings* were first published in German in 1913 and a selection from them, entitled *Cannae*, in 1925. His *Letters* were published in 1958. The only translation into English of any work by von Schlieffen is that of *Cannae*, published by the Command and General Staff School Press, Fort Leavenworth, U.S.A. (For this last mentioned information, I am indebted to Dr. Schneiders of the Bayerische Staatsbibliotek, Munich.)
[6] In a review of *FNM*, in the *Guardian*, 8 September 1967, Dr. Percival Spear justly remarks that Ayub Khan should 'neither be underrated as a politician nor overrated as a soldier'.

a book entitled *The Economic Problems of Pakistan* by one S. Inait Hussain.[7] In bringing to notice the work of a fellow-countryman, Ayub Khan was doing something worth while in itself, but it would have been wiser, in his own interest, and certainly of greater public benefit, had he attached his commendation to work of weightier substance. Again, years later, he once advised the revenue officials of West Pakistan to study the system devised by Raja Todarmal, Revenue Minister of the Mogul Emperor, Akbar. He explained, with an air of discovery, that he had been reading Todarmal's book and thought that his system of revenue collection should be adopted.[8] There is, perhaps fortunately, no indication that his advice was taken.

It was often said of him that he was, and claimed to be, one who read and enjoyed books. This may well be so, but it is evident that his reading had very little about it that was exhaustive or profound. A photograph taken of him when convalescing early in 1968 shows him with a current copy of the *Reader's Digest*.[9] To be sure, we do not expect to find an invalid, recovering from a serious illness, absorbed in a massive and abstruse tome. Further, the real point in placing the magazine in his hand was to establish the date on which the photograph was taken. This is all very well, but in using so light a journal for this purpose, the image of Ayub Khan as a deep-thinking man was belied and his public relations advisers obviously made a mistake. All this said, however, the *Reader's Digest* seems to be about the size of it. This view is, I also think, borne out by those references to literary interests mentioned in *Friends not Masters*. Evidently his taste was for good, readable, well-informed stuff, but without range or depth and nowhere do we find reference to any of the epoch-making books of this, or any, century, unless it be the *Quran*.

It is worth noting that in Pakistan it is the custom each year to award to distinguished and deserving artists and writers the President's Medal for Pride of Performance (whatever this latter phrase may mean), and the practice was certainly kept up in Ayub Khan's time. It is also the custom for recipients of this honour to receive cash gifts ranging from five to ten

---

[7] Pakistan, 1956. Published, it appears, by the author.
[8] *D*, 10 November 1967.
[9] This photograph appeared in many Pakistani newspapers on 4 March 1968.

thousand rupees. However, to the Bholu brothers, a well-known family of Punjabi wrestlers, Ayub Khan made a much publicized gift of Rs.100,000 in the form of Government of Pakistan Prize Bonds. For this munificent presentation no specific reason appears assignable apart from their generally recognized feats as all-in matmen. It was such circumstances as these that left little doubt in the mind of the Pakistani intellectual as to Ayub Khan's personal order of cultural priorities.

The truth of the matter is that Ayub Khan's intellectual pretensions were false and misconceived. They sprang from that element in his character which, in its exercise, so often betrayed him. It may be that leaders do not reach eminence without a touch of vanity[10] but this, like everything else, has its levels. The things about which a man is vain, as well as the manner in which he gives visible expression to this weakness, tell us a great deal concerning him and, with Ayub Khan, triviality and a readiness for self-display were unhappily distinctive features.

It seems possible that these trifling forms of conceit sprang from an inherent sense of inadequacy. Later, we shall discover other evidence of this. His origins were modest, if these be measured by rank and wealth, but his family belonged to the martial classes of the Punjab with honourable traditions on which to rely. His father, joining the former Indian Army as a *sowar*, rose to the rank of risaldar-major in Hodson's Horse. Ayub Khan, in his book, tells us something of all this, but manages to evade the need for telling the reader just what it all signifies. The glossary to the book vaguely states that 'risaldar' means 'commander of a cavalry unit' which, although correct, is quite misleading. In fact, to become the risaldar-major in a crack Indian cavalry regiment in those days was a substantially more difficult thing to do, and possibly a greater test of character and ability than to become, let us say, a brigadier-general in one of Europe's vast continental armies. Ayub Khan did not have to excuse or justify his father. He had only to say what he was.

Instances could be multiplied, but one other will suffice here. In *Friends not Masters*[11] he describes an incident, involving the famous Muslim educationalist Sir Ross Masood, which

---

[10] Kissinger, op. cit., p. 203.   [11] *FNM*, p. 7.

occurred when Ayub Khan, who was A.D.C. to the Resident at Hyderabad, says: 'I told the Resident, "You might think this man [i.e. Sir Ross Masood] is making a nuisance of himself...".' The whole story rings false. In the first place, it is conceivably possible that, at the time, Sir Ross Masood was on first-name terms with the Viceroy, leave alone the Hyderabad Resident, who knew exactly who Sir Ross Masood was. Secondly, A.D.C.s do not tell anybody anything. They stand smartly to attention and speak when they are spoken to.

In later years, as his time as President went on, vainglory and egotism grew upon him with ever-increasing effect. Mr. Fazlul Qader Choudhury, a Minister in Ayub Khan's administration after June 1962 and later a Speaker of the National Assembly, has described a meeting in 1965 of the Working Committee of the Pakistan (Convention) Muslim League at which Ayub Khan said that during the last fifty years, the Muslims had not witnessed a greater leader than he.[12] It is, perhaps, necessary to qualify this information by explaining that the circumstances in which Fazlul Qader Choudhury had earlier quitted the office of Speaker led to bad relations between Ayub Khan and himself. It also seems that Choudhury's virtual dismissal from office was attributable only to his own unwise conduct when acting as President of Pakistan during one of Ayub Khan's absences abroad.

From the very beginning, Ayub Khan took his publicity very seriously but, as time went by, it became more and more evident that he was doing so in more senses than one and was beginning to suffer from delusions of grandeur and omniscience.[13] His appetite for flattering praise was fed daily by a press only too well aware of official directives to the effect that reports of national progress and advancement, as well as of plans for the nation's security and prosperity, should be so stated as to make it appear that President Ayub Khan was the fountain of all wisdom and the source of all constructive

---

[12] *Urdu Digest*, Lahore, June 1969.

[13] In a review of *FNM* in the *Daily Telegraph*, London, 7 September 1967, it was said that the author verged on the paranoiac. There were other unpleasant remarks also, though strangely enough the Karachi newspaper *Dawn*, 10 September 1967 carried the headline 'Daily Telegraph lauds Ayub's biography'. *The Times Literary Supplement's* review (12 October 1967) described Ayub Khan as possessing an element of megalomania.

inspiration. This explained why, in most Pakistani newspapers of those days, it was common to find his name at the top of practically every column on the front page. Ultimately, it came to be said that the test of successful journalism in Pakistan was that when President Ayub Khan glanced at the morning papers, he should not be upset.

Still, it was not only his own countrymen who discovered in him talents of a far-ranging versatility. At various times he was the object of panegyric showered on him abroad, although most of it was ephemeral, keyed to the hour and the circumstances.[14] At other times, it was cleverly, and sometimes expensively, engineered. Nevertheless, it is also true that he won genuine esteem and confidence among many foreigners that he met. The former President of the United States, Lyndon B. Johnson, held him in high regard and, when the Mangla Dam was inaugurated, he addressed a congratulatory letter to Ayub Khan couched in the warmest terms.[15] It seems also that he enjoyed good personal relations with and even succeeded in impressing General Charles de Gaulle who, with his customary want of tact, made a prominent reference to the esteem in which he held Ayub Khan when addressing a letter to General Yahya Khan on the latter's assumption of office as President of his country.[16]

More usually, however, Ayub Khan's strong and affable personality did not convince people of an intellectual cast of mind. This is said to account for the coolness in his relations with President Kennedy. Certainly, it explains why, despite several determined and well-publicized efforts, he made little or no impression on the intellectuals of his own country. Of course, with people of intellectual inclinations who happened also to belong to the Ayub Khan establishment or were otherwise connected with his régime the matter stood differently,

[14] A British magazine, *The Eastern World*, November 1966, described him as a statesman 'as welcome in Moscow as he is in London'.

[15] The letter is quoted verbatim in *D*, 24 November 1967. Another American President, Dwight D. Eisenhower, said of Ayub Khan: '... I found President Ayub an agreeable, intelligent and persuasive gentleman.... Ayub is pleasant and modest, but incisive—characteristics that gave an aura of credibility to his avowed purpose of steadily developing healthy democratic institutions in his country.' Dwight D. Eisenhower, *Waging Peace*, Doubleday, New York, 1965, p. 496.

[16] Quoted verbatim in *D*, 16 April 1969.

and many of these were guilty of a painful sycophancy. These apart, the intellectuals of Pakistan found his ideas wanting in depth and they suspected him of seeking power for its own sake as well as its perpetuation. This was, to some extent, acknowledged by him in his broadcast to the nation on 21 February 1969, when he said that the intellectuals felt themselves excluded from the conduct of the nation's affairs.[17]

Among those groups of people in his own country whose status, comfort, security, and prosperity depended upon his ability to hold the ring, he was highly respected and, among those of feebler worth, virtually revered.[18] These groups included those with property, people in business, the managerial class and, of course, the civil servants, whose power and influence were so strongly buttressed and entrenched by reason of the Constitution he had introduced. It followed, also, that a natural sympathy for him was discernible among members of comparable groups in other countries and this explains, in large measure, the origin and reason for much of the praise showered upon him abroad.

For a long time, Ayub enjoyed the loyal support of the armed forces but, despite the material benefits which he was careful to confer on them, mistrust of him began to spread. This change of heart was probably aroused by whispers of the corruption practised by members of his family and other favourites, and mistrust took firmer hold as Ayub Khan tended to become more and more remote from the mass of the people and more and more identified with the wealthy few. It was probably the thought that he could, perhaps, no longer rely on the Army which strongly influenced his decision to relinquish office.

It has often been said of Ayub Khan that he hated politicians, and for a man who showed himself particularly *rusé* in the practice of political manœuvre and intrigue, there is irony in this. Whether his contempt sprang from his dislike of, and

[17] *D*, 22 February 1969.
[18] There is no doubt that in Pakistan there developed an Ayub Khan mystique with all the emotional involvement this implies. No doubt also after his fall from power, his devotees continued to be drawn from those who had been close to him and had been especially favoured. However, Ayub Khan would have done well to remember—or perhaps he did not know—that '... it is just those men in public life who most admire their leader who are usually most assiduous in using him to forward their own small interests and purposes'. (Palmer, *Political Characters of Shakespeare*, Macmillan, London, p. 219.)

disregard for, politics and politicians as such, or whether it sprang from the incompetence of other performers in Pakistan, when their performance was compared with his own, is a separate and interesting question. It is unnecessary to comment on the childish absurdity of professing a hatred for politicians or of saying so, and what matters here is something else. It is clear that Ayub Khan's dislike of politicians for what he took them to be in 1958, developed into virtual contempt several years later. He had discovered that he could do much better what they had long been practising, for the most part indifferently, and the hauteur with which he was wont to treat them arose from an entirely justified sense of professional superiority. The men who, from 1947 to 1958, had been playing ducks and drakes with the country's problems and prospects were unimpressive— the exceptions were unhappily too few—and when it came to the kind of tactics and manoeuvres in which they specialized, Ayub Khan proved to be a great deal better. If, then, it be asked, why did he fall, the answer is that these methods proved to be as fatal to him as to the men he had swept away in 1958.

It was all politics of the Tammany Hall kind—sordid, unprincipled and selfish in its obsession with the spoils of office and the division thereof—dissociated from the mass of the people and the true interest of the country. It had to do with personal intrigue; with setting one man or one group against another; with the distribution of rewards through import licences, permits to set up mills and factories, the grant of bank loans, secured or, more often, unsecured. These, and other money-spinning privileges were nothing more nor less than bills drawn by Ayub Khan on the nation's slender resources, entirely to promote his own purposes. No one knew better than he how to quieten dissidents, rally supporters or control his district bosses by these methods which at no time in the history of Pakistan had been used so widely, effectively or ruthlessly.[19] One of the

[19] In December 1966 Ayub Khan toured East Pakistan at a time when Sheikh Mujibur Rahman's 'Six-Point' agitation seemed to be gaining ground. In my diary, 26 December 1966, I noted that Ayub Khan's visit was held to have been a great success, and that by a judicious distribution of import licences and other favours many of Mujibur Rahman's supporters had been weaned away. However, Ayub Khan's then Law Minister, S. M. Zafar, made some observations in Dacca at that time on East Pakistan's claims for autonomy which were resented and there were student demonstrations.

main reasons for the want of efficiency in industry established in Pakistan lies in the fact that many permits to install factories of one sort or another were given simply out of regard for political considerations and with no regard for the ability or the desire of the recipient to set up such an installation, much less work it. Sometimes the favoured person tried his hand and, as often as not, failed. Otherwise the permits were usually farmed and this is one reason why so much of the country's industry is concentrated in comparatively few hands. At any rate, in the competition for economic privilege, merit counted little.[20]

In the end, it became impossible to believe in Ayub Khan's protest against corruption. On the contrary, it had become clear that he had abandoned himself to a substantial reliance upon it as a political instrument. No doubt, he was encouraged in this by his entourage and by his close political supporters. The argument was twofold. Many forms of corruption have always existed in the sub-continent—they are part of the culture, part of the way of life.[21] Secondly, if the supporters and workers of the régime were not rewarded, they would drift away and, eventually, merge with the opposition in the hope of better days. It has also been said that, on one occasion, Ayub Khan took the opinion of a visiting professor of political science —supposed to have come from the United States—as to whether corruption could be used as a political instrument. He was apparently given the pragmatic answer that all means are justified in the achievement of political ends.[22]

So far as concerns the argument in favour of corruption, advanced by the esurient wolves who surrounded Ayub Khan, no doubt their own interests were uppermost in their minds, but there was substance in their advice. In all countries, some accommodation of political supporters is necessary and this may

[20] Methods of dividing spoils are sometimes disclosed in unexpected ways. In June 1969 the Jama'at-i-Islam Party proposed a code of conduct for all political parties. It comprised eight points and included a pledge that all parties would abstain from the distribution of government patronage such as route permits for freight carrying vehicles etc. *D*, 15 June 1969.
[21] See M. A. Choudhury, *The Civil Service in Pakistan*, National Institute of Public Administration, Dacca, 1963.
[22] This was told me by a very senior member of the diplomatic corps stationed in Islamabad. I do not vouch for the truth of the story and I repeat it as it was narrated.

well extend to jobs and other forms of material advantage. The degree to which this is required and deemed tolerable is an index to the nation's political maturity, its political awareness, and political integrity. Thus, by way of example, the United Kingdom is credited with possessing a reasonably clean political life, yet it is undoubtedly true that the enormous patronage that lies in the hands of the Prime Minister arms him with great power when dealing with his opponents as well as with his own party men.

All this conceded, the fact remains that Ayub Khan allowed commercial malpractice and corruption of the crudest sort to expand and flourish and he used all of these without stint to purchase and retain the loyalty of his supporters. It was during his administration that, for the first time in the history of Pakistan, very high denomination currency notes were issued.[23] Whatever may be the commercial utility of these notes, the fact is that they are a godsend to smugglers and blackmarket operators.

Worse still, he allowed corruption to spread and grow within the civil service and, in some respects, can be said to have encouraged it. At least one instance is on record of a senior member of the Civil Service of Pakistan, with a long-standing reputation for corrupt practice who, on reaching retirement age in accordance with current service rules, was given an extension by Ayub Khan. Was this ignorance of the facts? Was it indifference, sheer perversity, or was there some other motive? It may not be possible to convict a man of corruption or even secure his dismissal or premature retirement on such grounds—the legal difficulties are well known—but where the bad reputation has long existed, what justification can there be for granting an extension of service? Another instance, concerning

[23] Notes in the denomination of Rs.500 were first issued in Pakistan in 1964. Previously, the highest denomination was Rs.100.

It is not suggested that notes of Rs.500 denomination were issued on the initiative or at the instance of Ayub Khan. Indeed, the proposal had been made in Pakistan before his administration first began and had been turned down for reasons that made it objectionable when these notes eventually came to be issued. Ayub Khan must, or, at any rate, should have been aware of these reasons because during World War II notes of Rs.1,000 were demonetized in India (notes of Rs.500 denomination were not then in issue), thereby following the example of the British Government which had demonetized £100 notes. The reasons were explicitly stated to be those of hindering profiteers and blackmarket operators.

an equally senior member of the same service, was publicly revealed after Ayub Khan departed from office. It was a case of a serious allegation of corruption made against an official who had once been Private Secretary to Ayub Khan when he was President. However, Ayub Khan would not permit the Special Police to pursue their enquiries in this affair.[24]

Inevitably this brings us to the question of Ayub Khan's personal involvement and that of his family, a subject which has been much publicized and which has provided plenty of material—however well-founded—for worldwide scandal.

So far as Ayub Khan is concerned, it may suffice to say that authority being what it is and men in power being what they are, it should be no cause for wonder if he quitted office a richer man than when he entered it. To know how far this is true is much more difficult. Reports and gossip on such matters as this tend always to be exaggerated and tinged with drama. As rumour goes the rounds, the embroidery that attaches to it is equalled in its variety only by the magnitude of the sums discussed. In this, as in most scandalous affairs, it is always astonishing to observe the assurance with which people, who cannot possibly have any direct knowledge of, or access to, the truth, sometimes profess the most exact and reliable information. This is certainly the case with much that has been bruited about concerning Ayub Khan and his family, the extent of their landed acquisitions and of their fortunes. I am not able to lay claim to any such certainty, but so far as Ayub Khan is concerned, it appears that his taste was for land and house property rather than for cash acquired through business transactions, surreptitious or otherwise.

That his name and reputation have been deeply stained by the money-making activities of members of his family, and by others who enjoyed his protection, cannot be denied, and as time went on and scandal proliferated, these matters became the subject of bitter criticism and stinging satire. A well-known

[24] *Daily News*, Karachi, 26 May 1969. This official had also been given an extension of service by Ayub Khan. In the course of an interview with the B.B.C. on 16 November 1967, the interviewer suggested to Ayub Khan that in Pakistan corruption was worse than ever. Ayub Khan denied this and said that his Government was doing its best to eradicate it!

writer of political lampoons rocked his audience with verses of which one example can be quoted here:

> *Ek bhai andar, ek bhai bahar,*
> *Bich men, hai bhai, Ghandhara!*
> *Pobarah! Pobarah!*

It is not possible for me to reproduce in translation the ringing contempt of the original which refers to the establishment of Ghandhara Industries Ltd. by Captain Gohar Ayub and his father-in-law, the retired Lieutenant-General Habibullah Khan Khattak. It may help if I add that the word *pobarah* means the winning throw at dice with which the thrower sweeps the board. The writer, Habib Jalib, was later arrested on charges of complicity in a murder case, and after a spell in jail in which to exercise his wit upon the prison walls, the poet was released.

I have selected this verse because it can be taken to suggest something which I do not believe to be true, namely that when Ayub Khan became President in October 1958 he more or less entered into a conspiracy with his sons and, maybe others, whereby they would despoil the country for as much as they could and for as long as they could. On the contrary, there is ample reason to suppose that Ayub Khan witnessed the retirement of his two elder sons Akhtar and Gohar from their careers as professional soldiers with the utmost reluctance, and particularly so in the case of Gohar Ayub for whom he entertained very high hopes. This, his second son, is a clever, personable young man and Ayub Khan had some justification in thinking that one day perhaps, Gohar would emulate his own achievement by becoming Commander-in-Chief. Unfortunately, events turned out differently, as they so often do.

When, much against his wishes, his two elder sons left the Army, it appears to have been Ayub Khan's plan that they should manage the landed property he had acquired and, for the rest, seek a career in politics. However, they soon discovered the potentialities of influence in the world of industry and commerce and, in collaboration with his father-in-law, Gohar Ayub proceeded to enter business on a very substantial scale. In Appendix B I have endeavoured to set out some indications of the scope of these affairs. In November 1967 it was reliably said that Ayub Khan had caused letters to be sent to various Government departments and to other organizations of an official or semi-official character, to the effect that if they were approached by any members of his family, seeking favours, a report was to be made to him. To what extent this made any difference it is impossible to say, but by then the damage was irreparable. The total wealth of Ayub Khan and his family, at the time of his giving up the office of President, was thought by Dr. Franz Pick to be in the order of $10 to $20 million,[25] and although Dr. Pick is a shrewd and well-informed observer who regularly visits Pakistan, this is a widely bracketed estimate. It is difficult to know how there can be any assurance of even moderate accuracy in such things, but the estimate of Gohar Ayub's wealth seems to indicate that the truth does lie somewhere between the limits suggested by Dr. Pick. If so, it represents no small reward for ten years' effort and whatever may be the odium attaching to Field-Marshal Ayub Khan because of it, it may well be that his descendants, if ever taxed with all this, would respond with the suggestion that to seek the bubble reputation, even in the cannon's mouth, when all this money was to be had for the asking, might be *sharif* (noble) but scarcely *hoshyar* (intelligent).

So far as concerns this odium, it has been the unenviable lot of Captain Gohar Ayub to be the object of most of it and, after Martial Law was declared in March 1969, he issued a statement to the press in which he said that he had been greatly and grossly maligned. He added that since Martial Law was again in force, it was open to anyone to address to the Martial Law authorities such complaint against him as was thought proper. This statement was not printed by the newspapers but the fact of its issue was mentioned in at least one of them, a daily published in Karachi in the Gujarati language.

Gohar Ayub might well say that he had unfairly been made the principal target of the criticism directed towards Ayub Khan's family and their activities. To be sure, he was deeply involved in the disturbances which took place in Karachi in January 1965,[26] and there was no gainsaying his single-minded approach to the task of making money. But whether he was responsible for most, or even a substantial part of the misdeeds

[25] *World Currency Report*, April 1969.   [26] See pp. 80-1.

committed by various members of the family and by others who basked in the sunshine of Ayub Khan's favour, is extremely doubtful. Quite apart from avarice, as such, these activities included land-grabbing, smuggling and various crimes of violence from which the possibility of murder cannot be excluded. Certainly, there was one case of seduction of a daughter of a senior official,[27] and, of course, the commoner forms of abuse of power involving the exercise of undue influence over officials, evading the net of justice and so on. It is probable that a complete list of all the tyrannies and villainies committed by these people will never be compiled and, perhaps, it is not necessary that it should be unless it were used as a reminder and a warning to others coming later. But it deserves to be said that there are those more deserving of the criticism and condemnation that have fallen upon the head of Gohar Ayub.

One reason for Gohar's misfortune in this respect is the conspicuous part he has played. Ayub Khan was ambitious for all his children and it has been said that such affection as he was capable of was entirely reserved for them. In particular, he reposed great hopes in his son, Gohar, and after Gohar had abandoned his army career, Ayub Khan did not conceal his endeavours to advance Gohar in politics. As so often happens, Gohar Ayub was probably the unintended victim of this paternal regard. The sedulous build-up and the undisguised intention to thrust Gohar into prominence and promote him in the public eye served to nourish envy and attract adverse notice. Still, Gohar was not the only one of Ayub Khan's children on whom ill-advised marks of affection were lavished and these, as it turned out, were to Ayub Khan's ultimate disadvantage.

In July 1966[28] it was announced that President Ayub Khan had been pleased to confer the style of 'Highness' upon the Wali of Swat and the Nawab of Dir, each of them thereby becoming entitled to a salute of fifteen guns. These distinctions were granted, it was explained, as rewards for great services rendered during the hostilities with India in September 1965. Not surprisingly, this evoked much opposition in Pakistan,

[27] It has, however, been said that the lady was easily seduceable.
[28] *D*, 9 July 1966.

especially among Ayub Khan's political opponents.[29] People enquired how it was that the President of a basically democratic republic could possess, or even assume, the power to create titles in the nature of royalty. Precedents existed, of course, in the history of those former colonial powers which happened also to be republics, but the more important question for us is how anyone bearing the heavy responsibilities that lay on the shoulders of the President of Pakistan, could concern himself with matters so unnecessary, so trivial, and so alien to the spirit of the times. To this enquiry, no rational answer presents itself and there is none. The explanation is that Ayub Khan's eldest daughter, Begum Naseem Aurangzeb, is married to the heir of the Wali of Swat. If, therefore, the naturally anticipated order of things prevailed, it was to be expected that a day would come when the granddaughter of the risaldar-major would be addressed as 'Highness'.[30]

Besides the question of Ayub Khan's ambitions for his family, his desire for various forms of personal distinction lend substance to the suggestion of a sense of inadequacy, to the suggestion that, inside himself, Ayub Khan was not quite *sure*. Indecision was part of his character and, indeed, within the external shell of firmness tempered by an amiable affability, there lay a man essentially lonely and sometimes troubled by doubt—a man who, in essence, kept his own counsel and made his own decisions. He was a case of the suspicious, wary, calculating villager, cunning rather than intelligent; a man much more withdrawn than many might suppose and one who did not recklessly entrust his fortunes and prospects to others.

However, for all this, there is one further point which, in fairness to Ayub Khan, must be elaborated. He has been heavily censured for what he allowed his family to do, or, at any rate, for his apparently silent acquiescence in what they

[29] The Karachi monthly magazine *Today*, August 1966, carried a highly critical article entitled 'Crown and Sceptre Again'. This magazine later ceased publication after it had drawn upon itself unfavourable notice by reason of an open letter, addressed to President Ayub Khan, in its issue of December 1966, on the subject of the freedom of the press.

[30] It may also be asked: Why, too, the Nawab of Dir? This relates to frontier politics. Historically, the houses of Swat and Dir are great rivals and Ayub Khan did not wish to appear to be favouring one against the other.

did, yet it is most improbable that he was alone in his encouragement, tacit or otherwise. The influence of the *zenana* must also be taken into account for this is often very powerful, particularly where sons are concerned.[31] To what extent the senior ladies in Ayub Khan's family encouraged his sons and other male relations to take advantage of his high position and pervading influence, is a difficult question to answer, but there can be no doubt that there was such encouragement. Nothing would be more natural, nor more consonant with eastern practice, than for them to invite attention to the great vista of opportunity that now awaited and to urge that it would be a mark of the greatest folly, calling down Heaven's wrath, if the golden harvest that good fortune offered, were allowed to go unreaped.

Difficult as are these things to prove, one instance can be cited, concerning which there is little room for doubt. This relates to Begum Ayub Khan's nephew and son-in-law, Najibullah Khan, an extraordinary person who earned for himself much unfavourable comment for several reasons. One of them had to do with various transactions and dealings in land which became a source of scandal. Eventually, his activities attracted official notice and became the object of official enquiry, but it appears that Begum Ayub Khan intervened and everything was suppressed until after Ayub Khan gave up the office of President. Legal proceedings were then initiated against Najibullah Khan in relation to the acquisition of land by a person who appears to have been his nominee and who was acting at his instance. This did not end his contact with the law for, later still, he became involved in charges relating to murder.

And now after so much that is adverse has been said, it is time to enquire what, if anything, has been the achievement of this complex, publicity-loving, egotistical character? What did he do for Pakistan and Pakistanis that can be stated to his credit and for which he deserves to be well remembered?

That he made positive and beneficial contributions to the

---

[31] I write this paragraph with some hesitation. Begum Ayub Khan has not appeared in public nor has she participated in public life and it may seem unjust to charge someone who has not so participated and who may not even care to answer for herself.

advancement and progress of his country cannot be doubted, and this contribution must now be summarized. It is true that he might have done more, if it had not been for the circumstances in which he worked. He was, in some ways, ahead of his time—at any rate, in Pakistan. He knew the dangers of confusing religion with politics and, in drafting the Constitution of 1962, he was anxious to eliminate any risk of such confusion. Changes which were made later, importing an Islamic emphasis, were against his better judgement. But it was a movement he could not resist and, eventually, he joined it, as a matter of political expediency. This need not, and should not be treated as a ground for criticism. Had he allowed himself to be defeated in the presidential election of 1965, or even later, on issues of this sort, it would not have prevented their adoption. The criticism that can be made is not that he was unaware of the dangers of the religious strait-jacket, or even that he was prepared to go along with those who desired it, but that all too willingly he allowed his own opinions to be cast aside.

Even as it was, his work in the field of social change brought him opposition from the orthodox and also some loss of support. His principal work in this respect—the Muslim Family Laws Ordinance and the impetus he sought to give to the Family Planning Movement—required distinct political courage. It is a fact that there are many women and children who have cause to thank Ayub Khan for instituting laws that have liberated them from injustice. His effort to encourage family limitation and to provide the means of education in its practice among all ranks of society, rural and urban, was a bold and praiseworthy attempt although, in his own time, it ended in substantial failure. This failure, too, can be partly attributed to him, since it was largely brought about by corruption and dishonesty, circumstances for which, as we have seen elsewhere, Ayub Khan cannot escape blame.

The extensive series of Commissions of Enquiry which he launched, particularly during the Martial Law period from 1958 to 1962, produced a vast body of solid information which has been applied and utilized, not always in a spectacular manner, for the reform and improvement of the public administration. It is far from true that all this information has been put to good use and equally far from true that all the recommendations of these Commissions have been implemented and the circumstances of non-implementation were not always to Ayub Khan's credit, but even where recommendation awaits adoption, it can still be said that it was the product of his initiative.

By concluding the Indus Waters Treaty with India, he made possible the removal of a major cause of dispute between the two countries and the elimination of an abiding risk of pressure from India under threat of withholding water. However, just as important, and perhaps more burdensome, was the task of ensuring completion of the works made necessary by the Treaty. It may be thought that once the Treaty was signed under the auspices of the World Bank, nothing remained but to let the engineers, the financiers and the contractors go to work and complete the necessary programme of dam construction, canals, canal links, realignments, headworks, and so on. It was very far from being so simple.

To begin with, the fact of having concluded the Indus Waters Treaty with India exposed Ayub Khan to criticism which was utilized against him during the election of 1965. It is possible to criticize the terms of the arrangement on technical grounds and certainly this view was held by some professional people in Pakistan. More difficult and trying, however, was the actual implementation of the Treaty which, having been signed, placed a great burden on Ayub Khan and his Government. The complexities of execution were very great, as is evident from a study of the water and power resources of West Pakistan, prepared for and under the auspices of the World Bank.[32] This study begins with the remarkable statement that the partition of the sub-continent took place in 1948 and proceeds to further statements just as remarkable and of very much more weight. It says: 'As engineers began to take a closer look at the proposed works following the Agreement, it became increasingly clear that the cost would far exceed the resources of the Indus Basin Development Fund.'

[32] Pieter Loftinck and others, *Water and Power Resources of West Pakistan*, Johns Hopkins Press, Baltimore, 1968, Main Report, Vol. I.

The Agreement here referred to was signed at the same time as the Indus Waters Treaty and the parties to it were Australia, Canada, Germany, New Zealand, Pakistan, the United Kingdom, the United States, and the World Bank. Its purpose was to provide funds for the works made necessary by the Treaty, and the countries named, along with the World Bank, were to provide the necessary money which, with India's agreed contribution of $174 million, was known as the Indus Basin Development Fund. Since the negotiations leading to the execution of the Indus Waters Treaty, and to the decision that the World Bank and the other signatories would, between them, contribute $721 million, had lasted some ten years, one may well enquire what they had been talking about all that time. Furthermore, the same Report, on page two, says that it had also become clear that the total cost of the Indus works would be not less than twice the amount available to the Fund and that there were 'unresolved problems' with regard to the 'precise works' to be built.[33]

Thus, if due and prompt effect were to be given to the Treaty which Ayub Khan had signed with India, it was necessary to find a lot more money and to find it on reasonable terms. It was necessary, also, to clear the way for action by settling the 'unresolved problems' which the engineers were now discovering. Whether all this was known to Ayub Khan and his Government when the Treaty was signed with India is not clear, but it seems unlikely. It is just as unlikely that it was known to any of the other negotiators either, and had these matters been elucidated earlier the terms of the Treaty, as well as of the Agreement, might have been different. India, for example, might have been asked to contribute more. Despite these insufficiencies in knowledge, the major part of the Indus Basin works was successfully executed during Ayub Khan's administration, the great Mangla Dam was completed, and work on the even greater Tarbela Dam was started.

It was during his administration that the public was made actively aware of the need for economic growth and for productive investment. Although Ayub Khan's own knowledge and grasp of financial and economic matters was limited, he

[33] Author's quotes.

was highly conscious of the need for determined economic activity, sedulously pursued, as a means of raising the general standard of living and of achieving economic independence. As in most developing countries, the enormous investments made in the public and private sectors have not been uniformly successful. For reasons already discussed, industrial inefficiency is common, costs are high and the financing has been expensive, due in part to many misconceptions as to the best methods by which economic progress can best be achieved. All the blame for these failings should not be laid at Ayub Khan's door so far as Pakistan is concerned. And they are common to all developing countries.

His much discussed Land Reforms are now generally understood for what they were and nothing need be said about them here. However, so far as concerns the utilization of land and the promotion of agriculture, he ultimately brought about a correction in the official stance, after a period of indifference to rural progress. In the latter part of his administration, he had the satisfaction of witnessing substantially increased crops and a rapidly growing fertilizer industry.

The main fruit of his work lay in what he did for economic and social progress and that he made a contribution is indisputable. In the field of education he was less successful, and so far as concerns his vague speculations on constitutional theory and foreign affairs the less said the better. It is true that by reason of an impressive and agreeable personality he succeeded in creating for Pakistan a better image than it had enjoyed for a long time, but this had little to do with his theorizing about bilateralism and so on. It seems never to have occurred to him that the pursuit of a policy of bilateralism may be little more than a euphemism for being in the international wilderness.

Ayub Khan's intellectual make-up and his stock of ideas were based on solid common sense and the ability to recognize, quickly and clearly, objective necessities. The limitations that lay heavily upon him consisted first in the inability to grasp that state policy must be a coherent whole and not simply adapted to the passing circumstance or event. He was fond of the word 'pragmatism', but confused its meaning with opportunism. Secondly, in those areas of thought and decision which call for broader knowledge and deeper penetration, common sense, while indispensable, is insufficient.

For reasons which are not difficult to trace Field-Marshal Ayub Khan has often been compared with General de Gaulle,[34] and in Pakistan they were often spoken of as 'the two soldier-statesmen'. It is true that in some ways they served their respective countries similarly, but the comparison goes little further. Despite General de Gaulle's unendearing quirks of temperament, he possessed a first-rate mind and a professional background that far exceeded anything Ayub Khan could claim. In the profession of arms, de Gaulle gave early proof of his exceptional ability with the publication of his treatise, *The Army of the Future*, one of the peaks in twentieth-century military writing. More than all this, however, is the fact that de Gaulle had been tried, as few men have, in the fires of adversity, an experience Ayub Khan had never known. An ardent patriot, de Gaulle witnessed the humiliating surrender of his country from which he was obliged to exile himself. Dependent upon the help and hospitality of alien nations, he lived under sentence of death and yet remained the living symbol of French defiance in defeat. Whatever may be the natural temper of a man's steel, it is only when its quality has thus been proved, that the keenest edge is possible. Compared with de Gaulle, Ayub Khan had it *khushi* all his life.

Still, whatever his limitations, Ayub Khan was by no means without ability. He had a flair for political manœuvre and the force of his personality was clear, as also his gift of leadership. He could win people to his side and did so. His ultimate fall cannot be attributed so much to his limitations as to an inherent weakness in his character and this brings us to the darker side of his career to which his downfall must be traced.

Power, success, and flattery spoiled him. Taken together, they form a heady nectar and Ayub Khan drank deep of it. Looking over events as they took shape and traced their course, particularly in the latter years of his administration, one may well ask if it is possible he knew nothing of the conduct of those people, some connected closely by family ties, who, under his protection, defied the law and lined their pockets with

---

[34] See, e.g. *The Economist*, London, 1 March 1969, p. 18.

insatiable greed? Is it possible he knew nothing of the rising tide of corruption in every branch of the public service and at every level? Is it possible he was ignorant of the burgeoning sense of despair among the educated classes, helplessly witnessing the methodical suppression of all liberty of thought? Is it possible he did not know that the political institutions he had devised, and in which he took so much pride, had degenerated into instruments of oppression and unlawful gain in the hands of his party bosses and their henchmen? Is it possible he had become so distant from the people that he believed a policy of repression could prevail so long as he cared to pursue it, that the tuneless music discoursed by his inept political orchestra fell with ever-growing sweetness on the public ear and that the upsurge, which followed the events of 9 November 1968, could be summarily put down by a bit of heavy-handed police work?

Well, all these things were possible. Whom the gods wish to destroy....

If ever a man, embarking on a career as leader of his nation, did so with the ball at his feet, that man is Mohammad Ayub Khan. When Iskander Mirza took his leave and Ayub Khan assumed his office, not a single dissentient voice was heard. This was so not merely because in those days dissent was forbidden by the recently imposed Martial Law, but rather because there was no spirit of dissent abroad. Today there are many who claim to detect, or to have detected, in the events preceding the Martial Law of October 1958, all sorts of conspiracies to which Ayub Khan himself was privy, but most of this has been revealed through hindsight. In the genuine and nationwide sense of relief felt in those days of political turmoil and unrest, the welcome offered to Ayub Khan was virtually total and utterly sincere. People were glad he came and they nurtured high hopes that he would serve to raise the country from the morass into which it had sunk.

Such was the opportunity vouchsafed him and such is the measure of his failure. He failed because he was corrupted by power in the full and precise sense of Lord Acton's famous aphorism. Thus is demonstrated the central infirmity of his character and thus it is proved that the most accurate, as well as the most charitable, judgement to be made of him is that the fibre of the man did not correspond to the manner of his address and was unequal to the necessities of his mission.

So it was that Ayub Khan lost his way in life. His misfortune has been aptly described in the concluding words of Professor T. Harry Williams' lecture on the late Huey P. Long, 'As we continue our constant quest to understand the politicians, perhaps we would be aided if we could realize that the greatest of them are essentially tragic figures.'[35]

[35] Inaugural lecture delivered at the University of Oxford, 26 January 1967.

Epilogue

At eleven o'clock on the morning of 25 March 1969, the Chief Martial Law Administrator, General Yahya Khan, broadcast an address to the nation. He spoke in English, his words brief and to the point. He promised direct elections based on universal adult franchise and a constitution that would be framed by the elected representatives of the people. On the question of administrative shortcomings, which had figured so prominently during the recent months of agitation, he was firm. 'We have had enough administrative laxity and chaos and I shall see to it that this is not repeated in any form or manner.' He continued with assurances to students, labourers and peasants. 'I am conscious of the genuine difficulties and pressing needs of various sections of our society. . . . Let me assure you that my administration will make every endeavour to resolve these difficulties.' He concluded by saying that the Martial Law Administration would not tolerate agitation or destruction and he appealed to everyone to 'do his bit to repair the damage caused to the economy and well-being of Pakistan'.

In both Provinces, the declaration of Martial Law was received by most people without serious demur, though in Dacca people came onto the streets. The feeling was that at the very time when East Pakistan was on the threshold of securing acceptance of its just constitutional and economic claims, Martial Law arrived in time to thwart them. The resentment thus created was in no way healed by arrests among the protesting crowds, but the arrests sufficed to restore and maintain order. What was to come thereafter no one ventured to suggest.

On 1 April Yahya Khan assumed the office of President of Pakistan, as from 25 March 1969, an obvious and, from every point of view, necessary step. On 4 April an order was issued that, with immediate effect, photographs of Ayub Khan in

Government offices were to be taken down and replaced by those of President Yahya Khan. It could thus be said that Ayub Khan's disappearance from public life was complete.

Shortly after he relinquished the office of President, it was announced that Ayub Khan would proceed to Swat, there to spend some time with the ruler of that state,[1] to whose son Ayub Khan's daughter was married. With an escort of one jeep, he travelled north, crossing the boundary that divided Swat from Pakistan.

Tamam Shud

[1] Swat is now part of Pakistan and is a District of the Malakand Division.

Appendix A

ALTAF GAUHAR—A PROFILE

Altaf Hussan Gauhar Janjua—or, as he prefers to be known, Altaf Gauhar—was born in Lahore on 17 March 1923, of parents in distinctly modest financial circumstances. It appears that the family has affiliations with the Ahmediya community, although there is little evidence that Altaf Gauhar has pursued these connexions. Still, it is worth noting that he shares that community's reputation for intelligence, application and a marked capacity for work.

As a student he distinguished himself, winning scholarships that took him to the Government College and afterwards to the Punjab University where he took a degree in English. He made a name for himself as a debater, particularly in inter-university disputations.

On leaving the university he found employment in Delhi and proceeded to look for entry into what was, in many ways, the most promising avenue of advancement for a young man of ability but slender means, the public service. He did so at a time during World War II when the future of the sub-continent appeared to be taking on a new shape. For a man of Altaf Gauhar's natural ability it was reasonable to look for a place in the premier service of those times, the Indian Civil Service. Unfortunately, for various reasons, administrative as well as political perhaps, no examination for that service was held in the year that was open to him and he sat, instead, for the Indian Finance Service and was accepted. In company with other probationers, he went to Bombay for training.

Not long thereafter came independence and partition, and Altaf Gauhar elected to serve in Pakistan where, as it happened, there was no Finance Service as such. Since recruits for the newly constituted Civil Service of Pakistan were needed and since he appeared otherwise suitable, Altaf Gauhar, along with some others similarly placed, was posted to this, Pakistan's top administrative cadre, usually referred to as the C.S.P. In this manner, Altaf Gauhar became a member of the C.S.P. without passing the usually required examination. By drawing attention to this, I do not in the least intend to disparage Altaf Gauhar's abilities, which are considerable. Had it been possible for him to sit for the Indian Civil Service, he would, in all probability, have passed well. Moreover, there were many among his colleagues in the C.S.P. whose beginnings were far less promising than those of Altaf Gauhar and who achieved the distinction of gaining entry into the C.S.P. without passing any Central Government examination at all. The point is that the good fortune which enabled him to enter the C.S.P. was of the kind that often goes with genuine talent.

As a member of the C.S.P. Altaf Gauhar went from one high-ranking post to another, the level rising as he advanced in seniority. He was, at various times, Secretary to the State Bank of Pakistan; District Magistrate, Dacca; District Magistrate, Karachi; Chief Controller of Imports and Exports. Ultimately, he went to a senior appointment in the Finance Ministry. In all these jobs, he established a well-deserved reputation for intelligence and grasp.

His promotion in September 1963, at the very early age of forty, to be the civil service head of the Ministry of Information and Broadcasting, placed him in close connexion with Ayub Khan. It is evident also that Altaf Gauhar had established a close rapport with Zulfikar Ali Bhutto and that both these men had similar ideas about China, India, and Kashmir. Moreover, as a man with some literary pretensions and with a genuine regard for, and appreciation of, the humanities, Altaf Gauhar's position at the Ministry of Information proved especially congenial.

He became, almost at once, a member of the small, top-level group which advocated a 'forward' policy with respect to Kashmir, and there is no doubt that he was a member of the intimate coterie which vigorously pressed such a policy on Ayub Khan. The others, including Zulfikar Ali Bhutto and the late Lieutenant-General Akhtar Malik, were not civil servants. In this respect, therefore, Altaf Gauhar began to acquire exceptional influence and power in the civil secretariat. The only man who appeared to rival him was Fida Hasan, a very much more senior member of the C.S.P. who later became Adviser to President Ayub Khan, but Fida Hasan though older, was less able than Altaf Gauhar.

At the time of hostilities between Pakistan and India in September 1965, Altaf Gauhar became very prominent in promoting and guiding a markedly aggressive wartime propaganda in which pro-Peking sentiments received emphasis. His machiavellian manipulation of the facts concerning a telephone conversation which took place between President Johnson and President Ayub Khan, together with the pro-Chinese emphasis, drew upon Altaf Gauhar distinctly unfavourable notice in other quarters and notably in the American magazine *Time*.[1] But the effect in Pakistan was to add much to Altaf Gauhar's influence, and breaking decisively with

[1] Issue dated 15 October 1965.

Bhutto when the latter left the Foreign Ministry, he became widely known as the *eminence grise*.

He had a great deal to do with the publication of Ayub Khan's book *Friends not Masters*. He applied himself actively to getting it translated into several languages and with its promotion in general, especially in Pakistan. Under his own signature, he circulated a letter to the heads of various important organizations in Pakistan, public and private, suggesting the desirability of purchasing an adequate number of copies to ensure that as many persons as possible in each organization should read it, if not possess it. Not surprisingly, the suggestion fell on willing and compliant ears.

It was Altaf Gauhar who conducted the campaign which celebrated during the year 1968 the Great Decade of Development and Reform which amounted, in fact, to a huge trumpeting of the achievements of Ayub Khan's administration during the preceding ten years. The idea was not a bad one, but it was overdone and went on too long. Eventually, people became tired of the Great Decade and the incessant references to it. Even official notepaper and envelopes carried the legend 'We celebrate the Great Decade 1958–68' and the whole thing ended by being wearisome and boring.

That Altaf Gauhar served Ayub Khan faithfully and, often, well cannot be denied, but the value of his services was marred by his love of power, his unbounded ambition and the tremendous self-confidence based upon his rapid advancement and, perhaps, the sense that fortune held him in favour. In these circumstances, the consequences cannot be thought surprising. Altaf Gauhar, whose personal intelligence apparatus appears to have been operated through the Bureau of National Reconstruction, was one of the principal architects of the policy of suppressing or blunting criticism and of centring upon Ayub Khan the prestige associated with great personal leadership and a personality cult.

It was during Altaf Gauhar's time that the policy of monitoring thought reached its apogee. His influence spread to all departments of the State, leading to a much resented interference in military matters, a development which was later to serve him ill. Eventually, it seemed that no limits were set upon the degree of invisible power that he exercised. The dangers were obvious.

These things being so, it is not remarkable that when Ayub Khan fell, Altaf Gauhar fell too. He disappeared from public notice, went on leave and his future was considered highly uncertain. Returning from leave, he was appointed Principal of the Finance Officers' Academy with the rank of Additional Secretary. It was a loss of position and a humiliation, but not the last humiliation he was to experience. In December 1969 Altaf Gauhar was numbered among the 303 Class I officials, many of them senior in rank, who were suspended from their duties and required to submit explanations of their conduct. It was understood that, in every instance, there were allegations of corruption as well as other forms of misconduct. On this question of corruption in relation to Altaf Gauhar I have no opinion to offer, although it is fair to add that no such reputation had ever previously disfigured the opinion people held of him.

However that may be, Altaf Gauhar submitted a reply to the charges made against him, in a written document running into three hundred or so pages. He declined to appear before the tribunal set up under Martial Law to deal with the cases of these 303 officials. In due course, he was dismissed the service.

In the influence which he came to exert on Ayub Khan, Altaf Gauhar occupied that place which Bhutto had previously held. It is evident that Ayub Khan had need of some highly literate person who could fill the gaps in his own knowledge and reading. Bhutto did this capably until he broke with Ayub Khan and, upon his departure, Altaf Gauhar, who had already displayed his own talent and energy, was there at hand.

In his determined effort to raise the stature of Ayub Khan in the eyes of his countrymen and of the world, it seems that Altaf Gauhar was imbued with the belief that every nation needs its heroes, especially those who are living, upon whom people can centre their emotions and energies. In thinking that Pakistan had discovered such a hero in Ayub Khan, Altaf Gauhar may well be forgiven for there were many indeed, both in Pakistan and elsewhere, who thought the same. How far this judgement was erroneous, events have plainly shown.

Appendix B

WEALTH ACQUIRED BY CAPTAIN GOHAR AYUB KHAN

The information set out below is taken from the files maintained, in accordance with the Companies Act 1913, by the Joint Registrar of Joint Stock Companies, Karachi.

At the end of July 1968, Captain Gohar Ayub Khan was:

Chairman: Arusa Investments Limited
　　　　　Arusa Industries Limited
　　　　　Hashimi Can Company Limited
Managing Director: Ghandhara Industries Limited
　　　　　　　　　Gohar Habib Limited (the managing agents of Ghandhara Industries Limited)
Director: Ghandhara Mineral and Trading Company Limited
　　　　　Janana DeMalucho Textile Mills Limited

As to his shareholdings in these Companies, the files maintained by the Joint Registrar at Karachi do not include all details since all these Companies are not registered there. However they do provide information as to Captain Gohar Ayub Khan's principal investments at the end of July 1968. These comprised:

(a) with his wife and two children　268,030 shares of Rs.10 each in Ghandhara Industries.
(b) Arusa Investments Ltd. held　65,250 shares of Rs.10 each in Ghandhara Industries.
(c) with his wife　5,000 shares of Rs.10 each in the Hashimi Can Co. Ltd.
(d) Arusa Investments Ltd. held　199,533 shares of Rs.10 each in the Hashimi Can Co. Ltd.

In August 1969 Captain Gohar Ayub disposed of his holdings in Ghandhara Industries Ltd. to the National Investment Trust and to the Investment Corporation of Pakistan Ltd. On the assumption that he also disposed of his family holding and that of Arusa Investments Ltd. at the then current price of about Rs.32 per share, the proceeds of this sale would be Rs.10,664,960.

It is also understood that he disposed of his half-interest in Gohar Habib Ltd. but for what amount is not known. It could be as much as Rs.25 lakhs but this figure is wholly conjectural.

In January 1970 the market value of shares in the Hashimi Can Co. Ltd. was Rs.18 and the value of his holding, along with that of his wife and that of Arusa Investments Ltd., was therefore Rs.3,681,594.

Taking these three items as they stand, therefore, the total value is approximately Rs.160 lakhs which is equal, at the then official rate of exchange to U.S.$3,346,560. If, therefore, his total wealth were taken to be U.S.$4 million, it would not be a wholly unrealistic estimate.

It is doubtful if other members of the family, including Field-Marshal Ayub Khan, were as successful in amassing wealth as was Captain Gohar Ayub. Nevertheless, on the basis of the figures given here, it seems reasonable to suggest that Dr. Franz Pick's estimate that the family's total wealth lies between U.S.$10 million and $20 million may well be correct. It is by no means a negligible reward for ten years of sustained endeavour.

Ghandhara Industries Ltd., undoubtedly Captain Gohar Ayub's biggest single venture, was registered in 1963, the certificate of incorporation bearing the date 23 February 1963. The initial capital was 750,000 shares of Rs.10 each. The Company was assisted in its operations, when commencing business, by loan facilities amounting to Rs.32·5 million provided by the American Express Company. Subsequently, the overdraft facilities were taken over by Pakistani banks.

The spelling *Gohar* is that which Captain Gohar Ayub himself favours although I think that *Gauhar* is the more appropriate transliteration. The word is Persian and means 'pearl'.

Appendix C

FORCES DEPLOYED BY INDIA AND PAKISTAN PRIOR TO HOSTILITIES IN SEPTEMBER 1965[1]

according to the estimate prepared by the Institute of Strategic Studies, London

India

Army
Total sanctioned strength: 825,000
16 full-strength divisions, including 9 mountain divisions and the armoured division. In addition, 4 infantry divisions on a reduced establishment have been sanctioned. It will take about eighteen months to bring the army up to its full strength.
Armoured forces include:
1 armoured division equipped with Centurion tanks
1 armoured brigade equipped with Sherman tanks
2 light tank regiments with AMX-13
2 light tank regiments with Stuarts
Territorial Army of 47,000

Navy
Total strength: 16,000
1 16,000-ton carrier
2 cruisers
3 destroyers
5 anti-submarine frigates
3 anti-aircraft frigates
6 other escort ships
6 minesweepers
13 light coastal vessels
2 amphibious warfare ships
5 survey vessels, training ships
Naval aircraft include 24 Sea Hawk strike-interceptors and 15 Alize ASW aircraft

[1] The following details should be read as of August 1965.

Air Force
Total strength: 28,000 (sanctioned strength 45 squadrons)
12 MiG-21 jet fighters
4 HF-24 Marut fighter-bombers
4 interceptor squadrons with 25 Mystère IVs each
4 interceptor squadrons with 25 Gnats each
4 bomber squadrons with 20 Canberras each
6 fighter-bomber squadrons with 25 Hunters each
Several Ouragan and Vampire fighter-bomber squadrons
1 reconnaissance squadron with 8 Canberras
The transport force includes 80 C-119s, 24 An-12s, and about 50 C-47s.
2 Il-14s, some Otters and Viscounts 723 and 730 Avro 748s and Caribous are being acquired.
The Auxiliary Air Force squadrons chiefly fly Harvard and Vampire trainers.

Pakistan

Army
Strength: 160,000–180,000
6 infantry divisions (1 in East Pakistan)
1 air defence brigade
The armoured forces include about 10 regiments with M-47/48 Patton and M-4 Sherman medium tanks and 2-3 regiments with M-24 Chaffee light tanks. These probably form 1 armoured division of 2 brigades and a separate independent armoured brigade.
Para-military forces
Frontier Corps: 25,000 (tribesmen)
West Pakistan Rangers: 10,000
East Pakistan Rifles: 10,000
Azad Kashmir troops: 25,000

Navy
Total strength: 8,000
1 light cruiser [at September 1965] appears to have been a cadet training ship
5 destroyers
2 ASW frigates
1 submarine
8 minesweepers
4 motor launches
8 other ships
There is a coastguard force of 1,500 men

Naval aircraft include Albatross and some UH-19 helicopters for sea/air rescue. (These aircraft are probably operated by the Pakistan Air Force.)

Air Force
Total strength: 20,000: 200 aircraft
2 B-57B Canberra squadrons
4 F-86F Sabre squadrons
1 F-104A Starfighter squadron (a second is to be formed)
RT-33As are used for tactical reconnaissance purposes
The transport force includes 4 C-130B Hercules and 10 Bristol Mark 21 and Mark 31 tactical freighters.
Some T-6, T-33 and T-37B jet trainers.

ACKNOWLEDGEMENT

I wish to express my gratitude to the Director of the International Institute of Strategic Studies for permission to reproduce this assessment of the armed forces of India and Pakistan and other extracts from *The Military Balance*.

Appendix D

KARACHI, SEPTEMBER 1965—
A BRIEF EYE-WITNESS ACCOUNT

As soon as hostilities opened on the Lahore front, the Government of Pakistan established a postal censorship, a Custodian of Enemy Property was appointed, and a scheme of War Risk Insurance set up.

In Karachi, complete calm prevailed and prices remained normal, although wealthier people undoubtedly laid in stocks of tinned provisions and, in some towns near the fighting, particularly Lahore, there was a certain amount of voluntary evacuation. The principal impact on daily life was caused by the black-out which was immediately imposed and black-out discipline in Karachi was well observed, at any rate to begin with. The usual spy stories rapidly became current and a number of people were arrested. Nothing more was ever heard of their fate from which it might be deduced that they were secretly tried and punished. The more likely explanation is that these unfortunate people were arrested simply on baseless suspicion and afterwards released. A joke went round that the same beggars had been arrested five or six times on charges of espionage.

On the day following the announcement of hostilities, an air-raid warning was sounded in Karachi at about 9 p.m., and anti-aircraft artillery opened fire. In the clear, dark sky it was easy enough to recognize the characteristic shell-burst pattern of eight heavy AA guns. Tracer shell from 40 mm. light AA guns put up the familiar display of rose-coloured fireworks and I estimated two batteries, possibly less. It was also evident that these guns were, quite properly, deployed in defence of the harbour and the oil terminal. A peculiar circumstance was that all these guns were firing at the same time and in the same direction which would have indicated attacks by hostile aircraft at high level and low level simultaneously, a very odd situation. I do not myself believe that any Indian aircraft visited Karachi during those days although there were rumours of parachutists and newspapers published what purported to be photographs of bomb-craters. From these pictures, one was led to conclude that the Indian pilots, if there were any, must have tossed out hand-grenades.

It appeared that the air-raid warning and the anti-aircraft fire were intended to create the atmosphere of a nation at war and to remind Karachi, 700 miles distant from the fighting, that the country was actually so engaged. For somewhat similar reasons, it is, of course, possible that not all the anti-aircraft guns in and around Karachi were fired, the object in this case being to deceive the enemy as well as interested observers like myself.

Some foreigners resident in Karachi managed to get out of the country immediately the Indian attack was known about. On reaching their home countries some of them spread wild stories of air-raids on Karachi, guns booming, searchlights stabbing the sky and so on. All these tales were, without exception, false. Pakistan may be an under-developed country but it is not so under-developed that, in 1965, it relied on searchlights to detect hostile aircraft. In fact, the principal hazard to personal safety in Karachi at that time was provided by bands of self-constituted *vigilantes*, comprising small boys aged from eight to thirteen or thereabouts. These urchins, armed with brushes and pots of black lacquer, summarily held up motorists in the streets in order to paint masks on head-lamps.

In Karachi the seventeen days of fighting had little impact although the public felt the utmost indignation about India's attack on the Lahore front and expressed the same patriotic fervour as was so noticeable elsewhere. The fighting was a long way off and the hostilities did not go on long enough for either economy, or social utilities or law and order to be affected. Prices did not rise, law and order did not deteriorate and perhaps the principal immediate consequence of those events lay in a somewhat dampening effect on social life. The despatch of foreign mail suffered delay and the postal censorship created inconvenience for those whose correspondence was not conducted in English.

What would have developed had the war continued, it is difficult to say, particularly as the fighting seemed to have settled down to a process of attrition. It is reasonable to suppose that supplies of consumer goods would have become short and that rationing would have been introduced in cities. As it was, petrol rationing was announced but there was hardly time for it to be organized. It is likely also that the stresses created by active and continued hostilities would have led to a decline in social discipline.

The real economic impact came later, partly through heavily increased defence expenditure and, more directly, through a surcharge on certain important taxes, customs duty, sales tax, excise and income tax. This surcharge was described as a 'defence surcharge' but inevitably these became a permanent part of the revenue and, in some instances, were integrated into the rates of collection prevailing, notably customs duty.

As things turned out, it was not the hostilities that brought trouble to Karachi, but rather the sense of disappointment caused by impending rumours of a cease-fire to begin on 23 September. The people, convinced that enormous and crippling losses had been inflicted on the Indian armed forces, and that their allies, notably the United States of America, had failed them utterly, were aroused to great indignation, which led to rioting and some burning of American and British property. The intensive propaganda launched in Pakistan as soon as the operations started had convinced most people—and many remain convinced—that the Indians had been overwhelmed, and to be confronted, by 20 September, with the prospect of a cease-fire, came as a crushing reversal to all belief and hope. But whatever the consequences to Pakistan's relations with the United States and the United Kingdom, there is no doubt that, as has been indicated in the text, the principal victim of the entire episode was its original architect, Field-Marshal Ayub Khan.

Appendix E

ZULFIKAR ALI BHUTTO

In a propaganda broadcast, made in the course of the Indo-Pakistan hostilities of September 1965, Mr. Frank Moraes, a senior Indian journalist and newspaper editor, when referring to Zulfikar Ali Bhutto, spoke of him, somewhat sourly, as 'that much-advertised young man'. We may be sure that this disparaging terminology was not intended to convey the impression that Mr. Bhutto had deservedly risen to early fame, but rather to invite attention to an evident fondness for the red carpet, camera flash-guns, the press of expectant newspaper men and the other exterior panoply that goes with high office. Still, this apart, Frank Moraes had a point as we shall see.

It is not intended, here, to write a detailed profile of Zulfikar Ali Bhutto whose good fortune it was, at the age of thirty, to be selected as a Minister in the first cabinet formed by Iskander Mirza, after the declaration of Martial Law in October 1958, and to be retained by Ayub Khan when a couple of weeks later, Mirza went into exile. The present purpose is simply to say something of the relations that subsisted between Bhutto and Ayub Khan and to suggest, if not to emphasize, the prominence that Bhutto acquired in Ayub Khan's administration, a prominence that the events of September 1965 served well to underline. It is in this context that the quotation was taken from Moraes' broadcast.

Speaking generally, a study of Ayub Khan's choice of Cabinet Ministers, during the ten years of his administration, would show that as regards the finance portfolio, this was always entrusted to competent, professional finance men, two of whom were in fact senior civil servants from the Finance Ministry. None of them—there were three in all: Abdul Qadir, Mohamed Shoaib and N. M. Uqaili—had any important qualifications in the political sense, but Ayub Khan was wise enough to ensure that the nation's finances were entrusted to trained men, trained, that is to say, as financial technicians which does not, of course, necessarily carry with it any pretensions to statesmanship. In all other ministries, his choice fell upon mediocrities and, as time passed, their mediocrity became drearier and drearier. To this statement, two notable exceptions must be mentioned—Ghulam Faruque and Zulfikar Ali Bhutto.

Something has been said about both of these men in the text and enough to indicate, perhaps, that each of them, in his own way and according to his own bent, was very well qualified. To that, there is nothing to be added here concerning Bhutto. As a Minister, and particularly as a Foreign Minister, he amply fulfilled the description of a well-educated, literate and articulate man. To these valuable assets, he added a marked arrogance of manner which brought him into collision with many people, both among his own countrymen and among foreigners. It was he who earned the distinction of being the first, and perhaps the only, Pakistani Cabinet Minister who procured the virtual expulsion of two senior British executives, both of them among the top representatives, in Pakistan, of the international oil business.[1] This unusual incident arose out of negotiations relating to the prices of petroleum products when Bhutto was Minister of Fuel, Power and Natural Resources. During these discussions it appears that heated words were exchanged or that Bhutto felt these two men were not sufficiently amenable to his persuasions and requirements. Offended by their attitude, it was at Bhutto's instance that they were invited to leave Pakistan at very short notice. Having tasted blood, Bhutto later sought to apply the same tactics to an American press photographer who, it was alleged, had not behaved well towards the Minister. On intimation of apology, however, Bhutto relented.

He displayed during the period considered a fierce antipathy towards India at all times. He seems also to have been influenced by a want of goodwill towards the United States and, to a less degree perhaps, towards the United Kingdom. He was, and remains, totally wedded to the policy of close ties with China and on these, it appears, he regards the future of Pakistan as depending.

The affidavit which he submitted to the Court, in February 1969, when his wife petitioned for his release from jail under Article 98 of the Constitution, tells much concerning his relations with Ayub Khan. At the time, Ayub Khan communicated to the Attorney-General, for submission to the Court, a simple denial of what Bhutto had stated in his affidavit, but although its language may be tendentious, the document bears every indication of substantial truth. Prior to September 1965, the two men were on very close terms and Ayub Khan relied greatly on Bhutto's knowledge and on his efforts to achieve the triangular containment of India. During the four years that Bhutto was Foreign Minister, he travelled widely in the pursuit of this aim and, for a time, appeared to have succeeded.

[1] Their names were Michael Condon and Norman Leslie.

His work was greatly featured in the Pakistan press and his frequent appearance on the front pages doubtless accounts for Frank Moraes' reference to publicity. The policy which he sedulously pursued collapsed with the fall of Sokarno and it is an interesting question whether, and to what extent, Bhutto was aware of Sokarno's weakening position and whether, and to what extent, he chose to ignore the fragility of Sokarno's Government, rather than admit to himself the possibility of failure. At any rate, during that time, he received much applause in Pakistan and was regarded, rightly, as one of the ablest of Ayub Khan's Ministers. However, the weight of this compliment was mitigated by the poor quality, on the average, of the men selected by Ayub Khan to serve in his Cabinet.

The cease-fire, in September 1965 and the Tashkent Declaration of January 1966 brought him his severest disappointment as well as the highest pinnacle of popularity he had yet achieved. Particularly among the younger, student generation, he was regarded as the real champion of Pakistan against Indian aggression, as well as the one courageous man ready to defy the serried ranks of the United Nations and, for that matter, to follow Sokarno in abandoning that international association altogether, if Pakistan's just claims were not fairly dealt with. This accounts for the many demonstrations in his favour when, having broken with Ayub Khan, he made his way by train from Islamabad to Karachi. At every stopping-place, crowds gathered to cheer and garland him and, at the same time, to raise slogans against Ayub Khan for his pusillanimous conduct. The image of this inflexible champion of Pakistan's rights and sovereignty, Bhutto has never entirely lost, although this does not mean that he is everywhere regarded as the man best suited to be entrusted with the administration of the country.

In his affidavit, Bhutto claimed that after his quarrel with Ayub Khan, he was threatened with the prospect that if he entered politics in opposition, Ayub Khan would *follow him to the grave*.[2] The possibility of such a threat is not only endorsed by what is known of Ayub Khan's conduct towards others who opposed him, but by the campaign of persecution which followed. Bhutto became the object of invective and animadversion from every man in public life, major or minor, who depended upon or sought the favour of Ayub Khan. But hard words break no bones and it gave Bhutto plenty of publicity. This sycophantic display, rather than injuring Bhutto, created sympathy for and interest in him and when, in due time, men like Choudhury Khaliquzzaman joined the chorus,

[2] Subsequently, it was enquired: *Whose grave?*

Bhutto, as well as many others, must have felt that the jackals were really barking at his heels.

In 1967, Ayub Khan's Government published details of documents which purported to show that, at one time, Bhutto was claiming to be an Indian national as well as a Pakistani. This, of course, was exactly what the Indian Government had been saying in September 1965 and so, two years later, the Indian Government had the satisfaction of witnessing Pakistan's endorsement. Not only so. The question naturally proposed itself how, when Ayub Khan and his Government actually knew of this—at any rate by September 1965—Bhutto was retained in the sensitive and important post of Foreign Minister.

This attack on Bhutto was, therefore, blatantly personal as well as stupid, but it could not be said that the Indian and Pakistan Governments were *in pari delicto*. In the case of the Indian Government, this statement, true or false, with respect to Bhutto's personality, could be treated as legitimate wartime propaganda tactics whereas, in the case of Ayub Khan, it was a clear attempt to smear a political opponent who could not be silenced. As it was, the attempt failed as it was bound to do for very good reasons. It could do no harm to Bhutto because, in the first place, everyone in Pakistan well understood the circumstances, to be touched on shortly, in which situations of this sort could arise. Secondly, it did no harm to him because, by 1967, nothing was more plain than that Bhutto was not only *not* an Indian national, but was as *non grata* in India as any man could possibly be. Unless Ayub Khan and his Government were prepared to assert that Bhutto had been guilty, and continued to be guilty, of the most extraordinary duplicity of conduct, for which neither ground nor reason had ever been apparent, it appeared simply absurd to suggest that something which related to events of twenty years before, had any materiality twenty years afterwards.

It is certain that there were many people in Pakistan of whom similar things could be said and the reason for this is both clear and well known. When partition of the sub-continent took place, there were many families with property in both of the two new countries. In many instances, families split themselves in order to avert the possibility of property falling into the hands of officials described as Custodians of Evacuee Property. One part of the family remained in India and another part in Pakistan. In other cases, different methods were adopted in order to retain landed and other possessions. It was for this reason that Bhutto, as a young man, found himself in the position of being, or having been, an Indian national when petitioning the Indian Supreme Court in relation to family property. It had nothing to do with politics or national affinities.

In adopting these shabby and futile tactics, Ayub Khan did poor service to his countrymen. He had, in fact, given specific shape to what I have referred to as *the Indian smear*. If one Pakistani wanted to injure the reputation of another, he could, among other things, spread whispers that the person he desired to injure was *probably an Indian National* or *held an Indian passport*. It had been done before, of course. Ayub Khan simply made it fashionable.

After leaving Ayub Khan, Bhutto's political future was uncertain for some time. It was thought he might join the (Council) Muslim League, but he said that that Party represented the country's landed interests whereas his interest was with the poor and the exploited. Eventually, in November 1967, he announced a convention for the purpose of forming a new party for which purpose the foundation documents were published in booklet form. As a production, this was very disappointing and did not promise well, especially when it was remembered that Bhutto, himself, is a well-educated, well-read man. The documents were in English, poorly written, ill-spelt and worse printed. Bearing in mind that some of Bhutto's colleagues in the Peoples' Party (later to become the Pakistan Peoples' Party) were as well-educated as himself, it seemed as if no one had taken the trouble to produce something impressive and designed to convey a sense of a really well-organized, well-established political party.

While not purporting to be an election manifesto, the documents contained statements of the Party's views on such evident matters as India, Kashmir, China, SEATO and CENTO. It set out a policy of economic and social reform to end the exploitation of the many by the few. There was special reference to regional cultures and so on and the claims of East Pakistan were mentioned. Among the documents was a curious litany based on the theme of *jehad*. Its tone may be gauged from some of the sub-titles. MAN HAS GONE ASTRAY. MAN IS ON THE BRINK OF DISEASE. THE SOCIETY HAS LOST ITS ANCHOR. Still, it is fair to add that subsequent Party publications were a considerable improvement.

Having launched his Party, Bhutto began to tour the countryside, holding meetings and making speeches mostly about the iniquities of Ayub Khan and his administration. His meetings were often interrupted by rowdies and by threats of personal violence. On one or two occasions he was the object of physical attack, either at a meeting or while travelling. At a meeting in Lahore, the electrical connexions were severed and water was used to disperse the crowd, then in darkness. This was typical of the violence that became the general feature of the closing years of Ayub Khan's administration until, in the last phase, the use of firearms, at meetings and against rivals or critics, became common.

The leading part that Bhutto played in the fall of Ayub Khan has been narrated in the text. There is no doubt that he was one of the few men who, having serious differences with Ayub Khan, had courage enough to oppose him actively and to criticize him publicly and bitterly. He was made to feel the consequences of this when in jail where he was badly treated.

It is for these reasons, as also his popularity with the younger people, that he remained prominent. In November 1968, when he initiated the campaign against Ayub Khan, he was much criticized in foreign newspapers and was described as not being at the centre of the political situation—a strangely false evaluation as events were soon to prove. If, at any moment, there was one plain, single, definable factor that could be isolated from the skein of events, situations and personalities that combined to bring down Ayub Khan, that factor was Zulfikar Ali Bhutto and his visit to Rawalpindi in the early days of November 1968.

The later success of his Party, in the elections held in 1970 under the administration of President Yahya Khan, forms part of Pakistan's history subsequent to 25 March 1969 and, as I have indicated elsewhere in this book, it is my intention and hope to write of them in a later work.

Appendix F

THE CODE OF CRIMINAL PROCEDURE
1898
(As modified up to 15 May 1968)

Power to issue order absolute at once in urgent cases of nuisance or apprehended danger

Section 144 (1): In cases where, in the opinion of a District Magistrate, Sub-divisional Magistrate, or of any other Magistrate (not being a Magistrate of the third class) specially empowered by the Provincial Government or the District Magistrate to act under this section, there is sufficient ground for proceeding under this section and immediate prevention or speedy remedy is desirable, such Magistrate may, by written order stating the material facts of the case and served in manner provided by section 134, direct any person to abstain from a certain act or to take certain order with certain property in his possession or under his management, if such Magistrate considers that such direction is likely to prevent, or tends to prevent, obstruction, annoyance, or injury, or risk of obstruction, annoyance or injury, to any person lawfully employed or danger to human life, health or safety or a disturbance of the public tranquillity, or a riot or an affray.

(2): An order under this section may, in cases of emergency or in cases where the circumstances do not admit of the serving in due time of a notice upon the person against whom the order is directed, be passed, *ex parte*.

(3): An order under this section may be directed to a particular individual or to the public generally when frequenting or visiting a particular place.

(4): Any Magistrate may either on his own motion or on the application of any person aggrieved, rescind or alter any order made under this section by himself or any Magistrate subordinate to him or by his predecessor in office.

(5): Where such an application is received, the

Magistrate shall afford to the applicant an early opportunity of appearing before him either in person or by pleader and showing cause against the order; and, if the Magistrate rejects the application wholly or in part, he shall record in writing his reasons for so doing.

(6): No order under this section shall remain in force for more than two months from the making thereof; unless, in cases of danger to human life, health or safety, or a likelihood of a riot or an affray, the Provincial Government, by notification in the official Gazette, otherwise directs.

Appendix G

THE PAKISTAN DEMOCRATIC MOVEMENT

The Pakistan Democratic Movement was formed on 1 May 1967 and was a fair reflection of the Combined Opposition Parties which had fought the election against Ayub Khan in 1964–5. It comprised East Pakistan's National Democratic Front; the Pakistan (Council) Muslim League; the Jama'at-i-Islami; the Pakistan Awami League and the Nizam-i-Islam Party. At the time of formation the Pakistan Democratic Movement issued its eight-point programme as follows:

1. There should be a federation of Pakistan with parliamentary form of government, a legislature directly elected on the basis of adult franchise, complete Fundamental Rights, free Press and independent judiciary.
2. The list of federal subjects should be defence, foreign affairs, currency and inter-wing communication and trade.
3. There should be full regional autonomy and residuary powers shall vest in Government as established by the Constitution in the two Wings.
4. Economic disparity between two Wings should be removed within ten years. Within this period all foreign exchange earned by East Pakistan shall be spent in that Wing after allowing for East Pakistan's share of defence and other agreed expenditure. All foreign exchange acquired by the Provincial Government should be at their absolute disposal.
5. Currency, foreign exchange central banking, foreign trade and inter-wing communication and trade should be managed by a Board consisting of an equal number of members from East and West Pakistan. These members should be elected by MNAs of their respective Wings.
6. Parity in all Central services, including autonomous bodies and the Supreme Court, to be achieved in ten years.
7. The effective fighting and fire power in the Defence Services in the two Wings should be brought at par, the Pakistan Navy headquarters should be shifted to East Pakistan and a Defence

Council appointed with an equal number of members from East and West Pakistan.
8. The Parliamentary National Assembly after election should first incorporate clauses 2 to 7 in the 1956 Constitution.

Appendix H

COUP OR CONSPIRACY?

After Ayub Khan's departure, much debate followed on the question whether he had, in any way, contrived to ensure fresh recourse to Martial Law in order to give 'a parting kick' to the politicians he so much disliked and who had harried him relentlessly and successfully during the preceding months.

The reasons adduced in support of this suggestion were three: that he had, by secret arrangement with various political agitators, among whom Maulana Bhashani's name was often mentioned, encouraged and spread the flame of dissent and violence; that he had deliberately restrained the Army and the police in the exercise of their duty to preserve law and order; and that the conduct of the Round Table Conference had been managed so as to ensure maximum disagreement among the participants.

Of these three reasons, only one appears to have any real verisimilitude and that is the suggestion that agitators were encouraged to sow discontent and riot. In the preceding text, reference has been made to the employment of *agents-provocateurs*. Of this, there is no clear proof, nor is there likely to be. Germane to this, however, is the certainty that rival factions within Ayub Khan's own party, the Convention Muslim League, were a source of trouble, especially in East Pakistan. In that Province, incidents involving violence at Dacca University could be traced directly to these internal factions within that party.

So far as Maulana Bhashani is concerned, it can only be said that his conduct, in touring West Pakistan, rather than his own Province, at a time when his arch-rival, Sheikh Mujibur Rahman, had just emerged as a triumphant hero from the Agartala Trial, seemed peculiar. And if, indeed, the Maulana was contributing to Ayub Khan's alleged policy of spreading disturbance, it can certainly be admitted that he succeeded. But there is another side to this coin. Perhaps Bhashani remained out of East Pakistan, when Mujib was released, simply from chagrin. Possibly in West Pakistan he was solely concerned with his rabble-rousing methods of re-awakening peasants, workers and students. And if, further, Bhashani found himself unjustly accused, that was because his enigmatic conduct so often invited several kinds of criticism. It cannot be proved that Ayub Khan tried by this method to ensure a return to Martial Law but if he did so try then this was a last, desperate plunge as the tide turned more and more strongly against him.

The other two reasons—restraining both Army and police, and the management of the Round Table Conference—can be argued both ways. The Democratic Action Committee called for the abandonment of police *lathi*-charges on students. There had been so much public outcry about the conduct of the police, whose reputation had fallen so seriously, that there was a distinct risk of civil disobedience which the police would have been unable to curb. This would have led to an exclusive reliance on the armed forces and, even there, evidence was not wanting of public defiance, particularly with respect to curfews and other restrictions. If, in these circumstances, restraints were placed on the Army and the police, it could still be said that the result was to encourage rioters and agitators. It remained equally true that had these restraints not been imposed, something akin to civil war might have resulted. Argument and counter-argument of this sort can proceed indefinitely. The truth of the matter is that Ayub Khan had sown the wind and during the period from November 1968 to March 1969 he reaped the whirlwind.

As to the management of the Round Table Conference, it did not require any contrivance on the part of Ayub Khan to bring about disagreement. Indeed, his readiness to meet the opposition at the conference table may have been partly inspired by the foreknowledge that there would be no unanimity except on the issues of the parliamentary system and of direct elections. It is possible that if any greater measure of agreement seemed likely, Ayub Khan might have had recourse to those occult measures of which he had shown himself a master, but this was never necessary. A study of the speeches made at the conference shows that, true to their unhappy traditions, the opposition leaders made ample contribution to the failure of the Round Table Conference.

The probabilities seemed to be either that Ayub Khan and his advisers concluded from a balanced appraisal of the situation that he would have to go and that Martial Law would have to be enforced or that Ayub Khan was confronted with an ultimatum in consequence of a *coup* by General Yahya Khan. Consideration of these alternatives, along with what is otherwise known, suggests the conclusion that, in all probability, the imposition of Martial Law and Ayub Khan's departure sprang from some combination of these two founded upon intelligence reports and appreciations prepared by the armed forces, and more particularly by the General Staff. These reports and indications led to the conclusion that Ayub Khan must go and that the deterioration in the state of law and order had gone beyond the capacity of any civilian government to repair it.

It can still be argued that this deterioration *was* the work of Ayub Khan and this amounts to asserting that he deliberately adopted such a policy in order that Martial Law might be declared. To this the answer must be that he was playing with fire and that he burned his fingers. In addition, had there been no initial discontent and disturbance springing from the nation's own volition and reaching a point at which it became uncontrollable, why should Ayub Khan have fomented and encouraged it in order to bring about the abrogation of the Constitution of which he was so proud and to which he ascribed all the triumphs of his administration between 1962 and 1969?

The habit of burrowing for secret, ulterior, and obscure motives is not a good one. No doubt they exist, and no doubt people pursue them, but a sole pre-occupation with their possibilities argues a shallow, not a profound, cleverness. Speculation about vaguely conceived hypotheses is quite different from the penetrating insight developed by men of genius or exceptional talent to perceive new and convincing relations between established facts. Thus, as we shall see, the course of events which culminated in Martial Law declared on 25 March 1969 was far less the product of Ayub Khan's machinations than of his administration. Never did he think it would end as ignominiously as it did.

If all the known factors are taken into consideration, it seems probable that Ayub Khan, in consultation with his advisers and the General Staff, decided that the situation had got out of hand and that recourse to Martial Law had become unavoidable. This was anything but a congenial decision for him, nor was it a snap, last-minute affair. The decision was probably taken after fully considering the whole situation and especially the grave point that this reversion to Martial Law would be deemed throughout the world to represent not only Ayub Khan's failure, but that of the nation too. President Yahya Khan was later to refer to its damaging effect on Pakistan's international status.

It is, of course, possible that Ayub Khan entertained hopes of continuing as President with General Yahya Khan as Chief Martial Law Administrator. (He could not have been blind to the possibility that, once stripped of all power and authority, he, and various members of his family and associates, might well become the object of attack, in the press, through the Courts and even in more sinister fashion.) If he nourished ideas of this sort, he was bound to be disappointed. He had lost the confidence of the armed forces for one thing, and for another it was foolish to suppose that General Yahya Khan would spring forward as a ready volunteer to pull his chestnuts out of the fire. It need not be doubted that with the decision to impose Martial Law, it was made known to Ayub Khan that he would have to go.

All this presupposes that the entire process, leading to a decision to impose Martial Law, was deliberate, logical, and founded upon a careful assessment of the entire situation and of the factors both for and against. Since Martial Law was declared at 7.15 p.m. on 25 March and since the morning newspapers of 26 March contained the first group of Martial Law Regulations, it is clear that the decision had been taken some days prior to the date of declaration, or it had been thought necessary to prepare for such a decision. It appears probable that matters were crystallizing about fourteen days before 25 March and certainly rumour about impending Martial Law was rife by that time.

But how does this fit in with the appointment of new Governors only four days before Martial Law was declared? Why expose the unfortunate Yusuf Haroon and the unfortunate Dr. Huda to the mortifying experience of being king for a day or, more precisely, four days? To me, it seems that two thought-processes were at work at the same time. The armed forces had already concluded that resort to Martial Law was becoming more and more certain. The state of the country was quite alarming and the performance of the political leaders at the Round Table Conference was clear proof of their inability to arrest the hastening decay. On his side, Ayub Khan was anxious, if he could, to do something that would either preclude Martial Law or, at any rate, retain a civilian presence that owed itself to him. The removal of the generally abominated Monem Khan, and of General Musa, mostly thought of as Ayub Khan's pale *alter ego*, was an obvious step but, as we have seen, the new men were powerless.

It is possible that Ayub Khan was urged by others to salvage as much of his power as he could for they well knew that his fall would place them in peril as later events certainly proved. Very soon after the declaration of Martial Law a strange thing happened. News was received, apparently in the form of an official communiqué, that Admiral A. R. Khan, Fida Hasan, and Arshad Hussain (who had been Minister of Defence, Adviser and Foreign Minister respectively in Ayub Khan's last administration) had been appointed advisers to General Yahya Khan. This, if true, simply meant that the new dispensation was nothing more than a continuance of

Ayub Khan's Government but without the Constitution. A couple of hours later, it was learned that this communiqué had been withdrawn and it never found its way into the press. The authenticity of this story cannot be doubted and it lent credence to the belief that Ayub Khan was obliged to go, relinquishing all authority and unable to safeguard his associates from whatever the future might have in store.

It remains perfectly possible that, in his own defeat and surrender, Ayub Khan was consoled by the thought that the politicians who had opposed him and who had contributed so much to his fall, were themselves thwarted. This may easily be so, but apart from the maliciously congenial sense of satisfaction of seeing *them* frustrated, the theory of the well planned 'parting kick' does not have much to support it.

Appendix I

THE FATE OF THE '303'

Proceedings against these officials were authorized by, and undertaken in pursuance of, Martial Law Regulation No. 58, promulgated in December 1969 and entitled The Removal from Service (Special Provisions) Regulation. Under this Regulation, the civilian officials concerned were served with notices calling upon them to explain their conduct with respect to the offences with which they were charged and to submit these explanations within a stipulated period. It appears that the offences alleged against them were supported by reference to specified matters. After submission of their explanations they were invited to appear before tribunals set up by the Martial Law Administration, in order to clarify anything which the written statement seemed not to have elucidated sufficiently or otherwise to answer such questions as might be put to them. So far as is known, all these officials submitted written statements but some, anticipating, perhaps, what lay in store, declined to appear before the tribunals.

The entire procedure was unsatisfactory in that everything was kept secret and *in camera*. Another important point is that the first list to be prepared of officials deemed to have attracted disciplinary action or, at any rate, enquiry, was considerably longer than that finally published and with respect to which action was in fact taken. The question at once arises as to how, and with what considerations in mind, the list was pruned? It is extremely doubtful if anything of a judicial character was involved in this process and, therefore, opinion seems to have been prominent throughout the course of these proceedings.

Nevertheless, I do not think there was any gross miscarriage of justice and I do think that the procedure used, in respect of these 303[1] officials, was more satisfactory than that adopted by Ayub Khan's screening committees.[2] The decisions taken in relation to some of the officials concerned caused eyebrows to rise among those familiar with them, their careers and reputations, but this seems to have been caused by a sense of undue lenience. There is no doubt

---

[1] But see later in this Appendix.
[2] See *Revolution in Pakistan*, op. cit., Ch. VI.

APPENDIX I

that at least one case of reinstatement was highly questionable. Even if, in the preponderating number of cases, punishment was, by and large, richly deserved, it is doubtful whether this kind of purge does anything, in the long run, to cure the evils to which it relates.

A complete statement of the result of these proceedings has not been made public at the time of writing. From official pronouncements it is known that of the officials concerned, 181 were dismissed from service, sixty-eight were compulsorily retired, and twenty-nine were reinstated. The fate of the remaining twenty-four does not seem to be publicly known. (The balance figure of twenty-four is correct because there was an error in the original total of 303 suspensions. One man's name was listed twice so that the true total was 302 and not 303. Nevertheless, the expression 303 stuck.)

One official who had fallen under the Martial Law Administration's disfavour, Mr. Qudratullah Shahab,[3] left the Civil Service of Pakistan at this time, in unusual circumstances. He was transferred from his position as Secretary to the Government of Pakistan in the Ministry of Education, to membership of the Central Board of Revenue, a move which could in no way be construed as advancement. At that very moment, however, Mr. Shahab was in Geneva, attending a UNESCO conference on behalf of the Government of Pakistan. He adroitly utilized this circumstance to secure election to the Executive Board of UNESCO but outside the Pakistan cadre. Thus, having stolen a march upon his employers, he sent in his resignation and took up residence in the United Kingdom where his wife was in medical practice. His resignation was later accepted by the Government of Pakistan with benefit of proportional pension.

[3] His name also figures in Ch. VII, notes 12 and 48.

Appendix J

TEXT OF THE TASHKENT DECLARATION OF 10 JANUARY 1966

The Prime Minister of India and the President of Pakistan, having met at Tashkent and having discussed the existing relations between India and Pakistan, hereby declare their firm resolve to restore normal and peaceful relations between their countries and to promote understanding and friendly relations between their peoples. They consider the attainment of these objectives of vital importance for the welfare of the 600 million people of India and Pakistan.

I

The Prime Minister of India and the President of Pakistan agree that both sides will exert all efforts to create good neighbourly relations between India and Pakistan in accordance with the United Nations Charter. They reaffirm their obligation under the Charter not to have recourse to force and to settle their disputes through peaceful means.

They considered that the interests of peace in the region and particularly in the Indo-Pakistan subcontinent and, indeed, the interests of the people of India and Pakistan were not served by the continuance of tension between the two countries. It is against this background that Jammu and Kashmir was discussed, and each of the sides put forth its respective position.

II

The Prime Minister of India and the President of Pakistan have agreed that all armed personnel of the two countries shall be withdrawn not later than 25 February 1966, to the positions they held prior to 5 August 1965, and both sides shall observe the cease-fire terms on the cease-fire line.

III

The Prime Minister of India and the President of Pakistan have agreed that relations between India and Pakistan shall be based on the principle of non-interference in the internal affairs of each other.

IV

The Prime Minister of India and the President of Pakistan have agreed that both sides will discourage any propaganda directed against the other country, and will encourage propaganda which promotes the development of friendly relations between the two countries.

V

The Prime Minister of India and the President of Pakistan have agreed that the High Commissioner of India to Pakistan and the High Commissioner of Pakistan to India will return to their posts and that the normal functioning of diplomatic missions of both countries will be restored. Both Governments shall observe the Vienna Convention of 1961 on diplomatic intercourse.

VI

The Prime Minister of India and the President of Pakistan have agreed to consider measures towards the restoration of economic and trade relations, communications as well as cultural exchanges between India and Pakistan, and to take measures to implement the existing agreements between India and Pakistan.

VII

The Prime Minister of India and the President of Pakistan have agreed that they give instructions to their respective authorities to carry out the repatriation of the prisoners of war.

VIII

The Prime Minister of India and the President of Pakistan have agreed that the sides will continue the discussion of questions relating to the problems of refugees, evictions and illegal immigrations. They also agreed that both sides will create conditions which will prevent the exodus of people. They further agreed to discuss the return of the property and assets taken over by either side in connexion with the conflict.

IX

The Prime Minister of India and the President of Pakistan have agreed that the sides will continue meetings both at the highest and at other levels on matters of direct concern to both countries. Both sides have recognized the need to set up joint Indian-Pakistani bodies which will report to their Governments in order to decide what further steps should be taken.

The Prime Minister of India and the President of Pakistan record their feelings of deep appreciation and gratitude to the leaders of the Soviet Union, the Soviet Government and personally to the Chairman of the Council of Ministers of the U.S.S.R. for their constructive friendly and noble part in bringing about the present meeting which has resulted in mutually satisfactory results. They also express to the Government and friendly people of Uzbekistan their sincere thankfulness for their overwhelming reception and generous hospitality.

They invite the Chairman of the Council of Ministers of the U.S.S.R. to witness this declaration.

Prime Minister of India: Lal Bahadur Shastri.
President of Pakistan: Mohammad Ayub Khan.

INDEX

Abbottabad, 242–3
Abdullah, Sheikh, 129–33, 140, 142, 149–50
Abdullah, Sheikh Tariq, 142
Achakzai, Abdus Samad Khan, 201
Adamjee Jute Mill, 269
Afghanistan, 102ff, 148, 156
Agartala Conspiracy Case, 63, 181, 185ff, 234–5, 252, 264, 266
agents provocateurs, 250, 265
agriculture, 43ff, 294
Ahl-i-Kitab, 104
Ahmed, Farid, 58, 174–5
Ahmed, M. Bashir, 74
Ahmed, M. M., 184
Ahmed, Mushtaq, 92, 94, 114
Ahmed, Sheikh Khursheed, 23
Akhand Bharat, 118, 128
Akhtar, Raja Hasan, 16
Aksai-Chin road, 95
Al-Aqsa mosque, 99
Ali, Choudhury Mohamed, 54, 56, 58, 68, 175, 178, 193, 199, 235
Ali, Mohamed (Bogra), 16–17, 22, 86–7
All-India Radio, 100, 143, 184
All-Pakistan National Conference, 160
All-Pakistan Textile Mills Association, 75
Amin, Nurul, 174, 180, 208, 235
Anthony, Frank, 145
anti-Semitism, 97–9
Arab countries, relations with, 96ff
Arabic script, 122
Arambagh mosque, 250
Army of Pakistan, 81, 137, 144ff, 155, 163, 241, 245, 254, 271, 275, 281
Asia: Chinese role in, 92
Aurangzeb, Begum Naseem, 289, 299
Aurangzeb, Prince, 13, 289, 299
Australia, 293
Awami League, 22, 68, 175, 182
Ayub, Captain Akhtar, 257, 286
Ayub, Captain Gohar, 77, 80–3, 286–8, 305–6

Ball, George, 114
Baluch, Mir Baqi, 191

Baluchistan, 194–5, 203, 205, 207, 211, 224
banks, 42, 47, 49
barley, 44–5
barrage land, 204, 206
Bata, 98
Bahawalpur, 195
Basic Democracies System, 1, 3, 13, 27, 39, 69, 76, 174, 177–8, 244, 255, 262
begar system, 37
Bell Mission to India, 116
Bengal, 119, 122, 198, 270
Bhashani, Maulana, 68, 71–2, 78, 174–175, 180, 235, 261, 266–7, 269–70
Bholu brothers, 278
Bhutto, Zulfikar Ali, as Foreign Minister, 16, 46, 71–2, 87; visits to Peking, 90, 93; visits Indonesia, 95; visits Moscow, 106–7; meets Talbot and Sandys, 113; comment on Humphrey's statement, 115; reaction to Woods mission, 116; accuses India of neo-colonialism, 127; leads delegation to Delhi, 129; claimed as Indian national, 143; comment on 1965 war, 148; warns that China might enter war, 152; anger with Malaysia, 153; address to Security Council, 154–5; on Tashkent Declaration, 158; leaves Government, 88, 159; opposed to Ayub Khan, 79, 184, 237; challenges Mujibur Rahman to public debate, 181; considered a spent force, 235; attended funeral of Hamid, 241; arrested, 238, 242; petition for his release 262–3; prayer to Court, 264; removed to Larkana, 265; declines to attend Round Table Conference 266–7
Biar Bet, 267
Bizenjo, Ghaus Baksh, 57, 201, 224
Bombanwala-Ravi-Bedian canal, 166
Bombay Presidency, 193, 197
British rule, 194ff, 206, 221, 224
Bugti, Akbar Khan, 207
Bugti tribe, 206

INDEX

bureaucracy in Pakistan, 39–40, 205–6, 235
Burki, Lieutenant-General, 10, 16
Burma, 96, 163, 275

Calcutta, 129
Campbellpur, 54
Canada, 293
cartels, 47–8
Census, 204
CENTO, 87, 90, 112, 129, 162, 242, 267
Central Intelligence Agency, 185
Central Statistical Office of Pakistan, 35ff
Chaklala Airport, 129
Chatan, 257
Cheema, Choudhury Afzal, 16, 29
Chen-yi, Marshal, 90
China, relations with, 91–6; Bhutto's policy on, 87–90; conflict with India, 86; freedom of speech in, 62; roads to, 94–5; economic aid from, 106; visit by Nur Khan, 110; air agreement with, 114; Humphrey on China and sub-continent, 115; seen as firmest friend of Pakistan, 123; encouraged Ayub Khan, 149; moral support for Pakistan against India, 152, 160; arms from, 161–2; Bhashani's sympathy for, 175
China-Indonesia-Pakistan Axis, 95–6, 149
Chittagong, 222, 267
Choudhury, A. K. M. Fazlul Qader, 15, 17, 279
Chou En-lai, 93
Civil Procedure Code, 157
civil service, 30–2, 40, 122, 169, 214, 245, 256, 281
civil war, threat of, 248, 270
Clausewitz, von, 276
Clemenceau, Georges, 59
Combined Opposition Parties, 4, 68–71, 78, 82, 261
Commonwealth, 66–7, 95, 134, 153
confederation as solution to Indo-Pakistan problem, 115
conglomerates, 48
Constitution, 1ff, 12–15, 18, 23, 24ff, 53, 164, 168, 176, 186, 208, 214ff, 227–9, 264, 291
Constitution, amendments to: First Amendment, 25ff; Second Amendment, 27–30, 69; Third Amendment, 30–1; Fourth Amendment, 31–3, 215–16; Fifth Amendment, 217–18; Sixth Amendment, 215–18; Seventh Amendment, 218–20; Eighth Amendment, 208, 219–20
Constitution Commission, 1, 4
Convention Muslim League, 20, 22, 55, 67, 75, 174, 262, 264, 279
Cornelius Report, 256–7
corruption, 70, 177, 205, 220, 231, 249, 259, 281ff, 295–6; anti-corruption Court, 239
cotton, 41, 45, 51
Council Muslim League, 20, 22, 68
Criminal Law Amendment Act, 66, 186
currencies, 179, 284
Custodians of Enemy Property, 218

Dacca, 66, 114, 173, 187, 222, 230, 237, 246, 253, 269–70
Dacca High Court, 187–9
dam construction, 43, 293
Daultana, Mian Mumtaz Khan, 68
Dawn, 113, 115, 139–40, 160, 183
decentralization, 209–10
Defence of Pakistan Rules, 181–3, 187, 221, 223, 232, 238, 242, 263–4
de Gaulle, General Charles, 105, 280, 295
Dehlavi, S. K., 113
Delhi, 129, 184
Democratic Action Committee, 261, 263, 266
Democratic Group in National Assembly, 22
Dewal Sharif, Pir of, 73
Dir, Nawab of, 13, 288

East Pakistan, economic situation in, 8–9; press freedom in, 59; movement for autonomy of, 118; problems of, 168ff; Safety Ordinance, 181–2; attitude towards One Unit concept, 209; army in, 254
economic factors, 7–8, 34ff, 258, 283; false economic miracle, 231; Ayub Khan's record, 293–5
Economist, the, 79, 152
education, 240ff, 291
Election Commission, 79
Elective Bodies Disqualification Order, 53ff

INDEX

Electoral College, 12ff, 27–8, 69, 226
electric power production, 41, 43
étatism, 49
European Common Market, 100
Evidence Act, 186
Export Bonus Vouchers, 9, 233

Family Laws Ordinance, 3, 6, 65, 76, 291
family planning movement, 6, 65, 265, 291
Farrakha barrage, 125
Faruque, Ghulam, 23, 60, 170–4
Fazlullah, Kazi, 238
Federation of Pakistan, 179
Federation of Pakistan Chambers of Commerce, 100
fertilizers, 41, 44, 294
feudalism, 39
Firyubin, N. P., 108
Five Year Plan, Second, 10, 111
Five Year Plan, Third, 107
flour, 46, 234
food prices, 45ff, 233–5
Force Gibraltar, 141
Foreign Affairs, 123
foreign aid, 117
foreign businesses in Pakistan, 75
France, relations with, 104–6
Friends not Masters, 192, 273, 277, 278

Gandhi, Mrs. Indira, 108, 110, 116
Gauhar, Altaf, 232, 257, 301–4
Gazdar, M. H., 63
General Motors Corporation, 77
General Staff, Pakistani, 141
Germany, 106, 293; German General Staff, 276
Ghalib, 121
Ghandhara Industries Ltd., 286, 305–6
gheraos, 258, 269–70
Gibraltar, 104
Gilgit, 95
goonda, 239
Government of India Act, 195–6, 221
Gracey, General Sir Douglas, 273
Great Decade of Development and Reform, 226ff
Gross National Product, 36, 40, 42–3, 48–9, 162
Gud du Barrage, 205–6
Gujarat, State of, 133

Habibullah, Khan Bahadur H. M., 57
Hamid, Abdul, 241
Hamid, Rana Abdul, 23
Haq, A. K. M. Fazlul, 175–6
Haq, Flight-Sergeant Zahurul, 252
Haque, Mohamed Abdul, 15
Haroon, Yusuf, 270–1
hartal, 265
Hashim, 242
Hawas, Youssef, 99
Hazara District, 54, 74, 81
Hindus, 119, 125ff, 157
Holiday, 182–3, 185
Home, Earl of, 90
Hossain, Tofazzal, 183
Huda, Dr. M. N., 270
Humphrey, Vice-President Hubert, 115
Huq, Dr. Mahbubul, 47
Hur community of Sind, 165–6
Hussain, S. Inait, 277
Hussain, President Zakir, 110
Hyderabad, 202, 230, 237, 265

Ibrahim, Sardar, 131
Iftikhar Khan, Lieutenant-General, 273
Independence Act, 195
India, relations with, 25, 125ff; bureaucracy in, 40; Indus Waters Treaty signed by, 43; Indian threat in election, 75–6; conflict over Kashmir, 15ff, 138ff; effect of Pakistan's friendship with China, 94; Soviet arms deal with, 106; Tashkent talks and Declaration, 108, 154ff; arms from the United States, 111; confederation proposed, 115; joint ventures with Pakistan suggested, 116; Pakistan's fear of, 118; communal relations in sub-continent, 119; cultural influence on Pakistan, 120ff; 1965 hostilities, 138ff; cost of war, 162ff; diplomat withdrawn, 184; resumption of fighting thought likely, 217; Ayub Khan on post-war India, 274; his attitude to India, 292
Indian Institute of Islamic Studies, 120
Indian National Congress, 130, 132
Indonesia, 95, 139, 152–3, 163
Indus Basin Development Fund, 292
Indus River, 196, 206
Industrial Development Corporations, 61, 171, 259

INDEX

industrial production, 41ff, 51, 282–3, 294
Indus Waters Treaty, 43, 76, 125, 292–3
Institute of Strategic Studies, 146, 162–163
insurance, 42, 47, 49
intellectual life in Pakistan, 122; intellectuals' attitude to Ayub Khan, 280–1
Iqbal, 121
Iran, relations with, 100ff, 152, 163 207
Iraq, 100
irrigation, 44
Irrigation Department, 206
Islam and the Constitution, 25–6, 291; Islamic socialism, 49; opposition to innovations, 64–5, 73, 260–1; Islam and foreign policy, 99–104; fusion with Hindu culture, 120; Islamic ideology as basis of Pakistan, 189, 211; anti-Islamic slogans, 250
Islamic College, 185
Islam, Nazrul, 121
Ismail, Abdel Fattaz, 99
Israel, 96–7, 99
Ittefaq, 183, 264

Jakrani, 206
Jalib, Habib, 286
Jama'at-i-Islami, 64–6, 68, 73
Jama'at-i-Talaba, 99
Jammu and Kashmir, State of, 131, 138ff
Japan, 106, 163
Jatoi, Hyder Baksh, 201
Jews in Pakistan, 98–9
Jilani, Malik Ghulam, 191
Jinnah, Miss Fatima, 4, 21, 63, 70–3, 235
Jinnah, Quaid-i-Azam Mohamed Ali, 4, 120, 132, 176–7, 193
Johnson, President Lyndon B., 156, 185, 280
Jordan, 152
Jung, 97
jute, 41, 45, 170
Jute Board, 171–2

Kabul, 78, 103, 156
Kahn, Professor Louis, 98
Kalabagh, Mohamed Amir Khan of, 56–7, 154, 190–1, 201, 262

Kalabagh steel mill, 109
Kalat Division, 195, 198
Kamal, K. M., 74
Karachi, 57, 64, 66, 74–5, 77, 80, 82, 88, 90, 138, 153, 155, 173, 185, 193, 203, 222, 230, 234, 250, 265, 269, 287
Karachi Chamber of Commerce, 192
Karachi Stock Exchange, 269
Karamatullah, Sheikh, 72
Kashmir, 85–6, 91, 99, 107, 113, 125ff, 132, 138, 154ff, 165
Kashmir, Maharaja of, 132
Kennedy, President, John F., 111, 280
Khaliquzzaman, Choudhury, 19
Khan, Abdul Ghaffar, 68, 78, 103
Khan, Abdul Jabbar, 229
Khan, Abdul Monem, 17, 23, 174, 177, 270
Khan, Abdul Qayum, 22
Khan, Abdus Sabur, 17
Khan, Air-Marshal Asghar, 79, 150, 244, 266
Ayub Khan, President, announces Constitution, 1ff; 1962 elections, 12ff; on Basic Democracy System, 4; personality of, 5–7, 294–7; credibility of, 10–11; address to National Assembly in 1962, 14; attitude to political parties, 18; saw himself as saviour of Pakistan, 20–1; attitude to Constitution, 24ff; economic achievements of, 34ff, 293–4; signs Indus Waters Treaty, 43; allows concentration of wealth, 46–8; re-elected in 1965, 77; speech at Campbellpur, 54; joins Convention Muslim League, 55; criticism of his administration, 51–2; differences with Kalabagh, 56–58; attempts to control press, 60–3; clash with Jama'at-i-Islami, 64–6; attends Commonwealth Conference in London, 66–7; presidential campaign in 1965, 68ff; defends son against charges, 77; foreign policy of, 85ff; rivalry with Bhutto, 88; attitude to United States, 114; relations with China, 115–16; article in *Foreign Affairs*, 123; relations with India, 125ff; meeting with Shastri, 138; policy on Kashmir, 139ff; summing-up of 1965 Kashmir policy, 148–51; Tashkent talks and aftermath, 156ff; declares emergency, 164; attitude to

INDEX

East Pakistan, 168ff; defeat on education issue, 173; refers to danger of slogans about autonomy, 181; visits to East Pakistan, 182-3; stand on Agartala Case, 185ff; four-point plan, 188; failure to retain One Unit concept in West Pakistan, 190ff; adopts repressive methods, 200-1; evaluation of his record in West Pakistan, 210-12; amends Constitution, 213ff; state of emergency continued, 218ff; use of Section 144, 223-5; the Great Decade, 226ff; illness, 226-9; accused by Bhutto, 237; assassination attempt 242; growing resentment of, 243; use of violence, 243-4; attitude to disturbances, 248; loses support of armed forces, 255; on welfare state, 259; opposition to, 261; broadcast on 21 February 1969, 266-7; resigns, 271; leaves for Swat, 297; assessment of, 272ff
Khan, Lieutenant-General Azam, 71-2, 170-1, 235, 266
Khan, Begum Ayub, 290
Khan, Haji Nawab, 57
Khan, Habibullah, 17, 65, 127
Khan, Liaquat Ali, 20, 142, 193-4
Khan, Maulana Akram, 19-21
Khan, Maulvi Tamizuddin, 16
Khan, Mohamed, 192
Khan, Najibullah, 290
Khan, Nawabzada Nasrullah, 261, 263-4
Khan, Air-Marshal Nur, 110, 207-8
Khan, Roedad, 80
Khan, Sabur, 174, 253
Khan, Sardar Bahadur, 18, 22-3
Khan, Major-General Sher Ali, 117
Khan, Major-General Tikka, 135-6
Khan, Wali, 68, 78, 242, 261
Khan, President Yahya, 110, 189, 195, 209-10, 271, 280, 298-9
Khanum, 250
Kharian Police Post, 58, 250
Khattak, Lieutenant-General Habibullah Khan, 77, 286
Khurshid, M. H., 131
Kodaicanal, 133
Kosygin, Alexei, 108-9, 156-7
Kotb, Sayyed, 99-100

labouring classes, 257ff

Ladakh, 142
Lahore, 61, 65, 82, 143, 147, 149, 157, 160, 166, 191, 230, 244, 265
Lahore Division, 198
Lahore Resolution, 176-9
Lakhem House, 63
Land Reforms, 5-6, 294
Larkana, 158, 265
lathis, 250-1, 263
Lenin, V. I., 39
Liaquatabad riot, 81ff
life expectancy, 31-2
Liu Shao-chi, 90, 116, 160
Lok Sabha, 143, 145
Long, Huey P., 297
Lyallpur, 65, 158

McNamara, Robert S., 112, 118, 242
Mahmudabad, Raja of, 19
Malaysia, 95, 153
Manchhar Lake, 37
Mangla Dam, 43, 280, 293
Mao Tse-tung, 91, 93, 175
Marambio, General, 156
Marco Polo, 95
Mari Indus murders, 191
Marri, Khair Baksh, 23
Martial Law, 1, 3, 5, 12, 21, 41, 53, 69, 165-7, 170, 209, 254, 271, 287, 291, 296
Marx, Karl, 39
Marxism, 260
Maudoodi, Maulana, 65, 68, 73
Masood, Sir Ross, 278-9
Mengal, Sardar Ataullah Khan, 63, 201
Menon, Krishna, 86
Mill, James, 39
Ministry of Information and Broadcasting, 232
Mirza, President Iskander, 21, 54, 296
Mohamed, Ghulam, 16, 20, 131, 193, 199
Moltke, von, 276
Morshed, S. M., 244, 266
money supply, 41-2
muhajirs (refugees), 211
Mujahid Force, 136
Munir, M., 2, 17, 23
Musa, General Mohamed, 141, 145, 191-2, 208, 227, 238, 242, 263, 270
Muslim Brotherhood, 99
Muslim League, 16, 18, 19, 20, 55; *see also* Convention Muslim League, Council Muslim League

338 INDEX

Muslims, 119, 176; see Islam
Mustafa, A. T. M., 16

Nanda, Gulzarilal, 130
Narayan, Jai Prakash, 130, 138
Nasser, Gamal Abdel, 97–8
nastaliq, 122
National Assembly, 3–4, 12–14, 18, 26–28, 53, 59, 69, 86, 128, 167, 200, 208, 214, 218–19, 227–8, 238
National and Provincial Assemblies Order, 13
National Awami Party, 22, 68, 72, 175, 183, 242
National Bank of Pakistan, 61, 259, 269
National Democratic Front, 22, 63
National Economic Council, 168
National Education, Report on, 173
National Institute of Public Administration, 117
nationalization, 49
National Press Trust, 60, 238
National Sample Surveys, 35, 48
Nawabshah District, 204
Nawa-i-Waqt, 61
Nazimuddin, Khwaja, 68, 174
Nehru, Pandit Jawaharlal, 91, 128, 130, 132, 142, 164
Nevard, Jacques, 83
New York Times, 42, 83, 113, 165
New Zealand, 293
Nizam-i-Islam Party, 22, 68, 175
North-West Frontier, 194–5, 211, 242
North-West Frontier Group, 68
nuclear project at Rooppur, 109

Oehlert, B. H., Jr., 98
Oil and Gas Commission, 106
Ojha, P. N., 184, 189
One Unit concept, 190, 192, 194, 198ff, 235, 242
Ootacamund, 133

Pahlavi, H. I. M. Mohammad Reza Shah of Iran, 100–1
Pakhtunistan, 78, 103, 242
Pakistan Democratic Movement, 237, 261, 321–2
Pakistan Labour Conference, 151
Pakistan Penal Code, 182, 224
Pakistan Peoples' Party, 79, 242
Pakistan Radio, 161

Pakistan Resolution, 176
Pakistan Tobacco Company, 269
Pat Feeder Canal, 206–8
Pathans, 80, 103, 204–5
Patton tanks, 165
Peking, 90
Peshawar, 109, 149, 242, 265
Philippines, 163
Pick, Dr. Franz, 287
Pindi Ghaib, 241
planning, 50
police, 58–9, 191, 238–9, 241, 249, 250–253, 265, 270, 285
Political Parties Act, 18, 20, 29
political parties, 12, 18
population, increase in, 40
Portugal, 104
poverty, 34ff, 46, 48–9, 52, 234
Presidential elections, 1965—70ff; 1970—226
President's Council of Ministers, 15
President's Medal for Pride of Performance, 277–8
press freedom, 59–60
prices, rising, 46ff, 233ff, 258–9
propaganda, 143
property, taxes on, 64
protein deficiency, 45
Protocols of Zion, The, 98
Provincial Assemblies, 12–14, 26, 59–60, 69, 219
provincialism, 196
Punjab, 142, 147, 159, 164, 192–4, 204–205; Punjabi language, 198, 211
Pushto, 198

Qader, Qazi Abdul, 174
Qadir, Abdul, 17, 23
Qadir, Manzur, 17, 106
Qasem, Abdul, 16, 20
Quaid-i-Azam—*see* Jinnah
Quetta, 63, 205, 208
Qureishy, Zamir, 191–2, 201

Rahim, J. A., 79
Rahman, Ahmed Fazlur, 182, 188
Rahman, K. M. Shamsur, 267
Rahman, Masihur, 23, 71–2
Rahman, Sheikh Mujibur, 68, 159–60, 174–6, 178ff, 209, 224, 235, 261, 264, 266
Rahman, Justice S. A., 253
Rahman, Tengku, 153

INDEX

Rajasthan, 165
Rajshahi University, 253
Rann of Cutch affair, 133ff, 146, 149, 267
rationing of sugar, 236, 240
Rawalpindi, 65, 88, 108, 113, 129, 157–158, 160, 230, 241
Rawalpindi Conspiracy Case, 186
Reader's Digest, 277
Regional Co-operation for Development, 100
Removal of Difficulties Order, 15
Reston, James, 111
rice, 44, 45, 234
'robber barons', 47
Round Table Conference, 245, 266ff
Rowlands, Sir Archibald, 193, 197, 199
Rural Works Programme, 3, 174, 178
Rusk, Dean, 90, 109

Saiyid, M. H., 72
Salinity Control and Reclamation Project (SCARP), 43
Sandys, Duncan, 90, 109, 113
Sanskrit, 121
sardari system, 194–5, 207
Saudi Arabia, 96, 152
Schlieffen, von, 276
SEATO, 87, 112, 162, 242, 267
secession of East Pakistan, 177, 182, 235
Section 144, 221–2
Security Council, 88, 95, 153
Security of Pakistan Act, 22
Settlement of Disputes Order, 14
Shah, Askar Ali, 151
Shah, King Zahir, 156
Shahab, Q. U., 113
Shahabuddin, Khwaja, 174, 232
Shahabuddin, M., 1–2
Shamsuzzoha, Dr., 253
Shastri, Lal Bahadur, 130, 134–5, 138, 143, 156
Sheikhupura murders, 191
Sher-i-Bangla—*see* Haq, A. K. M. Fazlul
Shoaib, Mohamed, 10, 23, 47–8
Sialkot sector, 114, 144, 158, 160
Sikhs, 164
Silk Road, 95
Sind, 192–4, 203, 211
Sind Abadi Board, 202
Singh, Swaran, 129
Sinkiang, 95

Six-Point Movement, 178ff, 268
smuggling, 205
socialism, 49, 260–1
social structure of Pakistan, 36, 49–50
Sokarno, President, 95–6
Speaker of National Assembly, 227–8
Srinagar, 132; Srinagar-Leh road, 142; Hazratbal incident, 150
Soviet Union, relations with, 76, 85, 106ff; arranges Tashkent talks, 108, 156; arms requested from, 110; purpose in sub-continent, 124; veto on Kashmir, 127
Stacey, Tom, 133
State Bank of Pakistan, 61
steel industry, 124
strikes, 258–61, 265, 269
students, 240, 247–8, 263–4, 269–70, 298
Subandrio, 95
Subramanyam, K., 148, 162
sugar, 10, 41, 45, 234, 236
Suhrawardy, H. S., 22, 63, 73, 110, 174, 179
Sukeri, Z. A., 262
Sukkhur, 239
Sunni sect, 198, 223
Supreme Court, 66
Swat, 108, 299
Swat, Wali of, 13, 288–9, 299
Sylhet, 181, 183
Syria, 152

Tagore, Rabindranath, 120, 267
Talbot, Phillips, 113
Tarbela Dam, 43, 293
Tashkent talks and Declaration, 88, 108, 156ff, 170, 178–80, 188, 238, 263
Tasnim-i-Islam, 72
Teheran, 153
television, 227, 229–30
Thailand, 163
Thant, U, 142, 152, 159
Tibet, 95
Tod, James, 39
Todarmal, Raja, 277
Tribal Areas, 27
tribal warfare, 206ff
tubewell schemes, 43
Turkey, 49, 100ff, 152, 163, 276
Twenty Year Perspective Plan, 51

United Arab Republic, 96, 99, 163

United Kingdom, relations with, 76, 85, 105; at CENTO Conference, 90; arms to India, 126; proposal for Kashmir partition, 113; mediation in Rann of Cutch affair, 134; British Information Services reading room damaged, 155; protests by Pakistanis in Britain, 182–3; stand on Baluchistan, 194; political life in, 284; Indus Waters Treaty, 293

United Nations, 85, 128, 131, 134, 139, 142, 147, 152, 218

United States, relations with, 42, 45, 111ff, 116; effect of arms sales to India, 76, 85–6, 126; criticism of, 104–5; lease of Peshawar base doubtful, 109; plan for partition of Kashmir, 113; economic assistance to Pakistan, 116–18; views on co-operation between Pakistan and India, 123; Embassy stoned, 155; military advisers withdrawn, 162; rumour of American involvement in Agartala Case, 185

universal adult suffrage, 18, 220–1, 268, 298

Urdu, 54, 61, 120–1, 157, 198, 227

U.S.S.R.—*see* Soviet Union

Usmani, Mahmoodul Haq, 72

Vice-Presidency, possibility of, 230

violence, 243–4, 255

Wahiduzzaman, 17, 174

Water and Power Development Authority, 61, 172

wealth, concentration of, 46ff

West Pakistan, problems of, 190ff; economic situation in, 8–9; authoritarian rule in, 56ff; press in, 59ff; dominance of, 168–70; Punjabis in, 198ff

West Pakistan Control of Goondas Order, 239

West Pakistan Government, 66, 160

West Pakistan Maintenance of Public Order Ordinance (1960), 66

West Pakistan Press and Publications Ordinance, 60

West Pakistan Provincial Assembly, 28, 66

West Pakistan Public Order Ordinance, 22

wheat, 44–5, 117; price of, 233–4

Williams, T., Q.C., 187–8

Williams, Professor T. Harry, 297

Wittvogel, Professor Karl A., 38–9

Woods, George, 116

World Bank, 116, 242, 292

Zafar, Bahadur Shah, 105

Zafar, S. M., 88, 153–4